S0-BKE-969

Show Me Thy Ways

Floyd O. Rittenhouse

This book is published in collaboration with the Youth Department
as an enrichment of the Morning Watch devotional plan.

REVIEW AND HERALD PUBLISHING ASSOCIATION
Washington, DC 20039-0555
Hagerstown, MD 21740

Editor: Bobbie Jane Van Dolson
Cover Illustration: Harry Knox

The publisher has sought to locate and secure permission for the inclusion of all copyrighted poems in this book. If any such acknowledgments have been inadvertently omitted, the publisher would appreciate receiving the information so that proper credit may be given in future editions.

Library of Congress Cataloging in Publication Data

Rittenhouse, Floyd Oliver, 1905-
    Show me thy ways.

    1. Devotional calendars—Seventh-day
Adventists. I. Title.
            242.2

Library of Congress Catalog Card Number: 83-61692

ISBN 0-8280-0209-6

DEDICATED

to NELLIE, DANA, and JUDY, without whose love this life would be a dreary wasteland, and to MY STUDENTS, who long since taught me that friendship is the only earthly paradise from which man cannot be driven.

FLOYD O. RITTENHOUSE

I was born on March 10, 1905, at Bozeman, Montana, the oldest of the seven children of Wilton Dana and Huldah LaFave Rittenhouse. I attended church school at Mount Ellis and graduated from Mount Ellis Academy in 1922. The following year I enrolled at Walla Walla College, where I continued through the school term of 1924. In 1928 I graduated from Emmanuel Missionary College.

In the early years of my service I taught at Sutherlin Academy in Oregon and at Mount Vernon Academy, attending Ohio State University in summer, where I was awarded a Master's degree in history in 1932.

From 1933 to 1938 I served as principal of Takoma Academy. In 1937 Nellie Blair Hubbard, of Brookneal, Virginia, and I were married in Takoma Park. In 1938 our daughter, Dana C. Rittenhouse-Dutcher, was born. We returned to the Washington area where I served as registrar and then academic dean at Washington Missionary College from 1942 to 1948. After the birth of our second daughter, Judith Ann (now Mrs. Tom Dybdahl), we were called to Southern Missionary College, where I served until 1952. During this time Ohio State University conferred on me the Doctor of Philosophy degree in history.

We returned to Emmanuel Missionary College, where I served as academic dean, and as president from 1955 to 1958, when that institution became Andrews University. I served at Andrews until 1963, when we accepted a call to Pacific Union College, where I was president until 1973. Since that time I have kept busy traveling, writing, and speaking.

Memberships include Phi Alpha Theta (honorary history fraternity), Rotary, and various organizations. I have written for a variety of periodicals, and in 1980 *Proving the Promises,* the life story of V. T. Armstrong, was published by Pacific Press.

FACING THE NEW YEAR

Teach us to order our days rightly, that we may enter the gates. Ps. 90:12, N.E.B.

New Year's Day is special for most people. Charles Lamb once remarked that no one ever regards it with indifference. And rightly so, for this particular day is the gate to the future and the finest time of all the year for new beginnings. Alfred Tennyson recalled that, as a child retiring early on New Year's Eve, he asked his mother to please

". . . wake and call me early, call me early, mother dear.

Tomorrow'll be the happiest time of all the glad New Year."

Charles Dickens likened New Year's Day to "an infant heir to all the world, waited for with welcomes, presents, and rejoicings." A modern poet, in a meditative mood, perceived New Year's Day as "reviving old desires" when the "thoughtful soul to solitude retires." Recently a newspaper poll indicated that, while not many people make formal New Year's resolutions anymore, the great majority do reflect thoughtfully on the past year and engage in at least some wishful thinking concerning the year just ahead.

One is reminded of the legendary Fortunas, whose wishing cap, when he put it on, could transport him instantly anytime, anywhere. Who wouldn't like to have that cap today so as to enable oneself to enjoy a delightful time every day of the year? However, Fortunas is only an imaginary figure. There is no real *place* where anyone can begin all over again. But, as a matter of fact, there is a *time* of beginning again—and this is the day.

A new year is one of Heaven's oldest gifts to man. In hopeful anticipation we may receive it as an alabaster box of precious things: talents of time to employ judiciously, jewels of faith, courage to enhance our Christian witness, occasions of service to those in need. It is exhilarating at the January gate to contemplate the pathways of the untrodden year. What an exciting prospect for a youth to sense that these days may well embrace one of the most momentous decisions of life! What a priceless privilege it offers for prudent parents to influence for righteousness their cherished children Heaven has temporarily entrusted to their care! With what gratitude can the mature believer envision the days ahead as priceless opportunities to perfect a character against the hastening day when we all shall know even as we are known! Let us resolve, with God's help, to make this New Year better than any that has gone before.

9

AN ETERNAL GOD

The Lord is the true God, he is the living God . . . everlasting. . . . Jer. 10:10.

As a boy growing up on a Montana homestead, I early learned to love the outdoors and the marvelous sights and sounds of nature. My eager, childish questions were always patiently heard and answered by my dedicated Christian mother. Under such favorable surroundings I came to accept the world about me and all natural phenomena as a part of God's universe, elements of His great plan.

Thus, even in childhood, the reality or nonreality of a great Creator seemed to me about the most important matter in life. Nor can I understand, even today, how any intelligent person can think otherwise. This is the one supreme question on which one must be sure. Actually, in one way or another, every decision in life depends upon it.

The skeptic holds another view, like the astronomer Lanland, who declared, ''I have swept the heavens with my telescope and have not found God.'' Likewise the Russian astronauts, having penetrated less than one ten-thousands of the distance to the nearest fixed star, announced, ''We were in the heavens and we found no angels there.'' Other scientists have written, ''We have examined the human brain with our microscopes and have not found the human soul.''

Nevertheless, in full confidence, I begin each day with the familiar prayer ''Our Father which art in heaven . . .'' I utter this petition, not as an outgrowth of any childish practice, but because I deeply believe it. Of course, this is an act of faith. Nor is any rational human being devoid of faith of one kind or another.

We have the record of the blind man of Galilee who believed and *then* his eyes were opened. Happily, the believer is not obliged to proceed in blind confidence, for by his faith he is led, step by step, into full knowledge and confidence. This is a divine paradox. We come to know *as* we believe and not before.

Like the nobleman whose son the Lord Jesus healed, your faith may sometimes waver. You will surely find strength and comfort if, like him, you will pray, ''Lord, I believe; help thou mine unbelief'' (Mark 9:24).

NO OTHER GOD

To you it was shown, that you might know that the Lord is God; there is no other besides him. Deut. 4:35, R.S.V.

With these words Moses was attempting to strengthen Israel's faith in God. The Christian believer today also needs to know that the Lord is God and that there is none else.

Aware of my religious conviction, some of my skeptical friends occasionally challenge it. "We know you believe," they say, "but you can't be *really* sure, can you?" But I do know, I assure them. This fundamental question of the reality of God is so important that one must be utterly sure. Certainly, if any belief doesn't hold up or prove itself in the fiery crucible of experience, it is of no value. The apostle Paul says they are blessed who believe even though they have not seen. This is clearly an act of faith, hence, *some* measure of faith must come first. But the man of faith cannot live on in blind credulity. Fortunately, he can have the concrete evidence he needs to back up his initial faith. The unbeliever, who has never known God, will call such spiritual confidence a delusion. But actually, it is not wishful thinking at all. Instead, it is a sublime reality.

Growth in spiritual faith is difficult to explain. It may be compared to trying to explain to a deaf man the stirring experience of hearing Haydn's majestic oratorio *Creation*. The man's misfortune does not make the music an illusion. Rather it is a vital, moving reality and a profound blessing to all whose ears and souls are open to its beauty. But while not everyone can hear a great oratorio, everyone *can* hear the voice of the heavenly Father. The supreme privilege of every soul is to know God.

In college I took a course in Christian evidence. The members of the class were deeply moved as the teacher convincingly presented overwhelming proof for the existence of God. At the final session, our teacher made this appeal: "Despite the weight of evidence, some of you may still have doubts. If so, will you now take the next step, which is to know God by personal experience. This is the most convincing evidence I know." The professor was right, for to know God through His indwelling Spirit is still the greatest proof.

WHO IS GOD?

There is one God, the Father, from whom all being comes. 1 Cor. 8:6, N.E.B.

To distinguish Himself from false gods, the true God called Himself Jehovah, *"the great I AM."* He commanded Moses to tell the people: "This is my name for ever; this is my title in every generation" (Ex. 3:14, N.E.B.). Recognizing God's eternal preeminence, the psalmist prayed, "Let them learn that thou alone art Lord, God Most High over all the earth" (Ps. 83:18, N.E.B.).

As the creator of all things, Jehovah God, the King of eternity, existed before all else. Although we cannot comprehend it, He exists "from everlasting to everlasting," which means that He had no beginning in time nor will He have any end. This Jehovah, the self-existent, uncreated, eternal One, is the source and the sustainer of all and as such is entitled to supreme and exclusive reverence. As such He is properly jealous of His supreme position. That men should recognize that He rules over all and that they owe Him their profound and undivided allegiance is implicit in the first commandment of the Decalogue: "You shall have no other god to set against me" (Ex. 20:3, N.E.B.).

It is this God, declared Job, "who commands the sun's orb not to rise and shuts up the stars under his seal; who by himself spread out the heavens . . . ; who does great and unsearchable things, marvels without number" (Job 9:7-10, N.E.B.). Without a living, all-wise God the universe could never have come into being, and without the constant exertion of His power it could not continue to exist or function. No wonder King David exclaimed, "The impious fool says in his heart, 'There is no God' " (Ps. 53:1, N.E.B.).

The themes of heaven's anthems hold deep significance for the Christian as he seeks to understand God's inscrutable purpose in creating the universe and as he strives to think God's thoughts after Him. In their exquisite melodies, celestial beings reflect God's unchangeable supremacy in His universe. As a forecast of paradise restored, heavenly angels are already singing the victorious Song of Moses and the Lamb: "Great and marvellous are thy works, Lord God Almighty; just and true are thy ways, thou King of saints" (Rev. 15:3). And so, in faith and trust, as we pursue our earthly pilgrimage, we too can say: " 'Thou art worthy, O Lord our God, to receive glory and honour and power, because thou didst create all things; by thy will they . . . have their being!' " (chap. 4:11, N.E.B.).

THE CREATOR AND HIS CREATION

Ever since the creation of the world his invisible nature, namely, his eternal power and deity, has been clearly perceived in the things that have been made. Rom. 1:20, R.S.V.

One of the most convincing answers to the question Does God exist? can be found in the book of nature. None will deny that on every hand are evidences of design, system, and order. "How," asks the believer, "can our boundless cosmos embrace such an unfathomable variety of complicated designs, all blindly conceived, yet without a Great Designer?" Or "How can the rational mind account for the multimillions of colossal orbiting spheres hurtling through space as the mindless achievement of chance? How does one explain the silent cycle of the seasons, the amazing intricacies of the human body, or the miracle of life itself?"

In his latter years, Albert Einstein, brilliant formulator of the theory of relativity, finally recognized the presence in the universe of a "superior reasoning power." To a colleague he wrote: "I cannot believe that God would choose to play dice with the world." Although not considered religious in the traditional sense, Einstein came finally to regard our cosmos as the outworking of a purposeful plan.

In his unshakable belief in God, the Christian logically equates this great, universal Planner with the Omnipotent One whose matchless wisdom and might "meted out heaven with the span" (Isa. 40:12), loosed Orion, and forever guides "Arcturus with his sons" (Job 36:32).

Thoughtful contemplation evokes convincing evidence that the entire, complex natural world did not just "happen." Rationality impels us to regard the whole cosmos as the masterpiece of an invincible Genius who "spoke, and it came to be" (Ps. 33:9, R.S.V.). How reassuring it is to own a faith that is based on the straight-forward Genesis affirmation that "in the beginning God created the heaven and the earth."

> "The spacious firmament on high,
> With all the blue, ethereal sky,
> And spangled heavens, a shining frame,
> Their great Original proclaim.
> The unwearied sun from day to day
> Doth his Creator's power display,
> And publishes to every land
> The work of an almighty hand."
>
> —Joseph Addison

FAITH BEYOND UNDERSTANDING

In the beginning God created the heaven and the earth. Gen. 1:1.

These are the first words of the Bible. Written under inspiration by the prophet Moses, they are the simplest and most satisfactory explanation ever given for the origin of the universe. Thus, Holy Writ begins with an everlasting, ever-living, all-wise, all-powerful God. He is introduced as the great Architect and Builder of all things.

Of God's creative power the apostle Paul wrote: "In him everything in heaven and on earth was created. . . . He exists before everything, and all things are held together in him" (Col. 1:16, 17, N.E.B). The psalmist explains exactly how God created: "By the word of the Lord the heavens were made, and all their host by the breath of his mouth" (Ps. 33:6, R.S.V.).

A cursory reading of the Bible shows that, with no exception, the authors of the Old Testament accepted without reservation the doctrine of Creation from nothing by Jehovah, the omnipotent Artificer of the universe. To such a degree was this accepted as the basic doctrine of Israelitish faith that, God came to be designated as "He who spoke and the world sprang into existence." Writing to the Hebrews, the apostle Paul stated categorically that the world was made of that which did not previously exist (see Heb. 11:3).

The Hebrew word *barah* means "abundantly to produce" and is invariably used to indicate an action of an astounding nature. It also means "producing something out of nothing." "Creative power is ideally great," says J. Profeit. "No greater work can be done." *

The original Creation can never be explained by science because science is incompetent to reason upon the formation of matter out of nothing. This is rather a kind of philosophy. Man reaches the utmost limit of his thinking capability when he admits that, because matter is not self-producing and eternal, it must have been created. All reasoning beyond this partakes of the nature of faith whether in Holy Writ or in human speculation. The atheist puts his faith in evolution; the Christian, in God. When asked to explain the existence of matter, the evolutionist is mute because he has no answer. The believer quotes Genesis 1, perhaps adding, "Beyond this I have no need to go."

---

* *The Creation of Matter*, p. 175.

14

THE AMAZING UNIVERSE

"By thee, Lord, were earth's foundations laid of old, and the heavens are the work of thy hands. . . . They shall grow old . . . like any garment. But thou art the same, and thy years shall have no end." Heb. 1:10-12, N.E.B.

With unanimous voices David, Job, Isaiah, Peter, and Paul, as well as the other authors of Holy Writ, speak convincingly of the starry heavens as indisputable evidence of God's omnipotent power and wisdom. Writing to the Colossians, the apostle Paul, speaking of the great Architect and Builder of the universe, declared, "By him were all things created, that are in heaven, . . . and by him all things consist" (Col. 1:16, 17).

Nothing is more reasonable to the rational mind than the Biblical assertion that God made the heaven and the earth. We live in the midst of a vast, swiftly moving, life-filled universe composed of billions of blazing suns and countless lesser wonder worlds. He, whose name "shall be called wonderful," has surrounded Himself with millions of orbiting spheres gloriously displaying His divine attributes. Is there any wonder that the agnostic philosopher Immanuel Kant declared, "Two things inspire wonder and increasing reverence the oftener and the more they are considered: the starry heavens above me and the moral law within me"?

Thinking similarly, Ralph Waldo Emerson once wrote: "If the stars should appear but one night in a thousand years, how men would believe and adore and preserve for many generations the remembrance of the city of God which had been shown!" To agree with Emerson one needs but to stand at midnight atop some towering mountain in the Rockies, there to watch in wonder as the silver moon in lofty majesty and fleets of glittering stars go sailing through the silent night. Under the magic spell of the starlit heavens a feeling of reverence comes over even the most skeptical doubter, who in the light of day seldom pauses long enough to consider "whence came all these things."

Hiram Maxim suggested that, "When your perspective becomes distorted by worldly worries, step outdoors and look at the stars. Consider their possible purpose, their size, their age; compare your affairs with theirs. Mayhap your troubles will shrink into comparative insignificance, and a certain comfort will be yours." The meditation thus evoked will enable the thoughtful person to look at things present and things eternal in better proportion.

STARGAZING

He [God] took Abram outside and said, "Look up into the sky, and count the stars if you can." Gen. 15:5, N.E.B.

In order to bolster his feeble faith, the Lord told His servant Abraham to step outside his tent; and there He asked him, "Canst thou tell the stars by number?" Abraham could not, and neither can anyone today, despite unnumbered years of diligent effort. The sum total of the stars remains to us as baffling as it was to Abraham.

Scientists now know many times more about the heavenly host than did the Lord's servant of old. But this increased knowledge has not answered God's direct question. Astronomers have become more and more frustrated because the more intricate the telescopes they develop, the greater the number of stars that burst into view. After centuries of the most intensive scrutiny, the greatest astrophysicists who work in the finest observatories can only make a very rough estimate as to the vast numbers of heavenly bodies. Neither can they measure the distances between them, nor even conceive the myriads of worlds that God has created and strewn through unmeasurable space.

With the naked eye today, man can see the same stars that Abraham saw. The passing centuries have not dimmed their luster. Storms of celestial intensity have not driven them off their predetermined courses. Not a hair's breadth have they deviated from their appointed paths. These ageless voyagers through uncharted space reappear nightly in the heavens just as they did when the patriarch Abraham watched them.

A quarter of a century ago, telescopes revealed one hundred times as many stars as were visible to Abraham. Palomar's newer 200-inch refracting mirror has increased that figure twenty-seven times. But even this fails to disclose all the heavenly bodies. Learned modern gazers perceive only boundless distance beyond as they peer into limitless space.

At evening the heavens seem to whisper, "Open your eyes and look." Although Wordsworth and Shelley tried, they, nor any other poet, have never adequately portrayed the genius of the stars to inspire confidence in the almighty Creator. But the marvel of marvels is that all this infinite humanly incomprehensible cosmos operates under the most precise control. None but an all-powerful Being could have planned it or called it into existence. Only such a God could uphold and guide it to this very hour. All other explanations have ever remained in the unreliable realm of speculative conjecture.

CARE AND PRECISION IN NATURE

See, and know, and consider, and understand together, that the hand of the Lord hath done this, and the Holy One of Israel hath created it. Isa. 41:20.

In the verses preceding our text for today the Lord had been explaining to Isaiah His great creative power and its materialization in planting the trees of the forest. He said, "I . . . plant in the wilderness the cedar, the shittah tree, and the myrtle, and the olive tree; I will set in the desert the fir tree, and the pine, and the box tree together" (Isa. 41:19). The Almighty is sure that if men will only think earnestly and look intently at the vast and precisely ordered universe of nature, they can arrive at but one conclusion: human wisdom could not possibly have created all these things.

But skeptics say, "We do not know who created these things." They reject the idea of a Supreme Being, yet cannot at all account for the origin of matter. So they theorize and more or less agree that life itself—which no one understands—probably developed in the distant past from some tiny one-celled organism or microscopic blob of jelly that they assume evolved of itself in the primeval ooze of the long ago.

Some agnostics admit that the mechanistic, evolutionary theory is untenable. Yet, having rejected the Scriptural account of the origin of life, they regard evolution as the most likely alternate explanation. One evolutionist concedes as much in these words: "The possibility of the appropriate essential elements coming together by chance seems remote indeed, but in a tremendously long, long period of time the impossible becomes the inevitable." This is astoundingly illogical reasoning. It is nothing but willful, blind credulity, utterly unacceptable to the rational mind.

Precision in nature alone rules out the possibility of evolution by chance. The ornithologist J. J. Audubon pointed out that there is an exact number of scales on the leg of each partridge, and that the American eagle invariably has seven tail feathers. This simple fact was overlooked when the first silver dollar was minted, and the artist inaccurately gave the big bird eight such feathers. Later, one feather had to come out. Reviewing such evidence, the believer humbly agrees with David that "such knowledge is beyond my understanding" (Ps. 139:6, N.E.B.).

Am I willing to doubt my doubts, believe my beliefs, and place my trust in the living God?

ARCTURUS AND THE PLEIADES

Can you bind the cluster of the Pleiades? . . . Or guide Aldebaran and its train? Job 38:31, 32, N.E.B.

The fortunes and misfortunes of Job constitute an everlasting lesson in trust and confidence in God. In his extremity of physical illness and broken in spirit, this good man engaged in a rambling and sometimes peevish argument by which he attempted to prove that God had treated him unjustly. Finally, the Lord broke His silence, but He did not attempt to answer Job's petulant questions. Nor did He refer to the mysterious happenings that had harassed and bewildered His troubled servant. Instead, He gave a vivid, verbal view of His power in Creation and the world of nature. The Almighty was attempting to lift the dejected patriarch out of his self-pity.

The questions put to Job disclosed scientific facts well-known today, but which only the Creator knew at that time. The sweet influence or bonds of the Pleiades had reference to the gravitational pull that holds together this mighty cluster of blazing suns. Of this remarkable constellation, Isabel Lewis, of the United States Naval Observatory, writes: "Astronomers have identified two hundred and fifty stars as actual members of this group, all sharing a common motion and drifting through space in the same direction." Dr. R. J. Trumpler, of the Lick Observatory, stated that the Pleiades are all bound together and "are flying like a swarm of birds." Here is a most striking confirmation of God's knowledge as indicated in his question to Job about the Pleiades. To look with naked eye at the seven visible stars in this luminous cluster is to comprehend their age-old message that the God of Job *was* and *is* the Creator of the universe.

In speaking of Aldebaran, the Almighty was asking Job about one of the most colossal suns in the universe. This brilliant luminary, burning like a taper in the sky, is actually a runaway, traveling at the rate of 250 miles a second. By comparison our sun sweeps along at the relatively sluggish rate of less than thirteen miles per second. A sixteen-inch cannon launches a projectile at twenty-five miles a minute; but Aldebaran is rampaging through outer space at more than fifteen thousand miles per minute. According to another astronomer, Aldebaran is so gigantic that "the combined attraction of all the stars we know could not stop him or turn him in his path." None but an omnipotent Creator could have asked the questions God put to Job.

EVIDENCE IN NATURE

The earth is full of the goodness of the Lord. Ps. 33:5.
Whoso is wise, and will observe these things . . . shall understand the
lovingkindness of the Lord. Ps. 107:43.

As a young man, David's duties as a shepherd kept him in the outdoors for months. While tending sheep he found ample time to contemplate the wonders of nature. In the early morning this perceptive youth observed the dew-covered lilies of the fields—each bloom a blaze of color intricately fashioned and possessing a shy beauty of its own. On a clear evening he could gaze upward in wonder at the dark and limitless sky studded with myriads of glistening stars. On occasion, no doubt, he walked among the giant cedars of Lebanon, with their gaunt and probing fingers pointing heavenward. Perhaps on many a lazy afternoon he peered intently westward at the ever-changing sea, with its restless waves moving relentlessly shoreward.

The psalms unmistakably reveal that the young poet reveled in the beauties of nature. He had his own expressive way of alluding to the wonders and mysteries of the natural world. The book of nature spoke to him continually of the Creator's omnipotent power. In the Shepherd's Psalm, David paints a word picture so vivid that the thoughtful reader can almost literally walk in those green pastures and then rest beside the still waters. Peace, calm, and tranquillity of mind are engendered as one envisions the pastoral scenes that speak persuasively and eloquently of God's power and goodness.

There is a lofty purpose in the natural beauty that surrounds us. "Whoso is wise, and will observe these things, shall understand the lovingkindness of the Lord" (Ps. 107:43). This inspiring truth has been admirably expressed in these words:

"The beauties of nature have a tongue that speaks to us without ceasing. The open heart can be impressed with the love and glory of God, as seen in the works of His hand. The listening ear can hear and understand the communications of God through the things of nature. There is a lesson in the sunbeam, and in the various objects of nature that God has presented to our view. The green fields, the lofty trees, the buds and flowers, the passing cloud, the falling rain, the babbling brook, the sun, moon, and stars in the heavens . . . bid us become acquainted with Him who made them all." *

---

* Ellen G. White, in *The Youth's Instructor*, March 24, 1898, p. 227.

THE TESTIMONY OF THE EARTH

O Lord, . . . the earth if full of thy riches. Ps. 104:24.

When God spake our world into existence, it was a chaotic, inorganic mass "without form, and void" (Gen. 1:2). But it did not remain so, for thereupon He proceeded to organize and collate it (see Gen. 1:1-28).

To the motorist hurrying along the highway on a close schedule, the undulating hills, monotonous flatlands and convoluted mountains may look like a disordered jumble. Actually, however, the landscapes, even the soil and stones beneath our feet, are anything but the confused aggregate they appear. Rather they are composed of complex materials compounded according to fixed laws and operating in amazing harmony. The desultory observer is often unaware that the myriad particles of earth all perform according to natural laws. The inflexible chemical law of definite composition requires that every element—few more than one hundred in all the universe—must invariably unite with other elements into innumerable but definite combinations. Every known substance is made up of particles, each composed of infinitesimal atoms (or ions) and electrons. Every atom is endowed with the capacity to coalesce with others, thus producing the endlessly diverse formations we see all about us. As inert, nonliving particles could not of themselves form combinations, the need of an original Compounder is clearly obvious. Since these particles making up the world are so infinitely small, as well as infinite in number, it follows logically that their Creator must be an infinite Being.

Isaiah speaks of "the treasures of darkness, and hidden riches of secret places" (chap. 45:3). Job refers to remote mine shafts where men find gold, silver, copper, and iron. We do not know why the Almighty elected to bury in such out-of-the-way places the choicest of metals and the most precious stones. But we greatly admire and enjoy their rare beauty once they are rescued from their deep and secluded havens.

Who has not stood entranced before a brilliant display of gold and silver and precious gems? How fascinating to view iridescent opals, flaming rubies, blushing garnets, evergreen emeralds, azure sapphires, and sparkling, well-cut diamonds! After poring over such radiance an observer may be gripped by a feeling of covetousness. The Christian, however, mindful of the gates of the eternal city, reluctantly turns away, awed that the Almighty could have fashioned and imprisoned in stones such superlative elegance.

MAN'S PHYSICAL ENDOWMENT

I will praise thee; for I am fearfully and wonderfully made: marvellous are thy works; and that my soul knoweth right well. Ps. 139:14.

Scientific understanding of the complexities of the human body has increased a hundredfold since David's time, and modern research continues to uncover new and unexpected intricacies of human anatomy. Such an ingenious arrangement of members and interplay of action the psalmist never dreamed of. Indeed, the more man learns about the body, the greater grows his admiration and awe for its consummate artistry, efficiency, and beauty. In 1966, Dr. W. W. Akers, a Rice University engineer who was working with surgeons to develop an artificial heart, declared: "The body is the ultimate in technological perfection. Almost any machine you can dream up, no matter how sophisticated, you can look into the body and find one better." * That inquisitive men should continue to discover unknown marvels in the human mechanism is exactly what the Christian expects, for its Creator is divine.

Of the mysterious formation of the baby in its mother's womb the psalmist wrote: "Thou knowest me through and through: my body is no mystery to thee, how I was secretly . . . patterned. . . . Thou didst see my limbs unformed in the womb, and in thy book they are all recorded" (Ps. 139:15, 16, N.E.B.).

It is humbling to realize that at one time you were but a single fertilized human egg no larger than the period at the end of this sentence. From such a minute beginning, extremely involved and mysterious developments gradually molded every tiny tissue of nerve, bone, and muscle until your entire baby body was complete with a brain to think, eyes to see, ears to hear, and every other organ perfectly fashioned.

Evolution offers no satisfactory explanation for the involved yet purposeful processes by which the human body is able to duplicate itself, transmit to its offspring countless inherited traits, and reproduce each intricate part with mingled characteristics of both parents. Of this higher Influence at work, Sir James Gray, an evolutionist, has observed that the procreative process seems "analogous to the process by which a house is built . . . in accordance with a predetermined plan . . . in a highly purposeful way." † The Christian recognizes here the handiwork of God.

---

* The San Francisco *Examiner*, Sept. 11, 1966, p. 30.

† *Science Today*, pp. 25, 26.

MAN'S MARVELOUS MENTAL ENDOWMENT

Thou hast made him a little less than a god, crowning him with glory and honour. Thou makest him master over all thy creatures. Ps. 8:5, 6, N.E.B.).

Man's original rank in the hierarchy of nature was one of eminence but little below that of angels. Although his physical endowments were marvelous to contemplate, he was never intended to climb like the monkey or to jump like the flea. But in the realm of the mind, man stood preeminently above every other member of the animal kingdom. Enabled to think God's thoughts after Him, the first man was fully competent to undertake his indispensable role in the grand design. Until sin disrupted his dominion, he remained the unchallenged master of the earth, a majestic personage "crowned . . . with glory and honour."

Evolutionists do not regard man as God's ultimate masterpiece. Instead, they propound the theory that he is but the latest product of a long, mindless, and purposeless evolutionary progression. Although uncertain as to whether this process is still continuing, they insist that man ranks just above some near-relative of the gorilla from whom he is supposed to have descended. By this hypothesis man is linked with the brutish creation and owes neither his origin nor his allegiance to any Higher Power.

Despite the negative view of skeptics, it is a fact that since World War II much astute research into the nature of the human organism points ever more clearly to an omniscient Master Designer. In the *Reader's Digest,* J. D. Ratcliff explains some newly discovered mysteries. For example, the thyroid gland in the neck, weighing less than an ounce, daily produces an infinitesimal quantity of a potent hormone. Yet this minute powerhouse of life directs the rate of growth in children, determines their size, and decides how much food the body's billions of cells shall convert into energy.

Likewise, the human brain, which is slowly yielding its enigmatic mysteries to scientific study, is now known to be infinitely more complex than was previously thought. It is staggering to realize that every mortal brain is composed of not fewer than 10 billion nerve cells. Each cell, once believed to be similar to a relay on a switchboard, is now known to be as complicated as a computer. Surely there can be no doubt that man is God's masterpiece.

THE CITADEL OF THE HEART

Keep thy heart with all diligence; for out of it are the issues of life. Prov. 4:23.

In the United States today heart disease is the number one killer. Last year more than a million people succumbed to this dread disease and 30 million others are currently afflicted with it. In spite of these appalling figures, the heart is the most essential and durable organ of the body. It is powerful, too, else it could not pump ten thousand quarts of blood through itself and out into the circulatory system every twenty-four hours—and keep this up constantly for a lifetime.

As the physical heart, which is actually a muscular pump, is the central source of life-giving blood for the body, the term "heart" was used by the ancients to identify the seat of spiritual life, the center of the moral sensibility of the soul. It is the focal habitat of personal life, the wellspring of desires, motives, and ethical decisions. The mental processes are also included, for the wise man said, "As he [a man] thinketh in his heart, so is he" (Prov. 23:7).

In the eighth chapter of Acts it is recorded that a man named Simon had a lofty opinion of himself. Simon was a baptized member, but he was not a regenerated believer. To further his own schemes he offered Peter money to buy the gift of the Holy Spirit. Peter replied sternly, "You have neither part nor lot in this matter, for your heart is not right before God" (Acts 8:21, R.S.V.).

The gift Simon wanted was good, but his motive was wrong. He wanted this power to spend it upon his own lusts and to further his own selfish ambitions. Peter told him his heart was wrong. Even after this sharp rebuke Simon, instead of praying for forgiveness, asked only for escape from punishment. His difficulty was not with his head but with his heart.

To assure its protection, the heart is set in the innermost sheltered place in the whole body. When it fails everything else succumbs. It is the spiritual heart that controls our thoughts, our words, and our actions. It makes our choices and decides our final destiny. What then can possibly be more important than the care and protection of the heart? Have you given serious attention lately to what enters and exits through your heart's door? If not, what better time than now to redress this fatal oversight?

THE PROUD HEART

Haughty eyes and a proud heart . . . are sin! Prov. 21:4, N.I.V.

Scorn, arrogance, and a haughty presence are evidences of a proud heart. And a proud, self-centered heart is displeasing to God. This spirit, which often accompanies those who in any way regard themselves as superior, is atheism of a sort because it honors the creature above the Creator.

It was this kind of self-aggrandizement, germinating in the heart of Lucifer, that fired his ambition to seek the highest place in heaven. War came and God banished Satan with this imperative: "Thine heart was lifted up because of thy beauty, thou hast corrupted thy wisdom by reason of thy brightness: I will cast thee to the ground" (Eze. 28:17). Solomon may have been thinking of this greatest of all tragedies when he wrote, "Pride comes before disaster, and arrogance before a fall" (Prov. 16:18, N.E.B.). In seeking to elevate himself and gain control of heavenly beings, to win them away from the Creator, Satan brought unspeakable woe into the world and eternal perdition on himself and all those who follow him.

It has been sagely said that discouragement and pride are Satan's sharpest weapons for separating men from God. Despite oft-repeated warnings that pride is a death-dealing trait of character, every generation is witness to human beings who grow proud and haughty, only to fall from the summit of supremacy to the depths of degradation. Some mortals—Nebuchadnezzar, Alexander, Napoleon, and Hitler, to name a few—each in turn with pride and power strode the world, only to meet disaster and disgrace in the quicksands of oblivion. Oh, why should the spirit of mortal be proud?

Harsh judgments have been pronounced on pride. Alexander Pope called it "the never-failing vice of fools." Martin Tupper referred to it as a "poisonous worm coiled about the foundations of the soul." "Spiritual pride eats out the vitals of religion," * wrote Ellen G. White. Horace Smith declared that "when a man thinks best of himself, then God and man think worst of him." It is this kind of pride that Satan inculcates.

Once I heard a young man say, "I would become a Christian if I could do just what I wanted to afterward." If you harbor such a self-pleasing heart it will give you no peace until you surrender it to God.

---

* *Testimonies,* vol. 3, p. 211.

THE MATERIALISTIC HEART

Take heed, and beware of covetousness: for a man's life consisteth not in the abundance of the things which he possesseth. Luke 12:15.

This text constitutes a warning to the wealthy and a comfort to those of limited possessions. Thrift, economy, and a healthy work ethic are laudable Christian virtues. But amassing vast material wealth is not. Jesus amazed His disciples by telling them that it is hard for those who have riches to enter into the kingdom of God. The reason, of course, is not that wealth is evil per se, but that great fortunes are seldom accumulated except by greedy grasping and other dishonorable means. A selfish, materialistic heart is never right with God.

To illustrate the catastrophic results of following the dictates of a covetous heart, Jesus told of a rich man who owned a most profitable farm. When his yield grew so bountiful that his storage places could not contain it all he began to question himself, "What shall I do, because I have no place to bestow my fruits?" Then he said, "This will I do: I will pull down my barns, and build greater; and there will I bestow all my fruits and my goods. And I will say to my soul, Soul, thou hast much goods laid up for many years; take thine ease, eat, drink, and be merry. But God said unto him, Thou fool, this night thy soul shall be required of thee: then whose shall those things be, which thou hast provided?" (Luke 12:16-20).

This unwise and unfortunate man tried to feed his soul on egoism, luxury, and license. He anticipated a long life of ease, gluttony, and self-gratification. He ignored God, eternity, and his own soul. His sudden, unexpected end came as the sole reward to his rapacious, materialistic heart.

In May, 1980, Mount Saint Helens, a majestic volcanic peak, dormant for 123 years, exploded in a towering eruption. Forty missing persons were presumed dead and twenty-five lost their lives, killed by noxious fumes and a layer of red-hot ashes that fell like flaming hail. Some could have survived had they fled. Among the lost was a grizzled old man who refused to leave his home on the mountainside. All his earthly possessions were there. Besides, he scoffed at the prospect of a holocaust. Today he and all that he owned lie under fifteen feet of ashes. How many there are who, similarly, will perish in the lake of fire because earthly possessions meant so much to them!

THE JEALOUS HEART

Jealousy is cruel as the grave. Its flashes are flashes of fire. S. of Sol., 8:6, R.S.V.

A jealous heart is not right in the sight of God. A brother to envy, and quite as corroding to the soul, jealousy is a green-eyed monster according to Shakespeare. John Dryden called it the yellow jaundice of the soul. Jealousy is the reluctant admission of inadequacy that betrays pettiness and penury of spirit. It is often the unintentional compliment the inferior pays his superior. William Wanley compared jealousy to Indian arrows, so "envenomed that if they prick the skin it is very dangerous: but if they draw blood, it is deadly."

Jealousy is a peculiar vice in that it is self-generated. Harbored in the heart it lives on suspicion and fear; yet, like a piece of ice concealed in the bosom, it chills none so much as the possessor.

How to account for a besetting sin so generally detested yet so well-nigh universal? Sacred Writ and the history of mankind since Eden explain it. It was jealousy in the heart of the archfiend that precipitated rebellion in heaven. Jealousy prompted the first murder. Blinded by jealousy of their brother, Aaron and Miriam stirred up trouble for Israel in the wilderness. The implacable and seething hatred Saul felt for David was prompted by jealousy for place and power. The ecclesiastical leaders in Jerusalem were jealous of Jesus' influence with the people. It was this that finally nailed Him to the cross.

Jealousy continues to generate vicious deeds of violence. Not infrequently the press reports shocking acts of malice, such as the torture and maiming of hapless victims. As suggested in our text, these atrocities result from incandescent tempers fueled by the green-eyed monster. All too often, sad to say, jealousy is the well-dressed, besetting sin that goes to church. No wonder, then, that jealousy, like its relative, covetousness, is a private, yet prevailing, frailty that few are willing to confess, a passion so full of cowardice and shame that hardly anyone will acknowledge it.

Although jealousy is more difficult to manage than "the fierce wolves of the wilderness," it is not beyond the reach of a determined will and the indwelling Spirit. Like other soul-corroding habits, it must be conquered, even if a full-scale warfare must be waged against it. For aid in this crucial struggle the Christian can take to himself the unfailing promise, "Ask, and it shall be given you" (Matt. 7:7).

THE INFIDEL HEART

The impious fool says in his heart, "There is no God." Ps. 14:1, N.E.B.

The original Hebrew word here translated "fool" suggests a person deficient mentally or morally, possibly both; someone colorblind to religious values. Faithless people sometimes make an outward show of respect for God for social or business reasons while in their disbelieving hearts there is no room for faith in Him.

Our text does not say that the infidelity is in the head but in the heart. The real problem of the infidel is not so much a defective head, a deficient intellect, as it is his flawed morality. So when a professed atheist says, "There is no God," he voices an inner, possibly subconscious, wish that this were true. And in many instances he hopes there is no God simply because he does not want to give up his sinful and selfish habits and practices. His stubborn will seeks escape from obedience to God's commandments, from the guilt of having broken them. This desire to escape responsibility for violating the moral law has turned many to willful atheism.

A striking example of the infidel heart can be found in the writings of the late, well-known evolutionist, Aldous Huxley, who explained, "I had motives for not wanting the world to have meaning. . . . For myself, as well as for many of my contemporaries, this philosophy was essentially an instrument of liberation . . . from a system of morality. We objected to morality because it interfered with our . . . freedom."

The infidel heart, loving sinful habits and comfortable with sinners, looks for excuses for continuing to relish and enjoy the pleasures of unrighteousness. But when the heart is turned toward Christ, belief and trust in an infinite God become the most reasonable things in all the world.

The study of history demonstrates that, in times of great peril, all men yearn desperately for protection and help from divine Providence. This assertion is confirmed by the widely publicized World War II observation that "there are no atheists in the foxholes." Even Plato, the pre-Christian Greek philosopher, recognized the universal temptation to look Heavenward in times of danger. He wrote that "few men are so obstinate in their atheism that a pressing danger will not compel them to acknowledge a divine power." Like Julian the Apostate, they cry out as he did on his deathbed, "O Galilean, thou hast conquered!"

THE UNFORGIVING HEART

Forgive, and you will be forgiven. Luke 6:37, R.S.V.

No principle of Christianity stands more supreme—and none is more contrary to the natural heart—than that of forgiveness. The spectacle of the Saviour, dying on the cross for the sins of men, will ever remain the most sublime example of the forgiving heart. He prayed, "Father, forgive them" (Luke 23:34).

The heart that will not forgive is not right with God, because it is a heart filled with bitterness, malice, and revenge. No teaching in God's Word is clearer than this: except you forgive men their trespasses, your heavenly Father will not forgive yours.

Caleb Young decided, after careful investigation, that a young man who was serving a life term in prison had been too severely sentenced. He brought the matter to the attention of the governor and finally secured a pardon for the criminal. With the pardon in his pocket he went to the penitentiary to give the good news to the prisoner. In the conversation Mr. Young asked, "If you were released from prison what would you do?" The young man replied, "If I were let out of here I would find the judge that sentenced me and I would kill him. Then I would 'get' the lawyer who prosecuted me and every last witness that testified against me." Mr. Young said not a word about the pardon in his pocket. Instead, he walked out of the prison cell and outside of the prison. Then, standing on the sidewalk, he tore the pardon to shreds.

John said, "He who says he is in the light and hates his brother is in the darkness still" (1 John 2:9, R.S.V.) and also, "Any one who hates his brother is a murderer, and you know that no murderer has eternal life abiding in him" (chap. 3:15, R.S.V.). The apostle Paul said, "Be kind to one another, tenderhearted, forgiving one another, as God in Christ forgave you" (Eph. 4:32, R.S.V.).

An unforgiving heart makes it impossible to worship God, because He cannot accept worship from such a heart. Someone has said wisely that "he who will not forgive others breaks the bridge over which he himself must pass, for all have need to be forgiven." If there is any ill-will, any desire to "get even," any vengeance in your heart, your worship is in vain. Furthermore, it is useless to seek God's mercy unless you show mercy, and the essential prerequisite for God's forgiveness is to come to Him with a forgiving heart.

THE NEW HEART

A new heart I will give you, and a new spirit I will put within you; and I will take out of your flesh the heart of stone and give you a heart of flesh. Eze. 36:26, R.S.V.

Not until recently has any heart-transplant patient survived. Even now, with the most skillful surgeons operating with the most sophisticated equipment, this operation remains the major of majors. Of the patients who have received transplants, only a few are alive today. But this transfer of the physical heart is not what the Lord spoke of when He said, "A new heart I will give you." The unbelieving, unconverted heart is so diseased that it is beyond mending. The only cure is the implantation of a spiritually new heart, which is exactly what the Lord promises to do.

Elder H. M. S. Richards recounts the story of the Indian chief Tedyuskung, who was sitting at the fireside with his devout Quaker friend. As they looked into the embers the Quaker said, "I will tell thee what I am thinking. It is the rule by the Author of the Christian religion which we call the golden rule."

"Stop!" said the chief, "don't praise it to me. Tell me what it is."

The Quaker replied, "It is for one to do to another what he would have the other do to him."

"That is impossible," said the chief. Again silence reigned. The chief arose, walked nervously about the room, and then stopped before his friend. He said, "If the Great Spirit that made man would give him a new heart, he could do as you say, but not else."

Tedyuskung was right. Only the new heart can please God. This is why David prayed, "Create in me a clean heart, O God; and renew a right spirit within me" (Ps. 51:10).

It is said that as Sir Walter Raleigh lay his head on the block, the executioner, before lifting the ax, asked, "Does your head lie right, Sir Walter?" Sir Walter turned his head toward the man and said, "You know, friend, it does not matter how the head lies if the heart is right."

Many who are not afflicted with physical heart disease suffer spiritual heart weariness. To all with this serious form of "tired heart" the Saviour says, "Be not afraid, only believe" (Mark 5:36). If your heart is not right before God it can be if you invite the Saviour in.

THE UNDERSTANDING HEART

Give therefore thy servant an understanding heart . . . that I may discern between good and bad. . . . Behold, I have done according to thy words: lo, I have given thee a wise and an understanding heart. 1 Kings 3:9-12.

New to the throne as successor to his father, David, the inexperienced Solomon realized his need of wisdom and understanding. He knew that human judgment was unequal to the task ahead, inadequate to decide fairly the issues before him, and to discern between right and wrong. It was then that the Lord appeared to the young king in a dream and said, "Ask what I shall give thee" (1 Kings 3:5). Solomon replied wisely, "Give [me] . . . an understanding heart." This was exactly what he needed to rule successfully over Israel. The Lord was so pleased to honor his request that the resultant extent of his knowledge, the depth of his understanding, and the glory of his reign became the wonder of the world.

Some years ago it was my pleasure to visit the home of the late plant wizard Luther Burbank, at Santa Rosa, California. The man in charge of this impressive old house and its splendid adjoining gardens told me that he had worked with Mr. Burbank for many years. I asked him what was the unique gift that so greatly distinguished this far-famed horticulturist. The superintendent replied, "It was his uncanny ability to discern differences that none of us who helped him could see. Mr. Burbank would go among springing flowers and mark just a few for special attention. No one else could tell any difference at all. But he could, and invariably the plants he selected proved to be the very ones that developed the unique characteristics we were seeking." Mr. Burbank's distinction was a rare, natural gift, a sense of texture and color beyond that of ordinary people. It was this special ability that made him successful.

The Christian in his daily walk does not so much need the kind of genius Luther Burbank had as he does the better wisdom from above, the clarity of vision to distinguish between good and evil, a distinction that often seems almost imperceptible. Yet if, like Solomon, we pray not for riches nor honor, but rather for the higher wisdom and spiritual discernment in our everyday choices, the Lord will surely honor our request. Then, with these precious, Heaven-sent virtues to guide us, we can walk safely through this "present, evil world" and come out finally "more than conquerors through him that loved us" and gave Himself for us.

THE DIVIDED HEART

A double minded man is unstable in all his ways. James 1:8.

Simply because we live in an unstable world and in the midst of uncertain times does not mean that we have to remain undecided or double-minded when it comes to the great issues of life. Faced with paramount choices, some are seized by paralysis of the mind, as if assailed by an acute attack of *anxiety*. The perplexed soul is no more able to follow a sound course than can a man sleep wondering whether he has wound the clock or bolted the door. Some seem divided by a bumptious *contrariness*, a complicated and difficult disposition of mind. We want to be kindly disposed and agreeable, but we are inwardly vexed by crosscurrents that make us discourteous and disagreeable. Thus we find ourselves torn between contending influences—one to be Christlike and gracious, the other to be edgy and unpleasant. Others are overtaken by a divided will when assailed by fitful *impulses*. Happy are those with the self-control to hold these sudden inclinations in check.

Young people are particularly susceptible to the divided-heart syndrome. Facing alternatives of great moment some agonize long between choices. With little experience to guide them and often having inadequate knowledge of the issues involved, it is easy to understand why they quail as they face a fateful decision. What career shall I follow? Whom shall I marry? What is God's will for me?

Such double-mindedness is not new. Augustine wrote that although he was greatly influenced by his mother, Monica, he was often swept back from the ideal by an outbreak of passion. John Bunyan told of his two selves continually at war within him. Even the apostle Paul worried because his better self longed to do the will of God whereas his natural self often brought him into thralldom. In near despair he cried out, "O wretched man that I am! who shall deliver me from the body of this death?" (Rom. 7:24). Yet, by the strengthening that comes from the power of God's indwelling Spirit the great apostle overcame this weakness of the divided heart. He declared, "I keep under my body and bring it into subjection" (1 Cor. 9:27). The record remains for our emulation.

What a thought that God brings a man into such a close connection with Himself that "the weak man may become strong . . . and the irresolute . . . become men of quick and firm decision"! *(Testimonies,* vol. 4, p. 614). This is the remedy for the divided heart.

THE CHILD HEART

Jesus called a little child to his side and set him on his feet in the middle of them all. "Believe me," he said, "unless you change your whole outlook and become like little children you will never enter the kingdom of Heaven." Matt. 18:2, 3, Phillips.

The Lord bids us to seek the child heart, not to be childish, but childlike. The illustrious soldier Naaman, a mighty man of valor, through the entreaties of a little captive maid came to the prophet Elisha, who told him that his leprosy could be healed by bathing in the murky waters of the Jordan River. He obeyed "and his flesh came again like unto the flesh of a little child, and he was clean" (2 Kings 5:14). A noble combination indeed—the stature and strength of the grown man united with the sweetness and winsome purity of a little child. Abraham Lincoln and Robert E. Lee are noted as having this rare amalgam, but not many men of large affairs attain this distinctive composite of virtues.

It is impossible for anyone to possess these two qualities without paying the price. The levels of rank in the kingdom of heaven are the opposite of those in the kingdoms of earth. Here men and women continually strive to outdistance and rise above their fellows, but in Christ's kingdom His followers stoop to serve and in this humbling they are crowned. Let us remember that the Master Himself girded His waist with a towel and, kneeling down, washed the feet of His disciples.

I have sometimes wondered who the child was, the one the Saviour called to His side. How happy he must have been as Jesus held him to His heart! "The simplicity, self-forgetfulness, and the confiding love of a little child are the attributes that Heaven values. These are the characteristics of real greatness."—*The Desire of Ages,* p. 437. These are natural traits of childhood. How sad that children early learn from us to seek notice, patronage, and favor!

Childlike hearts do not hold grudges and are quick to forgive. So do adults who are like them in spirit. Children love to sing together, as do all childlike Christians, who join in the symphony of prayer. One may go east and another west but beneath the touch of their spirit of love they remain in accord, in attuned fellowship with one another and with the masterful, yet childlike and compassionate, Saviour.

A FOUNTAIN OF JOY

These things have I spoken unto you, that my joy might remain in you, and that your joy might be full. John 15:11.

Surrounded by implacable enemies, the weight of the sins of all the world upon Him, Jesus walked offenseless among men. Each morning the unutterable anguish of the cross drew one day nearer. Despite the deepening shadow of His own impending doom, the Saviour spoke with radiant face of His joy. He strengthened His disciples with the assurance that this same joy might be theirs. Keeping constantly before Him the glorious consummation of His earthly mission, He could present an expression of gladness. He foresaw the travail of His own soul and was satisfied. In His ears already rang the voices of the redeemed singing the Song of Moses and the Lamb. Even though "unspeakable woe was upon Him; yet for the joy that was set before Him He chose to endure the cross and despised the shame."—*The Ministry of Healing,* p. 504.

The Saviour spoke of "my joy" and "your joy." If this "fulness of joy" could not be imparted to the believers He would not have mentioned it. He yearned for His disciples—of that day and of ours—to partake so bountifully of His joy as to become veritable fountains of happiness flowing out to bless others.

Does your Christian experience enable you to put on a happy face? We all know certain people who seem to make a room light up as they enter. A sunny disposition and infectious good humor impart an electrifying radiance that lifts the spirit and makes you feel that somehow everything is going to be all right. Such is the influence of fullness of joy.

After one of his many defeats for office, Abraham Lincoln was asked how he felt. He said, "Somewhat like the boy . . . who stubbed his toe, . . . The boy said he was too big to cry, and too badly hurt to laugh." Later he claimed he had "found that people are just about as happy as they make up their minds to be." Some people are not very good at laughing the outside while crying on the inside. They wear trouble like a badge martyrdom, spreading gloom on their closest friends and loved ones. a good way to dispose of friends and alienate people. Conversely, imparted by the Lord bestows neither heaviness nor gloom. It is a duty to be cheerful.

GOOD MEDICINE

A cheerful heart is a good medicine, but a downcast spirit dries up the bones. Prov. 17:22, R.S.V.

The average American Indian in his native habitat was—and is—surprisingly religious. To a degree little understood and seldom practiced by his white subjugators, the Indian in his daily life intermingled the secular and the mundane with the things of the spirit. Anything that promoted individual or general benefit was good medicine. The opposite was considered bad medicine. At long last modern, scientific medicine has come to realize that a cheerful heart, as suggested by our text, is among the most potent good medicines known.

One day a troubled man looked out on his world and back on his life. Distressed and surrounded by his enemies, he had the feeling that he was standing alone. He was obsessed with agonizing fear and dread of the unknown. But these were not to be the sum total of his life. Instead, the psalmist cried out, "This is the day which the Lord has made; let us rejoice and be glad in it" (Ps. 118:24, R.S.V.). The inspiring thought was good medicine to his faltering heart.

Another man was confined to the dull and debilitating routine of a dark prison cell. Through a tiny crack near the top of the wall he could see a slender slice of blue sky. Like a caged eagle he wished he might be soaring out there on vigorous wings. Then he bent down and wrote to his fellow believers, "Rejoice in the Lord alway: and again I say, Rejoice" (Phil. 4:4).

The gist of these and of many other scriptural references, even darkest pages, is the imperative Rejoice! There runs an underto cheer—good medicine, if you will—likely to burst forth unrestrained songs of praise and thanksgiving. Thus we joy is central to the Christian faith. Vital religion alw a cheerful outlook. Coming down the centu Christianity contains more praise than all "Endure life," says one. "What will "Struggle on, perhaps you can impro still another. "Appease the gods, distinguishes the Christian faith is tha being identified with a God who cares, stands before us in the midst of anguish medicine for the soul, "Be of good cheer."

JOY IN WORSHIP

Make a joyful noise unto the Lord, all ye lands. Serve the Lord with gladness: come before his presence with singing. Ps. 100:1, 2.

These verses, the psalmist's triumphant shout of joyous thanksgiving, are said to be the source of the well-known hymn, beginning, "All people that on earth do dwell, Sing to the Lord with cheerful voice." The melody, the Old Hundredth, was composed in 1551 by Louis Bourgeois, and the lyric was supplied ten years later by William Kethe. It is a hymn heard frequently in churches and at various gatherings all over the world.

As the crowning act of Creation, man is the only earthling with the ability to lift his voice in spoken words of praise to the Creator. We know that, when actuated by sentiments of the heart, a prayer of petition or praise is wafted swiftly on wings of song to the inner courts above. The psalmist knew this when in gratitude he emphatically declared, "I will praise the name of God with a song, and will magnify him with thanksgiving" (Ps. 69:30).

What of the nature of our collective worship? We can come reluctantly to divine services, inwardly struggling and kicking, as some do, particularly on a bright, warm day, and then suffer through it all. Or we can come with gladness and make our own sincere songs and prayers true vehicles of adoration. We can personalize our praise, concentrate on the thoughts expressed, and make song the highlight of the service. We can stand up to sing with heart and mind, with soul on tiptoe, which is the only right way when it is the risen Christ of whom we are singing.

All too often churchgoers plod through the week giving little thought to prayer or praise, quite as if God didn't exist. Some go so far as to rehearse their frustrations and even verbalize their complaints against Him. The Sabbath comes to such disheartened ones almost like a dare for God to do something. Shall we sit glumly through an hour of unattentive inconvenience or shall we attend to that which is central to living—praise to Him who has brought us safely through another week? "I will sing to the Lord as long as I live: I will sing praise to my God while I have my being" (Ps. 104:33). Since we know that heaven is filled with joy, should not the church on earth also be full of praise?

JOY IN SERVICE

And thou, Solomon my son, know thou the God of thy father, and serve him with a perfect heart and with a willing mind. 1 Chron. 28:9.

David's magnificent twenty-third psalm and his other sacred poems reveal his deep and abiding spiritual longings. Protected miraculously from death at the hands of Saul and in other countless ways as enemies pursued him, he truly "walked through the valley of the shadow of death." Yet he could say triumphantly of the Lord, "Thou art with me."

As King David came at last to the closing days of his long life he looked forward to the reign of his son Solomon, whom he earnestly admonished to follow the Lord, "the God of thy father, and serve him with a perfect heart and with a willing mind."

Some time or other in life a person is bound to be involved in tedious, unpalatable tasks. As boys, my brother and I had the job each spring of cutting bushels and bushels of seed potatoes for planting. We disliked the tedium. Our hearts weren't in it. That is, until we devised a simple gadget consisting of a sharp knife thrust through a thin board. After that we could sit and slice the potatoes by pushing them against the sharp knife edge. Immediately the routine changed. The work went faster and more easily, and from then on we cut potatoes with a "willing mind."

The hallmark of the early Christian church was the way the believers responded with all they had. Paul, the apostle to the Gentiles, drove himself like a dynamo all his days. He said, "Woe unto me if I preach not the gospel." Under persecution he spoke of the joy of suffering for Christ's sake. Unnumbered thousands since have counted it a privilege to offer themselves gladly in His service, not counting the cost, not holding back, not grudgingly but as cheerful givers.

There are two ways a minister can make a pastoral call. He can encourage the family by a cheerful half hour's visit or he can leave his card at the door. A teacher can prepare a lesson in one of two ways. He can diligently concentrate on it or he can give it "a lick and a promise" and vow to do better next time. The principle applies widely.

Does your attitude thunder, "Don't count on me. I'm too busy"? Or does it say, "Here am I. Send me"? "Not more surely is the place prepared for us in the heavenly mansions than is the special place designated on earth where we are to work for God."—*Christ's Object Lessons*, p. 327.

DEALING WITH DISCOURAGEMENT

Deep calleth unto deep at the noise of thy waterspouts: all thy waves and thy billows have gone over me. Ps. 42:7.

The Christian, as well as the worldling, can become victim of "the blues." There may or may not be a reason for this overwhelming sense of melancholy and abject despondency. At such times there is consolation in considering the experiences of the psalmist. Certainly David had reason enough for discouragement as he poured his heart out in the pathetic lament recorded in Psalm 42. He was a hunted fugitive exiled from the house of God where he had once found exquisite joy in the sacred services. Despairing of his life, he suffered the most poignant grief. "A sorrow's crown of sorrow is remembering happier things."—Tennyson.

Despite his peril, David, the fearful, harried wanderer, remembered the omnipotence of the Almighty even as he recognized the flood of his troubles as by God's sufferance. In desperation he lamented, "All thy waves and thy billows have gone over me." It may be that he had witnessed tumultuous, threatening torrents of the upper Jordan River, breaking in boisterous waves in flood time. His immediate peril seemed similarly threatening. Utterly discouraged, he sank down in deep despair.

Nevertheless, David's enduring faith prevailed as he prayed, "Thou art the God of my strength. . . . Send out thy light and thy truth: let them lead me . . . unto thy holy hill, and to thy tabernacles. Then will I go unto . . . God my exceeding joy: yea, upon the harp will I praise thee, O God my God" (Ps. 43:2-4). This anguished petition did not go unheeded. In succeeding months, as the minions of the jealous-hearted, murderous King Saul relentlessly pursued David to take his life, the God he trusted constantly safeguarded him. After many fiery trials, and in God's own time, the hounded fugitive ascended the throne of Israel as King David, a man "after God's own heart."

Through the ages God's servants, among them Job, Elijah, and Nehemiah, have been prey to discouragement. Whenever he suffered fits of despair, Martin Luther reminded himself that this was the work of the devil. Ellen White admitted that for years she "suffered peculiar trials of mind" "a weight of sadness and discouragement which cannot be uttered" (*Testimonies*, vol. 1, p. 346). For relief she endorsed hymns of praise: "Song is a weapon that we can always use against discouragement," she wrote, "as we thus open the heart to the sunlight of the Saviour's presence, we shall have health and His blessing."—*The Ministry of Healing*, p. 254.

FRET NOT THYSELF

Fret not thyself because of evildoers, neither be thou envious against the workers of iniquity. Ps. 37:1.

During my college years—and sometimes since—a relentless temptation has repeatedly assailed me. I refer to the unbidden impulse to lose heart and forsake the Christian pilgrimage because of the prominence and the prosperity of this or that dishonest, disloyal, or dissembling church member. Not a few of my cherished friends have become mightily troubled over what they perceive to be glaring inconsistencies in the lives of "the brethren." They ask questions. Why do some dishonest people flourish while many who are upright in heart barely eke out an existence? Why do students who cheat often get better grades than their conscientious colleagues who would rather fail than defraud? Why can certain persons of questionable morals capture the spotlight and lay hold of the prominent positions while other more capable and humble workers are passed over? Some have seen so much "wickedness in high places" that, to my sorrow, they "walk no more with us."

This spiritually withering influence of defectors from dedication and duty has plagued God's people from the day sin invaded Eden. The psalmist admitted that his feet had "well nigh slipped" when he "saw the prosperity of the wicked" (Ps. 73:2, 3). To stave off this temptation, David issued the solemn admonition to "fret not thyself because of evildoers." He provided three reasons to remain steadfast: It isn't good for us to become agitated when we see sinners getting away with their sinful practices (Ps. 37:1); we must not grow angry when we see dishonesty prosper (verse 7); and we must be on guard lest a resentful mood lead us to act wickedly ourselves (verse 8).

Looking steadfastly toward the future with eternity in view, the Christian can enjoy a peace of mind that sinners never know. How important it is to take the long view in the light of the Saviour's words spoken on Mount Olivet regarding the very days in which we live! He predicted that "because iniquity shall abound, the love of many shall wax cold" (Matt. 24:12). Let none forget that there is a judgment day coming when rewards will be made to the unjust as well as to the justified. "For yet a little while, and the wicked shall not be: yea, thou shalt diligently consider his place, and it shall not be" (Ps. 37:10). Without question and without exception, all transgressors, unless they repent, will end up in the lake of fire.

A HIDING PLACE

Thou art my hiding place and my shield. Ps. 119:114.

By the time I was 10, our family of seven included two brothers and two sisters, all younger than I. Our spacious kitchen, the busiest place in the house, served as a multipurpose room for the whole family. We loved one another dearly, but our noisy clamor often reached such levels that mother took refuge in her bedroom to read or sew; and father, ignoring the racket, would try to concentrate his thoughts behind his newspaper. Some distance back of the house beyond the garden lay an open cove, an overgrown lowland alongside Bear Creek. As a child I liked to explore this tangled wildwood looking for yellow bells and lavender shooting stars. There behind a huge, partly uprooted old tree I came upon a little open space. Here was a natural bower encircled with willows. Unkown to the others I laid down a crude floor of old lumber and, with leafy branches interwoven overhead, I devised a snug little den, my hiding place.

For several years this hideaway remained my secret. When sad or troubled I went there to be alone, to rest on my soft mattress of dry leaves, to listen to the woods, and to ease the hurts of childhood. There on my back I solved many a small problem, built fantastic castles in the air, and gravely pondered the unknown future. There I prayed for forgiveness and asked humbly for divine guidance.

How thankful I am today that, thus early, I found a kind of sanctuary, a quiet place where I could come alone to think, to heed the voice of conscience and commune with God. That hiding place is far away now and utterly lost except in memory. Decades have come and gone since I took comfort in the crude refuge. But the practice of contemplative solitude and of one-to-one communion with the Divine has endured through the years. When difficult times come, when disappointment shatters fond hope, when feelings of regret roll over me for opportunities neglected, wherever I am, in memory I come to my secret place and receive solace from God, quite as I did in the long ago.

When in need of special guidance I like to recall the significant statement from the pen of Ellen White: "Communion with God imparts to the soul an intimate knowledge of His will."—*Testimonies,* vol. 4, p. 534.

THE NATURE AND CHARACTER OF GOD

Then the Lord passed in front of him and called aloud, "Jehovah, the Lord, a god compassionate and gracious, long-suffering, ever constant and true." Ex. 34:6, N.E.B.

During Job's afflictions, his friends reviewed the futility of man's efforts to plumb the depths of God's wisdom and power. They asked, "Can you fathom the mystery of God? can you fathom the perfection of the Almighty? It is higher than the heaven. . . . It is deeper than Sheol; you can know nothing" (Job 11:7, 8, N.E.B.). And the apostle Paul, thinking of God's manifold and distinctive characteristics, exclaimed, "O the depth of the riches both of the wisdom and knowledge of God! how unsearchable are his judgments, and his ways past finding out!" (Rom. 11:33).

Today, the proud and arrogant mind of man, no less than in Job's time, demands to know God's attributes, His methods, and the way He deals with men. But, as in the days of Paul, His mysterious ways are "past finding out." Even so, from the things that are revealed, we can know God well enough to revere Him, faithfully obey Him, and even deeply love Him. As the presence of the universe proves His existence, so do the works of nature testify to His wisdom and power. His foreknowledge is seen in all the fulfilled predictions of Scripture (Isa. 46:9, 10). His mercy, long-suffering, and infinite grace are manifested in the plan of salvation (Ex. 34:6, 7). In fact, our Creator-God is infinite in all His attributes. Consequently, no finite being can fully comprehend Him. But since He is infinite, all His purposes must be infinitely just and perfect, and, therefore, quite above the judgments or criticisms of finite men. We would all be much happier if we could in simple faith believe that God is doing the very best He can for every one of us.

Thus, although the "secret things belong to God" (Deut. 29:29), although we cannot find all the answers to all the questions that dismay, nor always discern His purposes in His dealings with us, we can trust Him and keep confidence in His leadings. When perplexed believers cannot see the reasons for their calamities, let alone understand sudden death and disaster, we can take comfort in the assurance that His ways are not our ways and that the redeemed of earth will yet acclaim in unison: " 'Great and marvellous are thy deeds, O Lord God, . . . just and true are thy ways, thou king of the ages' " (Rev. 15:3, N.E.B.). My finite mind cannot fully comprehend God, but His infinity enables Him to fully understand me, and I will trust Him.

UNDERSTANDING OUR TRIUNE GOD

Without faith it is impossible to please him; for anyone who comes to God must believe that he exists and that he rewards them who search for him. Heb. 11:6, N.E.B.

Our text teaches that an award awaits those who "diligently seek" God (K.J.V.). Another verse reads: "The secret things belong to the Lord our God; but the things that are revealed belong to us and to our children for ever" (Deut. 29:29, R.S.V.). Accordingly, we study with enthusiasm and profit from the revelations of God in the Scriptures, the Testimonies, and the book of nature. But sometimes we fail to notice that certain things are not revealed, nor is it necessary for our salvation to know them.

From time immemorial philosophers and theologians have attempted to draw back the veil so as to more clearly see God's personality and better understand His nature and character. These secrets of the Holy Trinity have long remained a tantalizing mystery. Concepts of the Godhead have ranged from that of three nebulous entities to the belief that each One is a separate Being. But all the conjecture and philosophizing yields little beyond that set forth in the Scriptures.

Unfortunately, there are those who ardently seek to explore areas that God has not seen fit to explain to man—at least not yet. Sometimes such attempts to ferret out God's secrets are but harmless speculations; at other times, they may lead to futility, doubt, and skepticism. There is a vast difference between thoughtful meditation on the deep things of God and curious, pointless questionings that spring from a restless spirit. We must remember that heavenly things are revealed to our finite minds in the simplest essentials for our guidance and salvation.

With such precautions in mind, we turn again to the Scriptures to discover what is said about God. Jesus referred to a Triune God: the Trinity of the Father, Son, and Holy Spirit (see John 15:26). The apostle John says, "These three are one" (1 John 5:7). Jehovah-God is the first person of the Godhead. The second Member is Jesus Christ, the only begotten of the Father, by whom the worlds were made (Heb. 1:2). As the Son, He is of the same substance as the Father and as such is God. The third Person of the Trinity, also called the Comforter, is the Holy Spirit, who "proceeds from the Father" and influences men in the name of Christ (John 15:26). Each of the holy three is, therefore, a distinct personality, yet one in spirit and purpose.

SCIENCE VERSUS THE BIBLE

He is before all things, and in him all things hold together. Col. 1:17, R.S.V.

To the Hebrews Paul wrote that the work of Creation was finished "from the foundation of the world" (Heb. 4:3). But the power of God has been continually exercised ever since in upholding and operating this creation. Every breath, every pulsation of the heart, and every unfolding frond is evidence of the care of Him in whom "we live, and move, and have our being" (Acts 17:28).

Of God's constant working in His universe, Ellen White wrote: "It is by His power that vegetation is caused to flourish, that every leaf appears and every flower blooms. Every drop of rain or flake of snow, every spire of grass, every leaf and flower and shrub, testifies of God."—*Testimonies,* vol. 8, p. 260.

It has often been said that God speaks to man in His two books—the Bible and the book of nature. During the century since Darwin introduced the theory of evolution, scientific thought has turned largely in favor of mechanistic evolution as the best explanation of the existence of the universe. Such a view leaves no room for belief in a transcendent God. Hence, a century-long controversy developed. All this time scientists interpreted the book of nature as an irreconcilable disagreement with the Scriptures.

But as the weight of evidence in favor of a Great Designer has multiplied, more and more reputable and unprejudiced scholars have come to acknowledge that there may not be an irreducible conflict after all. Many scientific "facts" once thought to disprove the Bible are now "reinterpreted" so as to confirm it. Obviously, many evolutionists long misread God's revelations in the book of nature.

Recent and most exhaustive investigations point unerringly to nature as the product of a great creative mind. The intricacy and precision of the individual parts are as astounding as is the grandeur of the whole. After perceiving the skill and beauty with which the simplest organisms are fashioned, one overawed research chemist wrote: "The simplest man-made mechanism requires a planner and a maker. How this complicated universe, a mechanism ten thousand times more involved and intricate, can be conceived as self-constructed and self-perpetuating is completely beyond me."

TRUST IN GOD

The Lord is good. Nahum 1:7. Acquaint now thyself with him, and be at peace. Job 22:21.

To believe in God is the most natural thing in the world. Before the time of Christ, the renowned Roman philosopher Cicero declared that "Nature herself has imprinted on the minds of all the idea of a God."—*De nanatura deorum,* I. As the youthful David Brainerd was preaching to the inquisitive Indians about the existence of God, one astonished chieftain turned to Brainerd's associate and asked plaintively, "Does he think that we don't know that already?"

Two hundred years ago E. B. Condillac wrote: "The most perfect idea of God that we can form in this life is that of an independent, unique, infinite, eternal, omnipotent, immutable, intelligent, and free First Cause, whose power extends over all things."—*Traite des animaux,* vi. A half century earlier scientist G. W. Leibniz said: "God is to his creatures, not only what an inventor is to his machine, but also what a prince is to his subjects, and a father is to his children."—*The Monadology,* lxxxiv. All of which is quite as true today as it was then or when Nahum observed that "the Lord is good."

Job asked one of the basic questions of all time when he pleaded to be shown where he might find God. In due time he found the answer; whereupon, he was able to say, "Acquaint now thyself with him, and be at peace." The deepest needs of Job's life were satisfied through his growing understanding and appreciation of God. Strength, comfort, and inner peace come with knowing Him.

André Marois, noted French historian, observed that France began her decline when she lost God. The people generally continued their traditional religious practices, but they had lost their spiritual conviction. Many Frenchmen continued to attend church routinely, but their inner faith had evaporated. As a result, France experienced a disastrous downfall.

Sooner or later every society and nation faces decline when it individually and collectively neglects and disregards God. There is no need to wonder why, when for so many life has become a noisy, pointless, tedious round of meaningless activities. Engrossed in thoughts of progress and prosperity and harried out of mind with the problems and pressures of the day, the restless masses in this materialistic age have left no time to be still.

WHY SO MANY BELIEVE EVOLUTION

Knowing God they have refused to honour him as God. And their misguided minds are plunged in darkness. Rom. 1:21, N.E.B.

This text is both an explanation of disbelief in God and an indictment of those who reject Him. It is the most satisfactory explanation I know of the widespread belief in evolution. Disbelievers are charged with willful disregard of God's Word; whereupon, their "misguided minds are darkened."

The prevailing belief in evolution is a stumbling block to many, particularly to young Christians. This is partly because so much is written about it. Books and periodicals continually publish so-called scientific proofs of evolution. Perusing such literature, the reader is apt to feel that there must be some truth to it. He does not see that the problem lies, not in the facts, but in their interpretation.

Another reason is that evolution has long been taught as verified truth. Textbooks in history, science, philosophy, even religion, are full of it. Authors and professors believe and teach it. One authority writes: "We are permeated and saturated with this transformist idea . . . we learned it in our classrooms."—A. Rostand, *The Orion Book of Evolution,* p. 95.

A third reason for evolution's wide acceptance is that it is presented with a great weight of authority. The prevailing attitude is that only the ignorant refuse to believe it. Thus, the average student, having been brainwashed with evolutionary ideas, when he first hears the creationist arguments is amazed at the possibility of evolution being wrong.

A fourth reason for accepting evolution is the all-too-frequent failure of orthodox Christianity. The abuses, intolerance, and cruelty practiced in the name of religion; disharmony and enmity between religious groups, and pagan ideas such as eternal burning in hell are repugnant to rational minds. Therefore, many abandon religion altogether.

A final excuse or motive for embracing evolution is that "if man is created, then this implies a purpose" which suggests responsibility to one's Maker. Evolutionist Aldous Huxley wrote: "I had motives . . . for myself, as no doubt for many of my contemporaries, this [evolutionary] philosophy . . . was an instrument of liberation from . . . morality. We objected to the morality because it interfered with our . . . freedom." * Man's stubborn will does not want to obey God's commandments. Thus it becomes convenient, even welcome, to accept evolution.

---

* "Confessions of an Atheist," *Science Reports,* June, 1966.

EVOLUTION'S IMPACT ON SOCIETY

For this reason God has given them up . . . , because they . . . offered reverence and worship to created things instead of to the Creator. . . . In consequence . . . God has given them up to shameful passions. Rom. 1:25, 26, N.E.B.

Having rejected God, self-important man exchanged "the splendour of immortal God" for an image, or concept, embracing "birds, beasts, and creeping things" (Rom. 1:23). Thus, evolution presents an imaginary succession of creeping reptiles, birds, and beasts, presumably developed by natural selection and the survival of the fittest, in place of the Creator. And misguided men all but worship this so-called "ancestral line."

A recent volume announces with pride the story of man's beginning, stating that primitive matter, "on the edge of existence," slowly evolved into simple swimming organisms. Fish appeared eons later. Eventually dinosaurs took over the land, and the first mammals, small furry creatures, scurried about. Some took to the trees. According to this book, man found his forebears among these creatures.

Such is the beginning chapter of the evolutionists' Bible. Yet the agnostic Julian Huxley admits that "evolution is a series of blind alleys." Arthur Brisbane, prestigious newspaper columnist, described man's fanciful subhuman ancestors supposedly "hanging precariously from trees by their prehensile tails." Then he added, "You are not obliged to believe this."

When students ask whether God may have created the first living cell, with all higher organisms later evolving from it, I answer emphatically, "No, because creationism and mechanistic evolution are irreconcilable."

According to the Bible, man is obliged to reverence and obey God and follow the golden rule. Evolution obliterates Christian faith and rules God out of His sky. It disavows any binding human law, as well, and discredits any future judgment or punishment. The widespread increase of crime and violence is traceable directly to this pernicious teaching. Evolutionists logically insist that no one can commit sin, since where there is no law there can be no sin. Thus is fostered a lawless society. On this account, Christians cannot ever accept evolution. Evolution teaches the survival of the fittest, but the Bible teaches the survival of the faithful.

WHAT ABOUT THE FLOOD?

For the time will come when they [people] will not stand wholesome teaching. . . . They will stop their ears to the truth and turn to mythology. 2 Tim. 4:3, 4, N.E.B.

A leaflet published by the Gospel Tract Society is entitled, "Who 'Mythed' the Boat?" It explains why some scientist-scholars have branded certain Bible chronicles as unreliable legends rather than the true historical records the Bible declares them to be. Humorously, the author points out that when it comes to the account of Noah, the universal Flood, and the ark, the approach of these skeptics to the Scriptures is "mything" the boat. This attitude is the very antithesis of our text, which asserts that such thinking constitutes "mythology." The more important question is not "Who 'mythed' the boat?" but "Who missed the truth?" Our text answers this.

Unfortunately, this skeptical view has been accepted by many theologians who claim that only the Person of the Book is important. They say they are not concerned about the literality of certain Biblical stories that they consider of slight significance. But just how insignificant are such accounts, the one about Noah, for example?

The apostle Peter believed the Genesis record. He also predicted that in the last days men would arise who would willingly forget it (see 2 Peter 3:3-6). He called such persons "scoffers." Weightier still is the fact that to disbelieve the account of the Flood is to discredit Jesus Himself, who repeatedly quoted the Old Testament writers, whom He regarded as reliable authorities on people, places, and events already long past. Jesus believed that Moses really lived, that Sodom and Gomorrah were literal cities, and that Noah built an ark to escape from the universal Flood. Our Lord didn't "myth" the boat, and neither should we.

Another tragic consequence of treating lightly the historical records of the Scriptures is that in the process we lose sight of the reality of the redemptive work of God. Doubters of Noah also may question the reality of Jesus. And if He did not really live and finally die on the cross and rise literally from the grave, His person and His work are stripped of all meaning and significance. Whether it be Moses, Noah, or Christ, to reject one is to reject all. Tragic indeed are the consequences!

HOW GOD ANSWERS MAN'S QUESTIONS

They were to seek God, . . . and find him; though indeed he is not far from each one of us. Acts 17:27, N.E.B.

If you compare the philosophical and scientific advances of the twentieth century with the similar achievement of all previous time combined, you will be astoundingly convinced that there never was an age like this. In almost every field of human endeavor, eager, relentless, research-minded men have pushed back the frontiers of ignorance until they have almost literally discovered a new heaven and a new earth.

Yet, sagacious and masterful as modern man is and unquestionably able to do amazing things, the sobering fact remains that, in matters that really count, our current intellectual giants and wizards of the laboratory have never succeeded in prying open the door of divine knowledge. God's prime secrets remain as much a riddle to modern geniuses as they were thousands of years ago to the psalmist when he exclaimed, "Such knowledge is too wonderful for me" (Ps. 139:6).

Man's only hope, therefore, for solving his hardest problems and supplying his most urgent needs rests in a Power above and beyond himself. If this recourse is denied him, he is bereft of all that is most vital to him, and becomes miserable indeed. If, however, we accept the existence of an omniscient God and the claims He makes for Himself, it would seem reasonable that He should in some way communicate with man.

To provide man with an inquiring, rational mind and the capacity for delving into mysteries is pointless if the sources of knowledge are placed beyond his reach. If God does not indicate to man the reasons for his own existence, in justice He should not have created him as a rational being in the first place. Nothing is more intolerable to the reflective mind than the feeling of helplessness induced by the arbitrary withholding of the essential facts necessary to solve a given problem. And this is the case with incomprehensible life itself unless in some way God has supplied the missing factors.

How superlatively fortunate we are that the Almighty has not withheld the requisite pieces we need to solve our baffling jigsaw puzzle! These missing factors may be found in the Book that claims it came from God. There is no other book like it in all the world. Ellen G. White said that "every chapter and every verse . . . is a communication from God to men" (*Patriarchs and Prophets,* p. 504).

WITHOUT THE BIBLE

Blessed is the nation whose God is the Lord. Ps. 33:12.

Did you ever consider how much of all we believe and enjoy we owe to the Bible? Without this Book we would have only human speculation regarding the source of all things. We would know nothing of the origin of sin nor of the promised redemption. Except for a few scattered historical references, we would know little of the life, death, and resurrection of Jesus. With no Bible, there would be no Ten Commandments, no Sermon on the Mount, no psalms of David, nor any hope of eternal life. Without the Scriptures, the future would be dark and hopeless; and this darkness would be deepest of all in the human heart.

Without the Bible, the greatest literary productions would be somber and lusterless. There would be no *Paradise Lost,* no *Pilgrim's Progress,* and no *Desire of Ages.* Even Shakespeare would be emaciated and insipid if all his Biblical allusions were deleted. There would be no truly great music, no *Messiah,* no *Elijah,* no inspiring hymns, or any of the exalted oratorios that for centuries have profoundly stirred the human heart.

Exclude the Bible, and what would happen to art? Many great masterpieces would disappear. There would be no *Moses* or *David* by Michelangelo, no *Christ at the Door,* no *Last Supper.* Without the religious influence, little of value would remain from the great masters. And there would be no churches or cathedrals.

The honorable status enjoyed by women today is due to the Scriptures more than to any other influence. Without this advocacy, women would be subject to the lusts of men, degraded creatures with neither dignity nor hope. Except for Christianity, women would probably never have risen to a higher estate than they had in pagan Rome where, for the most part, only courtesans attained any social standing.

Societies that have never known the Scriptures survive by a kind of crude, distorted morality that often involves atrocious practices. Frequently innocent children, the old and weak, and the helpless are callously dispatched. The Bible enjoins a more noble way of life.

Finally, it is highly doubtful that the great American experiment in democracy could have survived without the moral undergirding of Christianity. George Washington, the first U.S. President, thought it could not. In his farewell address he declared: ''Reason and experience both forbid us to expect that national morality can prevail in exclusion of religious principle.''

THE FLIGHT OF BIRDS

"But ask . . . the birds of the air, and they will tell you. . . . Who among all these does not know that the hand of the Lord has done this?" Job 12: 7-9, R.S.V.

Even when in dire distress, the patriarch Job acknowledged God's omnipotence as revealed in His created works. If, in that distant day of limited scientific investigation, men saw God's hand in nature, how much more readily must modern man, with all his amplified erudition, recognize that certainly "the hand of the Lord has done this"! Microcosm and macrocosm alike testify to the wisdom of a Master Planner. The same ingenious might that swings the spheres through space is discernible in the lowly plants and flowers, the birds and insects, and in all other creatures, large and small, that inhabit our teeming world.

In Germany recently, an interesting experiment was undertaken with birds. Researchers there proved that each little warbler comes equipped with its own built-in, miniature directional finder. This microscopic radar is so accurate that it keeps the airborne wayfarer unerringly on course day and night throughout its long migratory flight. Furthermore, the brain of every little bird contains a minute chart of the starry heavens, a tiny device so efficient that, in some inexplainable way, it can register the seasons, the days, and the hours. With one glance at the sky, this curious instrument, no larger than a pinhead, instantly and automatically, points the right direction to take.

Experiments such as these explain certain behavioral patterns that have long puzzled ornithologists. They solve the riddle of the amazing accuracy of the flight of migratory wild fowl. As a child in North Dakota I remember hearing elderly cowboys tell how they marveled at the high-flying geese that invariably began to pass overhead on the same day every year. Now we know how they do it, as well as how the swallows return on the same day each year to Capistrano.

One night, after seeing a wild goose silhouetted alone against the darkening sky, William C. Bryant reaffirmed his trust in God in these oft-quoted lines:

> "He who, from zone to zone,
> Guides through the boundless sky
>   thy certain flight,
> In the long way that I must tread alone,
> Will lead my steps aright."

AN ANTIDOTE FOR ENNUI

But they that wait upon the Lord shall renew their strength; . . . they shall run, and not be weary; and they shall walk, and not faint. Isa. 40:31.

The letters and diaries penned on the way West by the pioneers make fascinating reading. They portray a saga of intrepid men, women, and children, who a hundred years ago and before turned their backs on the organized communities of the East and bravely set out toward the sunset, toward the Dakotas and Montana, "the land of the shining mountains." High on the lists of their recorded hardships appear expressions like these: "Too tired to eat." "Too exhausted even to sleep." "So utterly worn out I slept in my clothes and boots."

Their descendants often feel that their exhaustion is inherited. The patient says, "Doctor, why am I always 'bushed'?" The student excuses his lack of preparation by saying, "I was just too all-in to study." The timely message from the pulpit has little influence because those in the pews go to sleep, too toilworn to listen.

We live in an age of relentless drive, of speed, shortcuts, and accelerating efficiency. The never-ending demands of our tasks deplete our nervous energy until our frayed sensibilities no longer respond normally—or rationally. The solution to our problem, the tonic to tone us up for the treadmill, is not a faster pace but a calmer, more ordered one. To achieve this unruffled serenity we are admonished to "wait on the Lord: . . . and he shall strengthen thine heart: wait, I say, on the Lord" (Ps. 27:14).

Duties often accumulate faster than expected. Those who wait upon the Lord will not, on that account, curtail their daily devotions. They will not truncate the worship hour, singing only the first and last stanzas of the hymn, nor hurry through a short prayer—all because "there's a lot of work to do." From this waiting on the Lord and the resultant renewal of strength, a larger work will be done more easily, more efficiently.

> "Spin cheerfully,
> Not tearfully,
> He knows the way you plod;
> Spin carefully,
> Spin prayerfully,
> But leave the thread with God."
> —Anonymous

ABRAHAM LINCOLN AND GOD

Blessed is that man that maketh the Lord his trust. Ps. 40:4.

His fame has grown so great that Abraham Lincoln, whose birthday we remember today, is the best known and most highly honored personality America has yet produced. His rough-hewn features are recognized by the small child. His solemn countenance is etched on the penny, and his portrait adorns the five-dollar bill. More books have been written about Lincoln than about any other American, living or dead. Through intensive scholarship we know what he was—and also what he was not. While he lived he was thought of as a cross between a god and a clown. In reality he was neither. He was tall and angular but not always shabbily dressed and wrinkled. Nor was he a scarecrow made of a hoe handle and a stuffed shirt.

Research has hatched controversy regarding Lincoln's religious faith and experience. He has been called everything from an agnostic to a saint. His youthful uncertainty about God was not alleviated by the hellfire sermons of the unschooled itinerant preachers. Consider the miserable circumstances of his lowly origin, the dehumanizing effect of the grinding poverty of his family and the rough and ignorant community. No wonder he seemed "a youngun' without a chance." Yet from the first there was a spiritual character to his nature that indicates that, as he later said, he and the Almighty were on "good terms."

Abe was 10 when his mother died. The family buried her in a little clearing behind their crude cabin. An itinerant preacher came by and said a prayer over her grave. Abe felt better after that.

In many of Lincoln's speeches can be read reverent references to his faith in God's overruling providences. His tender heart and compassionate spirit went with him to Washington. Pardoning a wounded deserter, he wrote, "As the Scriptures say that in the shedding of blood is the remission of sins, I guess we'll have to let him off this time." As President he said, "Without God's help we cannot succeed. With it we cannot fail." He told his pastor in Washington, "I love the Saviour." His life proved he did.

IS ANYTHING HAPPENING?

Behold I will do a new thing; now it shall spring forth. Isa. 43:19.

A plain line drawing in an old reader attracted my attention. This simple sketch depicts two Kentucky pioneers meeting on a lonely, windswept road. It was a cold and snowy morning, February 13, 1809. One man asks the other if anything new has happened lately in his settlement. The man replies, "Nothing much. Nothing ever happens around here. Oh, there's a new baby over at Tom Lincoln's."

It appeared then that nothing new or important ever happened around bleak, frontier Hodgenville, Kentucky. On that particular morning everything was as usual except the birth, the day before, of a scrawny baby no one thought had much of a chance in life. Yet time proved that birth to be about the most important of the nineteenth century in America. Abraham Lincoln, whose origins could hardly have been more obscure or inconspicuous, grew up to reshape and ennoble a great nation's concept of human dignity and freedom. Also, as surely as was Washington that nation's founder, Lincoln was its savior.

Possibly, had two humble dwellers in Bethlehem met one morning two thousand years ago and had one asked, "Anything new?" the other might well have replied, "Nothing much, but I hear that a baby boy was born last night in a stable to itinerants from Nazareth."

Momentous events, often ignored at the time, have frequently proved to originate overwhelming consequences. Consider for examples the discovery of gold in 1848 in California, the drilling for crude oil in 1859 in Western Pennsylvania, the 1903 airplane flight of the Wright brothers at Kitty Hawk, North Carolina. Significant as they were, these were all human achievements. But the birth of the Saviour, quite ignored by most of the seers of His day, took place exactly as predicted by the Old Testament prophets. And the world has not been the same since.

When tempted to think that nothing significant ever happens where we are, should we not look for and attempt "new things" that our heavenly Father yearns to do in and through us?

TRUE LOVE

Many waters cannot quench love; rivers cannot wash it away. Song of Songs 8:7, N.I.V.

Pure love is so enduring that nothing can obliterate it. Although freely given, it cannot be bought or sold. The highest offer would be scorned as pointless. Today's text, which speaks of the invincible might and enduring constancy of true love, stands without a peer in all literature for forcefulness of expression. It is selected for today because for many thoughout the world this is a day to celebrate love. It is called Saint Valentine's Day.

Who was Saint Valentine? A creditable legend has it that he was a priest in Rome who took exception to an order of Emperor Claudius II forbidding the rite of marriage to his soldiers, believing that an army of single men was superior. Valentine, who thought this unfair, joined several couples in matrimony. For this defiance he was sent to prison, where he was beheaded in A.D. 270. In this way he became the patron saint of lovers. Centuries before this, however, the Romans celebrated Lupercalia, a lovers' feast at which young couples were paired off. In 496 Pope Gelasius changed this pagan festival into a Christian rite and named it Saint Valentine's Day. Formal valentine greetings date back to the fifteenth century and for almost two hundred years ribbons and lace and love symbols such as hearts, cupids, and doves have appeared on printed valentine cards. This year's card mailings will exceed 7 million.

Because of its pagan origin, the Puritans, and certain conservative church bodies today, have not recognized Saint Valentine's Day. Yet it is regarded in our society as the time for special expressions of affection. And, regardless of our attitude toward this day, Christians are reminded that there is a place in the Christian ethic for romantic love. The painter Vincent Van Gogh declared that ''love is eternal—the aspect may change but not the essence. There is the same difference in a person before and after he is in love as there is in an unlighted lamp and the one that is burning.''

This God-given romantic-filial love is the mystic tie that binds together the family, the fundamental unit of every Christian society. Within the family, when a child is born, a vast, fresh supply of love is sent down from Heaven's depthless reservoir: love of each parent for the child, of child for each parent, and between parents, too. Let this love abound!

LOVE EVOKES OBEDIENCE

Jesus answered and said unto him, If a man love me, he will keep my words: and my Father will love him, and we will come unto him, and make our abode with him. John 14:23.

An old gospel hymn, still sung occasionally, has these lines:

> "But we never can prove
> The delights of His love,
> Until all on the altar we lay,
> For the favor He shows,
> And the joy He bestows,
> Are for them who will trust and obey."

On a long-ago winter morning I stood with my father among other ranchers awaiting a livestock sale. Bundled against the cold, we stood around an open fire. One coarse fellow began to tell an off-color story. Suddenly he noticed a young minister, and breaking off his lewd anecdote, apologized, "Oh, I'm sorry, Reverend. I didn't see you." The minister replied mildly, "You need not heed me when you have no respect for the Lord I represent." A deathly silence ensued and the story was left unfinished. Nor was the pointed lesson lost.

When Saul, in his declining years as king of Israel, attempted to conceal his disregard of a specific command from the Lord by making a deceptive display of great sacrifice, Samuel, the prophet, pointedly omitted to commend the king for any good intentions he may have had. Instead, he fashioned his unanswerable rebuke in this well-known question: "Hath the Lord as great delight in . . . sacrifices, as in obeying the voice of the Lord? Behold, to obey is better than sacrifice, and to hearken than the fat of rams" (1 Sam. 15:22).

God is particular, and anything other than full obedience is unacceptable to Him. Does the character of those around you determine your demeanor and your words? Do you fit your conversation to please those within the reach of your voice? When with other Christians are your words softer and more carefully selected? Does your disposition improve when important guests are in your home? Our opening text teaches that Jesus is the unseen guest in every Christian home. He is the unescapable presence.

Dwight L. Moody once said, "There are two lives for the Christian, one before the world, and one alone with God." It becomes the believer to strive continually to blend these two lives into one.

THE SOURCE OF TRUTH

The whole Bible was given to us by inspiration from God and is useful to teach us what is true and to make us realize what is wrong in our lives; it straightens us out and helps us do what is right. 2 Tim. 3:16, T.L.B.

This text from *The Living Bible* may not be as accurately translated as in the *New English Bible* or as sublime as in the *King James Version,* but the purpose of Bible study was never better expressed.

In 1864 a delegation of black admirers brought President Lincoln a beautiful Bible as a token of their appreciation for his Emancipation Proclamation. His respect for this greatest of all books was expressed in his Thank-you speech as follows: "This great book . . . is the best gift God has given to men. . . . But for it we could not know right from wrong."

President Lincoln was correct, because the moral code of the Scriptures surpasses that of any other religion the world has ever known. Bible morality goes down to the root and fiber of life. In speaking to others, in expressing a wish, in writing a letter, in opening a door, in making the choices we face daily, indeed in every possible exercise of human thought, emotion, or act, the moral element is present. And, by illustrations and examples, this matchless Book provides unerring instructions for every situation and circumstance of life. Lyman Abbot said: "We sail upon an ocean whose distant bounds are far beyond our sight. The Bible gives every soul a chart to sail by."

The truths of the Bible are like gold in the earth. Whole generations of men walk over the earth not knowing what treasures are hidden beneath their feet. So do centuries of men pass over the Scriptures unaware of the rich veins of truth there awaiting discovery and incorporation into the life.

Henry Ward Beecher said of the Bible: "This book, without a spiritual life to exemplify it, is like a trellis on which no vine grows—bare, angular and in the way. The Bible with a beautiful spiritual life is like a trellis covered with a luxuriant vine, odorous and heavy with purple clusters of grapes shining through the leaves."

"Do you know a book that you are willing to put under your head for a pillow when you lie dying? Very well, that is the book you want to study while you are living. There is only one such book in the world."—Joseph Cook

THE SOURCE OF LIGHT

Thy word is a lamp to my feet and a light to my path. Ps. 119:105, R.S.V.

The little upland valley where we live is surrounded by heavily wooded mountains. Because of their natural sylvan charm, they have been interlaced with narrow, winding trails that run uphill and down in all directions through the precipitous terrain. Walking these paths by daylight presents few hazards to enchanted nature lovers, but when darkness falls these twisting lanes become a bewildering nightmare to the unwary pedestrian—unless he has a light. Passing along these byways at night, I have no fear, for I have the illumination of my trusty flashlight. The lighted way is safe. I think of God's Word in much the same way—a lamp to our spiritual feet and a dependable light on our pilgrimage path.

Electric power is said to ''light the world''; but if we were obliged to choose between the benefits of electricity and the Bible, the human race would be infinitely better off with the Scriptures. Anyone who earnestly wants to walk the perilous path of life in trust and confidence can do so with the Word of God as his light. I do not see how any sincere Christian can proceed safely or rightly, in this day of unsurpassed perils and pitfalls, along the pathway of spiritual progress, unless he whole heartedly accepts the illumination the Bible offers.

John Quincy Adams once made this entry in his diary: ''I have made it a practice for several years to read the Bible through in the course of every year. I usually devote to this reading the first hour after I rise every morning.'' Likewise, Abraham Lincoln said when found reading the Bible, ''Take all of this book upon reason that you can, and the balance on faith, and you will live and die a happier and better man.'' Decades later Herbert Hoover said: ''There is no other book so vital as the Bible nor one so full of wisdom. It instructs the mind.''

No book, other than the Bible, so effectively treats of both time and eternity; no other book can safely and adequately teach your soul. On this account, the apostle Paul, writing to the young Timothy, advised him that ''from early childhood you have been familiar with the sacred writings which have power to make you wise and lead you to salvation through faith in Jesus Christ'' (2 Tim. 3:15, N.E.B.). ''The Bible: read it to be wise; believe it to be safe; practice it to be holy.''

THE BOYHOOD OF JESUS

And the child grew and became strong, filled with wisdom; and the favor of God was upon him. Luke 2:40, R.S.V.

Although, according to prophecy, Jesus was born at Bethlehem, He spent His childhood and youth in the little mountain village of Nazareth. There He "advanced in wisdom and in favour with God and men" (Luke 2:52, N.E.B.). "His mind was active and penetrating, with a thoughtfulness and wisdom beyond His years. Yet His character was beautiful in its symmetry. The powers of mind and body developed gradually, in keeping with the laws of childhood."—*The Desire of Ages,* p. 68.

We usually think of Jesus as a grown man, not remembering that for more than half of His short life on earth He was child and youth. If our children and teen-agers today could think about Him as an admirable and exemplary young man instead of fixing their gaze upon some contemporary athletic champion or movie star, it would ennoble their thoughts. If they would meditate upon His obedient faithfulness as a son, it would inspire them to more cheerfully accept their proper role as loyal and dutiful sons and daughters. And it would surely reduce juvenile delinquency.

I once heard the story of a schoolboy named Jim who had been exposed to the injurious influences of pernicious habits such as swearing and stealing. In a dream one night an angel appeared and showed him some pictures of boys at play. The happy companions were racing and laughing. But one lad was different, for whenever he was present, things were special—there could be no cheating nor quarreling. That picture faded to be followed by one of a group of students in a classroom. And that same boy was there again with thoughtful brow, listening most attentively. A third scene revealed this same youth working in a carpenter shop. Light streaming through the open window showed that, busy as he was, his thoughts were moving in a higher realm. The next view showed him in happy conversation with his mother, and the last one represented him kneeling alone praying in deep reverence and youthful trust. When Jim awoke he recognized that the boy in his dream was Jesus. He was so impressed that he prayed that night with all his heart: "O Lord, help me to make my life like Yours. I want to grow in favor with You as well as with my friends." Have you ever been moved by Jesus' example? Surely the flower of youth is never more beautiful than when it turns toward the Sun of Righteousness.

ACCEPTING CHRIST AS GOD

In the beginning was the Word [*Logos*], and the Word was with God, and the Word was God. . . . All things were made by him. . . . And the Word was made flesh, and dwelt among us. John 1:1-14.

Many claims have been made for and against Christ. Millions of words have been spoken about Him. Libraries contain thousands of volumes dealing with every phase of His brief, controversial life. An endless chain of books links His day and life with ours. Obviously, the searching question of Pilate is as pertinent today as it was then, "What shall I do with Jesus who is called Christ?" (Matt. 27:22, R.S.V.). What do the Scriptures teach about this complex, enigmatic, yet strangely appealing, transcendent personality.

The Bible presents Him as its supreme, central figure. After carefully reviewing the available evidence, one is obliged to conclude that Christ is either all-in-all or nothing at all.

John the revelator lifts the veil of the infinite past and explains Christ's relation to the Godhead and the universe. "In him was life; and the life was the light of men" (John 1:4). Here is a unique revelation of the incarnate Word that became flesh through the virgin birth—"conceived by the Holy Ghost, born of the Virgin Mary" as set forth by Matthew and Luke and as incorporated in the Apostles' Creed. The life of Jesus unfolded a detailed fulfillment of all that had been foretold of Him in the Law and in the Prophets.

Although skeptics have ceaselessly challenged the historical Jesus, the multiplying evidence weighs ever more heavily on the side of His credibility. In his *Days of Our Years,* Pierre Van Paasen, modern author and publicist, sums up the evidence and concludes that it is far easier today to prove that Christ actually lived than to prove that He is simply a myth.

Evidences of Christ's divinity include His creative power, His sinless life, the miracles He performed, His resurrection and ascension and the fact that He now sits on the throne with His Father in heaven (Acts 2:33-36). It is profoundly reassuring to realize that the Scriptures undeviatingly present a living Christ always able and eager to "sympathize with our weaknesses," that "we may receive mercy and in his grace find timely help" (Heb. 4:15, 16, N.E.B.). Our faith depends upon what Christ does for us; our prospect of heaven depends upon whether we accept His salvation.

UNITY OF FAITH

Until we all attain to the unity of the faith and of the knowledge of the Son of God, to mature manhood. Eph. 4:13, R.S.V.

A careful reading of Paul's Epistle to the Ephesians makes it clear that the apostle did not regard faith, doctrine, and practice as separate entities. Rather are they interwoven in the body of his presentation of the great theme of Christian unity. Knowledge is inherently objective, facts on which faith is built. Yet, because human knowledge is incomplete, faith, resting on imperfect knowledge, is in part subjective and, therefore, variant. Christianity is rooted in imperfect knowledge comingled with subjective faith; hence the ever present possibility that believers will disagree in faith and doctrine. This very thing happened in apostolic times—and often since.

How then shall we attain this promised blessed condition, this unity in faith and doctrine? When a heated doctrinal controversy arose in the early church, the leaders, including Peter, James (the brother of our Lord), Paul, and Barnabas, gathered in Jerusalem for the first General Conference. After earnest prayer the issues were thoroughly debated. Finally, James arose and clearly stated the decision of the meeting. Under the influence of the Holy Spirit the matter was settled—and settled right. Unity of faith was preserved, and the gospel message blazed forth with renewed vigor and power. During all the centuries since that memorable council, whenever "new light" has threatened doctrinal unity and the procedures of that first Jerusalem Council have been followed, the decisions have been sound and the results salutary.

While we lived in Tennessee our family often visited Smoky Mountain National Park. There we found that imposing Mount Le Conte can be scaled by three different trails. The paths, divergent at first, draw closer together until they meet at the summit.

Believers, toiling along steep spiritual pathways, may be divided and far apart doctrinally at the lower levels; but there is divine sunlight and unity at the top.

"God is leading a people. . . . They will not be at variance, one believing one thing and another having faith and views entirely opposite. . . . They will all come to the unity of the faith."—*Testimonies,* vol. 3, p. 446.

THE SIN OF SILENCE

Whosoever committeth sin transgresseth also the law: for sin is the transgression of the law. 1 John 3:4.

The problem of sin disrupted God's plans and infected the earth from the moment Adam and Eve disobeyed in the Garden of Eden. Sin continues to be the fundamental problem of our day. It is the root cause of all wars, devastation, heartbreak, misery, and unhappiness in the world. Sin is most abhorrent to God. It is also the process that inflicts eternal damnation on the soul.

John Thomas, the Welsh evangelist, said that "sin is a current—the farther it goes, the swifter it runs. Sin is a habit—the longer it lasts, the stronger it becomes. Sin is a growth—rooting itself in the soul of our being. Sin is slavery—welding new chains around its unhappy victims."—*Spiritual Messages*, p. 17.

How many types and varieties of sin there are! There are family sins, social sins, and business sins. Sometimes people sin against their children, sometimes against their parents, sometimes against their neighbors, and sometimes against themselves. Every sin is against God. We may sin in what we do and in what we fail to do. Sometimes we sin by doing nothing at all. Among these sins of omission is the sin of silence. We can stifle our strongest convictions by denying them expression. About the strongest censure in the Scriptures is the denunciation Jesus heaped upon the head of the unprofitable servant whose excuse was "I was afraid, so I hid my talent in the ground." For this sin of omission Jesus called him a "wicked and slothful servant."

Any fear or negligence that prevents a righteous act is a sin. When we adopt timidity, reluctance, or inactivity as a way of life, we dishonor God and place our souls in jeopardy. A sense of inferiority, of weakness, deprives heaven of its rightful fruitage and lessens our faith, as does any act of belittling oneself. Self-induced paralysis of conviction must be regarded as any other dereliction of duty. When a policeman does not stop a crime he himself is adjudged as guilty. The longest list of criminals is found under the heading "accessory to the crime."

One of our greatest God-given talents is the ability to witness for the truth. To go about doing good and presenting the gospel by word and deed is to truly emulate our Lord. Beware lest timidity or cowardice induce you to sin through silence.

A DAY TO REMEMBER

For the righteous will . . . be remembered for ever. Ps. 112:6, R.S.V.

When we couple this text with Proverbs 10:7, "The memory of the righteous is a blessing" (R.S.V.), we can better understand and appreciate the numerous scriptural imperatives: the "remembers" and the "do not forgets." It is thus both appropriate and scriptural to recall that today is the birthday of the Father of Our Country, George Washington, who was also the first President. And although, to accommodate those who like extra-long weekends, February 22 is no longer regarded as a national holiday, it is, and always will be, Washington's real birthday. He was born on this date in 1732.

Washington's unfailing inner light was his unshakable belief in the overruling providences of God. As a late spring offered relief from the sufferings at Valley Forge, word was received that France had allied with the struggling colonies in their crusade for freedom. On notice of this momentous treaty, Washington issued a General Order to his pathetic little starving army. He said, "It has pleased the Almighty Ruler of the Universe to defend the cause of the United American States by raising up a powerful friend. . ... It becomes us to set apart a day for gratefully acknowledging this Divine Goodness." Throughout the changing fortunes of war and afterward, he never wavered in this trust.

Taking command of the Revolutionary forces, Washington said, "For this cause of freedom I pledge my life, my property [he was rich], and my sacred honor [which was dearer to him than the other two]." He kept that pledge.

The young nation's struggle for freedom ended on October 19, 1781, in the great victory at Yorktown.

"The army and the nation then arose as one strong man,
Responded to his leadership and followed out his plan.
They all fought on; they would not quit until the war was won.
George lost a score of battles but he won the last big one!"

—Adlai Esteb

THE WILL TO WIN

Take courage, and acquit yourselves like men. 1 Sam. 4:9, R.S.V.

Even though spoken by a heathen chieftain, the ringing words of our text epitomize the charge General George Washington issued to his troops as he assumed command of the untrained continental forces in the early days of the American Revolution.

It was a dark and threatening hour when the Continental Congress turned in desperation to Washington. He was the last hope to mold the untrained colonial men and boys into an effective military force. Without arms, ammunition, supplies, or money, the battered revolutionary cause seemed all but hopeless against the well-trained, well-organized, and well-equipped British veterans opposing it. Yet in Washington they found a leader worthy of the prodigious task ahead. The whole world knows the result.

George Washington and Abraham Lincoln, the two greatest American Presidents to date, stood poles apart in background and inheritance. Lincoln's ancestry could hardly have been more humble and obscure; Washington's family was aristocratic and eminent. Washington was born to wealth; Lincoln was poverty stricken. Lincoln grew up on the backwoods frontier; Washington had every advantage of culture and refinement. Despite these striking contrasts, they were remarkably alike in two significant characteristics: both possessed highest integrity and were reticent about their religious convictions.

Although he seldom spoke of his religious beliefs, Washington's biographers, almost without exception, characterize him as a Christian in principle and practice. Of him John Marshall wrote: "Without making ostentatious professions of religion, he was a sincere believer in the Christian faith, and truly a devout man."

Let all who love freedom everywhere thank God today for George Washington's steadfastness, his unbending will, and for his indomitable courage as we endeavor to emulate his virtues.

SOME STOOD FAST

"Our God whom we serve is able to deliver us from the burning fiery furnace; and he will deliver us out of your hand, O king. But if not, be it known unto you . . . that we will not serve your gods nor worship the golden image which you have set up." Dan. 3:17, 18, R.S.V.

One of my earliest childhood recollections is of my mother sitting in her rocking chair with my sister and me on cushions at her feet looking up to catch every word as she told us Bible stories. We came to know them by heart, but we never tired of hearing them repeated. The three Hebrews in Babylon held a particular fascination for us. Their invincible faith, their staunch courage before the autocratic monarch, their bravery in the face of death; these stirring scenes project a potent lesson for all who may be called to face desperate tests of faith. "Daniel and his three companions are illustrious examples of Christian heroism. . . . From their experience . . . we may learn what God will do for those who serve Him with full purpose of heart."—*My Life Today,* p. 68.

The arrogant and despotic King Nebuchadnezzar might have accepted a compromise such as kneeling down just once before the pagan idol. But the true God never compromises. He will accept no partial obedience nor accommodation with sin. Even a little yielding opens the floodgates to evil. To compromise is to foster weakness of character. We dare not be weaklings. Like the three Hebrews we must stand for right regardless of what happens. The tragic termination of the lives of Saul, Ahab, and Pilate demonstrate that those who compromise with sin gain only sorrow and ruin.

One all-too-common cause of compromise is the deleterious influence of unworthy associates. A bad potato spoils the good one touching it. The first psalm pronounces a blessing upon the man who "walks not in the counsel of the wicked, nor stands in the way of sinners, nor sits in the seat of scoffers" (Ps. 1:1, R.S.V.).

Compromise spawns spineless Christians unwilling to take a stand on much of anything. Compromise springs from the hope or prospect of wealth, position, power, or popularity. Gaining these fleeting pleasures, compromisers find they have won only ashes and have reaped only ruin in the end. The greatest want of the world is still "the want of men . . . who will stand for the right though the heavens fall."—*Education,* p. 57.

UP A TREE

And when Jesus came to the place, he looked up, and saw him, and said unto him, Zacchaeus, make haste, and come down; for to day I must abide at thy house. Luke 19:5.

Things look different from the top of a tree than they do at its base. Zacchaeus climbed the tree to get a better view. Elijah crawled under a juniper to hide because he was afraid.

Many wealthy people are deeply unhappy because their riches have been gained dishonestly. Zacchaeus, an extortionist, was one of these. Motivated by a deep conviction of heart, he wanted to see Jesus. Human nature is the same today. Even mere curiosity prompts some people to climb trees, poles, even high buildings, to see a visiting celebrity. But Zacchaeus sought "to see Jesus who he was" (Luke 19:3). For this little man it turned out to be a red-letter day, as is almost always the case when a person starts out to find the Saviour.

Coming to the place, Jesus "looked up, and saw him." This is still His way. No one else seemed to notice Zacchaeus and no one but Jesus cared about him. No doubt the tax collector was considerably embarrassed when called by name. But he promptly climbed down from his perch in the tree and joined Jesus. We don't know whether the crowd or Zacchaeus was the more surprised. But he soon overcame his embarrassment, for he received Jesus "joyfully." Jesus sought the hospitality of a home in Jericho, and when it was extended He brought salvation to its occupants.

In my life I have often found people sitting figuratively under junipers. Most of us have probably been there. But it is not a good place to be, and no one need stay there. The fearful pessimists under the juniper are not very good company. Discouragement, along with fear of Jezebel, drove Elijah there. His courage had been turned to cowardice.

Instead of upbraiding Zacchaeus for his disreputable past, Jesus simply showed love for him. During the dinner the little man's better self cried out for a personal reformation. Then and there he bared his heart before Christ and renounced his old life.

This experience beautifully demonstrates what conversion does. It takes Christ into the heart and gives man a true picture of himself. It starts him cleaning up his life and makes of him a genuine Christian. "Therefore if any man be in Christ, he is a new creature: old things are passed away; behold, all things are become new" (2 Cor. 5:17).

THE CHANGING AND THE CHANGELESS

Jesus Christ is the same yesterday, and to day, and for ever. Heb. 13:8.

This straightforward divine utterance constitutes the groundwork of the Christian religion. The everlasting constancy of the Lord Jesus is the rock-ribbed foundation on which the house of faith is built. By contrast everything in our world undergoes change. Even the so-called changeless hills are not really eternal. "Of old," said David, "hast thou laid the foundation of the earth: and the heavens are the work of thy hands. They shall perish, . . . but thou art the same, and thy years shall have no end" (Ps. 102:25-27).

The house where I was born caught fire and burned to the ground. The home in which I grew up was moved and grass grows on the spot. Even famous historic sites disappear. I went eagerly to visit old Jamestown where the first landings were made in Virginia, but the meandering waters of the James River have well-nigh obliterated the site. Sometimes I have gone to visit historic houses only to find a plaque or a monument marking the place. Sometimes there is nothing at all.

To our regret our friends and relatives also constantly undergo change. Some move away. Some pass away. Others come in and, to a degree, replace them. By painful experience we learn that the circle of friendship is highly unstable.

I knew of a wren that spent a day building her nest in a pile of orchard prunings. Cleaning up that evening, the orchardist scattered the twigs and straw. The same thing happened again the next day. On the third day the little bird built her nest in a rambling rose bush. Undisturbed, there she hatched her brood. Had she been allowed to finish her nest in the pile of prunings it would have been burned up long before the eggs hatched.

All earthly things inevitably change. But Jehovah remains the same. We may not be able to clearly trace His footsteps, yet, because He "changeth not," we can always count on His loving care and guidance. And even when He allows our friends and loved ones to go from us, when our nests of cherished plans and hopes are broken up, we can be sure His providences are ever wise, and, as we shall ultimately learn, they are wonderfully kind as well.

GREAT EXPECTATIONS

My soul, wait thou only upon God; for my expectation is from him. Ps. 62:5.

Many, particularly among the young, can scarcely wait to realize any pleasurable activity or event. I knew a high-strung boy whose father promised, after long entreaty, to take him to a professional ball game. The exciting prospect so stimulated the lad that he could not sleep a wink the night before the coveted event. Exhausted, he went to the game only to sleep soundly through all nine innings. Sometimes college students, and older people as well, entertain such great expectations of graduation or a wedding that debilitating fatigue robs them of the pleasure long anticipated.

Others, both young and old, grow so obsessed with the uncertainty of life that they wonder and worry continually about death. Psychologists insist that this is a natural apprehension. Such intense introversion, for any reason, paralyzes effort, weakens ambition, and often beclouds an otherwise sunlit day. Both overanxious anticipation and gloomy foreboding can be banished by meditation upon today's text, which explicitly declares that the expectation of the Christian rests with God. Jeremiah affirms that our heavenly Father thinks "thoughts of peace, and not of evil" (Jer. 29:11) toward His earth-born children and that He longs to give them "an expected end," or as one translation phrases it, "to give . . . [them] a future and a hope."

Still, in God's providences, some things require time. There is more than a passing suggestion of this essential time element in Jesus' parable as narrated in Mark 4. He said, "First the blade, then the ear, after that the full corn in the ear" (verse 28). Nothing in nature is in a hurry except man. Yet our lives do not develop with rapid strides. We need to learn that many of life's most precious attributes do not come suddenly.

Men of great faith are nearly always patient. It is essential to cultivate patience not only in temporal matters but with spiritual development as well. Dr. E. A. Sutherland, founder of Madison College in Tennessee, often voiced his unshakable trust in God's providences by quoting these lines from Mary Riley Smith:

> ". . . Then be content, poor heart!
> God's plans, like lilies pure and white, unfold:
> We must not tear the close-shut leaves apart—
> Time will reveal their calyxes of gold."

TO LIVE THIS DAY

As I passionately hope, I shall have no cause to be ashamed, but shall speak so boldly that now as always the greatness of Christ will shine out clearly in my person, whether through my life or through my death. Phil. 1:20, N.E.B.

Recently I visited an elderly friend, a physician, who was ill and not expected to live. Having known and admired him for years, I rather dreaded seeing him under such adverse circumstances. Yet I felt I ought to bring him some encouragement if I could. Although bedridden, he greeted me with a cheery smile and a surprisingly firm handshake. After speaking of our long friendship, I complimented him on his singularly beneficial life and thanked him for his spiritual encouragement to me when I was a college student. Then I asked him whether the thought of death frightened him. "Not at all," he replied convincingly. "As a Christian, I have done my best for the Lord Jesus, who has walked with me a long time. I have confidence that He will go on with me through the valley of death. I am not afraid to die. Yet sometimes I feel ashamed that I have done so little for Him who did so much for me. This is my one regret as I anticipate meeting Him face to face." On leaving, I told his wife that I had come to cheer him up, but that instead he had greatly cheered and encouraged me.

Christians properly speak often of the unimaginable bliss of heaven. What joy to be welcomed into Christ's presence never again to face the perplexities nor suffer the trials that plague this earthly pilgrimage! It is also an abiding comfort to realize that we need not fear the Grim Reaper when we are safe in the Saviour's care.

Thus, although the sincere Christian need never *fear* death, some may feel *ashamed* to face it, wondering whether they must meet their Lord with but little fruitage.

> " 'Must I go, and empty-handed?'
> Must I meet my Savior so?
> Not one soul with which to greet Him:
> Must I empty-handed go?"

This is a sobering question for all Christians, young and old, for we know that everyone must "give an account of himself to God" (Rom. 14:12). If today you were called to meet Him, how would you feel? If you have sincerely accepted His salvation, you can trust Jesus for eternal life. And you need not appear before Him empty-handed.

WHICH SIDE ARE YOU ON?

He [Moses] took his place at the gate of the camp and said, "Who is on the Lord's side?" Ex. 32:26, N.E.B.

While the children of Israel were camped before Mount Sinai, Moses was called up into the mountain to meet God. During his absence of forty days, the people reverted to the pagan practice of worshiping a golden calf. Warned of their sin and gluttonous reveling and fearing that in His anger the Lord would consume Israel, Moses hastily descended to the camp. After rebuking his unreliable brother Aaron for allowing this iniquitous exhibition, Moses seized the gilded image and hurled it into the fire. Then, turning to the multitude, he cried out, "Who is on the Lord's side? Come here to me"! The great majority of the vast assemblage responded. Those who refused to take their stand on God's side were slain.

Not many are called upon to choose so swiftly and dramatically whether or not to serve God. Yet by means of His just and inflexible requirements, the Almighty is continually testing the quality of everyone's loyalty to Him. Every mind is endowed with the power to discriminate between right and wrong. Daily the will must determine whether or not to obey God's commandments.

Once a deaf mute was asked by friends why he attended church so faithfully. "So," he replied in sign language, "people will know whose side I am on." As the end of time draws nearer, more and more people will be deciding day by day whose side they are on. At last, just as at Sinai, there will be only two sides—the Lord's and Satan's. The decision on this great question is the most momentous any person will ever make.

Do you want to make certain that you stay on the Lord's side? Here are seven helpful suggestions provided recently by a veteran minister:
1. Decide that you will stay with God come what may.
2. Learn to believe your beliefs and doubt your doubts.
3. Be confident and positive in your trust in God.
4. Determine that you will be a working Christian. Keep in mind that you don't have to be church employed to be a successful soul winner.
5. Read and study your Bible faithfully.
6. Know where you stand and why.
7. Keep your eyes fixed upon Jesus. Make Him your Friend, your Example, and your Guide.

THE FOUNDATION OF FAITH AND MORALS

For the word of the Lord is alive and active. Heb. 4:12, N.E.B.

The Bible is the most remarkable book ever written and unlike any other. Composed of sixty-six separate manuscripts, it stands as a harmonious whole. In it one may read a record of six thousand years past and find a sure guide for all time to come. Someone has said, "The New Testament is in the Old contained and the Old Testament is by the New explained." The apostle Paul wrote that "whatsoever things were written aforetime were written for our learning, that we through patience and comfort of the scriptures might have hope" (Rom. 15:4).

The influence of this great Book during the early decades of the American experiment in democracy is unmistakable. For at least the first half of our national life the majority of American statesmen were Bible readers and Bible believers. The venerable John Quincy Adams may be cited as a fair example. While President of the United States, he recorded in his diary that it was his practice to read meditatively each morning a portion of the Scriptures. He wrote, "I speak as a man of the world to men of the world: Search the Scriptures!" Until well into the twentieth century the *Congressional Record* was filled with speeches abounding in Biblical images and allusions. There is other indisputable proof that the Scriptures exerted a mighty influence on the mores and morality of the American people in the early years.

How then to explain the later dramatic decline in morality? In truth, until World War II the scriptural gospel was preached in nearly every corner of America. The pulpits were filled, and missionary activities were manned by those who regarded the Bible as the infallible rule of faith and practice. Today the situation is vastly changed. The massive assaults by evolutionists and higher critics have largely swept away the very foundation of integrity. Lacking vital moral underpinnings, millions now grope in a moral morass so deep that a leading national periodical asks, "Are we becoming a nation of criminals?" The latest statistics point clearly in that direction.

The inspired Word of God speaks volumes to any who will read and heed it. There you can find a word of peace for a time of peril, a word of comfort for distress and bereavement, a word of light for the hour of darkness.

THE BIBLE AS HISTORY

Speak to the earth, and it shall teach thee. Job 12:8.

For more than a hundred years a never-ending war of words has waged between defenders of Bible truth on one side and advocates of so-called scientific truth on the other. The argument still goes on, and the issue seems no nearer resolution today than when it began a century ago.

Archeologists generally side with modern-day researchers against a Biblical interpretation of history. But not all. In recent years Biblical archeologists have often been pleasantly surprised at finding unsuspected evidences of the historical accuracy of the Scriptures. One such "find" is the ancient pool of Gibeon, which to early Israel was a precious source of pure water (see 2 Sam. 2:13). But when Nebuchadnezzar's armies overran Palestine in the sixth century B.C. they dumped tons of stone and dirt into this great well, sealing it up effectively and erasing it from the memories of men. But the Bible did not forget. In its pages Dr. James Pritchard, of the University of Pittsburgh, found a clue that led to the rediscovery of the famous old well. Today the pool of Gibeon flows copiously again after having been lost for twenty-five centuries.

Another remarkable archeological discovery came to light in 1957, the work of Dr. Nelson Glueck, of the Hebrew Union College. Many eminent scientists had expressed the conviction that Ezion-Geber, one of the campsites of Israel in the wilderness (Num. 33:35), was a mythical place and that Solomon never mined copper. But Dr. Glueck and his researchers, using photographs taken from high-flying planes, located these ancient mines, along with crumbling remains of picks and the foundations of little smelters alongside veins of copper ore as yet unworked. These men proved that it is still true, as predicted in Deuteronomy, that "out of . . . [these] hills you can dig copper" (Deut. 8:9, R.S.V.). Today, the mines are back in production. Dr. Glueck also located without question the site of Ezion-Geber on the Gulf of Aqabah.

Another scripture, long disbelieved by scientists, states that King Ahab built an ivory palace in Samaria (1 Kings 22:39). While visiting that ancient citadel in 1967, I came upon a British team excavating the site. The leader proudly exhibited several fragments of ivory that had holes exactly matching round openings drilled into the massive, hewn stones that once comprised Ahab's palace. He explained, "This will forever silence those who deny that Ahab had an ivory palace. The Bible was right after all."

A FORM OF GODLINESS

Not everyone that saith unto me, Lord, Lord, shall enter into the kingdom of heaven; but he that doeth the will of my Father which is in heaven. Matt. 7:21.

Imposters don many masks, and pretense wears many faces. Though hard to understand, some people appear and act worse than they really are, whereas the vast majority of present-day, chameleonlike hypocrites want others to think they are better than they are. This peculiar paradox often confuses the Christian in his day-to-day relationships. But by far the greater danger is presented by feigned godliness.

Among the most perilous pitfalls in the religious experience is what Paul calls "a form of godliness." It is startling to find that the eighteen sins this apostle mentions in his letter to Timothy are committed by those who have "a form of godliness." He lists them as causes of the "perilous times" of the last days (2 Tim. 3:1-5).

In Matthew 7 Jesus declared that some who have taken His name on their lips and have even done wonderful things in His name will be rejected at last because He has never known them as His followers. Not only does the unconverted Christian deceive himself by a formalistic show of piety but his example leads others to laxness in their Christian experience. This fine-sifted leaven of worldliness in the church is sure to have a deleterious influence on all who come into contact with it. The Saviour illustrated this principle in the parable of the wheat and the tares. Even in the church both are to grow together until the harvest. Every member, therefore, should take care not to follow those in the church who have a tendency to liberalize the high standards and principles that distinguish the dedicated believer.

Jesus disclosed the essential element of worship when He said, "God is a Spirit: and they that worship him must worship him in spirit and in truth" (John 4:24).

For complete sanctification the body, soul, and spirit must unite in worship. It is not enough to be present for the church service. The soul must be alert to its spiritual needs and must come in the attitude David expressed in these words: "My soul longeth . . . for the courts of the Lord: my heart and my flesh crieth out for the living God" (Ps. 84:2).

Cold, rigid formalism imperils the church and brings even greater peril to the individual. Let us, therefore, worship with a contrite spirit and an open heart.

THE ILLUSION OF NEUTRALITY

He that is not with me is against me. Matt. 12:30.

On an unusually mild winter afternoon at Mount Ellis Academy in Montana I was eyewitness to a battle royal. Half a hundred teen-age boys had chosen up sides for a snowball fight. Each side had elected a captain with his lieutenants, designated sharpshooters, and bullet molders. They were in line behind compacted, yard-high breastworks of snow. Snowballs were flying thick and fast, and the laughter and shouts grew louder as the contest surged back and forth. Then I noticed one boy standing soberly aside watching the fun. When I asked him why he wasn't in the game he replied, ''Oh, I'm neutral.'' After walking on some distance I looked back. The ''neutral'' boy was still standing alone. He didn't seem very happy.

When World War II broke out in Europe a majority of the American people ardently hoped to escape the bloody conflict. President Roosevelt promptly declared for strict neutrality. Yet, despite rigorous efforts to remain ''neutral in thought as well as in deed,'' America was eventually plunged into the gory, costly fray.

In war itself, and even in ''play war,'' it is not pleasant or easy to remain neutral. And in the great conflict for the soul of man neutrality is impossible. There is no middle ground. In this momentous struggle, in which all must take sides, every soul is either a patriot or a traitor. He who is not wholly on the side of Christ is wholly on the side of the enemy. To be almost, but not wholly, on the side of Christ is to be not almost, but wholly against Him.

Some like to believe they can take a neutral way, can walk a middle road. But there is no such road. F. E. Belden expressed this eternal truth effectively when he wrote:

> ''There are two ways for trav'lers, only two ways:
> One's a hill pathway of battle and praise;
> The other leads downward; tho' flow'ry it seem,
> Its joy is a phantom, its love is a dream,
> Its love is a dream, 'tis only a dream.''

Reflection invariably leads to the conclusion that life's pathway would be infinitely more easily trod if it had no forks nor crossroads. But in all God's vast creation man alone was granted the power of moral choice. This is why destiny is not a matter of chance, but of choice.

VOICES: VOCAL OR MUTED?

We cannot but speak the things we have seen and heard. Acts 4:20.

These were the words of defense spoken by Peter and John when they were arrested and ordered by the chief priests "not to speak or teach at all in the name of Jesus" (Acts 4:18, R.S.V.). They and the other disciples never missed an opportunity to put their new-found faith into a lively witness. The phenomenal growth of the early church during the first century A.D. was the fruitage of the ringing testimony of the stalwart believers. In season and out they spoke "with boldness" and when the people "perceived that they were unlearned and ignorant men, they marvelled; and they took knowledge of them, that they had been with Jesus" (verse 13).

The vast amount of damage done to the Christian faith by moral laryngitis and the paralysis of convictions may never be known. No believer can allow himself to be tongue-tied with impunity, for in the judgment every soul will be held responsible for opportunities he has neglected. In a sense those who fail to take a stand for righteousness sentence themselves to slavery. James Russell Lowell wrote:

> "They are slaves who fear to speak
> For the fallen and the weak;
> They are slaves who will not choose
> Hatred, scoffing, and abuse,
> Rather than in silence shrink
> From the truth they needs must think;
> They are slaves who dare not be
> In the right with two or three."

Moral courage knows many compensations and delights that timidity can never even imagine. Unfortunate is the man or woman who has not known the bracing exaltation of taking a stand and then sticking fearlessly to his guns until the cause is won. Something like a shot of adrenalin, a little courage floods the spirit with vitality and ambition.

In the book of Samuel can be read the penalty meted out to the weak and indulgent temple priest Eli because he lacked moral courage. The Lord told Samuel, "I have told him [Eli] that I will judge his house for ever for the iniquity which he knoweth; because his sons made themselves vile, and he restrained them not" (1 Sam. 3:13). Eli's fate was sealed, along with that of his corrupt sons, when, in ease-loving indulgence and moral timidity, he failed to reprove them.

MORE STATELY MANSIONS

But grow in the grace and knowledge of our Lord and Savior Jesus Christ. 2 Peter 3:18, R.S.V.

Peter's Epistle to the churches closes with this admonition to "grow in the grace and knowledge." The text implies "keep on growing." In this life the Christian may aspire to continual advancement in understanding the ways and the will of God. It is inspiring—and challenging—to realize that, even here, there will ever be new worlds of mind and spirit to conquer, greater heights to climb, new adventures to exploit.

This concept of progression in the realm of the spirit actuated the mind of Dr. Oliver Wendell Holmes as he examined a shell found on the ocean beach. The poet was fascinated by the evidence of progressive living as the mollusk outgrew one chamber and moved on to the next. Admiring the pearly shell, Dr. Holmes realized that, like the humble crustacean, human aspirations must also continually move on, must grow and expand. Here was the theme for his marvelous poem, "The Chambered Nautilus." In a few telling stanzas he poetically compares the tiny, growing creature in its ship of pearl, moving from one chambered cell to the next, with the soul of man building for itself ever more stately mansions. He closes thus:

"Thanks for the heavenly message brought by thee,
    Child of the wandering sea,
    Cast from her lap, forlorn!
From thy dead lips a clearer note is born
Than ever Triton blew from wreathed horn!
    While on mine ear it rings,
Through the deep caves of thought I hear
    A voice that sings:—
Build thee more stately mansions, O my soul,
    As the swift seasons roll!
    Leave thy low-vaulted past!
Let each new temple, nobler than the last,
Shut thee from heaven with a dome more vast,
    Till thou at length art free,
Leaving thine outgrown shell by life's unresting sea!"

TOO MANY ALTARS

Take heed that you do not offer your burnt offerings at every place that you see. Deut. 12:13, R.S.V.

Along certain narrow, crooked mountain trails of Mexico, and in other countries as well, the wayfarer comes upon little open spaces perhaps with a wooden bench or merely a flat stone on which to sit and rest. Sometimes a brook or a trickle of water offers a cooling draft. Often an altar or a crude cross stands as an invitation to prayer. In some areas there are so many of these special open spaces that, were the traveler to turn aside at them all, he would never reach his destination. Obviously our text refers to such stopping places. The underlying principle, however, involves more than any temporary journey. Life's pathway is strewn with so many diverting side issues and distractions that to turn aside for them all will prove fatal to spirituality. On all sides, enchanting scenes beckon, and alluring voices call. An inflexible purpose and a determined will are required to disregard these beguilements.

When our daughter Dana was 5 years old, she made a trip with me from Washington, D.C., to California. While I was standing before the ticket window in the old railroad station in Chicago this wide-eyed child wandered away. For ten minutes I searched in vain. She had vanished. In near panic I persuaded the station guard to join the search. It took another twenty minutes to find her standing behind a huge pillar on the lower floor. She was calmly contemplating a huge fresco. With luck we made our train—but barely. Once settled down in our seats I asked my daughter, "Dana, what made you wander away like that?" She said, "Why, Daddy, those big pictures were *so* interesting!"

Children are not the only ones who forget where they are, what they are there for, and then wander off. Adults sometimes figuratively miss the train. Some kneel before so many shrines as to seem like devotees of a multideitied idolatry. But all who stop to worship before any pagan altar receive no response, save the echo of their own voices.

It is heart rending to see thousands pouring out their lifeblood and treasure before insensate things rather than before a prayer-hearing and prayer-answering God. When we kneel to pray let us make sure that we approach, not an idol or shrine fashioned of wood or stone or of precious jewels, but the living God, who loves us and gave His Son to save us.

THE TRIVIAL AND THE TRANSCENDENT

"As your servant was busy here and there, he was gone." The king of Israel said to him, "So shall your judgment be; you yourself have decided it." 1 Kings 20:40, R.S.V.

This text teaches a vital lesson for our day. Like his predecessor Saul, King Ahab chose to ignore God's specific instructions. Thereupon, through an ingenious disguise, the prophet of God induced the wicked king to pronounce his own sentence. His excuse was not the first, nor the last, attempt of shifty, deceitful-minded individuals to escape blame for dereliction of duty. By offering the excuse that they are too busy some hope to limp by. Here is a trap into which many well-intentioned people fall. While attending nonessentials, however innocent or interesting, they allow the best goals of life to slip by unnoticed. Often they do not realize this until these priceless opportunities are passed forever.

While attending graduate school I had a friendly, congenial roommate. He tried hard but strangely could not discriminate between the important and the unimportant. No matter how urgent the main tasks before him, he repeatedly failed to choose wisely between the vital and the trivial. Dallying over nonessentials, he cleaned the room when he could have been studying for an examination and carefully shined and reshined his shoes when a term paper was long overdue. This near-fatal weakness followed him. In later life he never achieved the levels of attainment his talents warranted. Doing daily the second best became his nemesis, his near undoing.

To those who realize that this life is brief at best, this matter of vital choices looms importantly. Actually, there is so little time available that we must omit much that has great appeal, must leave out many things that, of themselves, may well be good. When people ask, "What is wrong with this?" or "Why do you frown upon that?" the answer comes, "Nothing intrinsically, except that it crowds out what is infinitely more imperative."

Friendships figure prominently in our choices. But we cannot spend time with every interesting person we meet. There isn't enough time. A young man cannot marry every lovely girl of his acquaintance. There are too many of them. New books are published every day. But the most avid reader cannot scan even one in twenty. I have sometimes wished the government would certify good books as it does pure food. But no one certifies food for the mind. All the best choices of life are ours to make. God planned it so.

FEARFUL APPREHENSIONS

Say to them that are of a fearful heart, Be strong, fear not: behold, your God will come . . . and save you. Isa. 35:4.

With the intrusion of sin into Paradise a nameless fear seized our first parents. After their fateful initial transgression Adam and Eve hid themselves. When God came looking for them and calling, "Where are you?" Adam answered, "I was afraid." Ever since that disastrous day, fear, in a thousand guises, has stalked the steps of men. This "frightful fiend" walks daily unbidden at our side. Emerson wrote, "We are afraid of truth, afraid of fortune, afraid of death, and afraid of each other." Children fear the dark. Youth fear the future. Adults fear misfortune. The aged fear disease, decrepitude, and death. Is there no escape from this paralyzing power, this comfortless companion of our days?

According to Cicero, Dionysius, king of Syracuse, while presiding at a banquet taught a lesson on the constant perils of a ruler's life to Damocles, who was obliged to sit for hours beneath a naked sword suspended above his head by a single hair. This incident has come down through the ages as a striking illustration of the imminence of any deadly peril. We hear it quite often today. The whole human race may be said to be sitting on that chair with the naked sword of nuclear destruction hanging by a hair just overhead.

None of the perilous times of the past, horrible as they were, can compare with the potential terror of nuclear warfare. Within hours millions could be wiped out without warning. Great cities would become raging infernos, leaving only blackened ruins. Fertile fields would become radioactive and sterile. Watercourses would be contaminated and the air polluted and deadly. No wonder people worry. No wonder that a creeping fear seizes the hearts of men, including national leaders. Gradually the awful truth is dawning that any who might manage to escape such a cataclysmic destruction would find life not worth living. Disease, starvation, violence, and chaos would reign everywhere. No wonder those who look into the future are appalled by what they foresee.

But the Christian need not take so dark a view. In God's Book we can read how He has dealt with men in the past and we can learn of His wonderful plans for the future. With David we can say, "I sought the Lord, and he heard me, and delivered me from all my fears" (Ps. 34:4). Therefore, *fear not!*

77

PEACE OF MIND

Thou wilt keep him in perfect peace, whose mind is stayed on thee: because he trusteth in thee. Isa. 26:3.

Not everything Robert Louis Stevenson wrote is suitable reading for the Christian. But in one of his tales an incident is related that illustrates the lesson of confidence and trust. It tells of a sailing vessel caught in a storm near a rocky coast. One passenger, less terrified than the others, carefully made his way up to the pilothouse. There he found the pilot lashed to his post with his hands on the wheel and a smile on his face. The man took one look and hurried back to the others. Then he shouted, "All is well. We shall not be lost. I saw the pilot, and he smiled at me." That report calmed the panic and converted despair into hope. The ship made harbor safely.

In our day of mounting tension and anxiety, millions find it all but impossible to live calmly and courageously. Many recent books aim to encourage a quiet spirit. To inspire soul peace, Rabbi Joshua Liebman wrote *Peace of Mind*. Yet he failed to find it for himself and in despondency took his own life. Commenting on this sad end to a kind and gentle soul, one editor asked, "How can anyone have any peace anymore if he has any mind?"

The answer lies in our text: soul peace can be found only in absolute trust in God. The exercise of faith is the first spiritual function of the heart, and the Christian life from childhood makes this assurance the ceaseless contemplation of the soul.

One day a 19-year-old college girl, a dear relative of mine, asked me to take her for a drive. It was a bright spring day and I thought she wanted to revel in the colorful countryside. Instead, in an unusually grave mood, she asked me several penetrating questions that had been troubling her. She wanted to know my thoughts about the inscrutable providences of God. I did my best to explain to her why we can place in Him our everlasting, absolute trust. Satisfied and obviously relieved, she brightened and said with confidence, "Oh, I see it now. No matter what happens in this world, if you truly trust God, He will take care of you forever." I was thankful beyond words at hearing this simple, sincere confession of confidence.

If Jesus lived in our day of distress and doubt, He would be calm and cheerful in His confident trust in His Father. Let us be like Him.

STRENGTH DESPITE WEAKNESS

Three times I begged the Lord to rid me of it, but his answer was: "My grace is all you need; power comes to its full strength in weakness." 2 Cor. 12:9, N.E.B.

Many have speculated about the physical infirmity that afflicted the apostle Paul. It probably was poor eyesight. Obviously this condition caused him considerable pain and inconvenience. So much so that on at least three occasions he pleaded with the Lord to remove it. But instead of granting his request the Lord told him, "My grace is sufficient for you." The pain and inconvenience were allowed to remain, but God's servant was granted abundant grace to endure them.

This trying experience of the great apostle to the Gentiles shows that God has never promised to better circumstances or to release His servants from trying personal vexations. That bodily infirmities are of secondary importance to Him is evident through the witness of scores of sorely afflicted, yet richly fruitful, laborers in His vineyard.

While I was living in Tennessee I became interested in the life and ministry of David Brainerd, the pioneer missionary to the Indians of that region. This valiant man endured so many physical ailments that, throughout his short life of twenty-nine years, he seldom knew a well day. The story of his life as revealed in his diary and letters makes it clear that he did more for the Lord than many gifted, robust men do in seventy or eighty years. Often so ill and weak that he required help to mount his horse, he rode resolutely into the forest to bring the gospel to tribes whose language he could not speak. On one occasion scores were converted even though the interpreter was so drunk he could not stand unsupported. Writing to his brother of this experience, Brainerd quoted Paul, "My strength is made perfect in weakness."

Consider also the tubercular Robert Louis Stevenson, who wrote in 1893: "For fourteen years I have not had a day of health. . . . I have written torn by coughing, written in hemorrhage . . . yet I have done my work unflinchingly. . . . The battle goes on; ill or well is a trifle so long as it goes."

What is your attitude toward your physical defects and inabilities? Do you indulge in helpless self-pity? When tempted to cry out against affliction consider how much poorer the world would be without the works of John Milton and Fanny Crosby. Let us then accept God's will and serve Him as we can—and without complaint.

ALPHA AND OMEGA

I am Alpha and Omega, the beginning and the ending, saith the Lord. Rev. 1:8.

Suitably situated in the undulating uplands northeast of Los Angeles lies the lovely city of Azusa. Intrigued by the town when I first visited there some years ago, I asked a resident about its name. He replied proudly, "Our founding fathers wanted this to become the nicest place from A to Z in the whole United States. So they coined the name A-Z-U-S-A. Don't you like it?" I did like it and I still do.

The city fathers of Azusa were not the first to make the alphabet into a name. The Saviour used it to represent Himself when He said, "I am Alpha and Omega," the first and the last letters of the Greek alphabet. He said He was the entire alphabet, a figure of speech to express the completeness of His redemption.

Ever since the English language came into usage, authors have utilized the alphabet. Each writer has arranged the letters to express his particular thought or idea. Not one letter has been mislaid or worn out. Each one is just as good today as it ever was. The alphabet serves the historian and the poet, the minister in his pulpit and the judge on his bench. It enables the seeker to open and understand the wealth of knowledge stored away in any library.

The alphabet is all-embracing because there is no letter before A and none after Z. Likewise, in the experience of man upon the earth there is nothing out of the reach of or beyond our heavenly Father. In the distant councils of eternity, when the morning stars sang together and the sons of God shouted for joy, He was there (Job 38:7). He was there when the worlds were called into being and fashioned in perfection and beauty. When the distressed psalmist called out for Him, He was there. (Ps. 34:4). Most important of all, when the offenseless Lamb of God was called upon to yield up His life on Calvary's cross, He was there. And when this world with everything in it is gone, He will still be there.

As with lisping tongues we first pronounce the letters of the alphabet, so we compose our childish prayers. Then, as we pray, we come to know Him better, until in Him we find the answers to all our needs.

LOOKING BACK

Do not ask why the old days were better than these; for that is a foolish question. Eccl. 7:10, N.E.B.

Many people, particularly the elderly, find it easier and sometimes more pleasant to let their minds dwell on the events of the past, both good and bad, than to face the pains, pangs, and problems of the present. Listening to long, drawn-out, nostalgic reminiscences about days gone by, often petulantly particularized, I have suspected that memories grow blurred and that some word pictures paint roses of the past in overly bright colors while quite overlooking their thorns. So, when I hear glowing praises of "the good old days" contrasted with a dismal view of the present, I am tempted to remind the somber speaker that God puts our eyes in the front instead of the back of the head because He intends for us to look forward. It may be that the wise man had this in mind when he warned that to look at "the old days" as better than the present is foolishness.

Some find it hard to rise above the past. We all have our guilty memories that, if we let them, will come creeping back to haunt us with their sorrows. Mistakes and misconduct of yesterday return unbidden to flaunt their shameful faces. But it is not God's plan that we should bear this extra burden. All our yesterdays are now beyond recall. They are as cold and dead as the ashes of Carthage. The cheerful, courageous Christian will relegate regretful memories to the limbo of forgotten things and leave them there. He must believe that they are gone forever. We are told that our sins, once forgiven, are remembered against us no more (Jer. 31:34). If God forgives and forgets our sins, there is no reason for us to remember them.

A troubled man once confessed to me that he worried over his past heartless malignment of a good woman who died before he made the matter right. He said, "She was a noble soul whom God will surely save in His kingdom. But if I should be there, too, I will be too ashamed to meet her. Is there anything I can do about it now?" I reminded him that God abundantly forgives and that surely this good woman will forgive him also.

Dwelling unduly on past successes or failures is, like walking backward, a dangerous practice. Beware lest obsession with the past lead you unawares into a spiritual ditch.

WE HAVE TODAY
As thy days, so shall thy strength be. Deut. 33:25.

It is often said that the stream of time flows like a mighty river. At first our frail craft glides down the shallow channel past winding brooks that spill down their grassy slopes. Spring wafts her gentle fronds above us. Leafy trees shed blossoms on our youthful heads. Flowers on the banks offer themselves to our young hands. We are supremely happy as we eagerly enjoy the beauties that surround us. We move along. Then, before we realize it, the stream widens and hurries on. As it enters the sea we are surprised, as our journey ends, that we have grown old—and empty.

As mysterious as eternity to our finite minds, time spans past ages and the unknown future. Few realize that they are being borne along irresistibly every moment while the sun spins silently in its orbit. Life is being swept away by the ruthless hand of time. While it seems slow to youth, those of adult years feel that it flies. How exceedingly fast to the aged! Those who are older are tempted to say of our days, as was said of cherubims, that each one has six wings (see Rev. 4:8).

How strange that many, particularly among the young, spend this temporal life prodigally as if the supply of time were unlimited. All too soon the scant store proves too little, and many who kill time find at last that it kills them too. By then they would give worlds, if they had any, in exchange for just one more day.

Although time flows relentless and forever, we acquire it only in the brief and fleeting segments known as days. We live them one by one. Yesterday is gone. Tomorrow is yet to be. But we have today.

As we go forth this day let us do so with the confidence that we are not alone. The same Providence that watched over us through the night has promised to accompany us through the day. We will be provided with the energy needed to do today's tasks. Let us say to ourselves, "God has given me this new day. It will not be long. In its few, fleeting hours I can do right, meet the trials that beset me, and surmount the problems that present themselves. God has promised to give me strength for this day. I will keep His promise in mind and claim it until night calls me back to slumber."

Then let us go forth and face the day in confidence, knowing assuredly that we need not meet it in our own strength, but in His.

TOMORROW

I go to prepare a place for you. John 14:2.

Although the immediate prospects were appalling, far more terrible than His disciples could imagine, the Saviour reminded them that the future was bright. He wanted them to keep this so firmly in mind that, regardless of the calamities about to befall them, they would never lose hope. So He directed their attention to their certain glorious future. His promise is ours today.

Scrawled on a wall along a beach were these words: "Tomorrow has been canceled for lack of interest." What a fitting commentary on the attitude of uncertainty and despair that depresses many young people today! But the youth are not alone in this feeling of hopelessness. A noted scientist, lecturing at a great university, expressed his view of the future thus, "I see no way out for us all except through the little gray door at the end." For millions tomorrow offers no hope. They ask, "Why exist? What is there to live for? Might as well live it up while we can. We're in for nuclear extinction anyway."

This deep vein of pessimism infects a broad spectrum, rather than any isolated groups, in our society today. Some of the reasons can be listed:

1. The loss of faith by many professed Christians.

2. The decline of morality and accompanying burgeoning of crime.

3. Widespread loss of confidence in the ability of the statesmen of the world to prevent nuclear annihilation.

4. The failure of society to solve the problems of hunger, disease, and overpopulation.

5. The increasing love of ease, excitement, and pleasure.

It was not always so. Even as recently as the close of World War II, trusted men of science were promising an early solution to all our problems. They painted a roseate picture of a coming world utopia and of an American Great Society where there would be plenty of everything for everybody.

Their tomorrow is here and with it have come unprecedented problems. The Saviour predicted just such disappointments. But He also promised a glorious future. The eternal home He offers is free for the taking. This promise edges our present problems and foreboding future with rainbow hues. This radiant expectancy makes life eminently worth living. Tomorrow has *not* been canceled.

LOOKING FORWARD

Forgetting those things which are behind, and reaching forth unto those things which are before, I press toward the mark for the prize. Phil. 3:13, 14.

By these words the apostle Paul expresses the wisdom of looking toward the future rather than into the past. Solomon had a similar thought when he wrote: "Let thine eyes look right on, and let thine eyelids look straight before thee" (Prov. 4:25). These clear-cut admonitions do not admit of any misunderstanding. God's desire for His children is that they face ever forward, looking neither to the right hand nor to the left. When the heart is set toward righteousness the eyes will cease to rove. To keep the eye on the eternal goal and never stop until it is reached is the essential aim of every Christian.

A boyhood experience early impressed upon my mind the importance of constantly keeping in view an attainable goal. On a clear winter morning we were surprised to see that during the night a silent snowfall had spread a spotless four-inch blanket of white over all the land. As soon as my mother could bundle me up I hurried out to make a path in the untrodden snow. At some distance I saw a fence post on which I took aim with a view to make an absolutely straight track to it. For a while I kept my eye on the post and walked as straight as an arrow toward it. Suddenly my attention was diverted by a hawk flying low overhead. After it flew away I looked at the post again and continued in a straight line to it. Turning back to look I was surprised to see the exact spot where I had taken my eyes from the goal and wandered a bit, and also the place where I had resumed looking at it. The spiritual lesson has remained with me ever since.

Quite as important as a worthy goal is clear vision to keep it in view. A famous optometrist practiced near where we lived in Michigan. One day a prominent minister, whose eyesight seemed to be deteriorating alarmingly, came for a consultation. After testing his patient's eyes the doctor examined his eyeglasses. Smiling, he said, "There is nothing wrong with your eyes. One of the lenses has slipped around in the rim and your vision is out of focus." Relieved and grateful, the clergyman went away delighted.

If we focus our eyes ever forward and press on, we can, with God's help, like Paul, attain at last the everlasting prize.

WHAT TIME IS IT?

Walk in wisdom . . . redeeming the time. Col. 4:5.

Except perhaps for the familiar greeting, "How are you?" no question is heard more often than "What time is it?" When her husband stirs at dawn, the sleepy wife asks, "What time is it?" With stethoscope in hand, the family doctor asks it as he leans over a desperately ill child. The perspiring groom, awaiting his cue, inquires of his best man, "What time is it?" The soldier, awaiting the zero hour, asks it too. As does also the anxious patient facing delicate heart surgery. This is about the most meaningful question ever asked. "What time is it?" The offhand response is, "It is later than you think." But such a casual reply does not really answer the question at all.

Have you considered lately how slavishly civilization has come under the tyranny of the clock? We come into the world by it and leave the same way. We eat, sleep, work, and relax by it. Lovers court by the clock, schools operate by it, the wheels of commerce turn by it, and preachers preach under its frown.

"What time is it?" is a serious question. On a tower at Oxford, underneath the clock, these words appear in Latin: "They pass and are charged to our account." The Christian's duty is to count time, not by a dial or a clock, but by the accomplishments of each day. To redeem the time is more than simply refraining from idleness and frivolity. It involves taking advantage of every moment for positive action for good. "It is wrong to waste our time. . . . If every moment were valued and rightly employed, we should have time for everything that we need to do."—*Messages to Young People*, p. 322. "Young men and young women, you have no time to lose. . . . Seek to redeem the time."—*Ibid.*, p. 301.

Lord Chesterfield wrote his son, "Learn the true value of time. Snatch, seize, and enjoy every moment of it." In his *Poor Richard's Almanac* Benjamin Franklin included this gem: "Do not squander time, for that is the stuff life is made of." The aging Albert Schweitzer, famed doctor-missionary, still facing a formidable, unfinished task, sadly said, "I wish sometimes that I could stand on the street corner, hat in hand, that passers-by might toss me their wasted hours."

"Let us not pass in idleness the precious hours that God has given us in which to perfect characters for heaven."—*Testimonies*, vol. 3, p. 540.

GOD'S PECULIAR PEOPLE

Now therefore, if ye will obey my voice . . . and keep my covenant, then ye shall be a peculiar treasure unto me above all people. Ex. 19:5.

When I was a small boy ours was the only Adventist family living in the area. Especially because we "kept Saturday for Sunday," we were considered as distinctively different. Peer pressure is strong among children, and because we held unusual beliefs, which to us were sacred, and because in these things we were nonconformists, other children looked askance at us. To them we seemed strange, even queer. Of course, we were quick to sense this ill-concealed resentment, so we kept to ourselves as much as we could. The resultant spiritual and social isolation was hard to bear. But because to a large degree it was shared as well as understood by our parents, they lovingly watched over and encouraged us. They felt the pain too.

The word *peculiar* is not entirely negative. In Malachi 3 this Hebrew word, translated in Exodus as "a peculiar treasure," appears as "jewels." These texts show that in the sight of God no other nation was equal to Israel, also that every child of God, every consecrated Christian is a jewel in the crown of the Lord and is so considered by Him (see 1 Peter 2:9). Similarly, in Deuteronomy 26:18, 19 Moses declared that the Lord sets Israel apart as His peculiar people as long as they keep His commandments.

The New Testament also regards God's commandment-keeping people as peculiar. "But you are God's 'chosen generation,' his 'royal priesthood,' his 'holy nation,' his 'peculiar people'—all the old titles of God's people now belong to you. It is for you now to demonstrate the goodness of him who has called you out of darkness into his amazing light" (1 Peter 2:9, Phillips).

Jesus, in His day, was decidedly a nonconformist. He was not ordinary, nor were His disciples. When we take the name "Christian" we will no longer be ordinary. We will be different and will be considered peculiar by many.

If being "peculiar" means being out of step with the world, calmly disregarding hostile criticism and ridicule, then let us bravely ignore being called odd or strange. It takes courage to be distinctive, to remain aloof from all that is sordid and mean, and to faithfully keep God's commandments. But when we respond to Jesus we can bear what people call us—even peculiar.

BRIDGES

God was in Christ, reconciling the world unto himself. 2 Cor. 5:19.

During the Mexican War the battle of Buena Vista was fought between a six-thousand-man American army under Gen. Zachary Taylor and a much larger Mexican force. Among Taylor's subordinates was Col. Jefferson Davis commanding a regiment of Mississippi volunteers. Davis was married to Taylor's daughter and had been at enmity with his father-in-law for years. The hotly contested battle ended as an American victory largely through the courage and skill of the Mississippi Rifles and their brave leader, who was painfully wounded in the struggle. When word reached the victorious commander he hurried to the tent where his suffering son-in-law was being treated for his wound. A touching reconciliation took place, wiping out the ill feelings that had long corroded their relationship. The harmony and accord forged that day on the battlefield endured unbroken until the death of General Taylor while serving as President of the United States twelve years later.

Other moving reconciliations between long-standing enemies include that of Jacob and his brother, Esau. The sacred story says that "Esau ran to meet him [Jacob], and embraced him, and fell on his neck, and kissed him: and they wept" (Gen. 33:4). There is also the unforgettable parable told by Jesus of the prodigal son. The record is that, after a period of separation, "he arose, and came to his father. But when he was yet a great way off, his father saw him, and had compassion, and ran, and fell on his neck, and kissed him" (Luke 15:20).

Impressive as they are poignant, these reconciliations can in no way remotely compare with the sublime reconciliation set forth in our text: "God was in Christ, reconciling the world unto himself." The verse correctly implies that man once enjoyed a camaraderie with his Maker that was lost when sin sundered that close fellowship. Because there never has been enmity on God's part, the reconciliation is of wayward man to his God. The chasm carved out by sin has grown so wide that only the Son of God Himself can bridge it. He did this willingly when He offered Himself to die for sinners. In this way the gulf of sin can be crossed, for Christ is the living Bridge that links earth and heaven. There is no other way.

When next in your travels a mighty, high-arched bridge looms into view, let that beautiful masterpiece of architectural ingenuity symbolize for you the divine Bridge reconciling sinners unto God.

TURRETED TOWERS

Walk about Zion . . . number her towers, consider well her ramparts, go through her citadels; that you may tell the next generation that this is God, our God for ever and ever. Ps. 48:12-14, R.S.V.

Architectural masterpieces, particularly ancient castles with spires and steeples, turrets and towers, intrigue me—especially the towers. I was profoundly impressed the day I visited the lofty, lacelike Eiffel Tower, from which I viewed with ecstacy the far-flung city of Paris. Days later I stood on the frowning battlements of the ancient Tower of London, a gloomy, stone-walled city within a city, where not a few notable, but unfortunate, habitants had awaited execution. There was also the Tower of Silence, a crude stone pillar where the Parsees expose their dead until the bones are picked clean by vultures.

These I have seen, but not the tower that comes most often into my imagination. It must have been a tremendous pyramid, a magnificent, terraced edifice, for, according to the record, there was built in the land of Shinar "a tower," whose top was intended to "reach unto heaven" (Gen. 11:4). But when the Lord came down to visit "the city and the tower, which the children of men" were building, He was displeased and confounded their language. The resultant confusion caused them to leave off building, so the great tower was never finished.

If the student looks closely into history he may discern two multiple-towered bridges spanning the past to the present. One structure is supported by piers and towers of great violence. The other is held aloft by a series of piers of truth. The sadistic chief engineer of the first tower laced its catwalks with sharp and slippery hazards, so that with one misstep the unwise traveler falls to his doom. The other structure, built by a loving God, is a safe bridge of truth upheld by towers of divine strength.

The admonition to "walk about Zion" and to "consider well her ramparts" has been misunderstood by some critical church members as authorization for them to observe and pass judgment upon the performances and achievements of the brethren who direct the affairs of the church. This is a misreading of the text. Believers are urged to "walk about Zion" and "consider well her ramparts" for a far different reason. The observations are encouraged that they "may tell the next generation" that "our God" is "for ever." As we pass along the heaven-built bridge its unshakable towers provide assurance that God will be our guide to the end of life.

ENEMIES OF MAN: THE WORLD

Do not love the world or the things in the world. If any one loves the world, love for the Father is not in him. 1 John 2:15, R.S.V.

At first glance this injunction seems like a hard saying, especially to the young, whom John was immediately addressing. Young hearts thrill with wonder and delight at the beauty of natural things: spring flowers, a glorious sunset, a grassy meadow sparkling with dew when touched by the rising sun. Happily, this inborn appreciation of nature is not denied in this text. The Greek word here translated "world" does not refer to that which remains to us of the original loveliness of God's creation. Instead—fortunately for all Christians who dearly love the great outdoors—this text is a warning against something altogether different. It constitutes an injunction against all that is alien and hostile to God, all worldly affairs that lead away from Him. This is an exhortation to "love not" whatever earthly elements and powers Satan has arrayed in opposition to God and His plans for the salvation of men.

The three greatest enemies of Christian living are the world, the flesh, and the devil. As used by John, "the world" means the environment in which we must live all the days of our lives. This environment is a hostile enemy to almost every noble desire and purpose that springs from the converted heart. When we ask how man has generally related to this unholy atmosphere around him, the answer is that he has largely succumbed to it. How easy it is to accept the customs and practices of the world as the measure of all values! The common excuse is that "everybody does it." When conscience stirs, it is quickly quieted by reasoning that, even if the worldly ways are questionable, one can hardly be expected to swim against the current. From the days of Adam men have sought excuses for their unholy deeds and ungodly lives. Only thus have they been able to live with themselves and their unquiet consciences.

Man was originally created upright. But among his many perverted ideas is the morally paralyzing notion that we are hapless victims of the environment and that we must lie in this noxious bed of evil unable, even with God's help, to arise from it.

Fortunately, even now after many millenniums of this immoral habitat, free will, implanted by God Himself, is still ours. If we exercise this power of choice, His Holy Spirit is there to help.

ENEMIES OF MAN: THE FLESH

All that is in the world, the lust of the flesh, and the lust of the eyes, and the pride of life, is not of the Father, but is of the world. 1 John 2:16.

Of the three implacable enemies of the spiritual life—the world, the flesh, and the devil—the "flesh" is the most prevalent, for we must cope with it every day. The apostle Paul wrote, "I know that in me (that is in my flesh,) dwelleth no good thing" (Rom. 7:18). He also lamented, "What an unhappy man I am! Who will rescue me from this body that is taking me to death?" (verse 24, T.E.V.). The distress of the agonizing struggle between the will to righteousness and the evil influence of his natural inheritance brought out this cry of near despair. But Paul knew where to call for deliverance. The next verse expresses his thankfulness to "God through Jesus Christ our Lord" (verse 25).

The "flesh" specified here refers to the sin-polluted bodies where dwell the traces of all the characteristics inherited from our forebears. It has been said that "we are omnibuses in which our ancestors ride." Since Creation, every trait, good or bad, as well as physical resemblance, is blended into us and, according to one modern writer, "we are pitchforked into this world without let or hindrance." This is our natural inheritance.

The unrestrained works of the flesh are briefly defined in Galatians 5:19: "What human nature does is quite plain. It shows itself in immoral, filthy, and indecent actions" (T.E.V.). The sad fact is that we are born with this inherited nature so that there is within us all a natural proclivity for carnal things. Through the ages, down to and including our day, the overwhelming majority have taken for granted that those desires are altogether right and proper to express. In fact, the body is generally considered the appropriate agent for providing thrills.

But there is another side to this question. There is a marvelous solution available for dealing with this monstrous problem. With ready help from above we can bring every natural instinct and impulse under complete control and into subjection to the will of God. (See 1 Cor. 9:27, T.E.V.) "The body is to be brought into subjection to the higher powers of the being. The passions are to be controlled by the will, which is . . . under the control of God."—*Prophets and Kings*, p. 489. Thus, like Paul, we can thank God and take courage.

ENEMIES OF MAN: THE DEVIL

Be alert, be on watch! Your enemy, the Devil, roams around like a roaring lion, looking for someone to devour. 1 Peter 5:8, T.E.V.

Here the Greek employs the definite article *the,* which implies that the identity of the Christian's enemy is well known. This adversary is the devil, a sinister, slinking foe who through falsification and deceit succeeded in entrapping our first parents into sin. Thereby he brought unspeakable tragedy upon them and all their descendants. He is a venomous enemy who surreptitiously injects lethal poison into the bloodstream of his deluded devotees. He is a crafty enemy skulking around continually to trap and devour the unwary and the innocent. And he is an efficient, eloquent, and persuasive enemy, else he could never have induced a third of the angels of heaven to join him in rebellion against the Creator.

Satan is the archfiend of all haters. He hates all that is good, lovely, and beautiful in the world. Everything he touches corrodes. Every living thing he breathes upon dies. He plows wrinkles into the face, and pestilence into the soil. He puts poison in the pot, famine on the land, and murder in the hearts of men. He sows tares amid the wheat, discord among brethren, and prints a special edition whenever a saint goes wrong. He plots destruction to the righteous; and be the agent disease, accident, or disaster, it makes no difference to him, so long as he can bow down with grief the hearts of God's children. He lays pestilence on the people and his own troupers in the tomb. Even without the cooperation of the world or the flesh, the devil can make direct, sinister attacks on man through carnal whisperings and temptations to the mind.

The apostle Paul was keenly conscious of the presence of this formidable enemy, with this array of herculean temptations confronting the Christian every day. He warned the Ephesians that "we wrestle not against flesh and blood, but against principalities, against powers, against the rulers of the darkness of this world, against spiritual wickedness in high places" (Eph. 6:2).

Once more we do well to remind ourselves that this vicious adversary is ever near and ready to spring upon us as does a lion upon its unwary prey. "We have a powerful enemy, and not only does he hate every human being made in the image of God, but with bitterest enmity he hates God and His only-begotten Son Jesus Christ."—*Fundamentals of Christian Education,* p. 299.

THE MOST HONEST MAN

Show yourselves guileless and above reproach, faultless children of God in a warped and crooked generation, in which you shine like stars in a dark world. Phil. 2:15, N.E.B.

In the natural world as evening shadows gather, smaller lights, scarcely noticed by day, glow brighter, their beams illuminating more and farther as darkness falls. This is the illustration Paul used as he urged the Philippians to "shine like stars in a dark world." His admonition is highly fitting today.

It was probably no news to the Philippians to be told that they were living in a wicked and perverse age. Even so, the malevolent society of that first century of the Christian era could hardly have been more corrupt than ours—that is, if we can judge from reports of steadily mounting crime that pour forth continually from television, radio, and newsprint.

One day I walked about the old Oak Hill Cemetary in Battle Creek, Michigan looking for the graves of pioneers of the Advent message. To my surprise I came upon a modest tombstone inscribed "David Hewett, the most honest man in town." What a tribute! Later on a fellow teacher and I were looking for the country home of a prominent Adventist family in northern Georgia. As our directions were vague I stopped the car before a white-pillared mansion on a rise surrounded by a meticulously manicured lawn. There sat an elderly gentleman in a wicker armchair beside a table loaded with garden produce for sale. My companion got out and addressed the distinguished-looking individual, "Can you direct us to the place of Mr. S?" The thin man stood to his full height of above six feet and replied in a cultured Southern accent, "Do I know him! Do you know him? The man you want is a well-to-do Seventh-day Adventist and the best and most honest man in the county." He gave directions. We thanked him and went thoughtfully on our way. That night we were graciously entertained in the home of this "most honest man in the county."

Another time, inquiring for a Chattanooga businessman, I was told, "He is the smartest businessman in town and the most honest. He's a strict Seventh-day Adventist. I'd gladly trust him with all I own in the world."

Are you regarded as one of "the most honest"?

POINT OF NO RETURN

Ephraim is joined to idols: let him alone. Hosea 4:17.

This verse seems to me to be about the saddest in the entire Bible. Its counterpart is found in Genesis 6:3 in which the Lord, perceiving the preponderant wickedness of the antediluvian world, pronounced its doom, declaring, "My spirit shall not always strive with man." It is as if an anxious, compassionate physician, after long efforts to save a failing patient, finally leans away from the bed of the unconscious sufferer to utter the fateful words, "I have done all I can."

Ephraim, meaning "fruitful," was the younger son of Joseph. With his brother, Manasseh, he had received a special blessing from his grandfather Jacob. As you read the sacred story of God's gracious blessing on this favored son and his descendants, you are grieved to discern their gradual decline into depravity. The causes are clear. Ephraim became the chief tribe of northern Israel. Decade on decade of iniquitous folly engrossed the minds of the people until their hearts were forever welded to their idols. God's spirit no longer strove with them, for there was no hope. They had passed the point of no return. Persistently refusing God's gracious and repeated appeals, they were finally left to reap the fruits of their own choosing. When they made that choice their probation closed.

In this life there are many points of no return. Flying miles above the vast Pacific Ocean one night I heard the calm voice of the pilot, "We have just passed the point of no return." Parties to a contract can agree beforehand on every item; but until the pact is officially signed by both, it can be canceled with impunity. But once the signatures are affixed, the point of no return is reached. Even after a prospective groom and bride decide to wed either one can cancel their plans. But when they meet at the altar their troth there brings them to the point of no return. The crucial turning point is always fateful and its results far reaching.

For generations the Lord has borne with His wayward children. Even now, in the face of defiant rebellion, He longs to "reveal Himself as willing to save" *(Prophets and Kings, p. 285)*. But "fearful will be the doom of that soul of whom the pleading Saviour shall finally declare, he 'is joined to idols: let him alone.' "—*Patriarchs and Prophets*, p. 165. Let us be willing and obedient lest we pass the point of no return.

NOT NINEVEH, PLEASE!

Now the word of the Lord came unto Jonah . . . saying, Arise, go to Nineveh, that great city, and cry against it; for their wickedness is come up before me. Jonah 1:1, 2.

Nineveh, proud capital of Assyria, had flourished for 1,500 years. It had never been conquered. Rightly called a great city, it was surrounded by a wall sixty feet high, on which three chariots could be driven abreast. In common with most populous cities, Nineveh was riddled with crime. It was a place of blood, and "full of lies and robbery" (Nahum 3:1). But the people of Nineveh were not wholly given over to evil. "In that city many who were reaching out after something better and higher, and who, if granted opportunity to learn of the living God, would put away their evil deeds and worship Him."—*Prophets and Kings* pp. 265, 266.

God told Jonah to arise and go. But, thinking of the difficulties of that commission and of his own self-preservation, Jonah hesitated and then went the other way. His fear and distrust prevented him from realizing that the same God who had told him to go would sustain him and give him success. But the Lord knew where he was all the time and spoke a second time to Jonah, "Arise, go to Nineveh." How good it is that God speaks to us more than once! This time Jonah obeyed and cried throughout the city, "Yet forty days, and Nineveh shall be overthrown." From street to street he went, calling out the divine warning. The result was amazing. "The people . . . believed God, and proclaimed a fast, and put on sackcloth, from the greatest of them even to the least of them" (chap. 3:5). When the tidings reached the king "he arose . . . and laid his robe from him . . . and sat in ashes" (verse 6). When the entire city responded and was converted God changed His mind and reprieved the penitent. No doubt many will be saved in heaven as a result of Jonah's evangelistic campaign in Nineveh.

Jonah, whose convincing message led to the sparing of Nineveh, should have rejoiced at God's amazing grace. Instead, fearing he would be considered a false prophet, he grew so sorry for himself that he wanted to die. His weakness still was his self-concern, which overshadowed his awareness of duty to God and compassion for sinners. Jonah's eternal fate is not revealed, but the Saviour's reference to him indicates that, like his converts in Nineveh, Jonah repented and will be counted among the redeemed (see Matt. 16:4).

"PUT AWAY CHILDISH THINGS"

When I was a child, I spake as a child, I understood as a child, I thought as a child: but when I became a man, I put away childish things. 1 Cor. 13:11.

More than anyone I ever knew, the late Elder F. D. Nichol loved little children and babies. Many times he would stop after a church service, or even on the street, to speak to a mother and admire the child in her arms.

Most everyone loves babies. We smile at their innocent ways, and their childish traits intrigue us. But the very things that amuse us in babies we abhor in adults. About the most disappointing thing in the world is a grown-up baby. This is why the apostle Paul resolved that, as a man, he would put away childish things.

The adage that "adults are only children grown tall" is often all too true. Many carry their infantile ways over into adult life; and, because they continue to act like babies, they pout and complain. Something different is expected of grown-ups.

A baby announces his presence by crying. He quickly learns this is the easiest way to get what he wants. Sometimes he cries with little or no provocation. To be neglected or denied his own way induces tears. To cross him brings squalls, and even imaginary hurts evoke ear-piercing wails.

Adults sometimes are moved to tears too. There is "a time to weep" (Eccl. 3:4), but not all the time. Tears of joy or sorrow or for the misfortunes of others have their place. But to cry over unintended slights or trifles has no place in the lives of stalwart Christian adults.

Have you ever seen a thankful baby? I haven't. They take life's blessings as a matter of course and have to be taught to say "Thank you." We don't expect gratitude from babies because they are babies, but it is disappointing when men and women show no sense of gratitude either to God or other people for the blessings they receive. Writing to the Romans, Paul said of the ungodly that they did not glorify God "neither were thankful" (Rom. 1:21). Adults, not babies, are admonished to "in every thing give thanks" (1 Thess. 5:18).

The childish trait of seeking attention can be endured in children. But the adult who craves the spotlight makes few friends. Without considering others, the small child reaches for the biggest apple. But the selfish adult who demands his own way will find only bitter disappointment. Let us, therefore, "put away childish things."

HIS LEAF WILL NOT WITHER

And he shall be like a tree planted by the rivers of water, that bringeth forth his fruit in his season; his leaf also shall not wither; and whatsoever he doeth shall prosper. Ps. 1:3.

The trees I knew from my youth are the Western conifers: pine, fir, and cedar, also cottonwoods, aspen, and the sizable willows that thrive along the streams. Each kind is distinctive and admirable in its own way. But to my mind the towering Douglas fir, a truly noble strain, excels them all. If the expression "grow in grace" applies to trees, the Douglas fir best exemplifies it. How anyone can look steadfastly and thoughtfully at such a tree and fail to appreciate the handiwork of God is beyond understanding.

The redwoods of California are also an inspiring sight. More than two thousand years have rolled over their lofty heads and still they stand, living testimonies to God's power. There is at least one such tree that was already mature when David wrote our text for today. It was old when Jesus walked beside Galilee, and it was hoary and aged when Columbus discovered the new world. Nations and empires have come and gone, yet that soaring tree still lives and grows.

The child of God is to be like a tree planted by the water, always growing. This apt figure of speech beautifully represents the one who, like a great redwood, continues to grow. His life is a success because he "bringeth forth his fruit in his season." Because he is planted beside rivers of water there is no season of drought, no crop failures in the life of the one who continues to grow in grace. His life is ever green. His experience is fresh and invigorating. He is a shade for the weary and tired and provides protection for those buffeted by the storms of life.

The growth of a sturdy tree and its stability symbolize the life of the committed Christian. From tiny tendril to awesome giant the life of a sky-piercing tree is one continual process of receiving and growing. We are recipients of temporal and spiritual nutrients, neither earned nor deserved. Without the Source of strength and power we quickly wither and die. Yet, by God's help, our souls can be like the enduring strength of a tree. We, too, can bring forth fruit in season, which, after all, is what the tree was planted for in the first place.

MEN AS TREES WALKING

And he looked up, and said, I see men as trees, walking. Mark 8:24.

These words were spoken by a blind man who had once had sight. We are not told the cause of his blindness, but during his days of darkness he remembered the shapes and images of things he had previously seen. When Jesus touched him his darkness began to fade into indistinct glimmerings. Because he expected healing there may have been both surprise and disappointment in his voice when Jesus asked him, "What do you see?" He replied, "I see men as trees, walking." Jesus touched his eyes again. A moment passed, and then the man "saw every man clearly" (Mark 8:24, 25).

It was probably better to see men as walking trees than to see nothing at all. But Jesus, who never does things by halves, was not satisfied until His outpatient could see everything plain and clear.

More important than the restoration of sight to blind physical eyes is Jesus' ministry to the eyes of the soul. Few are troubled by imperfect physical sight today compared to the myriads whose soul eyes are dim and darkened.

There is an earthly philosophy of darkness that sees man as an amalgam of animal instincts, a coequal or counterpart of the horse and the dog. The poet Bryant called man "a brother to the insensible rock and the sluggish clod." Hendrik Van Loon looked on all humanity as "packed in a box" to be pushed over a ledge into oblivion. He wrote, "The human sardines in their mortuary chest will soon be forgotten." These are exponents of the darkened mind that sees only hopelessness and futility beyond.

The believer has clearer vision. In the collected Jewish legal writings, *The Talmund,* appears this illuminating passage: "Walking on the mountains one day, I saw a form which I took to be a beast; coming nearer, I saw it was a man; approaching nearer still, I found it was my brother."

One of the shortcomings of the Laodicean church was weak spiritual eyesight. That church was told, "Anoint thine eyes with eyesalve, that thou mayest see" (Rev. 3:18). Ellen White calls this eyesalve "the grace of God" *(Testimonies,* vol. 3, p. 254). It is given to the Christian, the eyes of whose soul are touched by Christ, to know that through regenerating faith, men may become sons of God and brothers.

BY HIS GRACE

For by grace are ye saved through faith; and that not of yourselves: it is the gift of God. Eph. 2:8.

The simplest definition of grace is: unmerited favor. The easiest way to explain God's grace is to say that it is the benevolent gift of eternal salvation conferred by faith even now upon repentant sinners. The significance of this verse is that the grace of God, which provides salvation, is solely and absolutely a free gift. We could never merit it however uprightly we live. We could not earn it with a lifetime of labor. It has nothing at all to do with what we deserve. It is God's way of manifesting His kindness to us because He loves us. The depth of that wonderful grace was shown when "Christ died for us while we were yet sinners, and that is God's own proof of his love towards us" (Rom. 5:8, N.E.B.). To express his gratitude to God, John Newton wrote the words of the well-loved hymn "Amazing Grace":

> "Amazing grace! how sweet the sound
> That saved a wretch like me!
> I once was lost, but now am found;
> Was blind, but now I see.
>
> . . . . .
>
> "Through many dangers, toils, and snares,
> I have already come;
> 'Tis grace hath brought me safe thus far,
> And grace will lead me home."

The beloved statesman Henry Clay was said to have held the hearts of the American people in his hands. When he narrowly missed the Presidency, strong men wept. But Clay was not a good businessman and neglected his financial affairs until he was hopelessly in debt. Facing certain ruin, he went to his banker and sadly confessed his plight. The banker seemed unperturbed. Then he said, "Mr. Clay, you owe us nothing. Your friends have paid it all." Senator Clay stood stunned and then, with tears coursing down his wrinkled old face, he turned slowly away, too moved to say another word.

"He [Christ] died for us. He does not treat us according to our desert. Although our sins have merited condemnation, He does not condemn us. Year after year He has borne with our weakness and ignorance, with our ingratitude and waywardness. Notwithstanding our wanderings . . . His hand is stretched out still."—*The Ministry of Healing*, p. 161.

NONE OTHER NAME

Neither is there salvation in any other: for there is none other name under heaven given among men, whereby we must be saved. Acts 4:12.

The key words here are *name* and *salvation,* two words linked together forever by the Saviour's sacrifice on the cross. This linkage stands out more forcefully when we remember when and by whom our text was spoken. The apostle Peter, a few weeks before, had denied his Lord and then forsaken Him. But there is another spirit in him now as he stands boldly before the priests and Sadducees to tell them to their face, "This is the stone which was rejected by you builders, but which has become the head of the corner" (Acts 4:11, R.S.V.).

Do we fully appreciate the apostle's words? What did he mean? He meant that no one can be saved from sin and its consequences except through Jesus Christ.

When the Flood came there was but one place of safety. It was Noah's ark. All other places and devices—mountains, trees, towers, caves, or rafts—were alike useless. Likewise there is but one hiding place for the sinner in the day of God when His wrath storms through the earth. That hiding place is in Christ. There is but one Name that will provide admittance when we stand at the gate of heaven. That name is Christ Jesus. This is the sublime truth uttered by the apostle Peter. It is a truth well spoken in these lines:

> "I know of lands that are sunk in shame,
> of hearts that faint and tire;
> But I know a Name, a precious Name,
> That can set those hearts on fire.

> "I know a soul that is steeped in sin,
> That no man's art can cure;
> But I know a Name, a precious Name,
> That can make that soul all pure.

> "I know a life that is lost to God,
> Bound down by things of earth;
> But I know a Name, a precious Name,
> That can give that soul new birth."
> —Author unknown

APRIL FOOL'S DAY

The fear of the Lord is the beginning of knowledge; fools despise wisdom and instruction. Prov. 1:7, R.S.V.

Originally April was month One of the year, the happy time when snow disappears and leaves burst out on shrub and tree. Burrowing animals reappear after their long winter's nap, birds return from the South, and bees begin to gather nectar from the early flowers.

April 1 was long known as April Fool's Day because some continued, after the calendar change in 1582, to regard it as the first day of the year. These were called "April Fools" by their friends who played jokes on them such as sending them on fool's errands or duping them into believing something absurd. In some countries this practice continues still.

The Bible speaks about fools. The word translated "fools" in our text refers to those who know right but have left it and abandoned themselves to wickedness. The wise man says, "Fools make a mock at sin" (Prov. 14:9). A fool is licentious (Prov. 7:22). Fools meddle in other people's business (Prov. 20:3). Fools are great in their own eyes (Prov. 12:15). A fool is devious and deceitful (Prov. 14:8).

Clearly, these texts refer, not to morons, but to those who ought to know better. A fool is not ignorant of God's law nor unaware of His love but, in his own inflated ego, considers himself self-sufficient. In rejecting the wisdom and the will of God he depends on his own wisdom and engenders unbelief in his own heart. The light that was in him turns to darkness and "how great is that darkness!" (Matt. 6:23).

Over the years I have known many gifted, even highly educated persons, who, in their pursuit of worldly wisdom and acclaim wandered from the Light of the World, "which lighteth every man that cometh into the world" (John 1:9). And I have been amazed and saddened to see them groping in their own self-chosen darkness. One such brilliant, former colleague announced to me that he had found in Oriental literature all the insight and comfort he needed. He died prematurely without hope of heaven.

The higher wisdom is to trust God and walk humbly in the light. The path we each take is not a matter of chance but of choice. Spend a few moments today comparing those who once knew God and yet rejected Him with those who know Him and follow Him. You may belong to either company you choose.

MORE ABOUT FOOLS

A prudent man sees danger and hides himself; but the simple go on, and suffer for it. Prov. 27:12, R.S.V.

One prevalent characteristic of the foolish is the tendency to disregard good counsel. "Fools despise wisdom and instruction" (Prov. 1:7, R.S.V.). "The mind of him who has understanding seeks knowledge, but the mouths of fools feed on folly" (chap. 15:14, R.S.V.). These and similar verses often came to mind as I have taught and counseled with students in Adventist colleges. This experience has convinced me that the wise counsel most often disregarded is that which deals with early, premature marriage and dropping out of school.

These two mistakes are often made in connection with each other. In the words of an experienced youth counselor, "My prime candidate for a fool's cap is the young fellow who leaves school to get married and his runner-up is the one who drops out to make money." Another youth advisor said, "All too often a boy falls in love with a dimple or a curl and then foolishly marries the entire girl." Young girls are as apt as are boys to make this mistake.

The *Testimonies* abound with strongly worded counsel to youth to avoid these blunders. "Young people are sent to school . . . to obtain an education, not to flirt with the opposite sex."—*Fundamentals of Christian Education,* p. 62.

"A youth not out of his teens is a poor judge of the fitness of a person as young as himself to be his companion for life. After their judgment has become matured, they view themselves bound for life to each other, and perhaps not at all calculated to make each other happy. . . . The young affections should be restrained until the period arrives when sufficient age and experience will make it honorable and safe to unfetter them."— *Messages to Young People,* p. 452.

"Many youth act from impulse. . . . Many will not listen to reason or instruction. . . . Thus thousands have sacrificed themselves, soul and body, by unwise marriages, and have gone down in the path of perdition."—*Ibid.*

For years I have been deeply distressed to see gifted youth with great potential in God's cause drop out of school never to return. If you are a student who is tempted to act foolishly in these regards, won't you reconsider your plans before it is too late?

DON'T PLAY WITH FIRE!

A prudent man foreseeth the evil, and hideth himself: but the simple pass on, and are punished. Prov. 22:3.

This text is almost identical with yesterday's. But a quite different application can be made by means of an illustration. When I was 9 our family lived on a dry-land wheat farm in central Montana. For some childish reason I liked to carry matches in my overalls pocket. One hot August afternoon mother sent me out to feed the chickens. There behind the barn I noticed a piece of porous cedar bark hanging loosely from a fence post. On impulse I touched a match to it to see if it would burn. It did and the flaming ember fell to the ground at my feet igniting the tinder-dry grass. I tried unsuccessfully to stamp it out. In no time a spreading grass fire, fanned by the wind, was burning rapidly toward a big field of ripe grain. Terrified, I called loudly to my mother. Seeing the danger, she ran out with two buckets of water from the horse trough and two empty grain sacks. With the wet sacks we were able to beat out the flames—but barely. It was a close call indeed. That night, in remorse, I promised my parents I would never again use matches carelessly. I have kept that promise.

From this dramatic, dangerous episode I early learned that it is not safe to play with fire. Nor is it safe to play with temptation or to linger in its presence. The longer Eve dallied the less was her chance to escape Satan's deception. Samson played with temptation in going to see Delilah and he did not escape the burning. Peter might have escaped temptation had he gone bravely with Jesus into the courtroom. But he dallied outside with the Roman soldiers.

Someone has said, "Those who deliberately place themselves in the way of temptation tempt the devil to tempt them." "While praying to be delivered from temptation do not peek at it through your fingers."

The wise person, who unfortunately often gains wisdom by painful experience, remains as far as possible from places and persons that invite temptation. Thus the believer can escape the sin of presumption. Taking chances in the presence of evil—along with overconfidence in our own ability to resist it—is to tread on Satan's ground, for in and of ourselves none of us is strong enough or smart enough to win out against the devil. Don't play with fire!

OUTLOOK ON LIFE

The lines have fallen for me in pleasant places; yea, I have a goodly heritage. Ps. 16:6, R.S.V.

Some scholars regard this text as referring to the "goodly heritage" God holds in reserve in heaven for the saved of earth. If so, David was exulting in this gladsome prospect. The pslamist may also have had in mind the apportionment of land by lot in Canaan, because in Hebrew the word here translated "lines" means a "length of rope" for measuring and alloting a field. Perhaps David considered his portion choice and his outlook bright.

There are almost always two ways to look at anything. Frank Stanton voiced the optimist's creed in these words: "You git a thorn with every rose, but ain't the roses sweet!" The pessimist says, "It's half empty"; the optimist, "It's half full." It's a question of basic outlook. We can look on life's dark side, count the discouragements, review our troubles, and lick our wounds. Or we can say with the psalmist, "The lines have fallen for me in pleasant places."

A troubled friend once wrote to Charles Lamb that the world seemed "drained of all its sweets." Lamb replied, "I don't know what you mean. Are there not roses and violets still in the earth and the sun and moon still reigning in heaven?"

A cheerful outlook does not evolve automatically. Nor is it the offspring of events. The same circumstances that plunge one person into gloom gladden the heart and lift the spirit of another. One fine morning I stood with a handful of other sightseers on the height of ancient Samaria. Recalling the historical significance of that deserted citadel and touched with emotion before the spectacular view, I was shocked to hear a gruff, disgruntled voice exclaim, "Nothing here worth looking at. Just a pile of ruins." The rest of us thought differently. To me this incomparable journey through the Holy Land was to read the Scriptures anew with enchanted eyes. To kneel by a manger in Bethlehem, to stand on Galilee's shore, to drink from Jacob's well, to gaze on Calvary, and to peer into an empty tomb—all this was to intensify the inner voice that said, "The Son of God was here. He did it all for me."

It makes a world of difference—and a heaven of difference, too—whether we look out on life in mistrust and gloom or in faith believing. To a large extent whether the day glowers or glistens depends on how we look at it.

RELYING UPON GOD

He brought them out of darkness . . . and brake their bands in sunder. . . . And delivered them from their destructions. Ps. 107:14-20.

It was my privilege to hear the late Ralph Parlette deliver his popular lecture, later set down in a book, "The University of Hard Knocks." Mr. Parlette described life as a kind of school in which the student experiences not only achievement and happiness but also setbacks, sorrows, and disappointments. According to him, the college colors are black and blue and the college yell is "Ouch!" The thrust of his impressive address was: If you wish to learn the art of successful living, learn how to take hard knocks.

Some people I have known have taken such hard knocks from life that for anyone to suggest to them that they should ever come up smiling would seem unfeeling, would appear to lack any idea of the dimensions of their trouble. We all have dark days. When buffeted by adversity to the point of despair it is encouraging to remember William Cowper, plagued by depression and tempted more than once to take his own life. At such times he exhorted himself:

"Beware of desp'rate steps. The darkest day
(Lived till tomorrow) will have pass'd away."

It is sad to contemplate that there are millions of intelligent people who do not know where to go, outside themselves, for inner strength and comfort when a staggering blow strikes them down. Greek mythology has a legend of Sisyphus ever rolling a huge stone up a hill only to have it roll back down again. It tells also of Atlas obliged to carry the world on his shoulders. Some, who never progress from Greek mythology to the New Testament, think they must go it alone. They have faith only in their own sufficiency and take no comfort and find no strength from the Father and His Son, Jesus.

Troubled Christians often ask, "Why does God sometimes allow darkness to enshroud His children?" It may be in order to sharpen their spiritual senses. When anyone walks without a light on an unfamiliar trail at night his senses come alive. His eyes peer keenly into the gloom, and his hearing sharpens. A greater sense of awareness comes upon him. Similarly God allows trouble to darken the life so that His child may be better aware of, and more guarded against, evil. "Yea, the darkness hideth not from thee . . . the darkness and the light are both alike to thee" (Ps. 139:12).

WHAT IS MAN?

When I consider thy heavens, the work of thy fingers, the moon and the stars, which thou hast ordained; what is man, that thou are mindful of him? and the son of man, that thou visitest him? Ps. 8:3, 4.

One of the Hebrew words for man, *enosh,* means frail and wretched, thus indicating man's condition in his apostasy from God. This is the natural man, the unrenewed person without the grace of principle in his heart, despite his reason, talents, or human accomplishments.

Modern science has revealed an immensity of space far beyond David's comprehension of the universe when, looking into the heavens, he stood in solemn awe before the omnipotent Creator. For example, David did not know that the star Rigel emits 18,000 times as much light as our sun and, while it takes only eight minutes for sunlight to reach our earth, the light of Rigel takes five hundred years. Even so, in David's day the overwhelming splendor and majesty of the night sky prompted him to voice his own insignificance. "What is man," he asks, "that thou are mindful of him?"

The sudden first realization of our own insignificance in the universe often comes as a paralyzing shock. It came like that to me at the age of 5. Near midnight one spring night my father roused me from childhood's dreamless sleep to look up into the dark sky. I was startled to see, stretching almost from zenith to horizon, a luminous curved cavalcade of stars in the wake of a glowing headstar, a fiery ball that far outshone any moon. With tremulous voice I asked what it was. Father replied earnestly, "That's Halley's comet. It makes a visit to our solar system about every seventy-five years. If Jesus doesn't come before then you may possibly live to see it again. I never will." We watched entranced until the cool April night air sent a chill down my spine. Father tucked me back in bed. But not to sleep. The puny insignificance and brevity of human life, when matched against the heavens and eternity, thus first dawned upon my child mind. That humbling revelation remains.

Man cannot match the horse in strength nor is he as long-lived as the redwood. He suffers more pain than the dragonfly and worries more than the worm. He is so small and puny that he cannot well protect himself from epidemics, famine, and pestilence—nor even from himself. Yet, in every extremity and prostrating crisis he can confidently plead for acceptance and safety, as did the psalmist, when in anguish of soul, he cried out, "Lead me to the rock that is higher than I" (Ps. 61:2).

IN HIS IMAGE

And God said, Let us make man in our image, after our likeness. . . . So God created man in his own image, in the image of God created he him. Gen. 1:26, 27.

Geneticists profess that daughters, more often than sons, inherit the characteristics of their fathers, whereas sons are more likely to "take after" their mothers. If so, I have known numerous exceptions. The old maxim, "Like father, like son" seems to me to be well-grounded. I have observed, too, that parents with talented children tend to believe in heredity, and that beautiful women like to point out how like them are their charming daughters.

Some years ago I became well acquainted with, and fond of, an unusually handsome and admirable man. While his two elder sons were growing up I watched closely to see whether either of them would inherit their father's good looks and genial personality. Neither one did. But years passed and recently I met again the youngest son who was but a child when I had last seen him. To my surprise and delight he looks much as did his father at that age. Actually the resemblance is more perfect than that of many twins. The same features, complexion, and hair color, and same clear blue eyes and friendly smile, even the manners and gestures—indeed his whole personality—all proclaim that he is his father's son. And he is glad and rightly proud of it.

More certainly and more faithfully than any earthly father-son resemblance was that between the Creator and Adam, who was made in the image of God. Adam and Eve came forth from the hand of their Creator in the perfection of every physical, mental, and spiritual endowment. Adam could reflect that he was created in the image of God, to be like Him in righteousness and holiness. His mind was capable of continual cultivation, expansion, refinement and noble elevation, for God was his teacher, and angels were his companions.

If we are destined for Paradise, we shall need greater defense against error than the sophistries of materialistic philosophy which makes man his own creator and takes his eyes off Jesus, man's perfect pattern of godliness in an evil world.

THE SURE PROMISE OF SALVATION

If thou shalt confess with thy mouth the Lord Jesus, and shalt believe in thine heart that God hath raised him from the dead, thou shalt be saved. Rom. 10:9.

In times of doubt when faith wavers and hopes recede this is a great text to tie to. There is no doubt about it: a willingness to confess Christ before the world in word and deed and to maintain this faith to the end will result in eternal salvation. How very simple it is!

Some years ago I called on a courtly, elderly man at his Ohio farm home. A distant relative, a most alert and intelligent thinker and conversationalist, and having a noble bearing, he impressed me deeply. After visiting awhile on his front porch I moved to leave. Raising his hand in dissuasion, he urged me to sit with him a little longer. I sat down again and there ensued a conversation I shall never forget. He said, "You know, I am a church member and have lived an upright life. Still, I must confess that I do not understand all the involved theology I hear from the pulpit. What's more, I cannot envision heaven as clearly as some say they do. But I believe that Christ died for my sins. Do you think I'll be rejected because I am not able to vividly anticipate what heaven is like?" I told him I was sure his belief and trust were all he needed to enter Paradise. He seemed much relieved in his mind and I left him smiling. I never saw him again.

Salvation is a free gift. The word itself can be conjugated in three tenses. In the *past tense* we were accepted the moment we came to Christ. Simple trust in Him made it so. "Being now justified by his blood, we shall be saved" (Rom. 5:9). For the *present tense* we have this: "to us who are *being saved* [accurate rendering] it is the power of God." (1 Cor. 1:18, R.S.V.). In the *future tense* we are kept by God's power for the salvation yet to come (1 Peter 1). Salvation embraces the forgiveness that remembers our sins no more, deliverance from the death penalty for our evil ways, emancipation from corrupting habits, the conforming of the character to that of Christ, and the restoration of the body in spiritual beauty and energy to be forever the companion of angels in the earth made new. This answers the question "Can I be sure?"

SOME SIT IN DARKNESS

It was not to judge the world that God sent his son into the world, but that through him the world might be saved. . . . Here lies the test: the light has come into the world, but men preferred darkness to light because their deeds were evil. John 3:17-19, N.E.B.

Ever since sin entered into the world the legions of darkness have been unremittingly at work perverting men's minds and distorting their vision so as to keep them from perceiving the light that streams from God's Word. As a result, throughout the ages, millions have sat a lifetime in darkness without hope and never knowing the Christ, the Light of the world. Paul reminded Timothy that the Saviour "was given . . . before the world began" to bring "life and immortality to light through the gospel" (2 Tim. 1:9, 10). And, in his Epistle to the churches, Peter wrote: "Ye should shew forth the praises of him who hath called you out of darkness into his marvellous light" (1 Peter 2:9).

There is a rare disease of the eye, hemeralopia, that affects the vision so that objects can be seen only at night. Are not some Christians afflicted with a kind of spiritual hemeralopia? They desire a little light but the bright rays from the Sun of Righteousness pains their eyes. They walk in some light but want no more. I have heard people say, "I don't want to hear any more. If I don't know these things are wrong my conscience can't hurt me when I do them."

The remedy for this distorted thinking is to realize that the blood of Christ can cleanse from all sin only the willing and the obedient. Those who knowingly remain in darkness cannot claim this promise. To the One with whom we have to do, light and the night are both alike. In the hour of judgment no one can plead ignorance if the light of God's Word has been neglected.

We have the assurance that the Creator will make the earth anew, that out of this sin-darkened world He will fashion a fairer one. In this glorious re-creation all nature will have a part. All darkness will flee before the radiance of that eternal dawning, for God is light as well as love. And every soul that comes out of the darkness of sin into the light of God's grace will live and reign forever in the light the Lord God will give. Will you come?

OUR FILTHY RAGS

But we are all . . . unclean . . . and all our righteousnesses are as filthy rags. . . . Thou hast hid thy face from us . . . because of our iniquities. Isa. 64:6, 7.

This is a humbling text. To be told that all our prideful goodness is only as filthy rags in God's sight is humiliating. No verse of Scripture more thoroughly strips away our feelings of superiority and self-sufficiency. Jeremiah makes it plainer when he says, "The heart is deceitful above all things, and desperately wicked: who can know it?" (Jer. 17:9). We would like to apply these texts to unbelievers, but Isaiah uses the pronoun "we"—that is, for himself and for Judah. It is disquieting to say the least.

One day at a family picnic that I attended while home from college, I met, and was considerably impressed by, a very prepossessing young woman who had come to this outing with one of my cousins. When we gathered at the open-air table these two girls sat me down between them. It was all very pleasant and this winsome girl seemed to enjoy the association as much as I did. One of my aunts had her eye on us—as aunts often do. Later, during the afternoon ball game, this perceptive relative sauntered over to me casually and said, "I don't know what's on your mind, but if you're thinking about having a date with————, I'd forget it. She's attractive, all right, but she is not a good girl. Take my advice and let her alone." I accepted this wise counsel. Later I learned that this girl, charming and appealing as she was, for reason enough had a bad reputation around town. And when I had a chance I thanked my aunt profusely for her interest in my welfare. Never was good counsel given more appropriately.

Filthy rags are unsavory and, at best, of little worth. In some places city workers go around gathering them for free. In the sight of God, who "seeth not as man seeth," our own righteousness is repulsive. Our best efforts produce only imperfection. There is nothing in us to commend us to Him. Recognizing this we cry out with Paul, "O wretched man that I am! who shall deliver me from the body of this death?" (Rom. 7:24).

Fortunately, we need not remain in this "filthy-rag" condition. All who sincerely seek deliverance from the bondage of sin can come to Jesus, who is the only one able to take away our filthy garments and clothe us in His resplendent robe of righteousness.

A PORTRAIT OF PERFIDY

Then entered Satan into Judas surnamed Iscariot. Luke 22:3.

To be filled with the Holy Spirit is a blessed condition possible only to the true believer who yields himself wholly to the will of God. Conversely, spurning the Holy Spirit leaves the soul a void into which the great deceiver, the father of lies, can enter. This is what happened to Judas Iscariot, and from that day to this the story of that infamous tragedy has echoed and re-echoed down the corridors of crime. The very name "Judas" has for centuries stood as a symbol of deception, perfidy, and betrayal.

Insight into the spirit that actuated Judas is provided by a glance at the original meaning of the word "devil" which is "slanderer." We find it also in the origin of the word "Satan" meaning adversary. Yet it need not have been so. Incontestable evidence discloses that Judas was tall, polished, and prepossessing. His impressive presence, business skill, and other obvious talents could have made him a blessing to the church. Instead, evil desires, revengeful passions, and sullen thoughts were cherished until Satan had full control and Judas became a representative of the prince of darkness.

Judas was a traitor, but he didn't look like one when he was chosen to be one of the twelve. A traitor rarely looks the part. Judas had a price. Lacking scruples, he went to the chief priests and asked, "What will ye give me, and I will deliver him unto you?" He also feigned concern for the poor. When Mary poured costly perfumes on Jesus' feet, Judas asked, "Why was not this ointment sold for three hundred pence, and given to the poor?" (John 12:5). And his crowning act of treason, his final betrayal of his Lord, was, astoundingly, a pretense of devotion. He tipped off the enemy by rushing up to Jesus crying, "Master, master!" (Mark 14:45).

When he joined Christ's disciples, Judas may have been partly actuated by laudable motives. But he lacked one indispensable virtue—assumed but never mentioned—in this most pathetic account. He lacked loyalty. He never dreamed that Jesus would submit to arrest, but when it happened Judas' belated realization of his relentless descent into treason so overwhelmed him that suicide seemed the only way out. The spectacle of a lost man overcome by self-destroying despair, hanging from a dry and leafless tree drives home the admonition: "Guard well the heart's door lest selfish ambition creep in and wreak eternal shipwreck on the soul."

"THY KING COMETH"

Rejoice greatly, O daughter of Zion; shout, O daughter of Jerusalem: behold, thy King cometh unto thee. Zech. 9:9.

This is the week when, throughout Christendom, the final awesome events of Christ's earthly ministry are remembered with reverence. This is thought to be the anniversary of the culmination of His thirty-three years among men, of His divine mission for their eternal salvation. This so-called "holy week" began with the most triumphant scene of His temporal sojourn and ended with the climax of the cross.

It was a calm, clear Sunday under an azure April sky. Jesus came from Bethany to Jerusalem, not on foot as before, not as an obscure, itinerant teacher and healer, but riding on an animal as a symbol of His royal right as a king, for thus temporal kings rode in triumph (see Zech. 9:9). He was accompanied by His disciples and an adoring palm-waving multitude shouting, "Hosanna to the Son of David!" Christ was following the Jewish custom for a royal entry. The people took this as evidence that their glad hopes of seeing Him established on the throne of David were soon to be realized. They gave Him homage, not with costly gifts of worldly splendor, but by the worship of happy hearts.

Down the stony slopes of the Mount of Olives the expanding procession came. To cover the stones the exultant participants threw down palm branches and their outer mantles. Such a day of rejoicing they had not known before—nor would again. Accompanying the Saviour were living trophies of His labors of love: the blind now with sight restored, the dumb now singing songs of praise, the cripples now running in full vigor, widows and orphans who had been recipients of His mercy. And Lazarus, whose body had known corruption in the tomb, walked in the strength of manhood leading the colt on which Jesus rode.

Jesus knew that the hosannas resounding that day throughout the countryside were only ripples of surface enthusiasm. And He knew the jealous hatred of the nation's leaders. Suddenly emotion surged up within Him. "As he approached Jerusalem . . . he wept over it" (Luke 19:41 N.I.V.). Fleetingly His thoughts left the current scene and raced ahead to the impending tragedy to be visited upon this beautiful but unholy city that was about to reject its one hope of salvation. He slipped away unnoticed amid the tumult and spent the night in prayer at Bethany.

CAME CALVARY

**And when they were come to . . . Calvary, there they crucified him.
Luke 23:33.**

Writing of the four days, Monday through Thursday, that preceded
the crucifixion on Friday, Luke says that Jesus "in the daytime . . . was
teaching in the temple; and at night he went out, and abode in the mount
that is called the mount of Olives" (Luke 21:37). We know that He spent
the night after His triumphant entry in solitary prayer in the olive gardens.
On the way to the city the next morning He cursed the barren fig tree,
which promptly withered. This was an enacted parable of the doom soon
to befall Israel for simulated godliness that produced no fruit for the
kingdom.

During these climactic days, Christ again drove the thieving
moneychangers out of the Temple. None questioned His right as
authoritatively, in trumpet voice, He demanded, "Take these things
hence" (John 2:16). He also taught the people in the Temple court and
healed the sick. Then came Gethsemane, the kiss of betrayal, the
shameful shams before Caiaphas, Pilate, and Herod, and the diabolical
shouts of "Crucify him! Crucify him!"

Came fateful Friday, a day of all days to remember, the washing of
the hands, the howling derision of men turned devils, and the pitiless
flogging, the first blood drawn by men from the Son of God. Then on to
Calvary where they crucified Him.

So we remember this crucial Friday, the day that darkness settled over
the land and the Shekinah faded away forever as the Temple curtain was
torn, top to bottom, by angel hands. There was gloom everywhere.

Why this Friday? It is the day Jesus was denied by one of His closest
friends, betrayed by a disciple and deserted by all.

Why this Friday? It is the day that church, state, rabble, and slave
rejected their Lord and shouted for His execution.

Why this Friday? It is the day He asked forgiveness for His heartless
killers and pardoned the thief who asked for it.

Why this Friday? It is the day the Son of God breathed a long sigh and
died with these words on His lips, "It is finished."

Why this Friday? It is the day they laid His body in the grave, and
sealed the hopes He had inspired, in a borrowed tomb.

"And the sabbath drew on."

IN JOSEPH'S TOMB

The women who had come with Jesus from Galilee followed Joseph and saw the tomb and how his body was laid. . . . Then they went home. . . . [And they] rested on the Sabbath in obedience to the commandment. Luke 23:55, 56, N.I.V.

At long last Jesus was at rest—and properly, too. Joseph of Arimathea had offered his new-cut tomb in a nearby garden. He and Nicodemus took down the lifeless body. With the aid of the two Marys and John, they sprinkled spices over the still form, wrapped it in a large, winding sheet, laid a white napkin over the placid face, closed the opening with a great stone, and walked away in silence.

Yet, if tradition be valid, the women could not bring themselves to leave that rock that separated them from Him whom they loved. So they lingered. But presently, chilled by the night air and the oppressive, unwonted blackness, they too departed with tearful eyes, stumbling among the stones and bushes, promising each other to return after the hours of the Passover Sabbath had passed.

The Saviour's work had been faultlessly finished and, with wounded hands folded in peace, He reposed through the sacred Sabbath hours, resting at last from the sublime summation of human redemption. Disconsolate grief reigned that day among those that loved Him on earth, but there was exultant joy in heaven. Glorious now in the eyes of all heavenly beings was the sure promise of the future. The question of man's eligibility for entering heaven was now settled. Every repentant sinner was henceforth free, if he chose, to live with his Redeemer in Paradise and dwell there forever.

As the blood-red sun of the crucifixion Friday went down, evidences multiplied that the One put to death between two malefactors was, in the words of the centurion who watched Him die, "truly . . . the Son of God." An all-pervading, uneasy feeling of fear, as of some terrible, impending doom, gripped the crowds that had gathered for the Passover. It lingered through the night and alarmed the chief priests who were still jealous of Jesus, even in death. They dreaded the dead Christ more than they had ever hated Him alive. Fearing that the people would attempt to steal away His body, they obtained permission to set a guard of one hundred Roman soldiers at the sepulcher. Then they sealed it with the Roman seal.

The Sabbath ended and the long night hours drew on.

HE IS NOT HERE

He is not here: for he is risen, as he said. Matt. 28:6.

The Sabbath hours held no heart balm for the disillusioned followers of Jesus. During the mournful hours following the crushing crisis at the cross all their hopes lay smitten in the dust. So distraught were they that in their dismay they forgot that, more than once, their Lord had told them distinctly of His approaching death and that He would rise the third day. The shock of His shameful death had driven from their minds the very predictions that, in this hour of sorrow, could have sustained them.

Early the following morning the two Marys came with the other women bringing precious spices to anoint the Saviour's body. In half-light they tremulously approached the tomb. Suddenly an earthquake struck. The Roman guards were knocked unconscious. Coming close the women found to their horror that the stone had been rolled away. In fear and amazement they went in to find an angel in the form of a young man. "Do not be frightened," he said. "You seek Jesus. He is not here. He is risen." Pointing to the shelf where the body of Jesus had lain, he added, "Behold the place where they laid him."

We do not know at what decisive moment during the dark hours of that climactic night the Saviour arose. The resurrection was not witnessed by human eyes. We do not know whether those saintly women, staggered with surprise, paused long enough to thank the angel, nor what became of the spices. But we know the Son of God arose from the dead and that knowledge suffices. We also know that three of the gospel accounts of the resurrection conclude with a footrace. The women left the scene in haste and joy. The disciples ran to the garden to view the folded graveclothes. And then they all raced away to be the first to tell others of Christ's victory over death.

We know that in the early morning darkness Heaven's mightiest angel brought a special commission, that it was his feet touching the ground that caused the earthquake, and that it was his glory that flattened the guards. Then he rolled back the great stone and sat upon it. Moments later the Saviour stood at the entrance and proclaimed, "I am the resurrection, and the life!" The angels and the Saviour departed together leaving it to the guards—and to us—to tell the story.

GREAT GOOD NEWS

Go quickly, and tell his disciples that he is risen from the dead. Matt. 28:7.

The trembling women quivered with terror and joy as the bright angel told them that Jesus had risen. For proof he showed them the shelf in the stone grotto where His body had lain. He added, "Go quickly!" They hastened to comply but, at the margin of the garden, Mary Magdalene stopped, whereas the others hurried on. We do not know why she remained behind. She may have wished to look again to make doubly sure that the tomb was truly empty.

Returning, Mary saw a young man outlined against the green of the garden and the sunlight, but she did not recognize Him even when He said, "Whom seekest thou?" Thinking He was the gardener, she replied, "Sir, they have taken away my Lord." Touched by her simple candor, He spoke only one word—her name—in the unforgettable voice which had often called her before, "Mary." At this, the despairing woman recognized her Lord. Falling at His feet in the dewy grass, she clasped His feet as she exclaimed, "Rabboni, Master." Thus the woman of ill-repute out of whom He had cast seven devils became the first to see the risen Christ.

This great good news that was noised abroad on the resurrection morning would have been published in banner headlines had there been a Sunday edition that day. It would have been flashed on television and radio around the world had these media been available. As it was, this most momentous event of the ages was not slow to be heard by the ears of the many faithful who had crowded into Jerusalem for the Passover. This electrifying news roused new hopes in the hearts of the disciples and struck terror to His adversaries.

The resurrection settled forever in heaven the eventual outcome of the conflict of the ages. But the struggle only intensified among men. The evidence was so overwhelming that only His enemies believed the clumsy lie about the disciples stealing away His body. The truth kept spreading and has kept on spreading ever since. If His followers are faithful, truth will go on advancing until time shall be no more. Shall we do our part?

HE LIVES

I am he that liveth, and was dead; and, behold, I am alive for evermore. Rev. 1:18.

In the Rodeheaver *Youth Hymnal,* a popular song book at youth revivals and camp meetings a generation ago, is a rousing hymn, *He Lives.* At Mount Vernon Academy, where I served as dean of boys, this devotional song of victory over death was called for very often whenever the students were invited to name a favorite hymn. Even now in my ears still echo the confident words of the chorus these students sang so joyously, a song of assurance that Christ is indeed risen from the dead:

"He lives, He lives, Christ Jesus lives today!

He walks with me and talks with me

along life's narrow way.

He lives, He lives, salvation to impart!

You ask me how I know He lives?

He lives within my heart.'' *

Thinking back to those years and the exuberant young people who sang these words so enthusiastically, I sometimes wonder whether their trust is as strong, and their walk with the risen Christ as sure, now as then.

But what of that confident faith? Is it still justified? Or is our hope of eternal life just wishful thinking? Consider first that every act and aspect of our Lord's life was a remarkable fulfillment of scores of Old Testament prophecies concerning His birthplace, His tribe and family, His virgin mother, His work, and His death. He was what He said He was. When challenged to give a sign that He was the Christ of God, He appealed to His future resurrection—and to that alone.

A careful reading of the Gospels and the Acts reveals that Jesus' resurrection from the dead was never openly challenged. The truth of it was so widely reported that it effectively stopped the mouths of His detractors. He had said, "I lay down my life. . . . I have power to take it again.'' And when He walked away from the tomb He left no doubt as to who He was. He had done what He said He would do.

For all our yesterdays we need a living Saviour. We need Him more today. Because He lives He is preparing for us a glorious tomorrow. Let us accept it.

POWER OVER DEATH

Forasmuch then as the children are partakers of flesh and blood, he also . . . took part of the same; that through death he might destroy him that had the power of death, that is, the devil. Heb. 2:14.

This is a masterfully vital passage for every Christian. It states categorically that by Christ's death on the cross He broke, for all time, the power of the devil to inflict death. At the cross Lucifer bared his fangs and, when the Saviour died, the exultation of demons knew no bounds. Satan and his hosts considered this death would make him victor in the great controversy between good and evil. But actually the reverse was true, for by humbly submitting to death and by arising the third day the Saviour entered the "strong man's house" and freed the captives there (Mark 3:27). Ever since that blessed day "old skull-face death" has no terror for us. Golgotha and the empty tomb provide full assurance of salvation. The sting of the viper was nullified and a song of triumph implanted into the heart of every prisoner of hope.

Death, man's last enemy, was fairly met. He was defeated in his own domain by the use of his own weapon. Until then this cruelest of all tyrants had brandished his cold scythe over every generation and laid it in the dust. And even those whom Christ raised—the widow's son, the ruler's daughter, Lazarus, whom Jesus loved—returned to the caverns of the dead.

But there was One alone of human form who grappled with the strong wrestler, Death, and thrust him down. He, like others, condescended to go down into the prison house of death. But death and the grave had never received such a visitor. The sepulcher couldn't hold Him. He bade the grave adieu that day to return to it no more forever.

Have you a personal interest in that empty tomb? Christ died, not for Himself, but for us. For us He arose the third day. The angel invited the women to enter Joseph's empty tomb. Other graves will become empty when another angel's trumpet calls the righteous dead. It was a blessed morning when the rising sun lit up Joseph's empty tomb. More blessed will be that other morning when the Sun of Righteousness returns to empty the tombs of His righteous ones. If we live now in Christ, or in death we fall asleep in Jesus, we will assuredly be numbered with the saved.

WALKING TO EMMAUS

While they communed together and reasoned, Jesus himself drew near, and went with them. Luke 24:15.

The evening of the resurrection day two sad and sorely depressed friends and followers of Jesus (one was Cleopas) were walking from Jerusalem to Emmaus, a distance of perhaps seven and a half miles. They were going to their homes to meditate and pray. Like everyone else in Jerusalem these two had heard the news of the strange disappearance of the body of Jesus from the tomb and of His appearance to the women. Their thoughts were in turmoil and perplexity as they talked over the events of the previous week and of the crucifixion. Hopelessly they walked with faces crestfallen and hearts under the shadow of the cross.

Shortly a Stranger was walking beside them, but they were so concentrated on their gloomy thoughts that they kept right on talking and did not closely observe the fellow traveler. They continued their conversation puzzling over the lessons Jesus had taught. Then, in an easy, inoffensive manner, the Stranger, who (unknown to them) was Christ Himself, asked sympathetically about their despondency. Their response was to pour out their hearts' grief and the underlying reason for it: "We had hoped that he was the one to redeem Israel" (Luke 24:21, R.S.V.).

Promptly the Stranger took over the conversation. His rapt listeners gave silent attention as He explained recent happenings so clearly that they felt ashamed not to have understood them before. The westering sun lengthened their shadows in the dusty road as the three approached the gate to Emmaus. There they stopped as the Third appeared as if He would go farther. But Cleopas and his friend were unwilling to part with their mysterious companion. They took Him by the hand and begged, "Abide with us." He went in with them.

When at table, as their Guest broke bread and gave a little to each of them, their eyes were opened. Springing to their feet, amazed and trembling, they finally knew Him. But they had no time, even to embrace Him, for Jesus vanished from their sight.

When these troubled travelers pondered the vital issue of salvation, Jesus drew near. When they bade Him be their guest, He responded. He will do the same today.

"TO MY FATHER AND YOUR FATHER"

And . . . while they beheld, he was taken up; and a cloud received him out of their sight. Acts 1:9.

The New Testament records ten appearances of Jesus during His forty days among men after the resurrection. All of them occurred among familiar friends and in familiar places. None questioned His identity in the end. Even doubting Thomas Didymus, upon viewing the nailprints in His hands and the spear scars in His side, could exclaim, "My Lord and my God!"

There is a mystery about this singular period in the life of the Redeemer. Why did He tarry for forty days upon the earth when His work here had been accomplished and had ended in darkness at Golgotha and in the triumphant brightness of the resurrection? The ten appearances reveal the reason. A busy forty days they were: explaining the prophecies, answering questions, promising the Comforter, delivering the Great Commission.

During these brief, memorable weeks, as the Lord intended, His disciples recognized a remarkable and subtle change in Him. In the twilight of the garden, underneath the olive shade, in the gray dawn of the lakeside, in the candlelight of the upper chamber, He was with them. Each time He spoke only a few sentences, then vanished as mysteriously as He had appeared. There could be no lingering doubt that the human Master they had known and loved was also the Lord of heaven and earth. In the blaze of His risen glory the humanity of the man Jesus was swallowed up in His divinity. Thus the Saviour's Godhead was indelibly imprinted in their minds.

The forty days had been well spent. But now the time had too soon come to say goodbye—as it always does in this world. Once more the disciples returned to Jerusalem, leaving their nets, this time forever, and accompanied their leader to the Mount of Olives.

The little group approached Gethsemane and ascended the familiar height. There Jesus paused and the disciples gathered round. Looking up, He raised His hands and began to speak. As His lips engaged in blessings, He slowly rose. Slowly He floated higher through the yielding air. But His eyes remained on the up-looking men as His words of benediction died away into silence. The eleven watched awestruck until the commissioned cloud bore Him out of sight. But there remained His promise, "I will come again."

GOD'S OMNIPOTENT POWER

Lift up your eyes on high, and behold who hath created these things, that bringeth out their host by number; he calleth them all by names by the greatness of his might, for that he is strong in power; not one faileth. Isa. 40:26.

If there were no other text in the Bible than this one about God's power, we would have ample proof of His existence. Note these reasons:

"Who hath created these things."

"That bringeth out their host by number."

"He calleth them all by names."

"He is strong in power."

Seven times in the Scriptures the word *power* is linked with *glory.* These twin attributes of sovereignty properly belong to God alone, for who else could perform any of these feats? Someone has well said, "If once there had been nothing, there never could have been something; hence something must be eternal and that something is God."

Dr. Leander S. Keyser, in his masterful book on *Why Believe in God: Christian Evidence,* sets forth the unanswerable argument that because God is unsearchable no man can understand Him fully or analyze Him, for, if we could analyze Him and completely understand Him, He would no longer be God. Job says God "doeth great things past finding out" (Job 9:10) and Isaiah declares that "as the heavens are higher than the earth, so are . . . [His] ways higher than . . . [our] ways, and . . . [His] thoughts than . . . [our] thoughts" (Isa. 55:9).

The more we study God's character, His divinity, His power, glory, and majesty, the more amazing and wonderful we find Him. Job asked, "Canst thou by searching find out God?" (Job 11:7). The answer, of course, is No.

All God's created works reveal His omnipotent power and majesty. To think of Him as the Maker of it all is a humbling experience, even for the wisest of earth. Some, however, like the deists, teach that God created the universe, then gave it over to the operation of inanimate secondary forces. Yet it is inconceivable that a good and wise God would desert the world and His beloved children therein, leaving them to sin and suffering. Instead, we know that He has a care for all His earth-born children and is "not willing that any should perish" (2 Peter 3:9). This watchcare is born of His love for them. Let us not forget that He expects us to tell others about Him.

HE MADE THEM ALL

For by him were all things created, that are in heaven, and that are in earth, visible and invisible, whether they be thrones, or dominions, or principalities, or powers: all things were created by him, and for him. Col. 1:16.

If a person early and unquestioningly accepts this verse of Scripture it will supply answers to many perplexing questions and will solve for him for all time many great issues of life. This categorical statement by the apostle Paul expresses positively that our earth is but one integral part of a mighty universe, visible to us as stars which, in reality, are vast solar systems, wheels within wheels as it were, planets and moons, all moving in perfect order about an enormous central sun. In turn, these systems, all intricately balanced, revolve according to plan about a central entity so remote as to bewilder the human mind. Paul speaks authoritatively of Christ as the Creator, not merely of our own galaxy, but of the totality of systems that constitute the universe.

That such a universe exists none will deny. And it would be unthinkable that an omniscient and omnipotent God would create such a universe without a grand, underlying purpose. Furthermore, from the Saviour's touching parable of the ninety and nine sheep safe in the fold and but one lost on the mountain (see Matt. 18:12-14), we can reasonably deduce that the universe is perfectly following this plan and that our world is the only one that has left the universal fold. The Revelator's statement that God's throne will be in the New Jerusalem (see Rev. 22:3) accords with Matthew's assurance of the triumphal joy over the return of that one lost sheep more than over the ninety and nine still safe in the fold. This indicates, too, how exceedingly great is the interest of the whole universe in the final outcome of the momentous conflict now in progress between good and evil.

As dwellers on this one lost world, we are participants in the great controversy. Each of us is a part of God's plan, worked out before the creation of the earth, to vindicate the wisdom and the reasonableness of God's government and to extol His goodness and love. This is no autocratic scheme, but it is the only plan that can win the favor of the beings in all the universe on the basis alone of its matchless merits.

Have you considered the importance of the responsibility entrusted to you? Have you thanked God lately for the privilege of enlisting under His banner?

WHY HE MADE THEM ALL

Thou art worthy, O Lord, to receive glory and honor and power: for thou hast created all things, and for thy pleasure they are and were created. Rev. 4:11.

Whether you peer with the aid of a powerful telescope into the measureless heavens or view with the naked eye the colorful world of nature about you, or look with the aid of a microscope at the infinitesimal creatures that swarm in the microcosm, an amazing display of enterprise is discernible everywhere. On realizing this the thoughtful person wonders about the underlying purpose of it all. He asks, "Why did the Creator design such an intricate, complicated universe?"

In a college science class such thoughts were running through my mind. Another student must have been thinking along the same line. He asked the professor, "Why did the Creator fashion such a complex universe?" Immediately the answer came, "For two reasons. First, to demonstrate His power, wisdom, and goodness; and, second, for His own pleasure." Then the teacher took up his Bible and read part of Revelation 4:11, "For thy pleasure they are and were created." The class seemed satisfied. I have never heard a better explanation.

The principles of justice and the well-being of every creature are the foundation stones of God's government. Although not foreordained by Him, God nevertheless foresaw that the fairness and saneness of His government would be called in question. Therefore, He designed the universe so that any attempt to thwart His original purpose would be made a means of demonstrating His worthiness to rule over the universe He had made.

Clearly these concepts were in the thoughts of the Creator as He designed our world. So He provided a plan, involving man and even the sacrifice of Himself, so that should sin appear the design would not require the least modification. In the end His glory, honor, and power would be clearly understood and more deeply appreciated than had not the interruption of sin ever taken place.

This wonderful truth is almost beyond the power of the mind of man to illustrate or explain. But it is within man's power to experience it. Do you altogether appreciate that God wants to use you as an integral part of this demonstration? Each life has a real bearing on the ultimate solution to the problem of sin. Are you willing to joyfully accept this responsibility?

HE MADE THE FIRMAMENT

God made the firmament and separated the waters which were under the firmament from the waters which were above the firmament. And it was so. And God called the firmament Heaven. Gen. 1:7, 8, R.S.V.

A theory that is gaining increased acceptance is that from Creation to the Flood a spherical layer of water completely encircled the earth above the atmosphere like a gigantic ball, that the greenhouse effect of this sphere of water equalized the earth's climate so that, instead of a torrid zone around the equator with frigid zones at the poles, the whole earth enjoyed a temperate climate suitable for the benefit and pleasure of all God's earthborn creatures, including man. If so, this would explain why three fourths of the earth's surface is now under seas due to the downpour at the time of the Flood when "the windows of heaven were opened." It would reveal why at this time only a fraction of the land surface of the earth—and only half of that hospitable to man—is above water. Thus the text above, that speaks of God dividing the waters from the waters, becomes explainable.

Whether one accepts the above theory or not, none will deny that there are three heavens: the atmospheric heaven composed of the air we breathe; the starry heaven; and the heaven where God dwells. For the time being mortals are more immediately concerned with the air we breathe which, as we climb mountains, becomes thinner as we ascend. This shows that the air has weight as referred to in Job 28:25: "To make the weight for the winds."

God made a part of the air oxygen, which is needed for respiration by nearly all forms of life. It also has carbon dioxide, which all plants require to create food for animals. The Creator also planned that this life-giving air should be constantly replenished by nature.

The wind, which is air in motion, "whirleth about continually, and . . . returneth again" (Eccl. 1:6). God flies "upon the wings of the wind" (Ps. 18:10). But, "as for man, his days are . . . as a flower of the field. . . . For the wind passeth over it, and it is gone; and the place thereof shall know it no more" (Ps. 103:15, 16). Yet notice that the judgments of God are compared to the wind (Isa. 27:8). He "tempers the wind to the shorn lamb" and assuages the fury of the storm. He mitigates the severity of His judgments and remembers that we are dust (Ps. 103:14).

HE MADE THE SUN

Truly the light is sweet, and a pleasant thing it is for the eyes to behold the sun. Eccl. 11:7.

Following my sophomore year in college I spent the summer as a carpenter's helper on the rainy Oregon coast. It was an unusually humid season and the constant drip, drizzle, and dampness grew depressing. Then, one morning after seemingly endless days of dismal semidarkness, the clouds miraculously parted and for the space of three hours sunshine held all below in welcome embrace. The following morning rain was falling again and the Portland *Oregonian* whimsically reported, "Yesterday the clouds parted briefly and a bright light appeared in the sky. When asked what it was an old-timer answered, 'Why that's the sun.'" If we do not miss the water until the well runs dry, we surely do not, nor can we, appreciate the sunshine until we are enshrouded in darkness.

The sun is the great luminary God created "in the beginning" to preside over the day. The Phoenicians worshiped it under the name of Baal and the Moabites under the name Chemosh. The Ammonites called it Moloch and the Egyptians called it Ra. These pagans paid it worship in revolting rites on high places, in groves, and upon the screened roofs of their houses. God sternly warned the Israelites against such heathen exhibitions in which men "worshipped and served the creature more than the Creator" (Rom. 1:25). He exhorts, "Take ye therefore good heed unto yourselves . . . lest thou lift up thine eyes unto heaven, and when thou seest the sun . . . shouldst be driven to worship [it]" (Deut. 4:15, 19).

Instead of worshiping the sun, as do many non-Christians today, it is our privilege to appreciate and enjoy it as one of the marvelous wonders of God's handiwork. Yet, were it not for darkness, we would never know what a pleasant thing sunshine is. The light and warmth from the sun provide untold pleasures. When touched by sunlight the dew on the grass sparkles like diamonds. It brings out the colors of the flowers and of the hummingbird as it whirls its gossamer wings before the blossoms. And sunlight intensifies the whiteness of the newly fallen snow.

Ian Maclaren wrote, "Climb the mast until you are above the fog which lies on the surface of the water, and you will see the sun shining on the spiritual world." We can add, Let your eyes behold the "Sun of righteousness." You will find it pleasant, and He will "arise with healing in his wings" (Mal. 4:2).

THE SPECTACLE OF THE SKY

And the heavens shall praise thy wonders, O Lord. Ps. 89:5.

From my earliest years the blue vault of the over-arching sky has been for me a source of fascination and wonder. To go out on a bright spring morning to lie on my back on a green carpet of new grass and there contemplate the infinite reaches of the azure dome of heaven was a delight inexpressible. The vivid contrast of the cobalt blue beyond with the fluffy white clouds lazing in the sunshine or floating along with a gentle breeze still evokes a pleasure beyond words.

From John Ruskin's impressive description in *The Sky* we have this:

"It is a strange thing how little in general people know about the sky. It is the part of Creation in which Nature has done more for the sake of pleasing man—more for the soul and evident purpose of talking to him, and teaching him—than in any other of her works. . . .

"There are not many of her other works in which some more material or essential purpose is not answered by every part of their organization; but every essential purpose of the sky might, so far as we know, if once in three days . . . a great, ugly, black rain-cloud were brought up over the blue, and everything well watered, and so all left blue again till next time, with perhaps a film of morning and evening mist for dew. . . . And every man, wherever placed, however far from other sources of interest or beauty, has this doing for him constantly."

There are those for whom the night sky is even more impressively moving than it is by day. This view has been well expressed thus:

"The nightly sky is more overwhelming than the bare blue vault of day. Light conceals and darkness unveils the solemn glories. The silent depths, the inaccessible splendors, spoke . . . of the God whose hand had fashioned them, and the thought of Him carried with it the assurance of His care for so small a creature."—*Expositors' Bible* on Psalm 8:3.

The encircling sky is a universal, worldwide medium of expression to every inhabitant of earth. There is no place on the globe but has its own particular heavenly glory. The Lord, in this way, leaves even the skeptic without excuse, for he has only to look up to believe.

THE STARS SHINE ON

Can you bind the beautiful Pleiades? Can you loose the cords of Orion? Can you bring forth the constellations in their seasons or lead out the Bear with its cubs? Job 38:31, 32, N.I.V.

In a subtle dialogue with His servant, the Almighty asks questions He knows Job cannot answer. Neither can any other created inhabitant of earth, for God alone directs the orbits of the stars.

Job evidently knew some of the constellations, since he mentions them by name. The Pleiades, a brilliant cluster of stars in the constellation Taurus, are particularly intriguing. This lustrous chain of pearls is still unbound. Tennyson described them as a swarm of fireflies caught in a silver braid. The Bear, Arcturus, and his cubs are still circling the pole as they were when, out of the whirlwind, God asked Job if he could guide this bright leader with its glittering, starry host on its distant way. Orion is still wearing his jeweled belt as he faithfully follows his incalculable circuit in the sky.

During the centuries these tremendous constellations have been upheld by a power men call gravity, which is only a name to cloak their ignorance of the power and force that belong to the eternal God.

"The stars also have a message of good cheer for every human being. . . . When the heart is faint and temptation presses sore; when obstacles seem insurmountable, life's aims impossible of achievement, its fair promises like apples of Sodom; where, then, can such courage and steadfastness be found as in that lesson which God has bidden us learn from the stars in their untroubled course?"—*Education,* p. 115.

These two stanzas from William L. Stidger seem singularly appropriate as we view the starry heavens:

> "I stood upon a hill one night
> And saw the Great Creator write
> His autograph across the sky
> In lightning strokes, and there was I
> A witness to this great event
> And signature magnificent!

> "One night I stood and watched the stars;
> The Milky Way and ranging Mars
> Where God with letters tipped with fire
> Had writ in rhyme and signed His name
> A stellar signature of flame."

HE UNROLLS THE SEASONS

While the earth remaineth, seedtime and harvest, and cold and heat, and summer and winter, and day and night shall not cease. Gen. 8:22.

As Noah and his family emerged from the Ark after the great Flood, the devastated earth that met their eyes was unrecognizable. The destruction they beheld was the result of the curse visited upon the world as the penalty for sin. The scene was indescribable. Nothing was the least familiar, for the entire earth was drastically changed. In many places hills and mountains, once symmetrical and beautiful, had disappeared, leaving no trace. Many vast and fertile plains had given way to jagged mountain ranges. It was anything but a pleasant or hospitable world.

The fear and anxiety that bore in upon these eight, bewildered survivors must have been overwhelming. Lest gathering clouds and falling rain, never known before the Flood, should overwhelm their hearts with livid terror of still another deluge, the Lord encouraged them with the promise that there would never be any more flood to destroy the earth. And as an everlasting surety of this promise He set His bow in the cloud as a token and reminder of the everlasting covenant between Him and every living creature. This covenant is still valid.

Not only did God assure Noah that there would not be another universal flood as long as the earth remained but also that no other cataclysmic interruption of the seasonal cycle would ever occur.

Since Creation the earth year has been conveniently divided into seasons of growth and seasons of dormancy (Gen. 1:14). Night follows day, the tide ebbs and flows, and sunrise invariably follows sunset. God's promise has not failed nor will it fail.

God designed that all nature, including man, should be undulatory. Intermittence was practiced by the Saviour. After meeting great multitudes He took His disciples "apart into a desert place . . . [to] rest a while" (Mark 6:31). It was essential to get away from the stress of their labors for rest and meditation. Peter, James, and John spent a few glorious hours in the Mount of Transfiguration with the Saviour, but it was necessary for them then to return to their work in the valley. We can do well to follow these examples.

HE BRINGS THE WIND

He causeth the vapours to ascend from the ends of the earth; he maketh lightnings for the rain; he bringeth the wind out of his treasuries. Ps. 135:7.

Having grown up in a breezy, blustery part of the country, the wind, this mysterious element out of God's treasury, has always intrigued me. Not so with my mother. Because she passed her early years in a milder climate, she heartily hated the wind and looked upon it suspiciously as upon an unpleasant intruder. But my father seemed to generally accept the gusting air currents as a friendly element, like the sunshine and the rain, as a part of man's natural endowment.

It may be that my affection for the wind derives partly from the plaintive strains of certain Western songs that have special appeal. I feel sorry for anyone who can listen thoughtfully to "They Call the Wind Moriah" or "Lean Your Head Over, Hear the Wind Blow" and not be deeply moved. To hear the wind moaning about the eaves on a cold winter night, to listen to it sighing in the tall grass on some isolated mountain meadow, or to observe its effects in the tall pines as it sings its weird song while arching and swaying them is an emotional experience everyone should know.

Perceptive writers have described the wind variously as harsh, soothing, searing, fickle, vagrant, whispering, wandering, caressing. W. H. Gibson in his *Pastoral Days* says it sounds like a long wail from some despairing soul "shut out in an awful storm." Longfellow mentions the "wailing winds," too, but he also wrote:

> "I hear the wind among the trees
> Playing celestial symphonies;
> I see the branches downward bent
> Like keys of some great instrument."

Several scriptural texts liken the mysterious moving of the wind to God's Holy Spirit as in John 3:8. This powerful, though unseen, third person of the Godhead quickens and restores the wavering heart to Him. We know the wind exists, yet we cannot perceive its source, how far it comes, not to what lengths it reaches. So are the spiritual changes wrought in the human soul by the Holy Spirit. There is nothing, therefore, more vital, either in this life or in the next, than keeping the heart open and sensitive to the movings of this Spirit.

HE CONTROLS THE WINDS

But the men marvelled, saying, What manner of man is this, that even the winds and the sea obey him! Matt. 8:27.

Elementary school children—and older youth, too—who live where the wind blows find it a source of endless amusement. It is exciting to see youngsters lately let out of school running as fast as their legs will carry them to open country, each clutching a homemade kite. In no time these "white-winged" birds of various colors, shapes, and sizes are let loose to sail aloft as if eager to join the turning, twisting kaleidoscopic display in the sky. The pulsing pull of a huge kite practically out of sight is a thrill to remember.

The wind gives great fun, too, when on ice skates or skis you can open your coat for a sail and be driven along like a bullet. In northern winters iceboating is widely popular, even for adults. Speeds of more than fifty miles an hour or more are not uncommon. Sailboating, too, offers an endless variety of enjoyments when the winds are right.

Lovers of wind-related sports may be blissfully unaware of the many practical uses of the wind. According to recent figures, windmills are still in operation in more than a half million homes and farms throughout America. And since their value has been proved for generating electricity, windmills are likely to multiply.

But winds are not always favorable. Wind was involved that far-away night when Jesus and His disciples, after a trying day, entered into a ship. Overcome with weariness, the Saviour lay down in the stern of the boat and soon fell fast asleep. Although the evening had been calm, darkness suddenly overspread the sky and a fierce tempest burst upon Galilee. Imminent death loomed certain and the disciples understandably panicked. In desperation they called their sleeping Lord. Knowing the danger, Jesus raised His hand and said to the angry waves, "Peace, be still." At once there came great calm. People in the nearby boats and those on the shore who had seen this miracle whispered among themselves, "What manner of man is this, that even the wind and the sea obey him!"

Let us remember that the winds and waves are ever under His control. He knows, too, how heavy our loads and how fragile our faith. When the surging winds of life overbear our strength, He will be there with easement and deliverance.

REJOICE IN THE LORD

Let the fields rejoice, and all that is therein. Then shall the trees of the wood sing out at the presence of the Lord. 1 Chron. 16:32, 33.

This text sets a gladsome mood for today and for the other days to follow in this month of May. There is no better time of year to lay aside last month's and last year's troubles, even the remembrances of dark days past and turn hopefully to the prospects of a brighter future. So wonderful is the thought of God's endless goodness and His love that even inanimate nature, by figure of speech, is called upon to rejoice at the presence of the Creator.

Poets have always found May a time for rejoicing, for gathering flowers, for singing and calling out jovial greetings to those they meet along the way. We find such genial good cheer in these: "It must have been a May morning when the world was made. Fancy the rapture of being there." "May is full of flowers," and, "Let all thy joys be as the month of May."

The celebration of May Day reaches back to ancient times when little children decorated May dolls with flower garlands. In the England of today songs of praise and thanksgiving welcome the May. Hymns are sung from the Magdalen Tower in Oxford. People gazing up from Magdalen Bridge and in boats on the river listen reverently. To conclude the ceremony church bells peal out their beautiful music.

As an impressionable eighth-grader in church school I vividly recall the dark, depressing days of World War I and the devastating Spanish influenza epidemic that followed. But when the war was over and the flu abated, a more hopeful mood spread over the land. Our gifted music teacher, Mrs. Victor Armstrong, organized a little student choir and led us in singing songs of praise and good cheer. The only lines I remember are these:

> "For it's May time, it's May time
> And all the world is bright,
> For love is in the sunshine
> And the golden stars of night."

Every returning May these words and their simple melody come back to me. Each time they uplift my spirit, for God's love is still "in the sunshine And the golden stars of night."

JESUS LOVES HIS CREATION
Come, behold the works of the Lord. Ps. 46:8.

The works of the Lord in His great outdoors constitute an appropriate theme for this time of year because right about now nature is at her loveliest in our land. But spring comes earlier in Galilee, where Jesus taught and where He joyfully beheld "the works of the Lord." In March in the Holy Land the early rain carpets the earth with green, while blossoming shrubs, trees, and flowers decorate it with glory.

Jesus loved the world of nature. He was country born and country bred. He was no child of city alleys, but of the wide world of wind and sky round about Nazareth. And later, whenever the ceaseless demands of His ministry lay overly heavy upon Him, He was away intermittently to the hills for the restoration of body and the refreshment of spirit. Perhaps for the very reason that He had made them, Jesus was as Wordsworth said of himself:

"A lover of the meadows and the woods,
And mountains; and of all that we behold
From this green earth; of all the mighty world
Of eye and ear."

Jesus was ever keenly aware of the mystery and wonder of His creation. When Nicodemus asked skeptically, "Can a man be born again?" he replied, "Yes. He can. Listen, Nicodemus, to the wind gently swaying the branches of that tree. It blows where it wants to, but you can't tell where it comes from or where it's going." So in this world of vaunted reality there are mysterious winds of the Spirit and you only have to lift your sails for them to be filled.

"Stay yourselves, and wonder," advised Isaiah (chap. 29:9). Although His hand had fashioned all nature, Jesus was constantly wondering. He wondered as He beheld the towering, snow-mantled Mount Hermon, at the miracle of the returning spring, and at the beauty of the little flower. He told His disciples to pray to the Father, "Hallowed be thy name," meaning, Bow down before Him and all His wondrous works.

We of today will do well to cultivate this much-lost sense of wonder. Are you too busy, too preoccupied, to stop and stand and marvel? Think about it!

CHRIST TAUGHT FROM NATURE

Consider the lilies of the field, how they grow. Matt. 6:28.

No one knows and understands an intricate machine better than its maker, nor any building better than the man who built it. We realize, therefore, why the Saviour could so deftly and beautifully illustrate His spiritual lessons with such apt parables from things that grow. He made them all.

"Consider the lilies!" This diminutive, low-growing wildflower was not our calla lily of cornucopia leaf and graceful finger of gold. Neither was it the lily-of-the-Nile or the lily-of-the-valley that resembles a string of little white bells. Rather was it a brilliant, serrated, wild anemone, the "lily of the field," one of the most common of Palestinian wildflowers.

We have noticed that Jesus taught from the wonder and mystery of the restless wind the mysterious workings of the Spirit. He also taught from the regularity and reliability of natural things. "Do men gather grapes of thorns, or figs of thistles?" He asked. They do not. Men gather what they sow. The soil into which the seed is sown is not unresponsive. It accepts the seed, nurtures it, and helps it do its work. So Jesus taught of something deeply spiritual in this universe that enables us to respond to faith and His Spirit and produce fruitage for the kingdom. "Unless the seed die," He said, meaning that, although it falls into the earth and seems to die, yet in time it will bear much fruit. So, despite the slowness of heart of some, in spite of the indifference of many others, Jesus could go forward with His saving work. He could even climb at last a skull-shaped hill and lay His body to the cross, certain that at last in God's own time His labors and sacrifice would bear "much fruit."

Another natural characteristic that must have appealed to Jesus was nature's peacefulness. In contrast with the noise and bustle of men, how quietly nature goes about its work! "Behold the fowls of the air," He said, and "consider the lilies." The birds have tasks, but they accompany them with music. In silence the flowers show us their bright faces and throw out their fragrance. Birds and flowers are quietly relaxed; men are strained and tense. Perhaps we should no longer cross bridges before we come to them or try to peer around the next corner. Instead, let us enjoy the current road we travel. "Consider the lilies!"

THE FAITHFUL CREATOR

So even those who suffer, if it be according to God's will, should commit their souls to him—by doing good; their Maker will not fail them. 1 Peter 4:19, N.E.B.

This is not an easy text to understand and no less difficult to accept and practice. Yet God is faithful and all His promises are sure. He is faithful in the regular return of the seasons and in the precise orbiting of the stars. He is faithful, as He promised, in prohibiting another flood and in providing sustenance for the myriad creatures He has made. Even that odd, extra sparrow, which Christ must have seen thrown in by the seller, when His mother bought the required four, cannot fall to the ground without His notice. Every daybreak is also a reminder of His faithfulness. Of the rising sun Thomas Hood wrote: "He never came a wink too soon, nor brought too long a day."

God is the faithful Creator and Sustainer in the heavens above and in His footstool here below. His everlasting faithfulness is a theme that permeates all Holy Writ. But why does Peter refer to Him as Creator in connection with what the suffering Christians may expect in life? Could it be that in the "fiery trials" all believers pass through we are apt to lose sight of the ever-welling springs of His tenderness and sympathy? He is there today as He was in the infinite silence of eternity when holy angels sang together and all the sons of God shouted for joy. Even then each of us was a distinct entity in His mind. From his bed of suffering Job declared, " 'Thy hands gave me shape and made me' " (Job 10:8, N.E.B.). In God's book, all our members were written "when as yet there was none of them" (Ps. 139:16).

The Christian's greatest security rests in the sure knowledge that God never forsakes His own. He provides protection from all harm and strength to suffer nobly. We must do the best we can and leave the rest to God. Through His grace we can become "more than conquerors" and find solace for our own frustrations and sufferings in sympathetic ministry for others.

PROJECTING AN IMAGE

And we all, with unveiled face, behold the glory of the Lord, are being changed into his likeness. 2 Cor. 3:18, R.S.V.

In the King James Version this verse is translated that we "are changed into the same image." The world today puts great store on projecting a favorable image. The family man wants his neighbors to regard him as a faithful husband. The politician takes pains to be photographed in working clothes chatting with working-class constituents. The minister acts in public so that his church members will consider him worthy of his calling.

Believers sometimes worry as to how their dress, their words, and their companions will look to others. Everyone likes to be thought well of. Yet this keen concern for our public image often proves to be sheer hypocrisy. We are all responsible for our influence, but we need to make very sure that what we appear to be to others is our true selves.

How then can we escape this "image syndrome" that can develop into a coercive burden? There is no sure way. We can behold "the glory of the Lord" and thus become genuinely changed into His image. As Moses talked with the Lord on the mountain his face took on a radiance from God's presence of which Moses himself was quite unaware. Abiding in the divine Presence produced a genuine transformation, and when he returned to the people it was so obvious that it was necessary for him to veil his face from them.

It is a well-known law of the mind that by beholding we become changed. What we behold alters us in its direction. If we contemplate the cheap and beggarly elements of this world (for example, the violence and wickedness so widely portrayed on the television screen), we subconsciously develop the unlovely, corrupt characteristics of those we see. Conversely, if we direct our thoughts toward wholesome, inspiring ideals, a pure desire springs up to live a life that will imitate the Saviour. The Spirit of God will then change the beholder "into his likeness" and we will no longer have any worry about our image.

JOY IN STRENGTH

Then Nehemiah . . . said. . . . "Let there be no sadness, for joy in the Lord is your strength." . . . So all the people went away . . . to celebrate the day with great rejoicing. Neh. 8:9-12, N.E.B.

Under the energetic leadership of Nehemiah, the great work of rebuilding the wall and renovating the city of Jerusalem had gone forward with dispatch. By the time this vast undertaking was finished, the time had arrived for the celebration of the three great feasts of the seventh month. The people assembled daily before the Temple for the solemn service of reading the law, for dedication and spiritual refreshment. But it was not all humbling solemnity. There were sacrifices of thanksgiving and festal meals with gladness and rejoicing.

It must have been an occasion of joy unrestrained as the returned exiles inspected the reconstructed protective wall that once more encircled Jerusalem. Their consciousness of a monumental task, now finished, heightened their joy. It is always an enormous satisfaction to review a Herculean achievement, carried to a successful conclusion to the best of our ability in spite of harassment and criticism. A thoroughly enjoyable holiday or vacation is made doubly delightful if we can look back on some worthwhile achievement lately finished, a piece of stonework, as it were, that will permanently endure in the edifice of our own characters.

The pain and sorrow of this sin-cursed world surround us. In many places the suffering and distress are far worse than we who are more favored know. Such degradation is the fruitage of sin and selfishness, a condition that Christians can only in part alleviate. But the singular joy that flows from doing what we can to mitigate these deplorable conditions remains all too often unknown to church members with the time and resources to ''go about doing good.''

There was also the Book of the Law which Ezra read day by day. The people gave attention. Does your Bible go along when you take a vacation? If not, try it and you will find there deeper meaning as you ponder its words by lake or mountain stream, along quiet country lanes or by the sea. One like unto the Son of man will stand beside you to illuminate its meaning until your heart burns within you and you are no longer sad.

KNOWING RIGHT AND NOT DOING IT

Therefore to him that knoweth to do good, and doeth it not, to him it is sin. James 4:17.

Divine precepts are both affirmative and negative. Inviting the Holy Spirit each morning to walk with us as our unseen Counselor will enable us to know and do what is right. Those who are hearers only but not doers show that their religion is vain (see James 1:23).

Not many years ago the eyes of a faithful servant girl in an upper class English home were filled with tears. Her scoffing friends had asked, "How do you know that you have been converted?" As the Bible was still largely a closed book to her, she could not refer to it. In desperation she finally exclaimed, "I know I am converted because I don't sweep the dirt under the mat anymore!" Her conversion was genuine because it had revolutionized her performance.

When Belshazzar was king in Babylon he "made a great feast to a thousand of his lords" (Dan. 5:1). When the revelry was at its height the intoxicated monarch boasted that the heathen Babylonian gods were greater than Jehovah. For proof he demanded that the sacred vessels of silver and gold that Nebuchadnezzar had taken from the Temple at Jerusalem be brought so the king and his lords might drink from them.

"In the same hour" a mysterious hand appeared and began to write strange words on the palace wall. All faces paled and Belshazzar, trembling with terror, called for Daniel to translate what he already sensed was a message of doom. Daniel did not hesitate. Slowly he spelled out, "Thou art weighed in the balances, and art found wanting" (verse 27). "God hath numbered thy kingdom, and finished it" (verse 26). He spoke of Nebuchadnezzar's debasement before God and added, "And thou . . . O Belshazzar, hast not humbled thine heart, though thou knewest all this" (verse 22). This momentous episode terminated, in the words of Sir Edwin Arnold, as follows:

> "That night they slew him on his father's throne,
> The deed unnoticed and the hand unknown;
> Crownless and sceptreless Belshazzar lay,
> A robe of purple, round a form of clay."

Belshazzar's knowledge of what was right and refusing to do it cost him his kingdom and his life. The lesson is ours.

YOUR CONSCIENCE

Herein do I exercise myself, to have always a conscience void of offense toward God, and toward men. Acts 24:16.

Paul knew, as do all men, that he could not live without making mistakes. "All have sinned," he said, but he was determined to live without guile. He wanted to look every man squarely in the face without shame or pretense in all good conscience.

The Bible describes conscience variously. There is the "weak," the "clear," the "defiled," the "seared," the "purged," the "good," and the conscience void of offense.

Every person in the world is endowed with a conscience. The wise man called it "the candle of the Lord, searching all the inward parts" (Prov. 20:27). Thomas Jefferson said, "The moral sense, or conscience, is as much a part of a man as his leg or arm." Abraham Lincoln spoke of it as his friend. In 1864 he told a committee of citizens: "I desire to so conduct the affairs of this administration that, if at the end when I lay down the reins of power, I have lost every other friend on earth, I shall have one friend left, and that friend shall be down inside of me." This persistent "inner counselor to the soul" is perceptively and powerfully portrayed by Francis Thompson in his "Hound of Heaven." He described with exquisite delicacy his flight from his persistent conscience as from an unshakable pursuing hound:

"I fled Him, down the nights and down the days;
    I fled Him down the arches of the years;
  I fled Him down the labyrinthine ways
    Of my own mind. . . .
    Adown Titanic glooms of chasmèd fears,
  From those strong Feet that followed, followed after. . . .
        They beat—and a Voice beat
        More instant than the Feet—
    'All things betray thee, who betrayest Me.' "

The one who harbors a guilty conscience lacks both peace and power. His inward life is like a troubled sea that cannot be stilled. He is weak and vacillating. But the person without guilt rests in peace. There is no bedfellow like a clear conscience.

CONSCIENCE IN LITTLE THINGS

Catch us the foxes, the little foxes, that spoil the vineyards, for our vineyards are in blossom. S. of Sol. 2:15, R.S.V.

During the times of David and Solomon foxes ran free in the vineyards of Israel. They were notoriously fond of the vines with their blossoms and budding grapes. Sly and cunning enough to keep out of sight, they caused endless trouble. This song of the Shulamite woman expresses concern with the minor irritations that threatened to spoil her marital happiness with Solomon. But, in a larger sense, the vineyard represents God's household and the story points out the effect of trifling with little sins that bring disaster to His vineyard.

A psychiatrist friend of mine once told me that I was overly conscientious in minor matters. He said, "I think you must have a New England conscience." I never found out just what he meant, but the fact is that life is made up of little choices that grow into habits which, in turn, are woven together to compose the tapestries of our characters. If we make the little decisions with the approval of a clear conscience and in the light of pure motives, we develop admirable characters. There is no other way.

There are those who excuse themselves—or try to—for cutting corners by saying, "It's just a little thing, so small it doesn't make any difference." But does it? A lady received a dollar sent anonymously to pay for a watermelon stolen years before from her father's farm. The sender said that, until then, when he prayed, that watermelon blocked his petition, and he wanted no hindrance to his prayers.

Once upon a time for several months I tutored two young girls in Spanish. Their parents asked for my help and promised to pay for it. But the family was in hard financial circumstances, and I told them to forget the pay, that I was glad to coach them. Years later a letter came from this man with a Thank-you note and payment in full, plus interest. He was a little man, but in God's sight I am sure he stood taller than many professing Christians twice his size.

Someone said perceptively that "trifles are trifles only to triflers." But to the thoughtful they are symptoms of peril or signals of hope. Because the world belongs to the God of the infinitesimal as well as the infinite, let us awaken to the significance of the insignificant!

BEHOLD THY MOTHER

Then saith he to the disciple, Behold thy mother! John 19:27.

There can be no more poignant, moving scene in all human history than that of the spotless Saviour dying on the cross surrounded by His cruel executioners. What makes it more heartbreaking still is the presence there of His mother, Mary, who in her deep love for her Son and in spite of her bitter grief, stood helplessly by and witnessed His agony. Before Jesus' birth Mary had puzzled at the prophecy of Simeon foretelling the divinity of her unborn child and then adding, "A sword shall pierce through thy own soul also" (Luke 2:35). Because, like most others, she anticipated her Son's sitting on the thrown of David, Mary long misunderstood His mission. Yet she witnessed His trials with sorrow and was a partaker of all His sufferings.

On that most fateful of days, when the Saviour's friends had all deserted Him, Mary and the other women followed her Son and the jeering mob to Golgotha. Standing at some distance for fear of the howling rabble, they became terrified witnesses to this greatest of all tragedies. There, before He died to provide eternal redemption for the human race, Jesus looked down upon Mary. He said to the beloved disciple who had come that far and was holding Mary in his arms because she was faint, "Behold thy mother!" What a legacy! John accepted it, took her home with him, and provided for her thereafter until, if we can believe tradition, she died and was buried at Ephesus.

Obviously Jesus loved His mother. If He were here today I am certain He would join us in honoring Mother's Day. If you are fortunate enough to have your mother still with you, rejoice, for you have the most precious of all gifts. If she is gone, remember her loving eyes, tender voice, and the healing touch of her hands. In my own case, I remember that the only unkind thing mother ever did was to slip away from us. You can multiply friendships, but you may never know love like that which she lavished upon you. Consider her Christian example. That and her guidance and prayers have resulted in much that is exemplary in her children. How ever much you give back to her, you can never hope to match all that she did for you.

If your mother still lives, are you providing properly for her? More than gifts, she needs attention, understanding, and affection. Today, with gratitude in your heart, "Behold thy mother!"

THE SCRIPTURAL AND THE SPURIOUS

You must teach what is in accord with sound doctrine. Titus 2:1, N.I.V.

Recently I noticed a newspaper account of a family tragedy. Husband and wife had been out gathering wild mushrooms of which they were very fond. When she served them he said, "These mushrooms don't smell quite right. Let's try them on the kitten first." This they did, and after a few minutes when the cat seemed all right, they ate some, too. But when they arose from the table their cat was dead. They rushed to the hospital, where both died within hours. Their fatal error was mistaking toxic toadstools for edible mushrooms. A lack of sound judgment cost them their lives.

Many people today are disbelieving the Bible, heaping ridicule on the virgin birth of Christ, denying the efficacy of His sacrifice, and casting aside other indispensable, fundamental truths of His Word. This loss of the underlying pillars of faith brings a sense of futility and hopelessness. There is such an erosion of the underpinnings of truth, so much depreciation of orthodoxy and fundamentalism, that millions of would-be Christians have lost the foundations of their faith.

The youth particularly demand more personal freedom. This is the brand of reckless abandon that carries the boat into the rapids and over the falls to destruction.

Of all the exponents of unbridled freedom of action and of independence of thought and deed, few have ever surpassed the melancholy German philosopher Friedrich Nietzsche, who thundered against religion and hailed the superman. He struck out at Christianity, calling it "a slave religion" and declaring that of all men he was the most completely free. But, at last, Nietzsche cried out, "Where is my home? For it I ask and have sought, but have not found it. Oh, eternal everywhere! Oh . . . eternal in vain." Certainly there is sting in all this, particularly in the last two words, "in vain."

It is not the wild rovers of the sea who find the highest and best in this life, but those who sail wisely with chart and compass. To become clever, independent thinkers denigrating the "thus saith the Lord" will neither win happiness here nor open the gates of heaven.

SINCERITY IS NOT ENOUGH

Prove all things; hold fast that which is good. 1 Thess. 5:21.

How often we hear people say, "It doesn't make much difference what we believe so long as we are sincere." Sincerity in anyone is a praiseworthy virtue, but, in and of itself, it can prove spiritually disastrous. As Paul admonished Titus, we must by all means be sincere, but sincerity must be combined and fortified with sound Biblical doctrine. Error is eternally fatal, and to sincerely accept error for truth is to lose your soul.

The trouble with sincerity is that a man can be as sincerely wrong and mistaken as he can be right and correct. While it rarely happens, it is not unknown for a football player, in the midst of the heady ardor of a game, to become confused and run the wrong way. I witnessed such an incident. The freshman quarterback was about the fastest member of his team. But he was easily confused and when, unexpectedly, he caught the ball, he outdistanced even his own teammates who tried to tackle him, and made a touchdown—for the opposing side. His team won, but he was not its hero that night.

A revered evangelist, whom I came to greatly admire, told of a happening that illustrates the limitations of misinformed or unenlightened sincerity. A merchant sold dry goods. To measure cloth he used an old yardstick that had been used for decades by his father from whom he inherited the business. Neither this storekeeper nor his customers realized that the long use of this measuring stick had worn it almost two inches short. Then one day a salesman gave him a new yardstick. In conversation with his visitor he idly placed the two sticks together, ends on the floor. Both men were surprised at the difference. The merchant had been sincerely cheating his customers. Knowledge of the truth corrected his sincerity. He put the old stick away and never used it again.

"Faith in a lie will not have a sanctifying influence upon the life or character. No error is truth, or can be made true by repetition, or by faith in it. Sincerity will never save a soul from the consequences of believing an error. Without sincerity there is no true religion, but sincerity in a false religion will never save a man. I may be perfectly sincere in following a wrong road, but that will not make it the right road, or bring me to the place I wished to reach."—*Selected Messages,* book 2, p. 56.

JESUS KEPT THE MORNING WATCH

And in the morning, rising up a great while before day, he went out, and departed into a solitary place, and there prayed. Mark 1:35.

More than most, this text is a key to the sinless life of the Saviour. He began each day with His Father. It was His custom to arise early and find a solitary place to pray. "As one with us, . . . He was wholly dependent upon God, and in the secret place of prayer He sought divine strength, that He might go forth braced for duty and trial."—*The Desire of Ages*, p. 363.

Morning is the best prayer time. One of my noblest colleagues in college administration made it his unwavering practice to "roll out of bed each morning on his knees." He loved to quote the psalmist, "O Lord; in the morning will I direct my prayer unto thee, and will look up" (Ps. 5:3). He liked also to quote the truism that "a five-minute prayer in the morning will save a half hour's confession at night."

One Sabbath morning, as was His custom, Jesus went into the synagogue. While teaching the people, He was interrupted by a man with a demon. He healed him. After the service He went to the home of Peter where He healed Peter's wife's mother of a fever. After sunset the sick came and He healed them all. Early the next morning He went away to a lonely place to pray. There Peter found Him and said, " 'Everybody is looking for you.' " Jesus said, " 'Let us go . . . to the adjoining country-towns, so that I may preach there as well; that is why I came out here" (Mark 1:37, 38, *Moffat*). How significant the words, "That is why I came out here." Alone with God He knew He could obtain wisdom and strength for the day. Morning by morning the Lord awakened Him so that He might commune with Him (see Isa. 50:4).

In no phase of His life did Jesus set a more faithful example for His followers than in His prayer habits. If we follow in His steps, we will be led every morning to the secret place of prayer. When we grow careless and spasmodic in this privilege, it is our sad loss. It has been rightly said that angels wonder why men pray so little. It is the hypocrite who never utters a private prayer. If we have allowed the cares of this life to crowd out this blessed communion, let us begin again this morning.

PALACES

And I will smite the winter house with the summer house; and the houses of ivory shall perish. Amos 3:15.

We know that before sin entered the world our first parents dwelt in a beautiful garden. Whether they had any other house or home is not disclosed by the sacred record. They may have had. Yet, after sin came—indeed, from time immemorial—even the oldest annals that have been salvaged from the ravages and rubble of time contain endless references to the habitations, the residences, the great houses, and other dwellings of men. Kings and lords, moguls and maharajahs, caliphs and khans, emperors and popes, and all the affluent of every age seem to have had like ambitions to rear for themselves mansions and palaces to dwell in, to impress their peers, and to memorialize their greatness once they have gone.

As a student in the field of history, my interest in houses induced me to pursue for three quarters, graduate courses in architecture. We studied the palaces of the Caesars, the castles of Europe, and the stately, imposing manor houses of early America, and, finally, the sumptuous mansions of our own time. Many are breathtakingly beautiful. Of these, the Georgian super-mansion at Santa Monica, built with no thought of cost by the late actress Marion Davies, outshines and outglitters the rest. This imposing edifice stands like a temple on a promontory overlooking the ocean. For years its exquisite charm enabled Miss Davies to reach the pinnacle of social eminence, the rarified stratosphere of fashion and elegance.

The Davies mansion contains ninety rooms, thirty-seven with fireplaces, four dining rooms, a drawing room with eighteen-carat gold ceilings and wall coverings imported from Europe. There are fifty-five bathrooms and two swimming pools. Marble bridges span quiet ponds that dot flower gardens. Here the scintillating hostess gave fabulous parties and eight-course banquets to muted music under subdued lights.

A devotee of pomp and pleasure, Miss Davies died of cancer in 1961. She enjoyed her mansion for only a few, short years. Like Uzziah and his pagan peers, whom Amos censured for wasting their substances on ivory palaces, Miss Davies built her great house in the wrong place. She could have invested in heaven.

When tempted, as some are, to overly admire these imperial palaces of earthly pride and their builders, let us remember Uzziah and his imitators—also their fate.

FOLLOWING THE CROWD

Thou shalt not follow a multitude to do evil. Ex. 23:2.

No doubt David's prayer to be delivered from secret sins (Ps. 19:12) was prompted by a sense of guilt. All secret sins need to be forgiven and forsaken, but the transgressions committed openly are far more numerous—and more serious, too, because of their pernicious influence on others. One of the increasing perils of our society is the tendency to follow the multitude to do evil and then offer the lame and unacceptable excuse that "everybody's doing it."

Wise Lord Chesterfield in a letter to his son advised the youth to "observe any meetings of people and you will always find their eagerness and impetuosity rise or fall in proportion to their numbers; when the numbers are very great, all sense and reason seem to subside, and one sudden frenzy to seize on all, even the coolest of them."

The psychology of crowds has been much in the news of late. Teachers are discussing it, psychologists are dissecting it, and pastors are sermonizing about it. No attentive person can observe the ludicrous behavior in evidence at a professional football game and fail to sense the opportunity there afforded for the release of primitive proclivities and animal passions. It is strange that some people act meaner in a crowd than when alone and are not ashamed to do in public what they would never do by themselves. All throughout a game the canons of good taste are repeatedly violated. The barbaric impulses of the heart show through and this makes a performance that is truly distressing.

The powerful "peer pressure" of the gang motivates youth of teen-age and younger to engage in wholesale robbery and vandalism. Under the whipped-up emotion of group psychology, so-called "good citizens" participate in lynchings and burnings, acts which under saner conditions of individual morality they would not even consider. In war men will kill strangers, although in other circumstances they would never do it. We react with sadness to see church members engaging together in reprehensible practices on the excuse that it benefits the church in the long run or is good for business. We need to be on guard lest, in our group or corporate capacity, we do anything that as individual church members we would refuse to do.

Let us dare to be Christians even in a crowd or when challenged by public opinion to "follow the multitude to do evil."

THE PLUMB LINE

The Lord said to me, "What do you see, Amos?" "A plumb-line", I answered, and the Lord said, "I am setting a plumb-line to the heart of my people." Amos 7:8, N.E.B.

The trowel is the bricklayer's best friend. He must have one. But no mason worth the name would attempt to build a wall without a plumb line as his second most important tool. A plumb line is inexpensive, just a stout string with a top-shaped weight at the end of it. With the aid of this simple device most any mason can build a perfectly vertical wall. Thus constructed, there is no danger it will lean and crush the builder or the people who will occupy the building after its completion. That little piece of lead at the end of the string points straight toward the center of the earth, and the wall built parallel to it will be exactly upright.

To build an upright life in this world, everyone needs a plumb line at the earliest age possible. And we need to use it every day. No one building character can do a successful job without it. Constant measuring with the plumb line will reveal whether the structure is upright and square. As the string and the weight serve the mason, so the conscience serves the purpose of the soul.

The parents of the late Chief Justice of the United States, Charles Evans Hughes, recognized in the boy an early awakening of his brilliant mind and tender conscience. So they provided a tutor to guide his childish studies. One day this private teacher found on the lad's little study chair a sheet of paper. On it, in plain block letters, was his outline of duties for the day, including prayer and meditation. He had headed his program, "Charles Hughes, Plan of Study." He was 4 years old. The life edifice of Justice Hughes, upright and honorable throughout, shows the repeated use of this plumb line as determined by himself at this early age.

Building without a plumb line is sure to entail misfortune sooner or later. It is far worse to live a selfish, independent life without reference to God's Word, His divine plumb line. In the final analysis we shall all be measured by it. The Lord told Isaiah, "Judgment also will I lay to the line, and righteousness to the plummet" (Isa. 28:17).

Do we feel uneasy at times over what we have done or said? Could it be that God is letting down His plumb line alongside our souls?

SCRUPULOSITY

By this we shall know that we are of the truth, and reassure our hearts before him . . . ; for God is greater than our hearts, and he knows everything. Beloved, if our hearts do not condemn us, we have confidence before God. 1 John 3:19-21, R.S.V.

The other day, in a bookstore, the title of a modern novel, *Scruples,* caught my eye. The story didn't interest me, but the name of the book did. So I looked it up in the dictionary. But I got no help there. The long, infrequently used word *scrupulosity,* simply means the quality of being scrupulous with overtones of excess concern, of being overly precise and particular in trifling matters. Then our text, which deals with this subject, came to mind. It speaks directly to the conscience of those who have a problem determining where lies the thin line between godly sincerity in following the will of God and excess concern for extremely small points.

An apt illustration of this problem is the experience of a boy hired by a neighbor to sort potatoes. He began to separate them, placing the larger ones in one bin and the smaller ones in another. His employer later found him in a hot, perspiring perplexity. Asked what was bothering him, the lad said, "Oh, it's not too hot in here. It's just that I can't decide which ones are big and which ones are little." The problem looms larger when our spiritual welfare is concerned.

We are assured that, when we go to God in deep sincerity of heart and ask forgiveness with a truly contrite spirit, forgiveness is certain. "If we confess our sins, he is faithful and just to forgive us our sins, and to cleanse us from all unrighteousness" (1 John 1:9). But some seem unable to accept this assurance and their consciences continue to disturb them. And so, feeling condemned for a sin that no longer exists, they continue under a cloud of their own devising.

Satan constantly tries to have us believe that our sins are not forgiven. He hammers away at our consciences, magnifying harmless oversights, unintentional blunders, and minor faults lacking any moral significance at all, until we misjudge them to be major transgressions. The resultant needless self-condemnation has darkened many a Christian experience. Our text speaks specifically to all who are afflicted with super-scrupulosity. For if our hearts condemn us, "God is greater than our heart, and knoweth all things."

THE CHRIST OF THE BIBLE

And this is the testimony, that God gave us eternal life, and this life is in his Son. He who has the Son has life; he who has not the Son of God has not life. 1 John 5:11, 12, R.S.V.

Christian faith is founded squarely on the Scriptures. Except for what the Bible says about Him, Christ would be all but unknown. Secular history mentions Him infrequently and grudgingly. In Him is life eternal, nonetheless, and in no other. He is the center and the circumference, the Alpha and the Omega, and the sole Fountainhead of orthodox Christianity. Simply believing that He lived does not make a person a Christian. Humanitarians go that far. Many extol His character and example as a worthy pattern to follow. But that is not enough. Just believing on His name is not enough. Even the mental assent that He is the Son of God is not enough. We are told that devils believe and tremble (James 2:19).

To regard Christ as a mere example is to misunderstand the entire theme of the Word of God. It strips away His divinity, His purpose in coming into the world, His accomplishments here, and the ministry that He now performs for us at the right hand of His Father. Christ must not be debased. He is more than an example worthy of emulation. He is Prophet, Priest, and King. At Calvary He made the essential atonement for sin; and, if we believe in Him at all, we depend on the efficacy of that sacrifice. "He was wounded for our transgressions" (Isa. 53:5).

It has been said that the three "R's" of the Bible are "ruin," "redemption," and "regeneration." We were all ruined in the fall and all lost through Adam's sin. We have been in ruin ever since through our selfish hearts and will be ruined eternally unless through God's grace we accept His great salvation. The "R" for redemption means that we are ransomed by His merits, redeemed by His strength, and rescued by His power.

Then there is the "R" of regeneration. No one can partake of redemption without regeneration of heart. In his own strength a man can serve God up to his highest ability; but until he has been regenerated and filled with the Holy Spirit, he will remain under the first "R," which is ruin.

These are divine truths and anyone who is in his right mind will realize that heaven is desirable, that death is diabolical, time is short, eternity is infinite, God is eternal, and His word invincible. Let us plan accordingly.

LORD GOD ALMIGHTY

And day and night they never cease to sing, "Holy, holy, holy, is the Lord God Almighty." Rev. 4:8, R.S.V.

Majesty and greatness are here expressed in words of magnificent dignity. They pertain to the eternal God. His all-embracing magnitude is set forth earlier as the Alpha and the Omega, the Lord God "which is, and which was, and which is to come" (Rev. 1:8). These two Greek letters represent all the intervening letters of the alphabet and enclose them as in a golden clasp. Likewise God's nature enfolds all creation, all races, the entire work of redemption, the final destiny of His children, and the ultimate triumph of righteousness and peace. An identical paean of praise made up the song of the seraphims in Isaiah's vision (see Isa. 6:3). Is there any wonder, then, that with ceaseless chant the angels sing, "Holy, holy, holy, is the Lord God Almighty"?

It is the custom of men to work by day and sleep by night, but the divine power that upholds the universe never relaxes. "He that keepeth Israel shall neither slumber nor sleep" (Ps. 121:4). Likewise, although night brings to a halt most earthly activities, it has no effect on the ceaseless praise to God issuing forth continually from the celestial choir.

In the fullest sense the Lord God Almighty includes God the Son, for Jesus is the complement to all human needs. From His bounty we may receive all the letters, the words, and everything necessary to make good all our deficiencies. Many who accept the Saviour do so only when they come face to face with their own needs and lost condition. To traverse the Alaskan ice fields you engage a recommended guide. But you come to fully appreciate him only after you have safely crossed the glaciers, bridged the abysmal ravines, and escaped a threatening avalanche by dint of his knowledge and skill. So, as we follow Jesus, we find Him more than sufficient for all our needs.

Although our needs be beyond counting, the resources of the Almighty are sufficient to meet them all. Paul promised that "God will supply every need of yours according to his riches in . . . Christ Jesus" (Phil. 4:19, R.S.V.). With such unlimited resources He can bountifully compensate for all our temporal losses of wealth, family, and friends. We are told that in the last days just before the second coming of Jesus losses will be heart-rending and suffering severe. Yet the bread and water of the believers will be sure (Isa. 33:16). None who serve Him now need fear that He will desert them then.

WHEN YOU ARE LONELY

I will never leave thee, nor forsake thee. Heb. 13:5.

Only those who have experienced the withering blight of loneliness can understand or appreciate how devastatingly sad it can be. It is especially prostrating if you are young. A promising, ambitious young man (or woman) leaves the familiar environment of his childhood home in high hopes to attend college many miles away or to take a job in some distant city. In the new locality everything is different. How he misses his parents, brothers, sisters, and friends now so far away. Every face is new and strange, and no one seems to care.

After a twenty-four-hour train ride a freshman, who had never spent a single night anywhere but under his father's roof, was assigned a room in a college dormitory. Within hours he grew so homesick he couldn't eat and, in spite of his determination to "brave it out," lay awake most of the first night wide-eyed and wishing that he could go back home the next morning. In his freshman composition class the first assignment was to paint a word picture—to write a brief essay on "the prettiest sight you can imagine." He entitled his, "The Face of the Old Hound Dog at Home." I roomed with this boy and did my best to console him, though I was almost as lonesome as he was.

Although loneliness is acute in youth and persistent in old age, the Christian is susceptible to its periodic attacks anywhere along life's journey. A lively sense of God's presence and the habit of conversing with Him can be a marvelous means of overcoming this intimidator of the soul. Those who have already learned to talk to God may still be lonely for human companionship. An effective solution is to take a helpful interest in others. Like many ministers and doctors, you can become so involved that you will not have any time left to be lonesome.

Loneliness can serve as an opportunity for Jesus to make Himself known to us personally. Our isolation makes a claim upon Him, and He will bear us company if we make Him welcome. Above the harbor at Smyrna is still visible the death site of the saintly Polycarp where Jesus stood by him, enabling him to be faithful unto death. And, like the beloved apostle in his lonely, rock isle, we can seem to hear hymns and prayers and join them in spirit. To all who in trust believe, the promise is precious, "I will never leave thee, nor forsake thee."

LET'S CONSIDER DIET—HISTORICALLY

God said, "Behold, I have given you every plant yielding seed which is upon the face of all the earth, and every tree with seed in its fruit; you shall have them for food." Gen. 1:29, R.S.V.

Originally the Creator, who designed our bodies, knew what kind of food would keep them running the best and the longest. He gave man "every plant . . . upon the face of all the earth, and every tree" It was a varied, toothsome diet that included grains, nuts, fruits, and vegetables. Then when the whole creation was completed, God looked it over and said "behold, it was very good" (verse 31).

Men lived vigorously and long on this original, wholesome diet. Well beyond the first thousand years of earth's existence the marvelous mental and physical vigor of the species enabled a person to anticipate a life span of five hundred years or more. Thus a man could set for himself a hundred-year task and, if he didn't get it finished in that time, he had every prospect of another hundred years, at least, to get it done. And all this was possible on a natural diet as provided by the Great Designer.

By the middle of the second millennium after Creation, divine laws and precepts were so thoroughly disregarded that men's thoughts were "only evil continually." So the Lord sent a deluge that cleansed the earth of the transgressors. But when men again violated His law and perverted the principles of a proper diet, they brought upon themselves a steady decline in physical size and life span. Later when the children of Israel were led out of Egypt under Moses by the Lord's mighty hand, God's purpose was to supply them with a diet superior to the feverish fare to which they had become accustomed during four hundred years of Egyptian servitude. "The perverted appetite was to be brought into a more healthy state, that they might enjoy the food originally provided for man—the fruits of the earth, which God gave to Adam and Eve."—*Patriarchs and Prophets,* p. 378.

The Lord could have as easily provided the Israelites with flesh as with the miraculous, nutritious manna. But they lusted after forbidden things until they were no longer willing to deny appetite and submit to divine leadings. Their request was granted, but God "sent leanness into their souls" and thousands died in a day.

This symbolizes the tragedy of many a life. When we get what we want we do not like what we get. How much better it is to listen to the Lord and follow His leadings!

LET'S CONSIDER DIET—CURRENTLY

The Lord your God . . . fed you in the wilderness with manna . . . that he might . . . do you good in the end. Deut. 8:14-16, R.S.V.

The coriander plant that grows wild in the Near East produces a small, round, grainlike berry. Moses described manna as being like this little grain, "and looked like resin" (Num. 11:7, N.I.V.). Every morning except Sabbath it fell with the dew and lay on the rocks and sand. Manna came in such quantities that, for forty years, it was sufficient to feed a multitude of more than a million people. Each one gathered enough every morning to sustain him for the day. David called it "angels' food," either because angels eat it or because it fell from heaven. The common Israelites, as well as the greatest nobles, fed on this delicious, energizing food until they came to the Promised Land, where the nonflesh diet provided Adam and Eve was again available.

Although a majority still believe otherwise, man is not now, nor was he ever, dependent upon animals to prefabricate his food for him. Henry David Thoreau, a nineteenth-century nature lover and author, visited a farmer who was plowing with oxen. As the two walked behind the plow they talked about diet. The farmer said, "You can't live on vegetables alone, for they furnish nothing to build bones with." Thoreau mused, "All the time he talks he is walking behind his oxen which with vegetable-made bones jerk him and his plow along."

Recent dietary research shows that plant foods are rich in vitamins and minerals that build strong bodies, not only for oxen, but for human bodies as well. Neither protein nor other essentials are lacking. Predominantly vegetarian diets provide seventy percent of the world's supply of protein. World champion swimmer Mark Spitz, and other athletic champions are vegetarians who lack nothing in physical fitness and stamina.

Can diet kill? Affluent countries where people consume large amounts of meat, milk, and eggs show a high level of heart disease. Scientists are only now rediscovering that the original diet given to man is the best after all.

Yes, diet can kill, and it is the special duty of every Christian to inform himself of true health principles and live accordingly. Sound, vigorous health does not depend on chance but on choice.

"Do you not know that your body is a temple of the Holy Spirit within you, which you have from God. . . . So glorify God in your body" (1 Cor. 6:19, 20, R.S.V.).

THAT GOOD PART

Jesus . . . said unto her, Martha, Martha, thou art careful and troubled about many things: but one thing is needful; and Mary hath chosen that good part, which shall not be taken away from her. Luke 10:41, 42.

Jesus spoke these well-known words in the house of Lazarus at Bethany. Mary was sitting at the feet of the Saviour storing up the precious words that fell from His lips. Martha was busily caring for the many household duties. The incident is a forceful reminder that womanhood has always been divided into two parts—the Marys and the Marthas.

There are many more Marthas than Marys. In fact, the world is filled with them. Martha represents those dear, well-meaning people who are conscientiously "troubled about many things." Most people who have too many things going at once have trouble.

There are many things that people desire, many things that contribute to our pleasure. But in the final analysis there is only one thing that truly matters. It is our personal relationship to God. This is what Jesus endeavored to impress upon Martha, who had become so absorbed in many good things that she overlooked that "one thing is needful." It was not the things she did, but what she failed to do, that called forth the pointed rebuke from the Saviour. In her concern for the other things occupying her mind she let slip the opportunity to commune with Christ.

Mary had a different set of priorities. She recognized what was important. She knew permanent values. She understood what would last. So she sat at Jesus' feet and heard His words. She wanted something that neither time nor man could take from her. Jesus called it "that good part."

When Jesus told His disciples to "take no thought . . . what ye shall eat, or what ye shall drink . . . what ye shall put on" (Matt. 6:25), He did not mean that no attention should go to our temporal needs but that those things should not be attended to at the expense of eternal life.

Throughout the Bible, God has set out warnings here and there. They are like flashing red lights and, if heeded, serve a very important purpose. We all know what happens when driving along the highway we disregard the traffic signs. Trouble, possibly disaster, follows, and not to us alone, but to others also. Shall we then take special care not to disregard the danger signals along life's highway?

OVERWHELMING CARES

Take heed to yourselves, lest . . . your hearts be overcharged with . . . cares of this life. Luke 21:34.

The unabridged text of our verse for today, according to Phillips, reads, "Be on your guard—see to it that your minds are never clouded by dissipation or drunkenness or the worries of this life, or else that day may catch you like the springing of a trap."

Once when Jesus was alone on Mount Olivet four of His disciples came to Him to ask how they could know when His return was drawing near. He gave a number of specific signs and described conditions that would exist just before the end of the world. He said that, as in the days of Noah, people would be engaged in a wild scramble for money and pleasure and would, therefore, forget God. As a specific warning to His followers in the last days, He said, "Take heed to yourselves."

The world in which we live is geared to an ever accelerating rate, to a tempo unknown a few decades ago. When the American pioneers reached the Forks of the Ohio (Pittsburgh), if a riverboat going down the river was late, they waited for it calmly and improved the time by washing and mending clothes, visiting with other travelers, and writing letters. But today people are so in a rush and so keyed up that they actually manifest impatience when they miss one section of a revolving door.

There is noise and confusion on every hand. Everybody seems on the move. These disturbing conditions make it imperative, both for our physical and spiritual well being, to shut oneself away occasionally to escape the debilitating effect of this endless turmoil and distraction. In times of less confusion the Saviour found it imperative to take His disciples to a quiet place "to rest a while."

> "This is the age of the half-read page
> And the quick hash and the mad dash
> The bright night with the nerves tight
> The plane hop with the brief stop
> The lamp tan in a short span
> The Big Shot in a good spot
> And the brain strain and the heart pain
> And the catnap till the spring snaps
> And the fun's done."

—Virginia Brasier

THEY WERE APPOINTED

"The God of our fathers appointed you to know his will, to see the Just One and to hear . . . [his] voice . . . for you will be a witness for him to all men." Acts 22:14, 15, R.S.V.

It is exhilarating to receive an appointment, particularly when it is to a better or more important position. In which case, it can also be sobering, requiring a deep searching of soul. The charge in our text was this kind of an appointment. It was more than simply man-to-man instruction. This was God's charge to the apostle Paul. His acceptance of it made him a minister of the gospel. The words are striking, meaningful. Every phrase is significant. The Lord said to Paul, "But rise . . . for I have appeared unto thee for this purpose, to make thee a minister and a witness both of these things which thou hast seen, and of those things in the which I will appear unto thee" (Acts 26:16). It was not just one appearance to Saul for a lifetime of service. He promised to appear again. The Lord kept this promise richly. Throughout his long life Paul had frequent revelations and new charges so that his service was ever according to the will of the Almighty. This is what made his work among the Gentiles the foundation of the gospel proclamation to all the world.

Throughout the ages the Lord's assignment to Paul has also been accorded to countless other men and women of all races under all circumstances. Their vicissitudes and trials are recorded that we may review them and be emboldened to follow their examples. In faded letters written on an old-style typewriter I found the following, unsigned:

"If you are impatient, sit down quietly and talk with Job.

If you are just a little strong-headed, go and see Moses.

If you are getting weak-kneed, take a good look at Elijah.

If there is no song in your heart, listen to David.

If you are a policy man, read about Daniel.

If you are getting sordid, spend some time with Isaiah.

If your faith seems below par, read Paul.

If you are getting lazy, study James.

If you are losing sight of the future, climb the stairs of Revelation and get a glimpse of the Promised Land."

YOU ARE APPOINTED

The people who know their God shall stand firm and take action. Dan. 11:32, R.S.V.

Interpreted within the immediate framework of its context, our scripture refers to the amazing achievements of the apostolic church and its subsequent development. Standing alone it serves as a concise summary of the divine operation. When individual believers truly know God, their trust and faith in Him grow until an inseparable companionship is forged. Through a submission of the will this sublime relationship imparts strength to meet life's struggles and temptations. It has always been so and will remain so until the end of time.

God has not yet gone out of the calling business. If He ever chose, called, and appointed men and women, He is doing so in these last days. He needs them to herald the third angel's message to a lost world. In the long ago the Lord made it plain that, while He blesses organizations and plans, He pours out His Spirit only on men and women who have heard His call. Just a few short years ago the subject of the end of time was highly unpopular. Now, suddenly and unexpectedly, the whole world has gotten interested in it. Books such as Hal Lindsay's *Late Great Planet Earth,* are on the best-seller lists, and have been for a long time. The reason is that today events are telling.

The world needs a convincing witness to the transforming power of God along with a disclosure to men of the true meaning of world developments. God has a "chosen generation" with a holy unction to proclaim that the last hour is at hand. The Spirit of Prophecy has said that, in the closing of the work, God's people will be seen going from home to home telling what God has done for them (see *Evangelism,* pp. 699, 700, *Christian Service,* pp. 124, 125).

Our call is to rightly represent Christ in our own generation. How would He act behind the wheel of your car? How would He spend your spare time? Would He grasp your opportunities to visit the sick and comfort the bereaved? Would He embrace your invitation to attend prayer meeting? Do you pray that He will reveal His will for you this day?

A look away to the Master's ministry in Galilee will help here. See Him unperturbed by Greek philosophy, Roman prestige, and ecclesiastical arrogance, quietly inviting humble men and women to previously unknown heights of moral dignity. We can remember that His work is still unfinished. He has called us to stand firm. You are appointed.

FAIRNESS VERSUS SELFISHNESS

But David said, "You shall not do so, my brothers, with what the Lord has given us. . . . For as his share is who goes down into the battle, so shall his share be who stays by the baggage; they shall share alike." 1 Sam. 30:23, 24, R.S.V.

These were the words of David, the warrior-chieftain, spoken to his soldiers after their surprisingly successful pursuit of the raiding Amalekites. To appreciate the significance of David's pronouncement we must note the episode that led him to make this decision. The pagan Amalekites had made an extensive incursion into Judah and made off with rich booty, including a great herd of cattle and many inhabitants to serve as slaves. The men were devastated with grief, as was their chief, David, whose two wives had been captured. When God advised David to go after the raiders and that all would be recovered, he selected six hundred of his bravest men and the pursuit was on. As they came upon the enemy camp they found their foes holding high festival eating, drinking, and dancing. The attack was made and a fierce battle continued all night and all day. It was a complete rout. "David recovered all that the Amalekites had taken; and David rescued his two wives. Nothing was missing" (1 Sam 30:18, 19, R.S.V.).

When the successful forces returned, these selfish soldiers wanted to be given everything that had been recovered. In thus displaying their greed they were very wrong. Thereupon David asserted a great principle. He declared that those who faithfully served the cause of Israel behind the lines must be rewarded equally with those who were actually engaged in the fighting. Thereafter it became a statute in Israel that all who were honorably connected with a military campaign should share the spoils equally with those who had engaged in actual combat.

In our day, as in David's, even in times of spiritual triumph, unsuspected selfishness can creep in to distort the sense of fairness in the hearts of the soldiers of the cross. Like covetousness, it blinds the eyes, magnifies our view of what we deserve, and depreciates the due rewards of others. Greed confuses the judgment and sometimes fills a church member with unholy ambition. All who are involved in promoting the gospel need to be on constant guard against inner demands for all the spoils. It should be here, as surely it will be in the hereafter, that all who serve the Lord, whether in the forefront of the conflict or behind the lines sharing in menial tasks, "shall share alike."

IN DEED AND IN TRUTH

My little children, let us not love in word, neither in tongue; but in deed and in truth. 1 John 3:18.

Since this gentle verse is addressed to "my little children," it was read early and often at our family worship when I was a child. The hymn "I Love Thee," which emphasizes this essential thought, we often sang. The words of the first stanza were meaningful then and they are meaningful now:

"I love Thee, I love Thee, I love Thee, my Lord;

I love Thee, my Saviour, I love Thee, my God:

I love Thee, I love Thee, and that Thou dost know;

But how much I love Thee my actions will show."

It is possible that John's readers were actually using loving words when loving deeds were needed, and he was telling them to stop such mockery. In any case, he makes a direct exhortation to practice true love and avoid the hypocrisy of saying one thing and doing another. There is no hint that to say a loving word is ever out of place or inadvisable. When those we love need only the comfort and assurance of a loving word, the kind word in season is highly laudable. But John warns against the loving word that stops there, when helpful deeds are needed.

The story is told of a Southern farm boy who became infatuated with the daughter of a rancher who lived two miles away. One afternoon he sent this girl of his dreams a love note: "You are so dear to me that I'd climb the highest mountain to spend an evening with you. I'd swim the deepest ocean to bask just an hour in the sunshine of your smile." Before sealing the letter and sending it by his little brother on horseback, he added this postscript: "I'll be over tonight if it doesn't rain." She was probably not much impressed.

The indwelling spirit of God should influence the head, the heart, and the hands. Having it in the head will keep us informed; having it in the heart will keep us humble and believing; having it in the hands will make us practical Christians. In this way we become "doers of the word, and not hearers only" (James 1:22).

"The completeness of Christian character is attained when the impulse to help and bless others springs constantly from within. It is the atmosphere of this love surrounding the soul of the believer that . . . enables God to bless his work."—*The Acts of the Apostles,* p. 551.

TRIALS AFFLICT ALL

All that will live godly in Christ Jesus shall suffer persecution. 2 Tim. 3:12.

A meaningful reference in a popular song recently took my fancy. It goes like this: "I never promised you a rose garden." This is the plaintive, almost defensive effort of a young husband to reassure his wife who has become disenchanted with their marriage. An all-too-frequent marital sequence, it parallels on a higher level the experience of many who on impulse lightly accept Christ, expecting this step to solve all life's problems. It doesn't. Contrary to the assumption of many observers, there is nothing easy about being a Christian. The Saviour never promised that it would be. The reason is not far to seek.

When one accepts Christ a deep conviction settles upon him that he must break with his old ways. He cannot compromise. This firmness leads to estrangements and separations. Friends, even loved ones, may cast him aside. Storms gather and their fury break upon him. The one who dares to stand up for principle must expect hardships. Jesus said that "in the world ye shall have tribulation." This is part of the price paid by all who follow Christ. But no investment has ever paid dividends like being a Christian.

We sometimes wonder why believers have so much trouble. It could not be otherwise. True conversion opens up a new world and with it come new horizons, new duties, and obligations never known before. The enemy of souls blows up stiff headwinds so that the new sea on which the believer has launched grows rough and tempestuous. This new faith flings the Christian into a world that seems now cold and unsympathetic where the winds howl and the storm rages. But the believer, like a kite, rises steadily higher when facing the wind.

In words that have lost none of their force through the ages, Jesus told His disciples, "If any man will come after me, let him deny himself, and take up his cross, and follow me" (Matt. 16:24). Although some crosses are heavier than others, none is anywhere nearly as heavy as was His. But none who sincerely follow is exempt from cross bearing.

Some in Christ's day found their crosses too heavy and the upward way too steep and narrow. "From that time many . . . walked no more with him" (John 6:66). When Jesus saw these vacillating ones giving up the struggle, He sadly asked the twelve, "Will ye also go away?" He asks this of us today.

NEVER FORGOTTEN

O Israel, thou shalt never be forgotten of me. Isa. 44:21.

On this Memorial Day, flags and flowers will decorate thousands of cemeteries throughout America. Originally it was known as Decoration Day, because right after the Civil War—probably on May 30, 1867—several women at Columbus, Mississippi, went out after church and placed flowers on the graves of the Confederate dead—their sons, husbands, and fathers. Noticing that nearby a few Union soldiers lay buried, these gentle women placed flowers on their graves as well. Word of this kindly gesture reached the ears of General John A. Logan, then head of the Grand Army of the Republic. General Logan was moved to issue an order on May 5, 1868, appointing May 30 "for the purpose of strewing with flowers the graves of [those] . . . who died during the late rebellion."

This felicitous proposal spread rapidly and soon May 30 became a legal holiday in most of the States of the Union. Since World War I this day has commemorated the dead of all wars. The day is often observed with parades of veterans, Boy Scouts, and other patriotic organizations marching to cemeteries for the solemn ceremony of firing a salute over the graves of the dead and playing *taps* on the bugle. Thus Memorial Day has come to serve as a day for decorating the graves of all our beloved dead who are mourned and remembered.

It is highly appropriate and salutary to observe one day each year to remember, in honor, those who are gone, including a vast host whose names are forgotten. This also embraces God's faithful servants and martyrs of all ages who were "stoned, they were sawn asunder, were tempted, were slain with the sword: they wandered about in sheepskins and goatskins; being destitute, afflicted, tormented; of whom the world was not worthy" (Heb. 11:37, 38). In more recent times thousands upon thousands of the truest of earth have gone down into nameless graves and already "the memory of them is forgotten" (Eccl. 9:5).

Yet the dead are not alone forgotten. Among us countless isolated or elderly individuals are unnoticed, sometimes even by their own children. But the Lord doesn't forget. He says, "Can a mother forget the baby at her breast and have no compassion on the child she has borne? Though she may forget, I will not forget you" (Isa. 49:15, N.I.V.). How wonderful that the Eternal One always remembers!

THE BENEFITS OF ADVERSITY

Behold, happy is the man whom God correcteth: therefore despise not thou the chastening of the Almighty. Job 5:17.

Never once did Christ minimize the price to be paid for serving Him. However severe our suffering or punishing our humiliation, these can never match His. Of Himself the Prince of heaven declared, "Foxes have holes, and the birds of the air have nests; but the Son of man hath not where to lay his head" (Matt. 8:20). "Ye shall be betrayed. . . . And ye shall be hated of all men for my name's sake" (Luke 21:16, 17). In the face of statements such as these, promising His followers sacrifice and hardships, He bade them, "Follow me." Only those with, or with the potential of, determination, resolution, and stout hearts, those possessed of undaunted courage, dare respond. There is no promise nor hope of reward to those who cower and compromise. Paul told the Hebrews, "If any man draw back, my soul shall have no pleasure in him. But we are not of them who draw back . . . but of them that believe to the saving of the soul" (Heb. 10:38, 39).

Some have been slow to harmonize hardships and sacrifice with the Christian life in this modern age in which every new discovery and invention makes life easier. "Why, then," they ask, "cannot the spiritual life be easier too?" We must not forget that we are dealing here with two different worlds: one is the natural and temporal; the other is the spiritual and the eternal.

The troubles of believers today, although hard to bear and harder to understand, can in no way compare with those of the patriarch Job. Consider that he was suffering from boils, he was bereft of children and property, and then his wife turned against him as a hopeless loser. She advised him to curse God and die (Job 2:9). But the record is that he still maintained his integrity and by God's help proved more than a match for all his woes. Can any doubt that when Job's fiery trials ended he came forth as fine gold and masterful in the majesty and uprightness of his character?

God has promised peace and joy to those who follow Him. These we have, even though surrounded with trials and tribulations. "Peace I leave with you, my peace I give unto you: not as the world giveth, give I unto you." (John 14:27). Like Paul, we may say, "We glory in tribulations."

THRESHOLD OF SUMMER

For now the winter is past, the rains are over and gone; the flowers appear in the country-side; the time is coming when the birds will sing, and the turtle-dove's cooing will be heard in our land. S. of Sol. 2:11, 12, N.E.B.

It must have been in early June that King Solomon awakened on a bright, clear morning to the cooing of the turtledove and the robin's song. Looking out on the prospects of a perfect day he may have noticed the flowers bordering and beautifying the palace grounds. Swept by these evidences of the regeneration of spring, he penned our text, perhaps in a mood like Wordsworth's when he wrote:

"All at once I saw a crowd,
    A host, of golden daffodils;
    Beside the lake, beneath the trees,
    Fluttering and dancing in the breeze.

"A poet could not but be gay,
    In such a jocund company. . . .
    And then my heart with pleasure fills,
    And dances with the daffodils."

This same revitalizing spirit of the season inspired James Russell Lowell to express his joy thus:

"And what is so rare as a day in June?
    Then, if ever, come perfect days;
    Then heaven tries earth if it be in tune,
    And over it softly her warm ear lays;
    Whether we look, or whether we listen,
    We hear life murmur, or see it glisten."

This is the time of year when it is easiest to read God's messages of love in the natural beauty that surrounds us. If we go out early in the morning into the woods, we can hear the birds praising their Creator. After walking one morning along the Itschen River where birds were singing, Izaak Walton exclaimed, "If thou, Lord, has provided such music for sinners on earth, what hast thou in store for the saints in heaven?" These and every other joy and blessing will be there. The invitation is given to all, "Come . . . inherit."

EXCELLENCE IN THE DESERT

The wilderness and the solitary place shall be glad for them; and the desert shall rejoice, and blossom as the rose. . . . They shall see the glory of the Lord, and the excellency of our God. Isa. 35:1, 2.

Traveling through the arid lands of southwestern America in early spring, the visitor is repeatedly impressed with the marvelous variety of God's creation. These vast stretches of desert are thought of by many as barren wastes of sand, immense reaches of hillocks and canyons where crawl the scrawny, graceless creatures of the wild and where a relentless sun beats down on the heads of forlorn travelers. This inhospitable region of merciless sun, largely avoided by cooling clouds, would seem bereft of flowers. But not so, for each spring the desert sands are carpeted with living color that flaunts dainty blossoms of the gaudiest hues. Lovers of beauty drive far just to feast their eyes on this riotous scene during the few short weeks it endures. These tiny blossoms, wrestling sustenance from shifting sands and flinty rocks, strike the beholder as accentuating the trackless solitude wherein they dwell. Thomas Gray observed that "full many a flower is born to blush unseen, And waste its sweetness on the desert air."

However, in God's sight, no fragrance or beauty, whether in nature or human life, blushes entirely unseen or is ever wasted. He takes delight in the work of His hands and His eye "seeth every precious thing." Each in its own way testifies to the beauty of His holiness. There are so many kinds of desert flowers that many varieties have never been classified. Likewise, there are thousands of ordinary people in the common paths of duty whose radiant lives of loving service must evoke joy in the Master's eyes.

The Scriptures promise that in God's good time what we call deserts now will blossom like the rose, that the curse will be removed from all nature, and that the redeemed will have no heartaches, sickness, or sorrows. They will love life and "long enjoy the work of their hands" (Isa. 65:22). Instead of deserts "there are ever-flowing streams . . . and beside them waving trees. . . . There the wide-spreading plains swell into hills of beauty, and the mountains of God rear their lofty summits. On those peaceful plains, beside those living streams, God's people, so long pilgrims and wanderers, shall find a home."—*The Great Controversy,* p. 675.

WHEN I AM AFRAID

O thou most High. What time I am afraid, I will trust in thee. Ps. 56:2, 3.

No matter how courageous we are or how deep our experience in the Lord, times come when the spirit is terrorized at the prospect of meeting some ghastly unknown enemy or suddenly having to face an awful, unexpected tragedy. The pervasive, creeping fear of wholesale nuclear destruction that admittedly stalks all mankind today is a shriveling, chilling contemplation which we try—often in vain—to put away. More than of ourselves we think anxiously of those we love, especially our dear children and the members of our families. And we are driven to near distraction when specialists in nuclear weaponry predict a worldwide, fiery annihilation within a decade. How can we carry on? How can we cope with such dread prospects?

Let us take a clear look at fear, which is admittedly, about the most devastating of all human emotions. The more we know about this dreadful enemy of all that is worthwhile in life, the better equipped are we to grapple with it and to overcome it. Fear is a corroding intruder which percolates through our thinking, warping our judgment, distorting the personality, and making everyone who harbors it landlord to a ghost. Worry is a blood brother of fear, and the two of them almost always travel together. They sleep together, too—and with us—robbing us of rest, plowing furrows in our cheeks, and fading prematurely to silver the ringlets on the brow. Our problem is how to banish these two horrible, unbidden guests.

The author of today's text was a valorous, stouthearted soldier, yet he was not ashamed to admit to fear. He said, "I am afraid." But the key to his courage was in his unshakable trust in God. "What time I am afraid, I will trust in thee," he said. "In God I have put my trust; I will not fear what flesh can do unto me" (Ps. 56:4). David had learned, as we must, that love for God and perfect trust in Him cast out fear (see 1 John 4:18). This is the invincible weapon against worry. Perfect love, which centers on our heavenly Father, cannot tolerate selfish fear, and does not have to, for "if God be for us, who can be against us?" (Rom. 8:31).

Thus we need to be concerned only when we lose faith in God. His mercy is over His children. His everlasting arms encircle the soul that turns to Him for aid. In His care we may rest safely, saying "What time I am afraid, I will trust in thee."

SAFELY THROUGH

When thou passest through the waters, I will be with thee; and through the rivers, they shall not overflow thee. Isa. 43:2.

When we depend upon the Lord, He does not leave us to flounder in the middle of the river. Twice in the above text the word "through" points to the other side. We are assured of passage through the rivers and through the waters, not left struggling alone where Satan would leave us. These promises must have been especially meaningful to ancient Israel because, at the very beginning of their journey out of Egypt, the Lord brought them miraculously through the waters of the Red Sea.

One could hardly wish to see a safer, gentler stream than the Yellowstone River in August. But in flood time its angry, turbid waters overflow its banks and rush in frightening billows toward its faraway confluence with the Missouri. One such time I stood in awe watching from a bridge as two boys were preparing to cross in a light canoe. It seemed terribly foolhardy to me until I saw a man in a large flat-bottomed rowboat bearing down on them from upstream. He tossed them the end of a rope, and, with that to hold and steady their frail craft, they were across the river in no time. His steady rowing did it safely; whereas, had he abandoned them at mid-stream, they would have swamped for sure.

The Lord has promised to bring us safely "through" whatever dangers may be best for us to His glory. He says to us as He did to Israel of old, "Fear thou not; for I am with thee: be not dismayed; for I am thy God: I will strengthen thee; yea . . . I will uphold thee with the right hand of my righteousness" (Isa. 41:10).

> "Seas of sorrow, seas of trial,
> Bitterest anguish, fiercest pain,
> Rolling surges of temptation
> Sweeping over heart and brain,
> They shall never overflow us,
> For we know His word is true;
> All His waves and all His billows
> He will *lead us safely through.* . . .
> For His promise shall sustain us,
> Praise the Lord, whose word is true!
> We shall not go down nor under,
> He has said, 'Thou passest *through.*'" *
>
> —Annie Johnson Flint

* Used by permission of Scripture Press Publications, Ltd.

NO TRUST IN MAN

They will besiege you in all your cities until they bring down your lofty impregnable walls, those . . . walls . . . in which you trust. Deut. 28:52, N.E.B.

As a result of Israel's unrepented wickedness, the Lord warned that their mighty strongholds would be reduced, that their defenses would fall, and that their trust in the human arm would prove futile.

Since World War II, as never before, man's trust in his fellow men has continually diminished until today personal security has all but vanished. According to FBI statistics, two persons in five will be assaulted in their lifetime, and city dwellers can expect it within five years. As crime rates soar, we find ourselves confronted with the question, "How can I protect myself? In his *Inquiry into Enoughness,* Daniel Lang writes: "If our era has a theme, it is that we are trying to stay alive. Clean bombs, dirty bombs, intercontinental missiles, space ships with warheads—these are the images that spin in our heads when we contemplate the state of the world." So many "certainties" on which man has always depended are in question, so many "ancient verities" have proved invalid that bewilderment in depth results. The products of modern science; the technological shrinkage of the world; rising international tensions; an increasing paradox of good and evil—all emphasize man's mass inability to cope with reality. For the vast majority the question is simple survival—that of staying alive.

Despairing of man's ability to solve his problems, the French philosopher, Jean Paul Sartre, has decided that "man himself is unauthentic, a phony," and T. S. Eliot admitted that

> "We are the hollow men
> We are the stuffed men
> Leaning together
> Headpiece filled with straw. Alas!" *

When our ancient bulwarks fail, what can we do? Confidence and trust in God remain. Fear can drive a man, but trust and hope can lead him safely. A rebirth of inner faith, a resurgence of hope and confidence, a rediscovery of the spiritual resources in each individual heart—these are the walls in which you can trust your faith. These walls will not fall.

---

* From "The Hollow Men" in Collected Poems 1909-1962 by T. S. Eliot, copyright 1936 by Harcourt Brace Jovanovich, Inc.; copyright © 1963, 1964 by T. S. Eliot. Reprinted by permission of the publisher.

TRUST IN THE LORD

The fear of man bringeth a snare: but whoso putteth his trust in the Lord shall be safe. Prov. 29:25.

Men of the world fear the future, illness, death, and, after that, the judgment. More immediately, insecure men seek and work like beavers for a kind of temporal security that eludes them. Those with more money than they need look for a safe place to invest it with high interest rates or dividends. Those who think they can do better play the stock market, in which they become so absorbed that they check with the exchange every morning and often cannot sit down to breakfast until they have looked up the latest quotations in the newspaper. I have known such men who are gracious and elated on the day their stocks go up and morose and depressed when they fall a few points the following day. The uncertainty of their holdings worry countless men and women of means into jumpy, premature old age and early death. The only sound course for those with means is to enter into a partnership with the Lord, paying a faithful tithe and trusting that ''he doeth all things well.''

Gnawing anxiety and a foreboding future induce in some such mental imbalance that they take their own lives. The suicide rate among teen-agers is high and constantly rising. Percentagewise it stands at a higher level among millionaires than among paupers. But the calm stability of mind and spirit that flows from an abiding trust and confidence in the Lord, come shadow or sunshine, casts out fear.

Along with other fears, some desperately dread the prospects of the second coming of Christ. Surely that momentous event that will terminate some six thousand years of human history will be overwhelming. It will be an awful day of retribution when all who are outside of Christ will cry in despairing anguish to the rocks and the mountains, ''Fall on us, and hide us from the face of him that sitteth on the throne, and from the wrath of the Lamb: For the great day of his wrath is come; and who shall be able to stand?'' (Rev. 6:16, 17).

Do you fear assault, robbery, accidental death, or atomic holocaust? You can commit yourself to the Lord for His safekeeping, knowing of a certainty that He has the will and the might to preserve you. If deliverance does not come *now,* it is sure to come *later.* Either way, you can assuredly come safely home at last with the saved of earth to the place prepared for you in the Holy City.

LOVE AND DISCIPLINE

For whom the Lord loveth he chasteneth, and scourgeth every son whom he receiveth. Heb. 12:6.

The sardonic author Mark Twain is credited with the observation that a man can endure any amount of ill-fortune so long as it afflicts someone else. No less pertinent, and certainly more helpful, is Longfellow's stanza:

> "Be still, sad heart! and cease repining;
> Behind the clouds is the sun still shining;
> Thy fate is the common fate of all,
> Into each life some rain must fall,
> Some days must be dark and dreary."

Emphasizing that hardships toughen a man for the battles of life, the evangelist Spurgeon said that "the Lord gets His best soldiers out of the highlands of affliction."

While we were young, in childish ignorance, most of us probably resented punishment for wrongdoing. Yet, when grown older, we understand, and even appreciate, the necessity of discipline for our guidance and direction. Also, we see now that it was in love that our parents administered it as an aid to character development. Likewise, from a heart of love, our heavenly Father allows the chastening of sorrow and difficulties to correctly guide us on the road to heaven.

This ceaseless, ongoing struggle of the Christian life, with its shaping and toughening of character, continues as new heights are mounted on our upward way. Christina Rossetti explained it well:

> "Does the road wind uphill all the way?
> *Yes, to the very end.*
> Will the day's journey take the whole long day?
> *From morn to night, my friend.*
> But is there for the night a resting-place?
> *A roof for when the slow dark hours begin.*
> May not the darkness hide it from my face?
> *You cannot miss the inn.*
> * * * * *
> "Shall I find comfort, travel-sore and weak?
> *Of labor you shall find the sum.*
> Will there be beds for me and all who seek?
> *Yea, beds for all who come."*

DO NOT RESENT TROUBLE

Despise not thou the chastening of the Almighty: for he maketh sore, and bindeth up: he woundeth, and his hands make whole. Job 5:17, 18.

It has been aptly said that the Christian life is like the face of a clock. The short hand represents discipline and the long hand, mercy. Slowly, but surely, the short hand of discipline must pass and God speaks in every stroke. But over and over again passes the long hand of God's mercy, bringing sixtyfold blessings for every stroke of trial and trouble. And all the time both hands are securely anchored to the central shaft—the great and changeless heart of a God of infinite love.

Both the hand of discipline and the hand of mercy play essential roles in the shaping of the Christian life. By the hand of discipline character is tested and formed and the radiant graces of the Spirit are developed. How can we learn the sweet graces of contentment if life runs on forever like a song? Or learn the relief of forgiveness if no one ever comes asking our pardon?

The eleventh chapter of Hebrews sets forth the many troubles which God's loyal servants suffered in ages past. Their trials were not removed, but the Lord's hand of mercy was outstretched to strengthen them until they became magnificent examples of faith. "Ah, happy he whom God is chastening! Spurn out the discipline of the Almighty; he binds up where he wounds, he hurts and heals" (Moffat). "The Hand that humbles . . . is the Hand that lifts up the penitent, stricken one. With deepest sympathy He who permits the chastisement to fall, inquires, 'What wilt thou that I should do unto thee?' " (*Prophets and Kings*, p. 435). The time will come when we can look back with gratitude upon the darkest experiences of our lives. Even now we can be glad for them.

The following lines seem appropriate here:

"Art thou weary, tender heart? Be glad of pain;
In sorrow sweetest things will grow, as flowers in rain.
God watches, and thou wilt have sun
When clouds their perfect work have done."

"The heart would have no rainbows if the eyes had shed no tears."

OUR AFFLICTION IS HIS

In all their affliction he was afflicted, and the angel of his presence saved them: in his love and in his pity he redeemed them. Isa. 63:9.

Here we have one of the most moving expressions in all Scripture. It reveals the loving compassion of the Lord for His earthly children in their trials and misfortunes. He was with them in Egypt and saved them from cruel oppression there. Today He is our great High Priest who is "touched with the feeling of our infirmities."

A companion text is David's comparison of God's sympathy with that of a father. "Like as a father pitieth his children, so the Lord pitieth them that fear him" (Ps. 103:13). When the parents of a large family were asked which one of the children they loved best, this was their reply: "The one who is away from home until he gets back, the one who is ill until he gets well, and the one who is disobedient until he repents."

Many of us know through apprehensive, firsthand experiences how the hearts of earthly parents ache when our little ones suffer from severe illness. Hour after hour, day and night, gentle hands minister to the prostrate little body while tired eyes keep vigil above the fevered form. It is impossible to say who suffers most—mother, father, or child.

Then comes the crisis. The twitching ceases, the fever breaks and is gone. The child opens wide his eyes but hardly recognizes the strained, anxious faces solicitously bending over him. At first he does not realize how great distress his parents have suffered during his illness. Looking again, he whispers, "I never knew you loved me that much." Nor does he know, until years later, when he goes through a similar experience, the mountain of consolation and gratitude his recovery generated.

It was through suffering far more acute than this that qualified Jesus to provide us the consolation that He alone can give. The Father, too, for six thousand years, has carried a burden of pain and suffering beyond comprehension. "Our world is a vast lazar house, a scene of misery that we dare not allow even our thoughts to dwell upon. Did we realize it as it is, the burden would be too terrible. Yet God feels it all."—*Education*, p. 264. So far does His pity surpass ours!

THE GOLD OF CHRISTIAN CHARACTER

I will make a man more precious than fine gold; even a man than the golden wedge of Ophir. Isa. 13:12.

Although the exact location of the ancient land of Ophir is not known today, the mines of that place were the chief source of the fine gold that enabled Solomon to decorate and embellish the Temple in Jerusalem in a manner and to a degree never equaled before and probably not since. This pure gold was refined and smelted into wedges, or V-shaped blocks, for convenient transfer to Jerusalem. Thus the symbol of extreme wealth and value became the "wedge of Ophir."

In our text the Lord evaluates a man of character and emphasizes that he is more precious than this golden wedge. Even today gold remains a metal of the highest value, but the character of a godly man stands higher still. The truly great of earth have always regarded character as the ultimate, conclusive measuring rod for all men. R. C. Winthrop wrote that "the noblest contribution which any man can make . . . is that of a good character. The richest bequest which any man can leave to the youth of his native land is that of a spotless, shining example." In similar vein we have this from John Todd: "A good heart, benevolent feelings, and a balanced mind lie at the foundation of character. Other things may be deemed fortuitous . . . but character is that which lives and abides. . . ."

The physical elements that compose the human body are of little value. One scientist concluded that it contains about ten gallons of water, enough fat to make seven bars of soap, enough carbon for a thousand lead pencils, enough phosphorus for two thousand matches, iron enough for one nail, a cup of lime, and the amount of sulphur needed to rid a dog of fleas. And this is as true of a moron as of a genius, a financier as of a pauper, a village idiot or an Einstein. "The value of the human agent is estimated according to the capacity of the heart to know and understand God."—*Counsels to Parents and Teachers,* p. 406.

In God's sight a man is of greater value than the gold-encrusted, sacred buildings of Solomon's Temple that shone with radiant splendor. Like that scintillating structure, the heart of the Christian may become the dwelling place of the Almighty, the sanctuary of the glorious Shekinah of His presence. What an exalted privilege this is!

A NOBLE CHARACTER

There lived in the land of Uz a man of blameless and upright life named Job, who feared God and set his face against wrongdoing. Job 1:1, N.E.B.

The prophet Ezekiel singled out Noah, Job, and Daniel as worthy of preeminent honor, and rightly so, for they were all conspicuous for their lives of blameless character. As was said of another, they "builded better than they knew."

Character has often been likened to a building with each individual serving as his own architect and builder. There is merit in this comparison because each of us determines the kind of character we wish to build. The word *character* comes from the Greek word meaning "to engrave." Thus character is, in a sense, what we engrave on life's tablet. Our thoughts and acts are our tools. Character, as it grows, becomes the essential part of each of us. Life "determines character; character determines destiny; as we live, so we are, so is our character."

An upright character cannot be inherited. It cannot be bought. But it is built by doing pure and noble deeds of moral excellence. "The formation of a noble character is the work of a lifetime and must be the result of diligent and persevering effort."—*Patriarchs and Prophets*, p. 223. In a sense character is a byproduct of aim and effort. Woodrow Wilson said that "if you think about what you ought to do . . . your character will take care of itself. Character is a byproduct; it is produced in the great manufacture of daily duty." Grenville Kleiser wrote that character building "demands the richest building materials: faith, courage, humility, integrity, magnanimity, nobility, self-abnegation. Wealth, influence, position, power—these are of little value without character. Grandeur of character is moral principle in practice."

> "We are building day by day
> In a good or evil way.
> And the building as it grows
> Doth our inmost self disclose.
> Till in every arch and line
> All our faults and virtues shine."

—*Selected*

WHAT'S IN A NAME?

A good name is rather to be chosen than great riches, and loving favour rather than silver and gold. Prov. 22:1.

When a worthy Puritan named his baby boy Praisegod Hallelujah Barebones Smith, his motives were the best. Obviously, name and hoped-for character were closely related in his mind. This relationship of name and character is illustrated also in an episode involving Alexander the Great and one of his soldiers. When it was reported to the Greek commander that this man was a coward and that his name was Alexander, the great chieftain had the fellow brought before him. In words admitting of no mistake, the commander in chief shouted, "One of three things you must do: fight, get out of the army, or change your name!"

The importance of a good name had Shakespeare put these words into the mouth of one of his players:

"Good name, in man and woman,
   is the immediate jewel of their souls.—Who steals my purse steals
   trash; But he that filches from me my good name,
   robs me of that which not enriches him,
And makes me poor indeed."

Everyone is properly jealous of his own reputation. The reason, of course, is that "as the tower is reflected in its shadow so is every man's character reflected in his reputation." Another has truly said that reputation is the cloak character wears.

Similarly, a reputable Christian family maintains a proper concern for its good name. This is an individual matter, too, because the family reputation is simply the combined reputation of its several members. Moreover, each one carries the obligation, not only to guard his own reputation, but to keep one another's reputation above reproach. Of this matter John Donne wrote: "No man is an island, entire of itself; every man is a piece of the continent, a part of the main . . . any man's death diminishes me, because I am involved in mankind, and therefore never send to know for whom the bell tolls; it tolls for thee."

Once I heard a good man say, "I do not traffic in scandal. When I hear ill of a person I ask myself, 'Is it true?' If so, why should I repeat it?" This is a practice worth emulating.

HOW ABOUT YOUR INFLUENCE?

For none of us liveth to himself, and no man dieth to himself. Rom. 14:7.

The significance of this text is in its emphasis on the solemn fact that the influence, however slight and whether intended or not, which every living person exerts on every other person, tells either for good or ill. It is a solemn truth that no one can live a wholly independent life. And the influence we exert is sure to lift up others or cast them down. It takes only one rotten apple to infect a whole barrel and one bad boy in a school can soon drag down others to his low level. On the other hand, as Shakespeare wrote, "How far that little candle throws his beams! So shines a good deed in a naughty world." Paul must have had influence in mind when he told the Galatians that "a little leaven leaveneth the whole lump" (Gal. 5:9).

J. D. Snider, in *The Vision Splendid,* tells of visiting an old monastery where the guide showed the guests a dungeon in which so-called holy men spend years in shut-in seclusion. A member of the visiting party spoke up to ask, "What's the use of being holy in a hole?" This question upset their guide because he had no answer. What the world desperately needs today are men and women of holy influence on the streets, in the churches and homes, in factories, and in every place where other men and women live and work, achieve and suffer, and die without Christ and without hope. There is a vast dearth of Christian influence among those we see every day, for the fields are ripe and ready for harvest. We need not wait to witness in lands afar. Whether a world can be saved if we make no attempt to save our neighbors is a serious question. Perhaps you consider your light to be only a little candle. Very well, there is a need close by. "Let the lower lights be burning."

> "As a pebble dropped in water
> Sends its waves out more and more,
> In an ever-widening circle,
> Till they reach the other shore;
> So a deed, a word, an action,
> Dropped upon the sea of life,
> Sends a blessing or a cursing,
> In this world of sin and strife."

—*Selected*

THE SHEPHERD AND THE SHEEP

The sheep hear his voice, and he calls . . . and leads them. . . . He goes before them; and the sheep follow him, for they know his voice. John 10:3, 4, R.S.V.

There could have been no question in the minds of His hearers as to the Saviour's meaning as He spoke of the shepherd and the sheep. They were accustomed to seeing the flocks and were undoubtedly familiar with the psalmist's references to God's people as the sheep of His pasture (Ps. 95:7). It was a suitable similarity then and it is also such today.

A few years ago this fitting analogy came vividly to mind when I visited the Holy Land. I was fascinated to see Arabian shepherds tending sheep on the Palestinian hills. The day was done and I watched as two shepherds came down a rocky hillside followed by a large number of sheep in single file. Well down where the path divided, one shepherd turned left, the other right. Presently one called out *"Menah,"* Arabic for "Follow me." The other called the same. At this parting of the way the line of sheep quietly divided into two columns, one going left, the other right, each one apparently following its swarthy, turbaned master. Each group followed on down to two separate folds.

Because we are weak and, like helpless sheep, not wise enough to choose our own way, we need to entrust our lives to the guidance of the Good Shepherd. He not only knows the right way for us, but He goes on ahead. If we humbly and trustingly follow His leading we will surely come to the safety of His fold.

In today's chaotic, bewildering society there are many shepherds, many paths, but only two folds. Some shepherds are false and would lead us down paths to eternal destruction. Yet, though we cannot always see the misted way ahead, His divine guidance is sure to lead us to green pastures and still waters.

How precious is the assurance that He will always be our Shepherd and we His sheep! As His faithful sheep we have one thing to do: Follow Him! He never wavers nor stumbles.

> "Then wherefore should I doubt
> My Shepherd's voice, or falter more?
> Not mine to choose the path,
> Yet mine to know He goes before!"

—Author unknown

IS HE YOUR SHEPHERD TOO?

The Lord is my shepherd; I shall not want. Ps. 23:1.

This is the first verse of the best known psalm, possibly the best loved chapter in all the Bible. It speaks to every race of men and to all ages. It is the delight of childhood and the consolation of age. Little children love to hear about lambs. When the youth leaves home his parents pray for the Good Shepherd to guide and protect him. Near life's journey's end the aging believer whispers, "Though I walk through the valley of the shadow . . . I will fear no evil: for thou art with me" (Ps. 23:4).

David was truly a shepherd of the hills. His twenty-third psalm has been variously termed the Nightingale Psalm, the Pearl of the Psalms, the Shepherd's Psalm. Saint Augustine called it the Hymn of the Martyrs. More poems and hymns have been inspired by it than by any other chapter of Holy Writ. Evidence indicates that, as originally composed, psalm twenty-three was a three-stanza poem. Yet it is far more than a poem, even more than a prayer. Its importance is that it remains for all Christians a guidebook for life, an anchor for the soul.

This felicitous figure representing the Lord as the divine Shepherd and His people as His sheep is repeated throughout the Scriptures. To fully appreciate the beauty and significance of this imagery a person must know the hazardous nature of the Judean hills which induces an intimacy between the shepherd and his sheep, also the singular devotion that is engendered between them during the hours of solitude spent together. Those who know sheep—and those who imagine they do—can visualize the gentle shepherd leading his flock through the perils of the wilderness to green pastures beside still waters and, when day is done, leading them back once more to the shelter of the fold.

As Jesus related the parable of the Good Shepherd, His hearers could look a little way beyond and see enacted before their eyes a scene depicting the very lesson He intended to teach: that in Him man's every need is provided for. The Lord desires the faithful to have every good thing, both material and spiritual. His bounties are ready for us, so that when we pray we can believe that we shall receive. For the present, the Lord is our Shepherd. For the future, we shall have no want. Is He your Shepherd today?

THE KINGLINESS OF KINDNESS

Be ye kind one to another, tender-hearted, forgiving one another, even as God for Christ's sake hath forgiven you. Eph. 4:32.

More Biblical expositors have emphasized the beauty of our text than have practiced its principles. Still, as Paul said of the doctrine of salvation through Christ, it is a precept "worthy of all acceptation" (1 Tim. 1:15).

A great and good man, a personal friend of mine, wrote a beautiful essay "The Kingliness of Kindness." He tells of his experience stranded in a strange city late at night and in need of transportation between railroad stations. When he called the telephone operator for information, she provided it in rude and discourteous language. Later he called her back to thank her for her help. Apparently it was something she rarely had happen to her, and the change in her voice and her whole telephone personality indicated that the expression of his appreciation had uplifted her spirit. How simple it is to say Thank you. Yet how much it means when spoken in sincerity!

An ancient Scottish proverb points out that "kindness will creep where it canna gang [cannot go]" and the Russians say that "a kind word is better than a big pie." Even better known is the little girl's prayer, "Please God, make all the bad people good and all the good people kind." Etienne de Grellet is supposed to have declared, "I shall pass through this world but once. If, therefore, there be any kindness I can show, or any good thing I can do, let me do it now; let me not defer it or neglect it, for I shall not pass this way again."

Nearly everyone appreciates those who are kind in dealing with their fellow men. We appreciate especially those who are largehearted as well as tenderhearted. Never a day passes that does not present opportunities to practice this virtue. "Let the tenderness and mercy that Jesus has revealed in His own precious life be an example to us of the manner in which we should treat our fellow beings. . . . Many have fainted and become discouraged in the great struggle of life, whom one word of kindly cheer and courage would have strengthened to overcome. . . . We cannot tell how far-reaching may be our tender words of kindness, our Christlike efforts to lighten some burden. The erring can be restored in no other way than in the spirit of meekness, gentleness, and tender love."—*Testimonies,* vol. 5, pp. 612, 613.

PUTTING ON KINDNESS

Put on then, as God's chosen ones . . . compassion, kindness, lowliness, meekness, and patience, forbearing one another. Col. 3:12, 13, R.S.V.

Paul's Epistle to the believers at Colossae, from which today's forthright text is excerpted, was written primarily to combat the twin heresies of Judaism, which were extreme asceticism, and paganism, which was unbridled license. Both misbeliefs had infiltrated the Colossian church. Paul pointed out that such heresies claim sovereignty for the human will and that worship of the human will is a false, inverted humility and, therefore, reprehensible and offensive to God.

The Scriptures speak, in various places, of "putting on righteousness" (Christ's spotless robe of righteousness), and of the Christian's need to be dressed in this holy raiment to cover or replace our own lamentable attainments which are in God's sight but filthy rags. In today's text the exhortation is more specific. We are told to put on compassion, kindness, lowliness, meekness, and patience. Since clothing oneself is purely an act of the will, the inference is that these particular meritorious characteristics are at the command of the believer. We may have them if we choose.

The word *kindness,* as used here, expresses love in action. It means gentle, gracious, kindly consideration, both in disposition and performance, toward the needs of one's neighbor. We are encouraged to "put on" a character manifesting greatheartedness, Christlikeness. We are to cultivate in ourselves the tenderest compassion for needy humanity. And we must emulate Christ in humility, developing a patient forbearance toward our detractors, overlooking their misrepresentations, misunderstandings, malice, and unfairness. This is the broader meaning of "putting on kindness."

"Kind words, pleasant looks, a cheerful countenance, throw a charm around the Christian that makes his influence almost irresistible. This is a way to gain respect, and extend the sphere of usefulness. . . . The plan of salvation is to soften whatever is harsh and rough in the temper, and to smooth off whatever is rugged or sharp in the manners."—*Our High Calling,* p. 238. "For to be a Christian is to be Christlike."—*Ibid.*

WALKING IN THE DARK

Which of you fears the Lord and obeys his servant's commands? The man who walks in dark places . . . yet trusts in the name of the Lord and leans on his God. Isa. 50:10, N.E.B.

There are at least two classes of persons who walk in darkness: those who willingly remain in the dark and those whose duties require it. Unfortunately, many young people prefer the blackness of their own devising to the guidance of the light God offers them. They do not trust his leadings.

"The Lord's hand has been reached out in tenderest compassion and love; but they [the youth] do not care to trust Him. They want to . . . devise and plan for themselves. . . . The Lord marks out a way in which He would have them walk. He has lent them talents to be used for His glory, to do a certain work for the Master; but Satan says, 'I will countermand the order of Christ. I will find another line of work for active brain and busy hands. . . . I will eclipse eternal interests before this youth, and attract his mind . . . with worldly allurements.' " * Thus they walk in darkness who follow the prince of darkness.

Some fear the Lord and walk in His truth yet on occasion encounter dimness and perplexity along the way. There are times in the experience of every Christian when darkness seems to settle over the soul. Unrest takes the place of peace, and the heart grows heavy, and spiritual barrenness blights the life. Why does God permit spiritual darkness to sometimes enshroud His children? It may be so that the doubting one will lean the more heavily "on his God." At such times God draws near. In a vision of His presence the veil is drawn aside and His trusting ones behold Him "who loved . . . [us] and gave himself for [us]." As in the experience of Jacob, God stands at the top of the ladder saying, "Behold, I am with thee" (Gen. 28:15).

During the dark days of World War II, King George VI quoted these words from Minnie Louise Haskins: "I said to the man . . . at the gate: . . . 'Give me a light that I may tread safely into the unknown.' And he replied: 'Go out into the darkness and put your hand into the hand of God. That shall be to you better than light and safer than a known way.' So I went forth, and finding the Hand of God, trod gladly into the night. He led me towards the hills and the breaking of day in the lone East."

---

* Ellen G. White, in *The Youth's Instructor*, March 23, 1893.

FEAR NOT

For I the Lord thy God will hold thy right hand, saying unto thee, Fear not; I will help thee. Isa. 41:13.

I knew of a woman who went shopping with her small daughter. At a busy street intersection the mother reached down saying, "Let me hold your hand." Her little girl clasped one hand with the other and replied, "Mother, I can hold my own hand." The Lord offers to hold our hand. Shall we spurn the offer and in our own self-confidence choose to walk alone?

Only those who weathered the great depression of the 1930s can appreciate the depth of discouragement and despair that gripped the nation. Sad and suffering citizens simply could not understand dire want encompassed with plenty nor national stagnation in the presence of unlimited potential energy. To alleviate the pervading paralysis of this fear and anxiety, President Franklin Roosevelt, in his First Inaugural Address, dauntlessly declared that "the only thing we have to fear is fear itself." He reiterated this assurance eight years later in his famous Four Freedoms message to Congress by listing, among the four essential human freedoms, "freedom from fear."

Despite valiant and repeated attempts, both before and since the Roosevelt era, to reduce the level of quivering apprehension in the hearts of men, a stealthy, stalking spectre of impending doom seems to persistently pursue the footsteps of all mankind. Speaking of these last days the Saviour predicted that men's hearts would fail them "for fear, and for looking after those things which are coming on the earth" (Luke 21:26). As added assurance, Jesus said, "Heaven and earth shall pass away; but my words shall not pass away" (Luke 21:33). Thus we know that the penetrating fear that pervades the world today is one more evidence of fulfilling prophecy. This injunction to fear not enables the Christian to face confidently the uncertainties of day-to-day existence and walk unafraid the hazardous pathways of life.

Cowardice goes hand in hand with fear, but faith is invincible. When we place our confidence in the Lord He provides assurance in times of trial; in times of danger, freedom from fear; in times of grief, comfort. "By prayer, by the study of His word, by faith in His abiding presence, the weakest of human beings may live in contact with the living Christ, and He will hold them by a hand that will never let go."—*The Ministry of Healing,* p. 182. To do the safe thing, accept God's helping hand.

JESUS OF NAZARETH PASSETH BY

Jesus . . . have mercy on me. Luke 18:38.

As Jesus, followed by His disciples and others, came to Jericho, a blind beggar sat by the wayside. His was a dark, dreary world. Because of his handicap he was forced to live humiliatingly on the alms of his none-too-generous countrymen.

Beggars have never been well received, even when blind. They are looked upon rather as parasites, and generally speaking, the world holds out small hope for them.

Bartimaeus had, no doubt, chosen a strategic position along the thoroughfare to be where the mass of men passed by. On this particular day traffic seemed heavier than usual. He could hear the shuffle of many feet. But he could only listen. Curious about all the excitement, he called out, "Why the crowd?" An unknown voice answered, "Jesus of Nazareth passeth by." The name "Jesus" startled him. He may have heard of the Lord's healing power, for Jesus' fame was noised abroad. Bartimaeus was suddenly seized with a passion. He may have thought, This is my chance. It is now or never. But what chance had a blind man in that crowd? Yet he was unwilling to let such an opportunity slip away. Although he was blind, he could talk. So he began to cry out, "Jesus, thou son of David, have mercy on me."

As soon as Bartimaeus began calling, those near him tried to hush him up. But he only called louder. Suddenly the procession stopped and there ensued a moment of silence. The Saviour had heard the poor man calling. Someone rushed over to Bartimaeus and said, "Be of good comfort, rise; he calleth thee" (Mark 10:49). Casting his garment aside, the blind man rose and came to Jesus. There was hope and expectation in his face. Jesus came right to the point. He asked, "What wilt thou that I should do unto thee?" Trembling, Bartimaeus replied, "That I might receive my sight." As quickly as the request, came the response. "Jesus said unto him, Go thy way; thy faith hath made thee whole. And immediately he received his sight, and followed Jesus in the way" (verse 52).

A whole new world opened before Bartimaeus now that he could see. He beheld buildings, people, the blue sky—all for the first time. But, best of all, he could look into the face of Jesus, who had shown him so great mercy. One day Christ's followers will all have this privilege. John climaxes the joys of the redeemed with these words, "They shall see his face" (Rev. 22:4).

A MIRACLE BY THE SEA

He said unto them, Give ye them to eat. Luke 9:13.

A modernistic Bible teacher told her class that Jesus didn't actually feed the five thousand that day beside Galilee, that this account is merely symbolical of the Saviour's fillng their minds with words of wisdom. One of her young hearers asked, ''How come there were twelve baskets left over?'' With a curt, ''We'll talk about that next week,'' she dismissed the class. She was confused because the question had exposed her blind unbelief.

Many hard-headed moderns refuse to accept anything miraculous. Especially do they reject out of hand the accounts of Jesus raising the dead and feeding five thousand people with five barley loaves and two small fishes. They say this and that could not be, therefore, the Bible lies. And if it lies about miracles, they reason that it does not tell the truth about anything else.

A careful reading of the four Gospels will draw the thoughtful seeker for truth to the interesting conclusion that the Saviour was always reluctant to perform miracles. Every time there was a proper reason for refusing, He refused. On the mount of temptation, He refused. At Nazareth when they attempted to kill Him, He refused to miraculously save Himself. Nor did He avail Himself of His miracle-working power at Gethsemane when they came to arrest Him, nor on the cross when they challenged Him to save Himself. Instead He reserved this power only for others, never for Himself. There are no exceptions.

The narrative of the miracle beside the sea rings true. The hungry five thousand had hung on the words of Jesus until night drew on. When He implied that they should be fed, His disciples told Him they had only a lad with five barley loaves and two small fishes. Philip thought the idea absurd. He said, ''Two hundred pennyworth [a large sum] . . . is not sufficient for them'' (John 6:7). But Jesus had the people sit down. ''Then he took the five loaves and the two fishes, and looking up to heaven, he blessed them, and brake, and gave to the disciples to set before the multitude. And they did eat, and were all filled: and there was taken up of fragments that remained . . . twelve baskets'' (Luke 9:16, 17). This was no allegory. It happened.

The true believer will not doubt the miracles of Jesus. After the miraculous delivery of Paul and Silas from prison, Paul told their terrified jailer, ''Believe . . . and thou shalt be saved'' (Acts 16:31).

OUR CARING FATHER

Cast all your anxieties on him, for he cares about you. 1 Peter 5:7, R.S.V.

This, along with many other Biblical entreaties, instructs us to roll our burdens, our cares, and our anxieties upon the Lord. He is not only able to help us carry the burden of our distresses, but He can remove them if He sees fit. He knows what is going on in the world, for His eyes "run to and fro throughout the whole earth, to shew himself strong in the behalf of them whose heart is perfect toward him" (2 Chron. 16:9). He, who marks the sparrow's fall and numbers the hairs on our heads, has not left anything beyond His control. No problem, however small, is too insignificant to call to His attention.

Our text for today and the words of the corresponding hymn, "Take It to the Lord in Prayer," were often in my mother's mind and on her lips as well. She was the young wife of a Montana rancher whose work required him to be away from home for days at a time. It was not very pleasing to be left with five small children alone on an isolated homestead on the prairie. At such time she calmed her fears by placing her trust in the Lord and imploring Him for our protection. Although the dangers were real, He never once failed us.

At a Southern camp meeting some years ago, C. L. Paddock told this story of Billy Bray, the Welsh evangelist, whose simple faith sent him to God with the daily perplexities of life. On the street Mr. Bray met a bighearted Quaker friend who knew the evangelist's needs. He said, "Mr. Bray, I have been watching thee. Thy unselfish life is an inspiration to me, and I believe the Lord would have me help thee. If thou wilt call at my house, I have a suit of clothes to which thou art welcome, provided they fit thee."

"Thank you," said Billy Bray, "but there is no doubt in my mind about the clothes fitting. If the Lord told you to give them to me they will fit me. He knows my size exactly."

When burdens press, remember that ours is an understanding Father and that we are His needy children. If perplexities arise or unexpected problems develop, He hears even the unspoken petition. In fact, you cannot shed a tear, breathe a sigh, commit an act—right or wrong—but that He cares. Let us talk over our anxieties with Him "in faith believing."

ROCKS

Trust in the Lord for ever, for the Lord God is an everlasting rock. Isa. 26:4, R.S.V.

Through the years I have had a lot to do with rocks. They have always fascinated me, particularly when they are of unusual size, shape, or color. As a boy I used a one-horse cultivator to kill the weeds that thrived between long rows of potato vines. I learned that by holding the plow handles in a firm grip I could cultivate even in rocky soil. But when I held the handles loosely, a rock would soon knock the plow out of the furrow and jar my teeth at the same time. There may be a lesson in that.

Sometimes the plow stuck in wet gumbo soil and I learned that a good way to free it was to use coarse sand, which is actually many tiny rocks working together.

Here and there all over America can be seen huge rocks that captivate and excite the eye: the great Stone Mountain in Georgia, Half Dome in Yosemite, Chimney Rock and Scott's Bluff in Nebraska, historic Independence Rock in Wyoming, Table Mountain in Oregon, Hole-in-the-Rock, Square Butte, and Pompey's Pillar in Montana, and many more.

Collecting strange and beautiful rocks has become of late a delightful hobby that has enriched the lives of many rock hounds. My preference, however, is to visit and enjoy those huge, mighty, fixed rocks that have stood unshaken through numberless ages. The Scriptures speak of a great rock in a weary land (Isa. 32:2). Its shadow provided a cooling refuge to the sun-scorched travelers.

Our text suggests that the love of God is the shelter of His people like a great rock that rears above the tumultuous sands of time. This is the Rock of Ages, a cleft rock cleaved by the lightning that flashed over Calvary. Spiritually speaking, in that cleft all repentant sinners may hide. Here is the safe and immutable refuge of the soul, the "Rock that is higher than I." Time may beat upon it but cannot dislodge it, for it is forever.

> "Rock of Ages, cleft for me,
> Let me hide myself in thee;
> Let the water and the blood,
> From thy riven side which flowed,
> Be of sin the double cure,
> Cleanse me from its guilt and power."
> —August M. Toplady

UNFINISHED

And I am sure that he who began a good work in you will bring it to completion. Phil. 1:6, R.S.V.

As a small boy I took a notion one fine spring morning to build a barn. I decided to have a double door in front, a second-floor hay mow, a hip roof, and to paint it red just like Father's barn. I laid out a plan and had in mind to use it as a dog house for my little terrier. For weeks I worked on it every day. But by the time the walls were only half up the July heat sapped my energy and dissipated by enthusiasm. Other interests took over and the barn never got finished. My dog continued to sleep on the back porch and when anyone mentioned "Floyd's barn," I was acutely embarrassed. So I tore it down. But the memory of it haunts me still. The house we had to pass on the way to town was also unfinished and a constant reminder that the owner had started something that he never completed. It was of no use to him or to anyone else.

Since those early years I have always felt ill at ease in the presence of any unfinished task—unless progress on it was being made. One wonders how many projects of the greatest possible value have never come to fruition because they were left unfinished. Have you ever wondered what Schubert's *Unfinished Symphony* would have been like had it been completed? Or what poetry Keats might have written had he not died at 26? Or how the sad tragedy of American reconstruction might have been avoided had not President Lincoln been cut down by an assassin in 1865?

Unfinished tasks are always distressing: a house lacking a roof, a fig tree without figs, the earth not yet become heaven. The Lord never intended it to end this way. Yet are not these too much like our past lives: incompleted projects, noble intentions never realized, stumbling on in frustration? Still, God began a good work in us and He has promised to help us finish it. We could never do it alone.

No one needs to wonder about the plans and purposes of God, because He finishes what he begins. In His great, last prayer, the Saviour said to His Father, "I have finished the work which thou gavest me to do" (John 17:4). God says, "I have purposed it, I will also do it" (Isa. 46:11).

WHO IS DRIVING?

But this is my plight. . . . I know, O Lord, that man's ways are not of his own choosing; nor is it for a man to determine his course in life. Jer. 10:19-23, N.E.B.

W. Somerset Maugham told a tale of old Baghdad that bears on the above text. One day, so goes the story, a merchant sent his servant to the market to buy provisions. Shortly the servant returned, pale and trembling, to say, "Master, just now in the marketplace I was jostled by a woman and when I turned to look I saw it was Death. She looked at me and made a threatening gesture. Now lend me your swiftest horse and I will ride from this city and so escape my fate. I will go to Samarra and there Death will not find me." The master lent him the horse and as fast as he could the servant galloped away. Then the merchant went down to the market and found Death and said, "Why did you make a threatening gesture to my servant?" Death replied, "It was not a threatening gesture. It was only a start of surprise. I was astonished to see him here in Baghdad for I have an appointment with him tonight in Samarra."

This legend strikingly depicts the hopeless fatalism that sees no future save that fearsome, impending appointment with the death angel that fate decrees. The bewildered worldling quakes before an obscure future. So, in a panic of fear, he risks a wild ride to Samarra in search of some hidden refuge where he hopes death cannot find him.

The aimless indirection of many lives came to mind when I read a news report in a Detroit paper. Late one night a traffic officer hauled three men into night court. Seeing their inebriated condition, the judge asked, "Now, men, which of you was driving?" One of them arose unsteadily to his feet and replied, "We have you there, Judge. We were all in the back seat." How many travelers on the road of life drift and waver because the driver's seat is empty!

"Infinite Love has cast up a pathway upon which the ransomed of the Lord may pass from earth to heaven. . . . Angel guides are sent to direct our . . . feet. Heaven's glorious ladder is let down in every man's path, barring his way to vice and folly."—*Our High Calling,* p. 11.

LIKE SODOM

Remember Lot's wife. Luke 17:32.

Because the comparison of our day to the times of Noah and Lot has been often repeated, the awful significance has become commonplace to many. We must not let this happen to us. Notice once more the setting in which the Saviour spoke this solemn counsel, "Remember Lot's wife." Lest the stupendous day of His second appearing come as an overwhelming surprise, as it will to much of the world, He described conditions to be expected as that great day approaches. His mind went to the fate of the proud, wicked, and doomed city of Sodom. He said, "They did eat, they drank, they bought, they sold, they planted, they builded" (Luke 17:28). These were the things the Sodomites were doing and Jesus said the same interests would absorb the thoughts of those who would be living in these last days. His description accurately reflects the main interests of most of the great cities of the world today, at least a hundred of them right here in these United States.

Sodom was a magnificent metropolis, a center of art and commerce. As wealth flowed in, the self-satisfied and self-serving inhabitants surfeited themselves in luxury and vice until the whole year seemed like one constant round of carnival. But the wicked city was not obliterated without ample warning. The anxious, urgent appeals of Lot and the angels were unheeded. The lovers of pleasure looked upon Lot as a simple-minded old fanatic. And the revelry went on.

Suddenly destruction fell from heaven like that which later struck Pompeii, where warnings were also ignored. In that city, many refused to leave their lavish homes and precious possessions, only half believing that disaster threatened. But the nauseous gases crept in as fiery lava and ashes rose at the doors. Cellars, yards, even upper stories provided no refuge and finally the pumice, cinders, and ashes covered the highest buildings. Pompeii was destroyed.

Lot and his wife did not come to Sodom by chance. They had chosen the city, a place of temptation. They set their eyes *toward* Sodom. Soon they were *in* Sodom and became *of* Sodom. Because their hearts were there, the angels had a hard time getting them *out* of Sodom.

The fate of Lot's wife, who became a pillar of salt, remains for us an example of inordinate affection for all material things. She left them reluctantly, and she loved them so much that she lingered and then looked back—her fatal mistake. Jesus says, "Remember Lot's wife."

FLEE YOUTHFUL LUSTS

Flee . . . youthful lusts. 2 Tim. 2:22.

The *New English Bible* has this rendition of Paul's practical advice for the youthful Timothy: "Turn from the wayward impulses of youth." Commenting on this wise counsel, Ellen White has written, "The Lord loves the youth. He sees in them great possibilities, and is ready to help them to reach a high standard, if they will only realize the need of His help." *

During my early years in Montana I learned about the wily coyote whose nocturnal depredations, particularly the killing of livestock, made him the hated enemy of the rancher and the farmer. To put a stop to this business, young men on horseback with greyhounds and rifles would ride out to run down and destroy these predatory wild dogs. It was relatively easy to get close enough to shoot the younger coyotes, but a different story entirely with the older, wise ones, particularly the huge, wolflike males. On first sight of the hunters these more experienced animals take off with great speed and never slacken their pace until they are out of sight. Their sole aim is to reach safety and they never stop to look back. These are rarely shot. The younger, more curious animals often pause for a backward glance and lose their lives.

The Scriptures abound in warnings to flee from sin. Curiosity about this enemy often proves fatal. To dally with it is to hazard one's soul. Lot and family fled Sodom in great haste to escape the infamous city soon to perish in the flames of divine wrath. The angel told them to take a one-way path to the hills and to make haste and not to look back. Lot obeyed, and went so fast that his wife and daughters could scarcely keep up with him. But Mrs. Lot's heart was still in the doomed city and, although her reluctant feet were already at the base of the mountain, she stopped to look back. That moment of delay was her last.

Holy Writ bids us to flee from idolatry, fornication, and "the wrath to come" (Matt. 3:7). Today's text concludes with this: "Follow righteousness . . . out of a pure heart."

---

* Ellen G. White, in *The Youth's Instructor,* Jan. 18, 1894.

A DAY OF RECKONING

Because sentence against an evil deed is not executed speedily, the heart of the sons of men is fully set to do evil. Eccl. 8:11, R.S.V.

Father used to tell of a vagrant hobo who came by a neat-looking farmhouse. As all was quiet he decided that no one was at home and that he could easily steal one of two shirts he saw hanging from the clothesline in the backyard. Just as he took it, the back door opened and the exasperated housewife, unable to prevent the theft, called out to the thief, "You are going to have to pay for that in the judgment." The tramp replied, "If it's going to be that long I'll take two!"

Whether ficititious or true, this anecdote correctly illustrates the attitude of myriads of sinners who do evil deeds because sentence against them "is not executed speedily." But the penalty is no delusion nor is it diminished by the lapse of time. This is one of Satan's most effective deceptions, like the familiar slogan, "Buy now, pay later," that traps many unwary people into financial stringency. Which is unfortunate enough, but this thinking becomes an eternal tragedy when the penalty of sin is considered.

God bears long with transgressors for He is "not willing that any should perish" (2 Peter 3:9). For four generations He bore with the idolatrous Amorites while giving them repeated evidence that He is the true God. For 400 years He held back His judgment on the wicked Amalakites. For 120 years His servant Noah pleaded in vain with the antediluvians to repent and be saved. Whenever His arbitraments are deferred it is to give the transgressors the opportunity for repentance.

Because of this delay of judgment sinners reason themselves out of repentance. They accept all God's benefits, presume upon His mercy, and regard the postponement of punishment as evidence that He doesn't intend to exercise vengeance—ever. They practice disobedience until sin holds complete dominion over them. Then, too late, they will find that God's forbearance is not without limit and that His provision for punishment to evildoers is as certain as His promise of salvation to the repentant.

"Though a sinner do evil a hundred times, and his days be prolonged," said Solomon, "yet surely I know that it shall be well with them that fear God . . . But it shall not be well with the wicked" (Eccl. 8:12, 13).

OUR FOREMOST OBLIGATION

Take heed unto thyself. 1 Tim. 4:16.

The context of this positive counsel in the *New International Version* provides this addendum: "Do not neglect your gift. . . . Be diligent." "The charge given to Timothy should be heeded in every household, and become an educating power in every family and in every school." *

When we hear a gifted vocalist sing or watch an Olympic champion perform, we marvel at such peerless ability. Seldom do we realize, however, the high price these people pay for their success or the countless hours they have devoted over many years to diligent practice. And to maintain the acme of perfection this exertion must never cease, not even for one day. Fritz Kreisler, the celebrated violinist, said that if he neglected practice for one day he noticed it, if he neglected to practice for two days his tutor noticed it, and that if he didn't practice for a week his audience noticed it.

Another famous personage who reached the pinnacle of prominence in his field was the eminent surgeon Dr. John Harvey Kellogg. His agile hands were never idle. Dr. Kellogg maintained his manual skills as a surgeon, at odd moments or while riding on a train, by making tiny stitches on little pieces of cloth he carried in his pocket for the purpose. This diligence enabled him to close an incision with astonishing speed and accuracy. His due fame was well earned.

In spiritual affairs—which are infinitely more important than any worldly accomplishment—success requires steady perseverance. The dauntless heroes of faith depicted in the Scriptures did not walk the broad path of self-indulgent ease. Well aware of this temptation, Paul warned Timothy to avoid spiritual and mental indolence. He said, "Give attendance to reading, to exhortation, to doctrine" (1 Tim. 4:13). Timothy was a promising young man, but he never could have become the influential force he was had he failed to follow Paul's admonitions.

Christian commitment lays an inescapable obligation upon all—particularly the youth—to develop whatever talents, visible or hidden, they may possess to their highest potential. It may be God's aim for you to surpass the attainments you now envision for yourself. Pursue that goal, never wavering. By His help, you can attain it.

---

* Ellen G. White, *The Youth's Instructor*, May 5, 1898.

THE GREATEST QUESTION

What shall I do then with Jesus?" Matt. 27:22.

This is the most important question ever posed by mortal man. It was asked more than two thousand years ago by Pontius Pilate, Procurator of Judea. The scene was so unique in human history, so charged with unspeakable pathos, so packed with unprecedented tragedy, that review it a thousand times, if you will, and each time you will be moved anew to the very depths of your being. This was the prelude to the climax of the ages, and it merits constant and careful review by every Christian.

Pontius Pilate was not an admirable man. Self-serving and suspicious, he was thoroughly disliked even by his fellow Roman officials. Yet draped in imperial toga, he posed as an impartial judge and tried to conceal his loathing for the bigoted, clamoring rabbis he detested as vermin. He rightly suspected that every word, every accusation, they spoke against Jesus was a lie. Such inoffensive innocence shone in Jesus' face that Pilate realized at once that here was no ordinary prisoner. Tremendously impressed, he determined not to condemn Him without a hearing. So he took the accused aside for a private interview. There the wavering Procurator heard the truth for the first and, as it turned out, for the last time. Despite a pleading note from his wife, Pilate didn't understand. Nor did he dream, even for a fleeting moment, that the obsure Jew who stood before him was the Saviour of the world who alone could reveal to him the truth. The shining moment of opportunity passed; and the cowardly Pilate washed his hands of the whole affair, left Jesus to His fate, and went to breakfast.

Pilate knew what he ought to do, but, unwilling to risk his dignity and his office, he delivered the Saviour of the world to be crucified. Instead of addressing his transcendent question to the rabble, he should have asked it of his own heart. No washing will ever cleanse Pilate's hands of the stains left on them by the divine blood of Christ.

For two thousand years each generation and each individual has faced this very personal question: "What shall I do then with Jesus?" Confirmed by history, enshrined in art, poetry, and music, and emblazoned in cathedrals, His name has inspired pilgrimages, pageants, and crusades. Yet, ever and always, the question of the day remains the personal query of Pilate, "What shall I do then with Jesus?" Your place in eternity depends on your response.

THE MORNING COMETH

And the evening and the morning were the first day. Gen. 1:5.

Reading over and over again the first chapter of Genesis and believing it implicitly, as do most Creationist Christians, one is impressed that God divided His creating into six periods of activity. "And on the seventh day God ended his work . . . ; and he rested" (Gen. 2:2).

Six times, at the end of six successive days, the words "the evening and the morning are repeated. This repetition makes it clear that God does not count days from midnight to midnight or the light first and the dark to follow. Neither did He sandwich in the light between two shorter periods of darkness, as man does. With the Creator, from the beginning it was first the dark and after that the light. God provided that each night end in daylight and that all the nights and all the days would end in one eternal day where there can be no darkness at all. The Revelator wrote, "There shall be no night there; . . . for the Lord God giveth them light" (Rev. 22:5). "In the City of God 'there shall be no night.' None will need or desire repose. There will be no weariness in doing the will of God. . . . We shall ever feel the freshness of the morning and shall ever be far from its close. . . . The glory of God and the Lamb floods the Holy City with unfading light. The redeemed walk in the sunless glory of perpetual day."—*The Great Controversy*, p. 676.

In John 3:19 we read that "men loved darkness rather than light, because their deeds were evil." It seems paradoxical that in this day and age, when artificial lighting prevails more than ever before, criminals boldly stalk the night, so that apprehension rises as the sun sets. Nightly assaults on the elderly and others unable to defend themselves have grown so vicious and widespread that thousands of innocent, inoffensive citizens dare not leave their homes after nightfall. It is at night that drunken drivers sow death on the highways. During the hours of darkness hope grows dim in the sickroom, and those who grieve sob alone in their sorrow.

Yet hope springs anew with the passing of the shadows. God does not forsake them who trust in Him. "Unto the upright there ariseth light in the darkness," said the psalmist (Ps. 112:4). And although "weeping may endure for a night, . . . joy cometh in the morning" (Ps. 30:3).

HELICOPTER OR JET PLANE
Let us go on unto perfection. Heb. 6:1.

One day I was stranded, along with four others, at a small airport ninety miles from Chicago, which was our intermediate destination. A gas leak had grounded our connecting plane.

The airport manager said, "We can get you to O'Hare by helicopter in an hour."

I said, "That won't do. I'm scheduled out of there for Vancouver in less than an hour."

He hesitated a minute, looked out on a perfect day and said, "I'll fly you there myself." He put his assistant in charge, and in ten minutes we were airborne in a six-passenger "baby jet" with this accommodating manager at the controls. Twenty minutes later we taxied up beside the Boeing 707 in final preparations for take-off to Vancouver. We had made our connection with minutes to spare.

On the way West I pondered the contrasts between a jet plane and a helicopter. The latter is maneuverable, capable of ascending and descending vertically, hovering motionless, and flying backward as well as forward. The swifter jet cannot stop or stand still in the air. Its safety depends on its continual forward thrust.

The "go on" admonition in our text regarding the Christian journey would seem to liken it to the flight of a jet plane. There can be no standing still, no reversing of our forward thrust, as we endeavor to mount ever higher levels of character development. Man was created to be a son of God. All who accept this high calling will go continually forward with no retreating or turning back.

Having accepted Christ as our personal Saviour, having the assurance that our sins are forgiven, we need to "go on" in our spiritual journey. Fundamental questions such as the existence of God, the divinity of Christ, the efficacy of His sacrifice, the sure promise of salvation, and many other indispensable doctrines should be settled once and forever. In confidence we can leave these "principles of the doctrine," as our text says, and go forward to the perfection of character.

Many current religious difficulties are due to questioning of truths long ago settled as indispensable to man's salvation. We need to get out of the wobbly, uncertain helicopter of doubt and board God's spiritual jet plane that goes on steadily to perfection. Pray that God will guide you on this forward journey.

SECOND FIDDLE

Among them that are born of women there hath not risen a greater than John the Baptist. Matt. 11:11.

After he had been the leading light preparing the way for Jesus' first advent, John began to fade out of the picture. When he said "I must decrease," he really meant it. No doubt this rare virtue helped make him the man Jesus said he was. Here is a splendid example of one who could step down from a leading role to a secondary position. He knew how to play second fiddle.

Some of the greatest people recorded in the Bible took a minor place. It is important to remember that a man's greatness in God's sight is judged not by his position but by the quality of his service. It is not how much we shine but how well we serve that counts. Sooner or later everyone must play second fiddle. No one can be first all the time. In fact, most of us must be second or lower much of the time. To do so is not belittling. It is the way of life. On the playing field, in the office, in the church, in the home, or wherever we are, most of us play a secondary role. There is no disgrace in this if we play our part well.

Taking second place is not easy. The natural thing is to cry out, "me first!" Only the grace of God can cause us to say, "He must increase, but I must decrease." Satan refused to occupy second place. He would have nothing to do with God's program unless he could be the leader. If he could not be first he would not play at all. "I will exalt my throne above the stars of God" was his egotistical boast. (See Isa. 14:13.)

Andrew showed how to take second place graciously. Anyone with an important father or brother has a certain handicap. Andrew's brother, Peter, was a gifted leader. But instead of envying him, Andrew tried to make Peter's work more successful. And he didn't complain when he was left out as Jesus took Peter, James, and John up the Mount of Transfiguration. Be it remembered that, while he could not be a Peter, Andrew brought that brother to Christ.

Talents are never improved by envy of others or being too proud to take a lesser place. Not until we have mastered the second fiddle can we expect the leading part. "He that is faithful in that which is least is faithful also in much: and he that is unjust in the least is unjust also in much" (Luke 16:10).

AUTHENTIC FREEDOM

If the Son therefore shall make you free, ye shall be free indeed. John 8:36.

This is the glorious fourth. Today a nation celebrates its birthday. Editors editorialize on it, newscasters elaborate on its significance, and ministers sermonize about it. Millions of Americans will use the long weekend to drive out to parks and mountains, share picnics with ants under trees, and swim in lakes, pools, and oceans. They will explode firecrackers by night and disturb the sleep of neighbors all around. There will be spectacular, luminescent displays that will light up the night sky like gigantic, lustrous kaleidoscopes for miles in every direction—to the delight of children and the recurrent wonderment of grown-ups. The odor of gunpowder will assail the nostrils, and not a few will imbibe alcoholic beverages and sink into a stupor or cause collisions in which some celebrants will die.

After all the noise has receded into silence and the last rocket has flared and faded, you may want to sit down and ask yourself, "What is freedom? How much did it cost?" You may even reflect upon the outpouring of toil and treasure, the suffering of the patriotic men who laid their good lives down. You can marvel how, under God's providence, the bravery and sacrifice of fewer than four million people won their independence from the greatest nation on earth and founded a new nation that now reaches "from sea to shining sea"—and beyond.

Our colonial forefathers were inspired by Washington's valiant few who left their bloody footprints in the snow at Valley Forge. They kept bravely on and finally won their freedom. They well knew, as we need to remember, that authentic freedom includes much more than physical independence. Today, as never before, we must keep uppermost in our minds that true freedom can be enjoyed only in Christ. John says, "If the Son therefore shall make you free, ye shall be free indeed." This is an infinitely higher kind of freedom—freedom of mind and spirit.

As we submit ourselves to the will of God, a fuller, richer liberty than was won by our forefathers becomes ours.

"Out of my bondage, sorrow and night, Jesus, I come. . . .
Into Thy freedom, gladness and light, Jesus I come to Thee.
Out of my sickness into Thy health, out of my want and
     into Thy wealth,
Out of my sin and into Thyself, Jesus, I come to Thee."

THE FIFTH OF JULY

Therefore, my beloved brethren, be ye stedfast, . . . always. 1 Cor. 15:58.

The title of today's reading has been chosen advisedly. The real significance of Independence Day is not so much how patriotic we are on July Fourth as the way we are today and tomorrow and on all the other days of the year. Anyone can wave a flag or stand up for "The Star-Spangled Banner." But it took more than this for our ancestors to win the American Revolution. And much more than that is needed to preserve our precious liberties that they secured in that conflict. There are "Fourth-of-July patriots," as surely as there are church members known as "Easter Christians" because they go to their knees only once a year.

A reading of history certainly teaches, among other lessons, that the nation that sets itself forward on a united front toward common goals is most often successful in attaining them. For example, such worthy national goals as the emancipation of the slaves and the extension of suffrage to women were secured, after years of controversy, when they developed into irresistible goals for the nation. Like a surging tide, the purposes of the people drove steadily forward until it became the national will to enact these reforms. Few today would dare to propose their repeal. Similar to a mighty national will is the life that is dedicated to God. It moves continually forward and with purpose toward its goal.

On that memorable night of the spectacular stellar display of November 13, 1833, Abraham Lincoln is said to have been visiting in the home of a gospel minister. Alarmed by the astounding celestial fireworks, the cleric, who stood with young Lincoln at the window, exclaimed, "The end of the world must be upon us!" Lincoln looked beyond the cascade of shooting stars and said, "No need for alarm. The great constellations are still in place." Like these constellations, we are to remain steadfast and unswervable even though others may falter and fail.

A living faith is constant. The dedicated life moves forward with steadfast purpose toward its goal. Delays and disappointments do not deflect it. He who wavers says, "I wonder." The child of God declares, "I know."

The constancy that really counts is that which lasts till death. But life's great crises, including the last one, cannot be faced courageously unless the life is trained to meet them. This steadfastness of purpose is noble and majestic. Our friends expect us to be faithful. God expects it too.

THE HAND THAT MADE US

The heavens declare the glory of God; and the firmament sheweth his handywork. Day unto day uttereth speech, and night unto night sheweth knowledge. There is no speech nor language, where their voice is not heard. Ps. 19:1-3.

One night, after viewing the stars brightly sparkling in the dark sky, Joseph Addison read the verses here quoted and then sat down to write a majestic poem for which he is justly famous. Franz Joseph Haydn, the noted composer, later fashioned a remarkably beautiful hymn no less exalted than the lyrics themselves. To hear this sublime hymn sung feelingly and at the same time to ponder the meaning of the words is an experience so inspiring that few can resist its message:

"The spacious firmament on high
With all the blue, ethereal sky,
And spangled heavens, a shining frame,
Their great Original proclaim.
Th' unwearied sun from day to day
Does his Creator's power display,
And publishes to every land
The work of an almighty hand.

"Soon as the evening shades prevail,
The moon takes up the wondrous tale;
And nightly to the listening earth
Repeats the story of her birth;
While all the stars that round her burn,
And all the planets in their turn,
Confirm the tidings as they roll,
And spread the truth from pole to pole.

"What though in solemn silence all
Move round the dark terrestrial ball?
What though no real voice nor sound
Amid their radiant orbs be found?
In reason's ear they all rejoice
And utter forth a glorious voice,
Forever singing as they shine,
'The hand that made us is divine.' "

THE SUN SHINES—AND SERVES

O Lord: . . . let them that love him be as the sun when he goeth forth in his might. Judges 5:31.

Our text for today is the closing refrain of the majestic song of Deborah and Barak, which commemorates the victory of the armies of Israel over the forces of the fleeing Canaanites and their chieftain, Sisera. It compares the total defeat of Israel's enemies to the rising sun going forth in his might. This is the glorious picture of all who love and serve the Lord. It is repeated in the prophecies of Isaiah (60:1), Daniel (12:3) and Malachi (4:2). The revelator used similar language to describe an angel ascending with the seal of God to be placed upon all who are prepared to receive it (see Rev. 7:2, 3). The saved of earth, sealed for salvation, appear "as if the sun had just risen from behind a cloud and shone upon their countenances, causing them to look triumphant, as if their victories were nearly won."— *Early Writings*, p. 89. The rising sun, going forth in his morning grandeur, symbolizes the eventual emergence of God's people from the conflicts of earth and poised to enter Paradise.

There is no more fitting figure than the sun, arising "in his might," to illustrate the reward of the righteous. Scientists and philosophers have outdone themselves in attempting to describe the incomprehensible power and greatness of the sun. Only by its prodigious energy can life be sustained on earth.

Although the sun's indispensability at the heart of our solar system has long been known, its importance has not always been appreciated as a health-promoting agent. "The pale and sickly grain-blade that has struggled up out of the earth in the cold of early spring, puts on the natural and healthy deep green after enjoying for a few days the health-and-life-giving rays of the sun. Go out into the light and warmth of the glorious sun . . . and share with vegetation its life-giving, healing power." * Little children who are kept indoors while the sun shines gloriously outside are to be pitied. Even today, some mothers do not realize that in order for their children to enjoy exuberant health, they need an abundance of sunlight along with pure air and physical exercise.

Shall we not henceforth more regularly appropriate the health-promoting sunshine and more faithfully encourage the Sun of Righteousness to shine in our hearts!

---

* Ellen G. White, *The Health Reformer*, May, 1871.

"SUNLIGHT IN THE HEART"
I will be glad and rejoice in thee. Ps. 9:2.

In several places the Scriptures speak of the blessings of the sunshine and then suggest that this outward manifestation of God's love should be reflected in the cheerful face of the Christian. "Rejoice" and "remove sorrow from thy heart," advises the wise man (see Eccl. 11:9, 10). For nearly a hundred years happy Christians have been singing the gladsome hymn, "Sunlight in the Heart." The first stanza and refrain go like this:

> "There is sunlight on the hilltop,
> There is sunlight on the sea;
> And the golden beams are sleeping,
> On the soft and verdant lea.
> But a richer light is filling
> All the chambers of my heart;
> For Thou dwellest there, my Saviour
> And 'tis sunlight where Thou art.

> "O the sunlight! beautiful sunlight!
> O the sunlight in the heart!
> Jesus' smile can banish sadness;
> It is sunlight in the heart."

During the late 1930s I was serving as principal of Takoma Academy. My office was downstairs, and the sill of the window was even with the lawn outside. One Sabbath after church I went to my office, opened the window, and looked out to enjoy a beautiful spring day. Presently a little girl, perhaps 6 years old, came by. Curious to see the window open, she peered in. She was startled to see me sitting there looking straight at her. She started away but hesitated when I smiled and asked her if she had been to church.

She said, "Oh, I was there."

I asked her if she enjoyed the sermon.

She replied seriously, "Yes. I like to hear Elder Spicer."

I then said, "What about it did you like?"

She said, "I like to hear Elder Spicer because, well, when he talks he is always so glad."

The sunshine of God's love in the heart instills an inner cheerfulness that invariably shines out in the countenance of every human soul in which His presence abides.

"LIKE A TREE"

He is like a tree planted beside a watercourse, which yields its fruit in season. Ps. 1:3, N.E.B.

Nearly all the great poets have written feelingly about trees. Perhaps the most widely known is Joyce Kilmer's poem, "Trees." Most of us can repeat Kilmer's famous lines from memory.

Well known, too, are these words from Bryant: "The groves were God's first temples." And this from Longfellow speaks meaningfully to all tree lovers:

"This is the forest primeval. The murmuring pines and the hemlocks,

Bearded with moss, and in garments green, indistinct in the twilight,

Stand like druids of eld, with voices sad and prophetic,

Stand like harpers hoar, with beards that rest on their bosoms."

Another much-loved poem by G. P. Morris contains these lines:

"Woodman, spare that tree!

Touch not a single bough!

In youth it sheltered me,

And I'll protect it now."

All who love to rest from exertion under a leafy bower can appreciate General Stonewall Jackson's reputed last words before losing consciousness when mortally wounded at Chancellorsville, "Let us cross over the river and sit under the shade of the trees."

The growth of a tree symbolizes Christian living. From seedling acorn to towering oak, its life is one continual process of receiving and giving, of absorption and dispensation.

Like a tree, we receive undeserved blessings, both temporal and spiritual. By serving God and our fellows we can manifest our appreciation. But unless output accompanies intake, a deadening of soul results, and the inner life withers. Any tree will quickly dry up if it is deprived of its nutrients. Spiritual life, too, ceases to be fruitful if the channel of God's grace is closed off. It is a marvelous privilege to put forth abundant foliage and, by God's help, bring forth rich fruitage in season.

DRIFTING WITH THE WIND

We have all withered like leaves and our iniquities sweep us away like the wind. Isa. 64:6, N.E.B.

The appearance of the first little apple-green leaves in spring foretells the early return of summer with all its seasonal blessings. But as summer wanes, the leaves gradually lose their vivid green, slowly turn brown, and then shrivel and die. One by one at first, then in clusters, they lose their hold on the branch, and the quickening Autumn wind sweeps by and carries them away to mold in some fence corner or depression. There they lie in dead heaps disintegrating under the rain and snow of winter. During the summer even a lively gale could not dislodge them, but with the seasonal cooling some subtle inner deterioration of the cells loosens their hold on the branch and they are swept away.

There is an unmistakable similarity between the withering leaf that loses its hold on the tree and is then swept away by the wind and the uncertain Christian whose wavering grasp of spiritual things is so fragile that it can be broken by the winds of worldly interests, whereupon he is swept away from God. As I travel I often meet them: former church members, former colleagues and students, former trusted religious leaders. Usually the recognition is a surprise, yet mostly cordial; sometimes restrained or embarrassing; occasionally poignant.

While crossing the nation by plane not long age I noticed a young woman scrutinizing me. I did not recognize her. Minutes later she got out of her seat and came down the aisle and spoke my name. I still did not recognize her. Then she told me who she was, a former student at a college were I had been academic dean. Then I remembered her. She told me, "I married a good man but not a Christian. We have two daughters, and the greatest regret of my life is that I left the church. If I had remained faithful I could bring these girls up in a Christian home, which they need more than anything else in the world." I assured her that it was still her privilege to make this reformation. She sighed, saying thoughtfully, "Perhaps. Sometime." I have not seen her since.

As the wind tears a leaf from the branch and carries it away, so trangression separates the sinner ever farther from God. But there is one difference. The severed leaf is gone forever from the tree, but the prodigal who repents is always welcome to return to his Father's house.

OASES

They came to Elim, where there were twelve springs and seventy palm-trees, and there they encamped beside the water. Ex. 15:27, N.E.B.

The long wandering of the children of Israel through the wilderness was exceedingly trying. What relief and rejoicing this oasis of Elim must have meant to the weary and footsore travelers! Not only were their tired bodies rested and refreshed but their courage was renewed.

Every so often along the pathway of life are located oases that mean much to everyone who is marching to Zion. But for them, few would ever reach the Promised Land. Yet when the Israelites came to the oasis of Marah, they could not drink because the waters were bitter. (See Ex. 15:23.) The believer today comes likewise to Marahs. But however bitter the waters, the Elims far outnumber the Marahs.

The Elims of life, resting places that refresh and strengthen, are not always properly appreciated. Some wayfarers pass by without seeing them. If men could but see and appreciate the Elims along the way, it would revitalize many lives.

One goodly Elim of life is the home. Not surprisingly, home is most appreciated by the homeless. The noted song "Home, Sweet Home" was composed by a man who had no home. Even the Saviour had no place to lay His head. Every Christian home ought to be an Elim, a place of refreshing for all who enter there.

But homes are not the only Elims God provides for us. Some wayside church, hidden away from the turmoil and bustle of the world, can be an Elim. The Christian farmers in one remote region inscribed over the door of their humble chapel the words, "Elim—the Place of Springing Waters and Shady Palms."

Christian schools can be Elims for dedicated youth needing refreshing water from the Fountain of Life rather than the bitter waters from the broken cisterns of Marah. We do well only when we provide a wholesome environment and God-fearing teachers who will give our youth every advantage in their struggle against the world, the flesh, and the devil.

In looking for the Elims along the pathway of life, we often overlook one. This is the place of private prayer. How many miss it! This living spring, with its welcoming, overshading palms, never fails—and it is available to all. Nothing can ever supplant it, for it is the place of power.

IN THE MAKING STILL

This also we wish, even your perfection. 2 Cor. 13:9.

The key word here is *perfection,* which could as well be rendered *completeness.* In this letter to the Corinthian believers Paul recognizes that these recent converts have only begun their journey toward perfection. He expresses the longing that they may achieve Christian maturity as they develop every gift, faculty, and talent to their greatest usefulness. Living Christians, like living plants, must either grow or die. The Lord desires each of us to grow characterwise "unto the measure of the stature of the fulness of Christ" (Eph. 4:13).

When God made the earth, He was so pleased that He pronounced it all "very good." But it wasn't fully developed. He could have finished it. But He didn't. He left a garden to till and many other tasks to be done. He placed various raw materials in the earth to challenge man, to set him thinking and experimenting. In doing this we enjoy supreme satisfaction and pleasure.

Have you ever noticed that children often will ignore their pretty mechanical toys in order to build, with spools, blocks, and sticks a domain of their own imagination? So it is with grown-ups. God gave us a world unfinished so that we may be like Him. He shares with us the joys and satisfactions of creating.

The Creator left the copper in the rock, the crude oil in the shale, and the electricity in the clouds. He left the mountains untrailed and the rivers unbridged. He left the forests unfelled, the diamonds uncut, and the schools unbuilt. He left the music unplayed and the poems undreamed. He gave us all these challenges that we might not be bored but stimulated and excited with creative tasks and so "think His thoughts after Him."

In multiple and magnificent ways men have met these creative challenges. Great satisfactions are ours as we view the gorgeous, glittering gemstones that have been cut to display every pleasing facet and hue. Graceful bridges of concrete and steel arch breathlessly over impassable chasms with such symmetry as to delight the eye, however often they come into view. And cold indeed must be the shriveled, mundane heart that is not moved by the deathless music of a Brahms or a Beethoven. But character building is the one challenge that transcends all others.

THE GOD OF CARE AND COMFORT

I waited patiently for the Lord; and he inclined unto me, and heard my cry. He brought me up also out of an horrible pit, out of the miry clay, and set my feet upon a rock, and established my goings. Ps. 40:1, 2.

Although the enormity of his troubles fell short of the afflictions of Job, David was no stranger to danger, nor was his life a bed of roses. A victim of enmity and jealousy, more than once he had to flee to the recesses and caves of the mountains. Even there he was hotly pursued by his murderous enemies. Later on, the psalmist described these perils as a nightmare in which he was groping in a dark, deep cavern. In this "horrible pit," can't you imagine the eerie sounds, the echoes of rushing, unseen waters, also strange, crawling creatures. Underfoot—nothing but slippery mud.

But the Lord protected David and brought him up. He set his feet on a solid rock, and the alarming sounds in the cave gave way to the song of birds and the voices of his friends. David's feet, which had been slipping in mud, were set on solid rock. His song of gratitude is understandable. Now he could walk securely in the light of day.

In his gratitude David exclaimed, "I waited patiently for the Lord; and he inclined unto me, and heard my cry." At first God seemed not to hear David's plea. Then He bent forward and listened. This is an apt, exquisite figure representing the loving fatherliness of our God. (See Ps. 31:2.)

In Romans, chapter 15, verse 5, the apostle Paul speaks of the God of patience and consolation. We all need patience and consolation in our times of stress and trial. We need patience under endless strain and worry, and we need consolation when the heart reaches the breaking point. Ours is a God of consolation. "As one whom his mother comforteth, so will I comfort you," says Jehovah (Isa. 66:13).

Paul also speaks of the "patience and comfort of the scriptures" (Rom. 15:4). What the Bible has meant to the myriads of martyrs, to the sufferers in prison, prison camps, and on the rack, to the harried Covenanters on the Scottish moors, to the Waldenses in their fastnesses, to lonely exiles and to bereaved hearts of all generations can only be revealed when the books are opened.

The most sympathetic human comforter may die or be removed but the Lord's ministry abides. "The God of all comfort" never fails.

PEACE PROVIDED AT THE CROSS

Having made peace through the blood of his cross, by him to reconcile all things unto himself. Col. 1:20.

It has been said that the worst peace is better than the best war. Those who have known first hand the horrors of war will agree. Yet even when the nation is at peace, many individual citizens do not have peace at heart. Some simple sources of peace are well known: a serene spirit, a happy home, honest, well-earned success, and the respect of our fellows. When a man is conscious of these, he can say with Job, " " "I will die in my own house, my days as numerous as the grains of sand" ' " (Job 29:18, N.I.V.).

Job's abiding peace is understandable. But there is a "peace . . . , which passeth all understanding" (Phil. 4:7). It is a peace too deep for words, like the pillowed depths of the ocean, undisturbed by surface storms.

When sin invaded Paradise, an alienation, like a wedge, was driven between earth and heaven. The cause of this separation was sin. Isaiah said, "Your iniquities have separated between you and your God, and your sins have hid his face from you" (Isa. 59:2).

A husband and his wife disagreed and quarreled. Finally they separated. Years went by, and then one day the husband came back to his hometown on a business trip. While there he went out to the cemetery to visit the grave of the couple's only son. As he stood in melancholy reverie by the grave, someone came up behind him. Surprised, he turned to face his estranged wife. On recognition, they both started to turn away. But their common interest in the grave of their cherished son made them hesitate. Then the husband gently took into his arms the wife of his youth, and they became reunited. It took the death of the son they both loved to reconcile them.

At Calvary, Jesus provided pardon for man and freed him from the penalty of sin. When He came, men were enemies of God. When He returned to heaven, He had reconciled the world to His Father. Thus He "made peace through the blood of his cross." No other such peace was ever made. Nor can it be.

"What a treasure I have in this wonderful peace,
    Buried deep in my innermost soul,
So secure that no power can mine it away,
    While the years of eternity roll!"

—W. D. Cornell

OUR GOD OF HOPE

Now the God of hope fill you with all joy and peace in believing, that ye may abound in hope. Rom. 15:13.

We all need hope because it is the inspiration of the soul. Hope is the light that leads us on, "the lively anticipation of things to come." Faith fills us with peace and joy, which overflow in hope. Faith enlivens expectations from God's Word and spreads their bright hues on her palette. With a few, deft dashes of her brush, she delineates unfailing, unfading hope. Faith energizes hope and does her finest work until the walls of the soul become replete with radiant frescoes.

A few years ago a young couple, attempting a winter plane flight over western mountains, were forced down by a storm in a remote, uninhabited area. Although unhurt, they had no idea where they were. When attempts at radio communication failed, the young man decided to go for aid. After covering his companion with blankets and placing what food they had—a box of cookies—within her reach, he struck out on foot through the deep snow. It took three days to find help, and two more days passed before the rescuing party could reach the stranded plane. To their surprise they found the young woman alive and in good spirits. While recuperating in a hospital from her ordeal she said, "I never once gave up hope. I just knew they would come." The attendant doctor said later that this girl's remarkable survival and rapid recovery were due as much to her superb courage and trust as to her physical vigor. Her hope and courage helped her come through.

Christian faith rests securely on the promises of God, and hope rests on faith. It is the sheet anchor of the soul. Hope enters within the veil and points unerringly to the shores of eternity. For the Christian there is a silver lining to every cloud, a patch of blue beyond the blackest sky, a bend in the longest lane, a breathless view to compensate for the steepest climb. What is otherwise impossible becomes possible through hope, for all things are possible with God.

Like any light, hope may flicker at times and even grow dim. We can brighten it by adding fuel, a daily surrender to God for a new infilling of His Spirit. The presence of Christ, when welcomed in, will keep the light of hope burning forever in our hearts. The God of all hope is with us.

PRISONERS OF HOPE

Turn you to the strong hold, ye prisoners of hope: even to day do I declare that I will render double unto thee. Zech. 9:12.

This title, "Prisoners of Hope," is not a fanciful one. To the Israelites it held a triple significance. When under the yoke of a foreign despot and longing to be free, the Jews were promised freedom. When bound in chains of sin the repentant ones were invited to flee to the stronghold of God's forgiveness. To all faithful believers, when tempted to feel imprisoned in unfulfilled prophecy, comes the assurance that the day star will arise.

In the Christian faith there can be no imprisonment without hope. In trials there is promise of deliverance. Even to sinners in wickedness a way is offered to escape the penalty of offended justice. No case is hopeless with God. In the atonement every hindrance is removed and every provision is made for deliverance.

The promise of our text, "I will render double unto thee," offers double blessings. Every mercy is a pledge of another to follow. There is safety in the stronghold of God, the immovable Rock of our salvation. And it is open to all who seek refuge there.

In various ways we remain "prisoners of hope." Until our mortal bodies are redeemed, we are subject to illness and infirmity. Some are prisoners to appetite, some to anger. But hope anticipates the possession of a perfect and immortal body. We are also prisoners to a limited, superficial knowledge. "Now I know in part" is a kind of bondage. "But then I shall know even as also I am known." That is freedom. We are prisoners to the brevity of life and its hidden elements. Hope anticipates a solution to the dark enigma of human existence.

We are prisoners also to a circumscribed fellowship. The great family of God is widely scattered. Those we know personally and love supremely, even close friends and relatives, are largely separated from us by distance—or by death. Hope anticipates a reunion in which a universal fellowship and everlasting association are promised.

Finally, we are imprisoned within an imperfect vision of Christ. We see now only as "through a glass, darkly." Human nature is incapable of more. How thrilling it is that hope anticipates, not only a perfect, personal vision of Jesus, but a perfect nature capable of full understanding! Although estranged here by time and distance, all may become prisoners of hope—"that blessed hope" (Titus 2:13).

THE MYSTERY OF REGENERATION

Jesus answered and said unto him, Verily, verily, I say unto thee, Except a man be born again, he cannot see the kingdom of God. John 3:3.

Nicodemus was a prominent man, a Pharisee, a ruler among the Jews, and a member of the Sanhedrin. He had credentials and no doubt looked the part. But he was so sensitive and so protective of his standing in the world that he came to Jesus at night. He was seeking the answer to a nagging question. He wanted to know how to regenerate his stagnant spiritual experience.

Jesus did not hesitate to speak candidly. He said, "Ye must be born again."

Supposedly mystified, Nicodemus asked, "How?"

Jesus replied, "Except a man be born of water and of the Spirit, he cannot enter into the kingdom of God."

When Nicodemus still couldn't quite comprehend, the Saviour told him, "Marvel not." In other words, accept it by faith. Experience the new birth. Then you will understand. The revitalization of his spiritual life became his. Nicodemus got the answer and the results he sought.

Although the Saviour told this sincere Pharisee to "marvel not," it is difficult not to ponder the wonder and the mystery of the new birth. Nicodemus was thinking of natural birth. Christ was illustrating spiritual rebirth. The figure is apt, for there are similarities. There is quickening in both cases. This comes in natural birth. In spiritual birth there comes a marvelous quickening of conscience, a renewed sensitivity to right and wrong, a new way of living, coming into being. No other experience is remotely like it. This is the miracle of conversion.

Natural birth, as we know it, is wonderful. It is emergence from compressed quiescence. From close confinement in darkness, the tiny creatures come into a colorful world, the yellow sun in an overarching sky, the earth in its mantle of green, the prospects of growth. So it is with human birth—a new life, a new member of the human race. The newborn baby is a person, a personality, an adult in embryo.

We ponder the deeper significance of this discipline of childbirth: of pain and weariness intermingled with joy and gladness. Its mystery quite eludes us. But it is never so marvelous as that inner awakening, the mysterious spiritual regenesis by which we come to belong to the eternal world through Jesus Christ the Lord.

LIKE THE EAGLE

He satisfies my desires with good things, so that my youth is renewed like the eagle's. Ps. 103:5, N.I.V.

Without foundation, except perhaps in myth, is the Indian legend of the phoenix, a great bird that was believed to live a long life and then, in old age, to retreat alone to some isolated crag, construct a nest of pine needles, sing a melancholy dirge, flap its wings to set fire to the pile, and consume itself in the flames. Thereupon, from the cooling ashes arose the reembodied phoenix, eager to fly away on youthful wings and in this new life reproduce its kind as instructed by the Great Spirit. Indian mothers told this tale to their children, and even today some people believe it.

The basis of this age-old story may be the fact that the eagle periodically molts its plumage, and when new feathers have grown, its strength and vigor gradually return. Perhaps the psalmist observed that this phenomenon gave the eagle an appearance of renewed vigor. Like a new bird, the refeathered eagle soars through the sky after this annual molt. David drew from it a descriptive picture of what it means to a Christian to experience new life through God's grace.

There is immense satisfaction in the assurance, "who satisfieth thy mouth with good things," as the King James Version words it. The Lord always satisfies the soul hunger of His servants. And apart from Him, the wants of man's great soul hunger can never be satiated. He, and He alone, can respond to the deep needs and gratify the boundless, unspoken desires. His presence and grace fill us with delightful satisfaction. "He satisfieth the longing soul, and filleth the hungry soul with goodness" (Ps. 107:9).

In the several verses preceding our text, six blessings are promised to God's children: forgiveness, healing, redemption, crowns, satisfactions, and renewal. For all these benefits David ascribes gratitude and praise to God, not only with tongue and pen but with the heart and soul as well.

It is important to notice that these blessings, especially forgiveness, are adapted exactly to man's needs. David's gratitude enlists every thought, faculty, power, the will, the affections, the conscience, even the reason. This embraces all that is highest and best in man in his outpouring of loyalty to God. Comparing our manifold blessings with his, how can we possibly do any less?

THE SOURCE OF AUTHORITY

Let every soul be subject unto the higher powers. For there is no power but of God: the powers that be are ordained of God. Rom. 13:1.

It is both profitable and practical to review from time to time the mighty undergirding principles of the Christian faith. Certainly no man's judgment exceeds his knowledge. Hence it is judicious and appropriate to reexamine, on occasion, the guidelines set forth in the Holy Scriptures regarding our daily walk among men.

"Order is Heav'n's first law," said Alexander Pope. Shakespeare was more specific when he wrote:
"The heavens themselves, the planets, and this centre,
   Observe degree, priority, and place,
   Insisture, course, proportion, season, form,
   Office, and custom, all in line of order."
How, then, shall we relate to civil government? The Supreme Court once ruled that the United States is a Christian nation. Actually this was incorrect—and still is. No authority of any kind should—except by persuasion and example—ever attempt to establish on earth a Christian nation as such. The Constitution of the United States guarantees to every citizen the right to worship God according to the dictates of his own conscience—or not to worship if he so chooses.

Does this set Christians at odds and at enmity with civil authority? By no means! In fact, by living an upright, honorable life the believer can be, and ought to be, a most exemplary citizen and member of his community, state, and nation. Our authority for this affirmation is the mandate of the Saviour when He said, "Render therefore unto Caesar the things which are Caesar's; and unto God the things that are God's" (Matt. 22:21).

Writing to the Roman believers, the apostle Paul further elucidates this great principle regarding relationships. He declared that civil authorities are "God's ministers" to do good and that the Christian owes the duty to be lawful and obedient "for conscience sake" (Rom. 13:4-6).

Thus all authority, which is essentially power—whether in mayors, governors, presidents, ministers, teachers, parents, and all others—derives from God. It is a delegation from Him. It is important to understand this, for unless we begin with the axiom that there is no authority except from God, everything else falls apart, and we are left with anarchy. The Almighty ordained it.

AUTHORITY IN THE CHURCH
For he is the minister of God to thee for good. Rom. 13:4.

To aid others as a servant is at the heart of all true ministry. Jesus definitively expressed the true enterprise of all authority when He said, ''I am among you as he that serveth.'' He also declared, ''He that is greatest among you shall be your servant'' (Matt. 23:11). There is no equivocation here.

The call to leadership in no way detracts from the authority or the majesty of the supreme Source of all sovereignty. So we sing with reverence:

> "Before Jehovah's awful throne,
> Ye nations, bow with sacred joy;
> Know that the Lord is God alone;
> He can create, and He destroy."

Heaven has provided that all authority exercised by temporal powers originates with God, whose agents they are. Thus all kings and presidents, all potentates and prime ministers, govern because God has delegated some of His authority to them to exercise temporarily. Because of this, the obligation devolves upon Christians to be obedient and subject to the laws of the land.

Similarly the authority of the church does not reside inherently in itself but in the Lord. The Saviour Himself founded the church on earth and delegated to it His authority to administer in His absence. God's servants are ordained of Him to do His work on earth. Thus the line of authority is duly established, on which account the faithful render cheerful obedience and proper respect to His ministers.

In times of ancient Israel, God was the supreme authority. As His representative, Moses administered the laws in His name. Lower officials: the Council of Seventy, the priests, and later the apostles functioned in their prescribed order. In church elections today the officers chosen receive their authority from God. Like the apostles, they administer the work of the church in God's name.

God's faithful agents are due the respect of the believers. An old Scotch prayer reads thus, ''God grant us the grace to respect our leaders; grant them the grace to deserve it.''

AUTHORITY IN THE HOME

Train up a child in the way he should go: and when he is old, he will not depart from it. Prov. 22:6.

The *New English Bible* translation of this verse suggests a more continuing upright life: "Start a boy on the right road, and even in old age he will not leave it." In either version the meaning is clear. The finger points to the years of youth as reliably predictive of the adult life. This proverb is so well known that for some, words may have blurred its significance. Still, its wide acceptance commends its meaning to our attention.

While it is not 100 percent certain that correct training in childhood guarantees, without question, an adult of commendable character, the correlation is so great as to be astounding.

Mrs. Hazel Woodruff tells of a young mother who took her 3-month-old baby to church. There she was asked why she brought so young a child. She replied, "I want him to get into the habit of going to church." When Mrs. Woodruff saw him assisting in the communion service forty years later, she recalled his mother's words.

For as long as I can remember a lively controversy has raged over which is the greater factor in character building: heredity or environment. Evidence indicates that both play a part. Whichever, the overpowering influence of the home on the child in tender years is above dispute. Some day every parent will be asked of God, "Where is the flock that was given thee, thy beautiful flock?" (Jer. 13:20).

Elder H. M. S. Richards tells of a thoughtful child who was asked why a certain tree in a garden was misshapen. He replied, "I s'pose someone stepped on it when it was a little fellow." All of us, especially parents, must be careful not to step on the little fellows.

Memory presents these lines from an unknown author:

"A pebble in the brooklet scant
Has changed the course of many a river.
A dewdrop on the baby plant
Has warped the mighty oak forever."

The fifth Commandment directs children to honor their parents. Because they stand in the place of God to their children, fathers and mothers are entitled to a degree of respect due no others. This entails obedience to parental authority. The combined influence of authority and love will ensure the child's obedience and make pleasant "the way he should go."

AUTHORITY IN THE SCHOOL

Go through the gates; prepare ye the way of the people; . . . lift up a standard for the people. Isa. 62:10.

The confirmed lines of authority under God embrace civil governments, church organizations, the home, and since the time of the prophet Samuel a system of education first launched as "the schools of the prophets," one at Ramah and one at Kirjath-jearim. During the days of Elijah and Elisha additional schools were set up at Bethel, Gilgal, Jericho, Samaria, and probably at other centers as well.

These schools were not to take the place of home education but were designed to carry forward the earlier instruction of the parents and the influence of the home. They were schools *of* the prophets and *by* the prophets, but not exclusively *for* the prophets. A careful reading of the sacred records reveals the subjects taught in these schools: the sacred Scriptures, sacred history, poetry, sacred music, and agricultural and industrial education. Subordinate subjects included writing, reading, and perhaps science and mathematics. This educational program proved to be highly successful. Great prosperity prevailed in Israel as the prophets, priests, sages, teachers, and lawyers trained in these schools assumed posts of leadership in the nation.

The purpose of this system of schools was "to serve as a barrier against the wide-spreading corruption, to provide for the mental and spiritual welfare of the youth, and to promote the prosperity of the nation." *(Education,* p. 46). The well-chosen teachers taught successfully that "righteousness exalteth a nation." Marvelous prosperity ensued. "It may be seriously doubted whether any nation has ever produced a group of religious and moral teachers comparable with those of Israel. . . . They were the public conscience, . . . the creators of public opinion, its most revered . . . teachers." *

Authority in these schools went quite unchallenged. Considering the well-chosen curriculum and the character of the carefully selected teachers and the dedication with which they taught, the tremendous respect and the profound appreciation accorded them are understandable. Where they are maintained, these same standards produce similar results today.

---

* F. H. Swift, *Education of Ancient Israel,* p. 37.

WORTH MORE THAN MONEY

Instruct those who are rich . . . not to fix their hopes on so uncertain a thing as money, but upon God. 1 Tim. 6:17, N.E.B.

Not many decades ago it was a prevailing practice for an editor or writer to collect and publish, usually in several volumes, a history of the county with which he was concerned. Many libraries in the county seats of America contain such histories. These compilations usually consist of a life sketch, often with a flattering picture, of each of the outstanding propertied citizens of the county. With a few exceptions their indifferent lives hardly warrant remembrance. Nor would they be included, except that they were almost all purse-proud possessors of property.

In his letter to Timothy, Paul recognizes that there were wealthy believers in the church in their day. These were neither included nor excluded because of their abundance, but their wealth exposed them to spiritual dangers from which their less affluent brethren were exempt. The apostle warned that the best things in this world are not for sale. They do not come with a price tag attached. It would be interesting, perhaps surprising, to sit down and list the really important things that money cannot buy.

Nearly everyone, whether owning a home or not, desires one. With money you can buy a house, but not a home. You can buy a stately, palatial residence, furnish it lavishly, and landscape it to perfection and still be without a home. Unless love, companionship, sympathy, and friendly neighbors go with the place, it remains an unresponsive building.

Some try to purchase friendship, but all the money in the world cannot buy one true friend. G. D. Prentiss wrote truly that "a friend that you have to buy won't be worth what you pay for him." Wealth may attract and surround its possessor with smiling, fair-weather friends like those that gathered around the prodigal son. But when the money is gone, these friends soon follow.

Money cannot buy happiness. One man, four times a millionaire, lost half his wealth. His future on only two million dollars looked so bleak that he leaped to his death from the top of his ten-story hotel.

Inner peace comes from God. Jesus said, "My peace I give unto you." Everyone yearns for greater security, but even gilt-edge investments sometimes fail. As society crumbles about us we realize that nothing is secure in this world but things money cannot buy. The eternal security found in God is free for the asking.

CHRIST IS HEAD OF THE CHURCH

The God of our Lord Jesus Christ, the father of glory, may give unto you the spirit of wisdom . . . that ye may know . . . what is the exceeding greatness of his power . . . which he wrought in Christ, when he raised him from the dead, and set him . . . in the heavenly places, far above . . . every name that is named . . . : and gave him to be the head over all things to the church, which is his body. Eph. 1:17-23.

This sublime declaration of the apostle Paul to the believers in Ephesus emphatically recognizes the exalted office of the risen Saviour as head of His church. The apostle was further inspired to declare that Christ sits at the right hand of the Father, "far above all principality, and power, and might, and dominion . . . in this world, . . . [and] also in that which is to come" (verse 21).

As sovereign Lord, Christ Jesus is superior to every heavenly and earthly power. He has supreme, universal authority quite above all other beings. As a result of His submission to the cross, His universal exaltation is supreme both in this age and in the age to come.

More important, as far as you and I are concerned, Christ is now and forever the head of His church on earth. This church body is composed of a group of human believers who have been inducted through repentance and baptism into this select and beloved organism, His church.

It is customary to think of a church as a building, constructed of brick, stone, wood, masonry, or adobe—as a local structure with perhaps a steeple and stained-glass windows. Paul likened the true church, the collective believers, to a stately edifice when he said to the Gentiles, "Ye are no more strangers and foreigners, but fellow citizens with the saints, and of the household of God; and are built upon the foundation of the apostles and prophets, Jesus Christ himself being the chief corner stone; in whom all the building fitly framed together groweth unto an holy temple in the Lord: In whom ye also are builded together for an habitation of God through the Spirit" (Eph. 2:19-22).

It is a priceless privilege to have Christ unite with His church through the Holy Spirit. His indwelling quickens and inspires each member to overcome temptation and to triumph over all the beggarly elements of the world. Christ's living presence meeting with the assembled believers lends sanctity to the meeting place and inspires reverence there. Let us cherish this precious privilege!

ONE HEAD AND ONE BODY

There is one body, and one Spirit . . . ; one Lord, one faith, one baptism, one God and Father of all, who is above all, and through all, and in you all. Eph. 4:4-6.

It is an exciting pleasure to observe closely the concentrated efforts of the contestants at a track meet. It is thrilling when the winners win to see the ecstatic expressions on their faces as they are awarded their prizes. It is fascinating and also informative to notice the symmetry and grace of a well-formed body, with every muscle alert and moving in consummate harmony. Such perfection is not soon forgotten.

In the above verses from Ephesians, the apostle Paul explains how Jesus Christ dwells within His church by the power of the Holy Spirit. After representing the body of the believers as a church edifice, he continues to elucidate by using another simile: the human body with the head representing Christ and the members as parts, all smoothly functioning together.

The manner in which the church body is developed is exemplified by the events of that great day of Pentecost (see Acts 2). Peter preached a powerful sermon that memorable day, convincingly declaring that he and his fellow disciples were eyewitnesses of the Resurrection; that they had seen Jesus alive on many occasions after His death at Golgotha; and that it was indeed the Christ who had been crucified. Thousands in the crowd who heard Peter's inspired words were stricken in their hearts. They asked worriedly, "Men and brethren, what shall we do?"

Peter responded by urging his convinced hearers to repent and be baptized and receive God's Holy Spirit. He made it clear that by this induction into the church they would become members of His body. Those who accepted this appeal were "added unto them." Thus they were joined to the other believers and received the Holy Spirit, the Comforter, as promised by the Saviour before His ascension. In this way, more than three thousand souls were received into the church.

Paul expounded this blessed relationship to the Corinthians by saying that "as the body is one, and hath many members, and all the members of that body, being many, are one body: so also is Christ" (1 Cor. 12:12). Notice that this is no artificial designation of any humanly devised body but an accurate expression of Scripture describing those who are members of the church, the body; Christ being the head. In this sacred relationship, and in no other, is there salvation.

UNITING TOGETHER

O God of our salvation, . . . gather us together, . . . that we may give thanks to thy holy name, and glory in thy praise. 1 Chron. 16:35.

David's first psalm did not first appear in the book of Psalms but in 1 Chronicles 16. Our text for today is a part of it. This is a hymn of gratitude which, in order to be most effectual and offer maximum praise, required the people to come together and sing with mingled voices. Their chorale, or paean of praise, must have made the countryside ring. Their anthem of joy was a delight to the God of their salvation.

Many melodious voices singing in harmony are much sweeter and carry farther than a solo, however talented and well-trained the singer. In this, as in many other things, numbers make for strength. The principle applies well beyond the music department. A delegation, for example, is more impressive than a single suppliant, and a petition bearing a thousand signatures carries more weight than a lone request.

It has been said that ours is a nation of joiners. I was amazed recently to see listed hundreds of organizations—local, state, and national—with literally thousands and thousands of members. Obviously people take great pride in "belonging." Comparatively speaking, my memberships are few: as a boy, the 4-H Club; later the national honorary historical society Phi Alpha Theta; still later the American Historical Association, Rotary International, and a few others. I had the experience one time to be named an "honorary Kentucky Colonel." Each organization issues its own insignia, pin, or button. I wear mine occasionally—with pride.

However much men and women enjoy belonging to an alumni association, the DAR, the American Legion, the Masonic order, or any other such group, each of these memberships terminates with the death of the member. Apparently there is no exception.

One mystical organism, however—the body of believers, of whom Christ is the head—stands above and beyond the vicissitudes of the world. It extends over all the years. Membership in this choice fraternity is voluntary. For admittance, there are no conditions of age, race, or prior standing. The noblest of earth hold membership in it. Once listed, no name, except by one's own will, can ever be erased, for they are all inscribed in the books of heaven. Someday not far from now will come the rare opportunity to examine that list. If you are not yet enrolled, why not join now?

MOODY CHRISTIANS

A merry heart maketh a cheerful countenance: but by sorrow of the heart the spirit is broken. Prov. 15:13.

Some people have sunny dispositions. We can count on their cheerfulness regardless of weather or the problems of the day. Others I know tend to be morose and gloomy, their lot always a sad, discouraging one. Speaking to a friend of one such person, I ventured that "he has at least an even disposition."

My friend replied, "Even. Yes. Gloomy even when the sun is shining." We encounter both types of people every day.

There is another class, good people generally but up and down like a yo-yo. One day, buoyant beyond utterance and viewing the Promised Land from Pisgah's height. Soon, perhaps the very next day, their souls sink to the depths and their feet into the Slough of Despond. When this mood overtakes them, they cast a dark shadow over themselves and everyone else.

Controlled by their feelings, these moody Christians are like a candle, burning bright and clear one minute, then faint and flickering the next. Their unstable moods are often born of selfishness denied, of sullen, unforgiving tempers that seek to draw others into their castles of despair.

There are other moods to avoid: The mood of sullen indifference leads to dabbling in sin until the possessor drifts away from forgiveness and the hope of heaven. The mood of suspicion tempts one to think that every man's hand, and even God, is against him.

King Saul became a man of moods: a cordial friend today, a bitter enemy tomorrow. Envy and jealousy drove him farther and farther from God until there was no hope for his crazed mind and shriveled soul. He died a sad and shameful death.

In my earlier years I was occasionally subject to "the blues." At such times any minor annoyance or disappointment loomed large out of all proportion. Most people experience seasons of despair. Youth particularly suffer distress and trials, unable through tear-dimmed eyes to see the sun beyond the clouds. The Scriptures relate how some of noble faith felt depressed at times too.

All Christians need to see that the severity of our troubles is nowhere nearly so important as the spirit in which we meet them. The mood of despondency must not be allowed to gain the ascendency. Faith unleashed can triumph over all our moods.

PASSING THROUGH TUNNELS
Whereas I was blind, now I see. John 9:25.

One day in spring I was going from Chicago to San Francisco by train. Beside me, as my traveling companion, sat my little daughter, Dana. It was a never-to-be-forgotten trip. Threading its way up a Colorado mountainside, the train suddenly entered a tunnel. Without a word, Dana, who was standing in the seat at my side, tightened her arm about my neck. As suddenly as darkness had fallen when we entered the tunnel, we came out into bright sunlight. My little girl put her face close to mine and exclaimed, "Daddy, now it's tomorrow!"

Life is like going through tunnels on a train. From liquid sunshine and in delightful surroundings, suddenly and unexpectedly we are plunged into midnight darkness. We have entered one of life's tunnels.

Some Rocky Mountain tunnels are long. Yet if the train keeps going, we have confidence that we shall eventually reach the light. So also is life. Trusting God, we know there is light ahead.

The man who spoke our text was born blind. For him there was no light until he met Jesus. Something wonderful always happens when a person really meets Jesus.

Seeing this blind man, Jesus came up to him, lay a mud plaster over his eyes and said, "Go, wash in the pool of Siloam." He obeyed. Out of a lifetime of darkness he came into noonday light. When he was asked about this miracle, he said, "I went and washed, and I received sight."

Because what Jesus told him to do seemed foolish to some, this happy, healed man was ridiculed. And because he gave credit to Christ for his good fortune, the angry Pharisees "reviled him" and "cast him out." But he could see. There would have been no light had he refused to obey Jesus. Neither is there spiritual light for any who refuse to obey God.

When the Lord's obedient servants do His bidding, ridicule and opposition usually follow. Persecution comes next. All who go resolutely from darkness to light can expect mistreatment and abuse. The fearful, who are unwilling to face such hardness, are destined to continue in darkness.

Whenever anyone experiences the personal healing and saving power of Jesus, no argument can convince him that he is mistaken. He knows better. There is nothing like an infilling of the Holy Spirit to bring the recipient out of darkness into God's sunlight of love.

EXPECTATION OR HOPE?

"For I know the plans I have for you," declares the Lord, "plans to prosper you and not to harm you, plans to give you hope and a future." Jer. 29:11, N.I.V.

Some years ago the noted economist Stuart Chase, wrote *The Most Probable World*. In this captivating book the author discusses the population explosion, energy, nuclear weaponry and confrontation, one world, and many other pressing problems currently confronting and bewildering mankind. He made carefully calculated predictions for the immediate and long-term future. Many of his sophisticated prognostications have already proved out; many others have proved to be far from the mark.

The favorite, current occupation of many popular writers is making bold, staggering predictions about the home, the family, education, health, the economy, government, whatever. Whether we agree or not, all of these projected visions of the future influence our thinking. So pervasive has become his anxious absorption with the frightening future that colleges are developing courses in futuristics. The big question seems no longer to be ''What is the world coming to?'' but rather ''What is coming to the world?''

The followers of Jesus ought also to be involved in futuristics. Not to be is to deny the power of His continuing watchcare and revelation. As we peer into the obscure future do we expect or hope? There is a distinct difference. Hope is of God, a spiritual confidence that trusts in His goodness to do what is best for our eternal happiness. Hope is always centered on the Giver rather than the gift. In many ways hope stands in contradiction to what many perceive to be the present reality. Its opposite is despair, always wearing a forced smile of resignation but with no power to give life.

Expectation is different. It looks to satisfaction from a predictable process, what we think we have a right to. To live by expectation alone is to be unlinked from hope. Christ is the person in whom Christians hope. This hope exceeds all anticipation. The Christian must value it, cherish it, and in essence realize it already, according to the promises of God. This is our hope of glory.

HE PLANS FOR US IN LOVE

Blessed be the God and Father of our Lord Jesus Christ, which . . . hath begotten us . . . unto a lively hope by the resurrection of Jesus . . . to an inheritance . . . reserved in heaven for you. 1 Peter 1:3, 4.

In the present unprecedented international confusion, when world leaders admit that they are baffled, the individual feels so puny and ineffectual that he is tempted to cry out, "it's hopeless. There's nothing I can do." All that is decent and upright in him protests against the brutal abuses of power in nations and among men. It is no wonder that many settle in helpless resignation, pondering whether any one person or his individual faith has any significance at all.

The fact is that it is only the individual that counts with God. The church is the apple of His eye only because it consists of a communion of individual hearts. Our God is a personal God. He maintains a relation with me quite as personal as if I were the only one for whom Christ died.

The Holy Spirit dwells in the heart of every believer and provides him with a foretaste of heaven. This indwelling Spirit is called the earnest, or pledge, of the inheritance awaiting God's people through His grace (see Eph. 1:13, 14). In Bible times the word *earnest* was used with reference to the bridegroom's betrothal gift to his fiancée. It was a token that she would soon be a joint owner with him of all his possessions. Likewise, the joy shed in the heart of every Christian by the Holy Spirit is a sampling of the inheritance God will bestow upon His bride, the church, after Jesus comes again.

When we give way to dark and haunting fears, even to the possibility of nuclear obliteration, we betray our faith in the Lord Jesus, for He says, "The thoughts that I think toward you" are "thoughts of peace, and not of evil." An earthly father, in disclosing to his son some special favor, says, "I've been thinking about you, son." Our heavenly Father thinks of us in the same way. His plans for us are so manifold and magnificent that we scarcely can comprehend them. Like the lame man at the Gate Beautiful, we tend to think of life only in terms of beggary.

God's majestic plans make every believer a child of the King. This relieves us of feelings of inferiority and enables us to exult as we diligently serve Him.

WHERE DO YOU LIVE?

They said unto him, Rabbi, . . . where dwellest thou? John 1:38.

The day after John baptized Jesus in the river Jordan, he looked upon Jesus, and, pointing, proclaimed, "Behold the Lamb of God!" Andrew and John heard these words and followed Jesus. When He turned to inquire why, they asked, "Where dwellest thou?" He took them to His place, and they "abode with him that day," which was exactly what they wanted. As it turned out, this was the greatest single day of their lives. This one day with Jesus made Andrew and John His devoted, lifelong disciples. Those few hours with Him changed the whole course of their lives. They were never the same again.

There is no record that anyone else ever went to visit Jesus at His dwelling place. This was because He had no home, not even a place to lay His head. But this lack has never been a barrier to any who covet converse with Him. Now, as then, men cannot visit Him at His home, but He can visit us where we live. He says, "Behold, I stand at the door, and knock: if any man hear my voice, and open the door, I will come in" (Rev. 3:20). When we open the door it becomes a very personal visit. Paul expressed the wish "that Christ may dwell in your hearts" (Eph. 3:17).

It doesn't make much difference what kind of house you live in. It may be large or small, old or new. It may be a mansion or a cottage, a row house, a duplex, a condominium, or maybe a mobile home. It may be built of brick, wood, or stone, it may be trim and neat, with flowers at the door, or it may be on a side street with no flowers at all. The outward appearance is not what counts, but the character of those who live within.

Who are your guests? Is Jesus among them? He longs to be. When He knocks at your door of flesh, He may ask, "Who lives here? Who is that looking out the window?" And if you invite Him in, He will not go away without leaving a blessing, as He did in the long ago when He called at the homes of Zacchaeus and Lazarus.

Jesus' visits are the same today. When He knocks at the door of your heart will you let Him in?

HAVE YOU CONSIDERED LOVE?

Beloved, let us love one another: for love is of God; and every one that loveth is born of God. 1 John 4:7.

Have you ever paused to consider how vital is the role of love in every aspect and act of life? As you reflect upon it you come to appreciate why love is what "makes the world go round." Love is an energizing emotion with which even the sun, in all its glory and overwhelming power, cannot compare. Philosophers have gone to great lengths to explain this most pervasive of all emotions. Poets innumerable have racked their minds and exhausted their vocabularies in unsatisfactory attempts to describe it accurately. All of this serves to emphasize love's preeminence. On all levels of existence, love is unquestionably the "grand emotion." And, as has been proved a thousand times, when love is done, life loses all relevance, meaning, and purpose. As its last vestige ceases, life itself dies. Francis W. Bourdillon has expressed it thus:

"The night has a thousand eyes,
The day but one;
Yet the light of the bright world dies
With the dying sun.

"The mind has a thousand eyes,
And the heart but one;
Yet the light of a whole life dies
When its love is done."

This grandest of all emotions, love, comprehends so many interrelated elements and is so all-embracing that to fully enjoy all its benefits and to appreciate its subtle nuances we must try very hard to rightly understand it. Basically our English word *love* embraces three different concepts: concupiscence, or sensual love; filial, or affectionate family love; and brotherly love, a favorable feeling for others motivated more by principle than by sentiment. All three components of love are surely God-given, in order that man, as a child of God, might properly employ them and in this employment experience the finest joy and greatest happiness, as was intended by the loving Creator.

The apostle John had this third principle of loving in mind when he wrote, "Let us love one another." This is the love that joins Christian hearts together. It leads the possessor to follow the golden rule and sacrifice for the good of others. Let us cultivate this divine love.

THE MAGNITUDE OF GOD'S LOVE

That Christ may dwell in your hearts by faith; that ye . . . may be able to comprehend . . . what is the breadth, and length, and depth, and height; and to know the love of Christ, which passeth knowledge. Eph. 3:17-19.

This all-encompassing affirmation emphatically declares that the love of God extends beyond the farthest reach of human understanding. Even so, our finite minds can grasp a limited perception of that affectionate, all-embracing regard as we contemplate these confident assertions. In breadth His love takes in the peoples of all the world, for "God so loved the world" (John 3:16). In extent His love has no date of origin nor will it have any conclusion. "God is love." His tender attachment is thus expressed in the perpetual present tense—indissoluble, unchangeable, everlasting. In height, like the waters of the flood overtopped earth's highest mountains, so His love more than covers our highest sins. Its depth touches the bottomless pit of sin and debauchery, of sorrow and need. In all the universe there is nothing with which to fittingly compare God's love.

The apostle John employs hyperbole when he prays that we may attain to a knowledge of the knowledge-surpassing love of Christ. While we cannot gauge Christ's love, we can consider it. We can gather some idea of it by observing human love. There are many touching examples.

Whatever else may be said of President Andrew Jackson, he left an unsurpassed example of conjugal love in his devotion to his faithful wife, Rachel. And when word came that she was mortally ill he drove his carriage horses furiously in hope of reaching the Hermitage while she still lived. On arrival he strode in and mounted the steps to her bedside. She had only just then breathed her last. Attendants removed the wedding ring she had worn since their wedding day. Inscribed within they found the words, "Love is eternal."

For the most part we can understand, appreciate, and highly esteem human love. But the depthless love of God extends far beyond all finite comprehension.

THE LOVE OF FATHER AND SON

[Jesus therefore said to them,] The Father loves the Son and shows him everything that he does himself. John 5:20, Phillips.

Since we know that God is love, the supreme love uniting the heavenly Father with His Son, Jesus, should not surprise us. The Saviour's eternally close relationship with the Father was divinely attested at Jesus' baptism. It was the Father's voice from heaven that proclaimed, "This is my beloved Son, in whom I am well pleased" (Matt. 3:17). Identical words of approval and affection were voiced by the Almighty at the Transfiguration (chap. 17:5). And at the close of Jesus' ministry, as He departed from the Temple for the last time, the Father's voice was heard again in reassurance that the Son's imminent sacrifice was acceptable and that His name would be glorified (John 12:28).

In the preceding councils of eternity, Father and Son were associated in an everlasting fellowship through which the world was made (chap. 1:3). This intimate relationship was not broken but was rather intensified, if possible, while Jesus walked among men in His incarnate state. Here in this world, for the divine love of both Father and Son, Jesus "took upon him the form of a servant," lived as a human being, and submitted to death on the cross. Jesus' prayer life kept close His relation to the Father, and during His ministry He explained their cooperation in these words, "My Father worketh hitherto, and I work." When requested to manifest the Father more clearly, He said, "He that hath seen me hath seen the Father."

Nothing is clearer in the gospel story than that the perfect love between Jesus and God the Father forged a confidence and a trust so strong that even the supreme tragedy at Golgotha made no difference. In Jesus' matchless prayer in Gethsemane the divine will shows through clearly as the dominating motive in Jesus' life on earth. Thomas W. Manson wrote: "In this prayer His absolute trust in the Father and complete obedience to His will overcame the natural shrinkage from the approaching ordeal." This unbreakable trust demonstrated that "perfect love casteth out fear." And when our love toward the Father is based, as was Jesus', on constant communion and complete surrender to His will, our fears will fade because we know that "all things work together for good to them that love God" (Rom. 8:28).

THE SAVIOUR'S UNDYING LOVE

Now before the feast of the passover, when Jesus knew that his hour was come that he should depart out of this world unto the Father, having loved his own which were in the world, he loved them unto the end. John 13:1.

At last the hour of the Passover feast had come. Century on century the sacrificial lamb had been dutifully offered as an act of faith that the Messiah would come. Now the Lamb of God was about to offer Himself as a sacrifice for sinners. As the prophetic hour drew nearer, Jesus' thoughts were with His disciples. His clear eyes veiled in the loving sadness of parting, He said, "With desire I have desired to eat this passover with you before I suffer" (Luke 22:15). For a few precious minutes He turned His eyes from Calvary, gazed affectionately upon these who were His friends, and gave voice to His love for them. He loved them to the end. His controversy with evil was a fight to the finish. But toward His disciples it was love to the finish.

Up to that moment such love had not been expressed by any words of Christ to His friends: such a longing for the day of perfect union, for the ultimate feast destined to follow so great a sublimation. They knew that He loved them. But until that hour their bruised and troubled hearts had not realized how deep and poignant was that love. Willing to submit Himself to the cross through the love He had for all mankind, He had ardently desired to eat this climactic Passover with these few who were His closest friends. Someone has said that as He disclosed this love, His face "shone with that noble sadness which is strangely like joy."

About to be torn from those He cherished, Jesus wished to give them a supreme proof of His love. All along He had loved them with a love too bountiful for their narrow hearts. Now, although He was their Master, He humbled Himself and knelt to wash their feet. Only a mother or a slave would have done it, the mother for her child, the slave for his master. By this act He left them a memory of complete humiliation and of perfect love. This love is ours to share.

> "O dearly, dearly has He loved!
> And we must love Him too,
> And trust in His redeeming blood,
> And try His works to do."
>
> —Cecil Frances Alexander

THE WONDER OF GOD'S LOVE

For God so loved the world, that he gave his only begotten Son, that whosoever believeth in him should not perish, but have everlasting life. John 3:16.

This is the most wonderful and best-loved verse in all the Bible. There are reasons enough—and more—to wonder, all compressed in this choice verse. One is the wonder that God loved and loves the world. We can believe that He made the world because, except for the ravages of sin, it is so beautiful. We can even believe that He created the heavenly hosts, for He called them all by name and brought them out by number. By comparison, how small is our world! Yet it, too, is belted, encompassed, and entirely surrounded by the love of God.

We wonder too that the only begotten Son of God would come to this earth and dwell with men. Here He was the child of Bethlehem and the Carpenter of Nazareth. It is here where He incorporated the human with the divine and on this earth we walk the paths that were trodden by His blessed feet. Our world thus became the pivot and focus of the universe, not only for time, but for eternity as well.

The wonder of God's love will continue into eternity. "Tongue cannot utter it; pen cannot portray it. You may meditate upon it every day of your life; . . . you may summon every power and capability that God has given you, in the endeavor to comprehend the love and compassion of the heavenly Father; and yet there is an infinity beyond. You may study that love for ages; yet you can never fully comprehend the length and the breadth, the depth and the height, of the love of God in giving His Son to die for the world. Eternity itself can never fully reveal it."—*Testimonies,* vol. 5, p. 740.

In our text is still another wonder: that eternal life is reachable by "whosoever." Our finite minds can comprehend time. But an endless, eternal life of love and light and joy without end we can only accept by faith—and wonder at it. This "whosoever" in our text is like a blank line in a fabulous deed. How wonderful that we can write our name on that line, and by doing so we can make this greatest of all promises our own!

WHILE WE WERE YET SINNERS

But God commendeth his love toward us, in that, while we were yet sinners, Christ died for us. Rom. 5:8.

A highly successful evangelist announces his campaigns with this arresting title: *Amazing Facts*. With compelling logic he shows that the most amazing fact of history is that God loves sinners.

It is understandable that a heroic man might die for his friend. Although to do so demands love unlimited, men have done so. "Greater love hath no man than this, that a man lay down his life for his friends" (John 15:13). "Scarcely for a righteous man will one die: yet peradventure for a good man some would even dare to die" (Rom. 5:7). Few indeed have ever attained to such self-sacrificing devotion.

To die willingly for a friend requires the acme of human, selfless love. But to die for your enemies who are sinners is Godlike. Because of our narrowness of mind we find this hard to appreciate or even to understand.

> "There's a wideness in God's mercy,
>   Like the wideness of the sea;
>   There's a kindness in His justice,
>   Which is more than liberty."
>
> —F. W. Faber

Some years ago a devoted mother we knew was left a widow with a headstrong, heedless son. She could not control him. As a wayward teen-ager, with dissolute companions he engaged in various villainies in total disregard of the prayers and the pleadings of his sorely distressed mother. Taken in armed robbery, he was tried, convicted, and sentenced to a term in the state prison. The sympathy of the neighborhood for this disgraced mother exceeded their antipathy toward her felonious son. In their compassion my parents took this woman to the railroad station to bid him goodbye. I went along. Even now I can recall vividly the tear-stained anguish on her face as she held her manacled son in a parting embrace. She might have forgotten him, but she never did. She had borne him. Nor does God ever forget His wayward children of earth. Christ died for them.

"All the paternal love which has come down from generation to generation through the channel of human hearts, all the springs of tenderness which have opened in the souls of men, are but as a tiny rill to the boundless ocean when compared with the infinite, exhaustless love of God."—*Testimonies,* vol. 5, p. 740.

GOD'S LOVE OVERCOMES TROUBLE

Because he hath set his love upon me, therefore will I deliver him: I will set him on high, because he hath known my name. Ps. 91:14.

This amazing assurance of personal care and protection is made to God's children, not because any of us are deserving, but because He loves us in spite of all our frailties and failures.

The psalmist set his love upon his God. We need often to consider where our love is set. Is it on God or on ourselves? Do we know Him? Do we know His name? Some do not love Him simply because they do not know Him. To truly know Him is to love Him, for He first loved us. And He manifested that love in Jesus through sacrifice to salvation. "Thou shalt call his name JESUS: for he shall save his people from their sins" (Matt. 1:21).

A few years ago, in company with Dr. Alstrup Johnson, a long-time friend, I checked in for PanAm Flight 843, San Francisco to Honolulu. The Boeing 707 four-engine jet held a full complement of passengers and a crew of ten. It was a bright July day, and with a feeling of confidence we bade my wife and daughter goodbye and went aboard. There was nothing to indicate trouble ahead. The takeoff was routine, and within minutes the giant plane was rocketing westward toward the vast Pacific Ocean. At that instant, Flight 843 became a nightmare. I felt a shock, then a shudder, and looking out from my window seat over the wing, I saw the right outboard engine aflame. The plane inclined sharply to the left, yawed wildly to the right, and the fire-alarm bell sounded. Terror-stricken passengers screamed. As we watched, the fiery engine burned loose and hurtled to the earth, leaving the stricken wing curling upward in ghastly trailing flames. Seconds later almost half the weakened wing fell off. Aerodynamically, Flight 843 should have crashed.

My companion and I clasped hands and prayed earnestly that God's will would be done. A half hour later, with piloting later praised as "masterful," Captain Kimes set the crippled plane down smoothly at Travis Air Force Base. Asked about it, he replied with feeling, "I had help from above." I agree with Captain Kimes.

We felt from this harrowing episode that God had "set His love" upon us. May this lesson come to all who read of our experience.

GOD'S LOVE EVOKES OUR RESPONSE

The Lord hath appeared of old unto me, saying, Yea, I have loved thee with an everlasting love: therefore with lovingkindness have I drawn thee. Jer. 31:3.

A personable young man I knew was thinking of marriage. Then he met and gave special attention to a talented, attractive young woman in our community. Because of her admirable character, gracious ways, and reputation for integrity, she had become a favorite of young and old. When she responded warmly to his attentions, the young man began to waver. Coming to me for advice, he said, "She is all you say, but I am not really sure I love her."

I quoted to him my father's oft-repeated remark, "There is nothing sweeter in all the world than the unselfish love of a faithful woman." He went away in a thoughtful mood. Later, after their very happy marriage, I asked him what had induced him to accept her. He said, "She loved me, and I knew it. I could not keep from loving her too. I simply could not let her go."

True love begets love. The Saviour reached to the heart of the matter when He admonished His followers to love God. "And thou shalt love the Lord thy God with all thy heart, and with all thy soul, and with all thy mind, and with all thy strength: this is the first commandment" (Mark 12:30).

God's everlasting love for spiritual Israel is a most stupendous thought. Before we had any objective being, He loved us. The moment we were born we began to live in the love of God. The ray of light from a distant star has been streaming down the measureless path of space long before earth was peopled by man. But before the light wave that made that starlight shine in the heavens was started in the ether by the pulsations from that remote star, God was already loving us. What a vast eternity of love!

In His constant, conscious passion the Lord yearns with strong ardor over His earthborn children. This love, which is stronger than all the lusts of the flesh, meant Calvary, nothing less. That love was bestowed in the ultimate at the cross. When we understand and accept this ultimate in divine love, He will set [us] up on high above the Slough of Despond, above the fog of doubt and fear. May we realize our sacred responsibility to cherish, to respond to, and exemplify His love in every aspect of life.

YOU NEED LOVE

He that loveth not knoweth not God; for God is love. 1 John 4:8.

Love has so many facets and has been described in so many ways by so many people that we tend to think of it as a common endowment, like sunlight and air, from the "everywhere spirit." Yet, when the last spoken word has receded into silence and the ink on a thousand pages has blurred and faded, we still must recognize love as the most essential ingredient of life. The Christian enjoying buoyant health needs love to sustain the optimistic glow. The little child, seeking assurance, needs it as he comes to his mother, inquiring, "Mamma, do you love me?" The hard-pressed student and the overburdened worker need love to energize their flagging efforts. The aged need love to relieve the monotony and pain of their loneliness and give them something to live for. And distraught patients in mental hospitals all over the world sit hopelessly in psychiatric wards because somehow love has been leached out of their hearts.

The famous psychiatrist Dr. Karl Menninger said, "Love is the best medicine for the ills of mankind; we could all live if we had love." Suicide notes confirm this. Those who, despairing of life, end it for themselves, particularly the young, usually blame this last desperate act on their total bankruptcy of affection. The most frequent phrase to be found in these pathetic farewells to life is "No one cares for me."

Unfortunately, the mentally disordered are not the only ones who suffer from this sad deficiency of love, which is the severest famine overspreading the world today. You can observe the symptoms in the faces of people in the street, in offices, in classrooms, in stores, even in church. Loveless faces look out to us in endless variety everywhere.

This innate longing for love is so intensely personal that it is usually hidden or disguised so that the ordinary passer-by does not suspect that it exists at all. Sometimes it takes the form of a defensive mask that is mistaken for selfishness. We hear it said of such a one: "He loves only himself." But this is not so. Deep down he likely loathes himself and needs love desperately.

When we turn discerning eyes inward, what we see is apt to make us wonder that God can love us at all. But He loves us, not because we are lovable but because He is loving. Let us love Him, for He first loved us.

EXPANDING OUR LOVE TO GOD

Jesus said unto him, Thou shalt love the Lord thy God with all thy heart, and with all thy soul, and with all thy mind. Matt. 22:37.

The Master said explicitly that the first commandment of His kingdom is to love God supremely. Yet many who wish to do so find it difficult to love God. Why is this? The reason is that man, in his fallen state, feels at enmity with his Maker. Consequently, in various ways, members of our rebellious race dislike God, distrust Him, resist Him, and try, in every possible way, to avoid and escape Him. Many professing Christians, too, often feel alienated from, and at variance with, their Creator. Martin Luther once said that the separation by sin is so great that man has developed a passion against God. The unbelieving H. G. Wells called God "The Antagonist." Elder Walter Beach tells of a faithless surgeon who declared that, if he ever appeared before the Most High, he would present Him with a cancerous bone and demand an explanation.

Such volatile enmity toward God is seldom voiced. Yet, in the face of the Saviour's admonition to love God, how few seek Him or hold fast to Him as they do to their earthly treasures! Our desire for Him is infrequently felt and less often expressed. For this reason a shallow spirituality prevails to the point of being almost a mockery. Many minds are so filled with thoughts of self, of daydreams and idle fancies and of the problems of the day, that neither time nor room remains to think of God. Professing Christians absorbed in such thoughts can well ask themselves, "If my love of God were real, would not my mind dwell upon Him?"

Most people consider love to be a function of the emotions, with little relationship to the intellect. Yet our text exhorts us to love the Lord with the mind. In truth we can love God if we have a mind to. Francis G. Peabody expressed it thus: "It is a great thing to love God with the heart and soul, to let the emotions of gratitude to Him or in joy in His world run free; but to rise in sympathetic interpretation of His laws, to think God's thoughts after Him, and be moved by the high emotions which are stirred by exalted ideas—to love God, that is to say, with the mind—that . . . is the highest function of human life." *

---

* *Mornings in the College Chapel*, p. 175.

A MEMBER OF THE FAMILY

Behold, what manner of love the Father hath bestowed upon us, that we should be called the sons of God. 1 John 3:1.

It was as His Son that God sent Christ into the world. Many times throughout His ministry Jesus emphasized this close relationship. He also frequently called His disciples "my brethren," signifying a family connection they could understand and appreciate. He specifically taught this close family tie in the touching parable of the prodigal son. Although this ungrateful, disgruntled son was long away from his father's house, he knew all along that he was his father's son. And knowing the changeless persistence of that paternal love, he finally "came to himself" and returned to his father, whom he should have never left in the first place.

The graphic experience of the prodigal son is that of all sinners who, fortunately, before it is too late, become reconciled to God. This includes you and me, for "all have sinned." By our disobedience we broke the ties of love. We rejected our inheritance, choosing willfully "to enjoy the pleasures of sin for a season." Soon followed bewilderment, then disillusion, as we wandered in the wastelands of despair. We had sold out to the enemy. He rewarded us with swine for companions. To stave off starvation, we partook of husks, only to find them bitter in our mouths. We were clothed in filthy rags. In this sordid state we could find no hope of betterment in ourselves. We had relinquished our place in the family of God.

But when we turned our footsteps back toward our Father's house, He came running. Even our emaciation and rags could not dissuade His embrace. This compassion melted both hearts. In tears we asked to come back as a servant. Then the Father said, "My son." We could scarcely believe our ears. Once more we became "sons of God." The reconciliation was complete. We were restored to the family of heaven.

This changeless love of the Father is the power that draws modern prodigals to Him and their heavenly home. In this way the alien and the stranger, wandering unhappily and unloved in a world of sin, can "come home," where—received with open arms—he can be restored to his proper place in the family of God.

This wonderful message of salvation offered freely to all men is the "good news" that Christians are privileged to proclaim everywhere.

"With arms wide open He'll welcome you.
It is no secret what God can do."

OUR EXAMPLE IN ALL THINGS

I have given you an example, that ye should do as I have done. John 13:15.

The entire life of Jesus was an object lesson, a pattern to follow. It was a living manifestation of the character of the heavenly Father. Since the Saviour is our example, "it would be well for us to spend a thoughtful hour each day in contemplation of the life of Christ."—*The Desire of Ages,* p. 83.

As an academy teacher, it was my duty to teach as best I could whatever classes were assigned to me by the principal. For three years my teaching included a class in New Testament history, which was largely a study of the life of Christ. To get my students to study, the inspirational book quoted above was chosen for auxiliary reading. However, instead of routinely assigning the volume to be read, chapter by chapter, we concentrated attention on topics. Each student was to find and paraphrase references dealing with a specific subject and list them for class discussion. This simple procedure stimulated interest and proved to be a spiritual blessing to the members of the class—and to the teacher as well.

One highly rewarding subject proved to be "The Manifestation of Christ's Love." A sampling of the statements the students picked out appears below, together with the page references concerned.

The Saviour always manifested a loving interest in men (86).

He relieved every case of suffering that He saw (87).

He spoke words of sympathy when He saw people bearing heavy burdens (90).

He showed an interest in men's secular affairs (151).

He spoke with such sympathetic tenderness that sinners took no offense when they realized their humiliating position (173).

When men refused His message of peace, His heart was torn to the very depths (255).

His love was not limited to any one race (402).

His mission was not to condemn the world but to save it (462).

His gentle, kindly manner won the love and confidence of little children (511).

His enemies read love, benevolence, and quiet dignity in His calm, solemn face (581).

The love of God flowed from Him in irrepressible streams (678).

Jesus is our example in all things.

THEY HEARD HIM GLADLY
And the common people heard him gladly. Mark 12:37.

In his popular story *A Christmas Carol,* Charles Dickens aptly depicts various classes of people: the rich, the poor, the weak, the strong, the greedy, and the generous-hearted. None is more appealingly portrayed than crippled Tiny Tim, whose loving heart embraced everybody. In James Whitcomb Riley's words,

> " 'God bless us every one! prayed Tiny Tim
> Crippled, and dwarfed of body, yet so tall
> Of soul, we tiptoe earth to look on him,
> High towering over all.
>
> * * * * *
>
> "And thus he prayed, 'God bless us every one!'—
> Enfolding all the creeds within the span
> Of his child-heart; and so, despising none,
> Was nearer saint than man.''

What a touching illustration this is of the spirit that the Saviour manifested in all His relationships! His love was not awarded according to wealth or standing, position or influence. He looked upon all men, high and low, as candidates for His kingdom. In the expression of His countenance and the music of His voice the common people sensed the irresistible drawing power of His presence.

Christ accepted all who came to Him—as they were and where they were. He could have restricted His ministry to the "nice" people, those having the approval of their peers. He could have ignored the common people in favor of the well-dressed whose reputations were as spotless as their attire. Consider the rude, unlettered fishermen He called at the lakeside. What a contrast they made when compared with the learned scribes and the proud Pharisees! Consider Mary Magdalene. He might have considered it jeopardizing to His influence to talk to a street walker. Was it wise to waste His time on sordid chaff when He needed every precious minute to devote to His prodigious task on earth?

Fortunately for the tarnished Mary—and for us—the Saviour does not restrict His love. It was extended as freely to the beggar and the thief as to anyone else. His love knows no barriers. It does not condemn but reaches out. Only as we comprehend its boundless abundance can we reflect its fullness to others.

THE BONDS OF CHRISTIAN LOVE

Finally, be ye all of one mind, having compassion one of another; love as brethren, be pitiful, be courteous: not rendering . . . railing for railing: but . . . blessing. 1 Peter 3:8, 9.

Of the closeness of Christian fellowship at Pentecost inspiration records: "They rejoiced in the sweetness of communion with saints. They were tender, thoughtful, self-denying, willing to make any sacrifice for the truth's sake. In their daily association with one another, they revealed the love that Christ had enjoined upon them. By unselfish words and deeds they strove to kindle this love in other hearts."—*Acts of the Apostles,* p. 547.

This is the kind of love God's indwelling Spirit fosters among believers. Of the special sense in which this love should be cherished, the apostle John wrote, "He that loveth his brother abideth in the light, and there is none occasion of stumbling in him. But he that hateth his brother . . . walketh in darkness, and knoweth not whither he goeth, because that darkness hath blinded his eyes" (1 John 2:10, 11). "This is the message that ye heard from the beginning, that we should love one another" (1 John 3:11).

One day when I was 12 years old I went with my father to help an impoverished neighbor construct a needed room onto his small home. Because the family was in want, this free labor was deeply appreciated. We did not know that another church member, a carpenter, had not gotten this job because there was no means to pay. Later this man happened by. Hearing pounding, he came in. Seeing father doing work he wanted, he flew into a rage, shouting, "If you didn't have that hammer, I'd knock you down."

Father calmly let the hammer fall to the floor. The irate fellow raised his fists. But then he hesitated. A few tense seconds later they began to talk. The fists came down. As father explained that his help was for free the excitable man wilted and broke down sobbing. Father accepted his abject apology. A friendship was then born that lasted to the end of their lives.

This unforgettable episode has remained a priceless lesson for me. Our text speaks of having compassion one for another.

WHAT LOVE CAN DO

And above all things have fervent charity [love] among yourselves: for charity shall cover the multitude of sins. 1 Peter 4:8.

All the graces of Christian virtue flow naturally from the wellspring of love. This attribute generously forgives the mistakes of a wayward brother, understands his weaknesses, and stands ever ready to come to his aid when he is in need. Love prompts the believer to weigh his words lest his tongue speak gossip, and applauds the nobility evident in the lives of others. Love is sacrificial, even risking life itself when in a crisis conscience dictates it. "Greater love hath no man than this, that a man lay down his life for his friends" (John 15:13).

The history of the Salvation Army is studded with accounts of singular love and sacrifice. None surpasses that of the officers of that admirable organization who booked passage years ago on the ill-fated ship *Empress of Ireland*. The liner foundered, and over a thousand lives were lost. Among them were more than a hundred Salvation Army leaders. When their drowned bodies were recovered, not one of them had a life belt. Survivors of this disaster told how these noble men responded with calm courage when they learned that the ship was sinking. Not enough life belts had been provided. So the officers, to a man, removed their belts and gave them to other passengers they felt were not prepared to meet their Maker. One of them was heard to say, "Because we know the Saviour, we are prepared to die." Then, as the ship went down, these confident soldiers of the cross stood prayerfully on the deck until they were engulfed by the sea. "Greater love hath no man . . ."

Few Christians are ever called to face the ultimate, definitive decision these men met. Fewer still are willing to yield up their live so that others may have the opportunity to repent and be saved. Yet Jesus went even further when He laid down His life, not for His friends, but for His enemies. How unspeakably moving it is when we realize that by this incomparable sacrifice the gates of heaven were flung open to receive every sinful apostate who will repent and accept the Saviour!

"Dear Saviour, we would know Thy love
Which yet no measure knows;
For us it led Thee once to die;
From thence salvation flows."
—Harold A. Miller

LOVE IS FORGIVING

Forbearing one another, and forgiving one another . . . : even as Christ forgave you, so also do ye. Col. 3:13.

For many Christians the practical daily exercise of the divine principle of forgiveness constitutes a vexing problem. How contrary to the inclinations of the natural heart is this noble virtue! Instead of forbearing to retaliate and generously forgiving or overlooking the slanders, slights, and injuries inflicted upon us, we are inclined to resent them hotly, and we plot and plan to take revenge on the perpetrators of these grievous wrongs.

When a person feels that he has been dealt a low blow, he is more than likely to exclaim, "I can forgive, but not forget." Such a spirit is wrong, but the truth is that a very thin line separates forgetting and forgiving. In fact, no one can truly forgive and forget. God Himself is not the Great Forgetter some think He is. We know that He removes our transgressions from us as far as the east is from the west. But He does not altogether forget them. He redeems our checkered past by healing our wounds and covering our sins. But He has not forgotten them.

Likewise, for us to forgive is to accept other "travelers" along the pathway of life, including their past life styles. Forgiveness brings peace and gratitude and enables us to love those who have injured us.

One time a friend asked General Dwight Eisenhower how he dealt with base deceit and injury. He replied, "When I find that a man is utterly untrustworthy I write his name on a sheet of paper and put it in a little pigeonhole in my desk. Then I try never to think of him again." Apparently this worked well for the general, but Godlike forgiveness goes further. When an unworthy son breaks his father's heart and shames the family name, his father forgives him although he can never forget.

Before coming to the throne, Louis XII, king of France, had been imprisoned in chains. On becoming king, he was expected by many to take revenge on his enemies. He then drew up a list of names and placed a cross in red ink opposite many of them. Fearing for their lives, those so indicated fled France. Then the king explained, "The cross I drew beside each name was not to punish. It is a pledge of forgiveness granted for the sake of the crucified Saviour, who upon His cross forgave His enemies and prayed for them."

Are you holding a grudge against anyone? Remember Paul's words, "as Christ forgave you, so also do ye."

CHRISTIAN LOVE INCLUDES FEELINGS

Rejoice with them that do rejoice, and weep with them that weep. Rom. 12:15.

The compassionate Christian will not stand aloof but will enter into the joys and sorrows of others. This active, sympathetic sharing is Godlike, for of ancient Israel Isaiah said, "In all their affliction he was afflicted, and the angel of his presence saved them: in his love and in his pity he redeemed them; and he bare them, and carried them all the days of old" (Isa. 63:9). The Saviour wept in sorrow with them that mourned and rejoiced with those who forsook their sins and joyfully accepted His offer of salvation. He was reflecting the delight of the sinless host above when He said, "Likewise joy shall be in heaven over one sinner that repenteth" (Luke 15:7).

Loneliness depresses the spirit, because man desperately needs fellowship, not only with God, but also with his fellow human beings. This is the reason that one of the severest forms of punishment is solitary confinement. When incarcerated alone, a perfectly normal human being becomes a victim of hallucinations, undergoes subtle personality changes, and sometimes eventually goes insane.

This feeling of isolation can break down the strongest personality. In his hour of need the psalmist's robust spirit faltered. Deserted and friendless, he cried out, "Refuge failed me; no one cared for my soul" (Ps. 142:4). On another similar occasion he plaintively wrote, "I watch, and am as a sparrow alone" (Ps. 102:7). Because loneliness is so devastating, all Christians are admonished to "visit the fatherless and widows in their affliction" (James 1:27). Nor are we to neglect the aged and infirm in their loneliness.

In his little book *Living God's Love,* Douglas Cooper tells of a lonely widow living in a twelve-story apartment house. One day, with no apparent intimation, she opened her window, smiled at the janitor, and then leaped to her death. The note she left in her room said, "I cannot stand one more day of this loneliness. I have no friends. I receive no mail. No one calls me on the telephone. I cannot stand it any longer." Her surprised neighbors said, "We did not know she felt that way."

How about your loved ones and friends? Do you ever speak to them about your love for the Saviour? If you fail to witness to them now, what will be your feeling in the judgment when they turn accusing eyes on you and say, "No one cared for my soul"?

TRUE LOVE RESTRAINS AND REFRAINS

I have refrained my feet from every evil way, that I might keep thy word. Ps. 119:101.

Although they are not exactly synonymous, the words "restrain," "refrain," and "withhold" are alike in meaning and often appear with like intent throughout the Scriptures. Job asked, Who is able to put a "restraint on words?" (Job 4:2, N.W.T.). Gamaliel warned the Sanhedrin to "refrain from" troubling Peter and other early converts. (See Acts 5:38.) Writing to scattered believers, Peter declared, "He that will love life, and see good days, let him refrain his tongue from evil" (1 Peter 3:10). Begging for her husband's life, Abigail insisted to David that the Lord had "withholden" his hand from shedding blood (1 Sam. 25:26). In each of these instances a hasty, unwise, or sinful act was avoided because of the divine Spirit of restraint intervened.

The wise man spoke for self-control when he wrote "He that is slow to anger is better than the mighty; and he that ruleth his spirit than he that taketh a city" (Prov. 16:32). The advantage of holding one's temper is universally recognized. An old adage has it that "temper is so fine a thing no one should ever lose it." Another says that "temper is singular in that it improves the longer it is kept."

It is one thing to decry an angry spirit, but quite another to develop enough self-control to overcome it. Still, many have done so. In his youth George Washington had a well-attested reputation as a hot spur. He was regarded as harboring a fearsome, towering anger that sometimes got out of hand. Recognizing this weakness he set his violent temper under his iron will and won the victory.

Long in the educational endeavor, I have learned that, without God's indwelling love in the heart, any victory over evil habits is short-lived. A boy from the back streets of an American metropolis was sent to us by his stepfather in hopes that our Christian school could reform him. He wanted him to make good, so we accepted him. But his language was so vile that he could scarcely utter one sentence free of vulgarity or profanity. We labored with him in vain. Then came the Week of Prayer. Deeply touched by the moving messages, he gave his heart wholly to God. His new life testified to the depths of his conversion, and he swore no more.

The conquering love of the meek and gentle Saviour gives strength to keep His word and refrain our feet—and our mouths—from evil.

LOVE OFFERS POWER TO OBEY

For it is God who works in you, inspiring both the will and the deed, for his own chosen purpose. Phil. 2:13, N.E.B.

Along with this solemn assertion that God's indwelling spirit is an inner enabling power, the apostle Paul admonishes, "So you too, my friends, must be obedient, as always; even more, now that I am away, than when I was with you. You must work out your own salvation in fear and trembling (Phil. 2:12, 13, N.E.B.). The injunction is not to work *for* our own salvation, for that is God's gift. But each of us has a part in working *out* our salvation. Even the Saviour said he could do "nothing of himself" (see John 5:19).

"The words that I speak unto you I speak not of myself: but the Father that dwelleth in me, he doeth the works" (John 14:10). In the same way Christ, dwelling in our hearts by His Holy Spirit, works in us "both to will and to do of his good pleasure." With this unlimited power within we are able to work out our own salvation. We must not fail to notice that "it is God which worketh *in* you," not *among* you.

We have the tremendous assurance and admonition: "Fear not, little flock; for it is your Father's good pleasure to give you the kingdom" (Luke 12:32). This is the sure heritage that makes the Christian a child of the King. It is His deepest desire that we be satisfied and saved. But we have a part to play. Like the farmer who plows the field and prepares the ground to receive the seed, we must make our hearts ready to accept His will for us and then welcome in His power to produce the harvest. But the husbandman's diligence would be fruitless were it not that God works through the sunshine and the rain and the germinating seed. Likewise in the spiritual life, God works and we work. Writing to the Ephesian believers, Paul said his prayer was that God "grant you, according to the riches of his glory, to be strengthened with might by His spirit in the inner man" (Eph. 3:16).

Some seem to think all they have to do is to pray for the Christian virtues and God will do the rest. But heaven is not that easy. Of course we must pray—and earnestly too—whereupon our heavenly Father answers our prayers by enabling us to develop the graces of the Spirit as we *work out* our salvation with fear and trembling. This is God's way. There is no other.

OBEDIENCE IS THE PROOF OF LOVE

If ye love me, keep my commandments. John 14:15.

Our little twenty-student church school at Mount Ellis did not enjoy a high reputation for good conduct. For various reasons teachers seldom remained for more than one term, often less. As another school year drew near, rumor had it that our incoming teacher was inexperienced and not yet 20 years old. Naturally, we were all very eager to see her. As nine o'clock approached on the opening day noisy excitement reached a fever pitch. Then she came in. At once an uncommon silence prevailed. Our new teacher, Miss Olive Smithwick, was impressively lovely. Such a gracious, winsome young woman we had not known before. From that moment she held the school in the hollow of her hand. In fact, she was so beautiful that it was a joy just to look at her. Because she was as kind and as gentle as she was charming, in no time students were vying with one another to sharpen her pencils, empty the wastebasket, erase the blackboards, and eagerly run errands at her least suggestion. That proved to be a banner year, and our sincere sorrow was deep when, as school closed in the spring, our beloved Miss Smithwick announced that she was leaving Mount Ellis to be married. But we always remembered her and how our love for her prompted us to obey with satisfaction and pleasure.

Like Miss Smithwick, the Lord does not demand obedience. He makes it crystal clear what we ought to do and then leaves it to us whether to obey. When out of a spirit of love we respond, He is pleased, and we enjoy His blessing. This freedom of choice on our part is implicit in His reminder that "if any man will come after me, let him deny himself . . . and follow me" (Luke 9:23). No doubt John remembered this when he wrote, "We receive of him, because we keep his commandments, and do those things that are pleasing in his sight" (1 John 3:22).

In speaking the words of today's text, the Saviour did not hint of any disloyalty in His disciples, for He knew that they loved Him. He was simply reminding them that willing obedience is the test of true love.

A man once asked his friend, "How would you like to live where no one drank or smoked, nor stole nor cheated?" "There is no such perfect place," came the reply. "Oh, yes, there is," said the first man. "You will find it in any well-operated penitentiary."

Voluntary obedience alone is acceptable to God. This is the test that will decide our eternal destiny.

TRUE LOVE CONSTRAINS
For the love of Christ constraineth us. 2 Cor. 5:14.

Years ago, when the Youth Department of the General Conference was known as the Missionary Volunteer Department, the text above was the constant, conscious motto of every Missionary Volunteer Society in the world. Does the love of Christ still activate and motivate Adventist youth? It does when they soberly contemplate the price that was paid for our souls' salvation, the sacrifice that was made on Calvary. When any of us consider that love and its consequences, which ensures salvation for all who accept it, our hearts are intensely moved. The more we study about His self-denial, His humility, condescension and mercy, the deeper burns our love for Him.

When we truly love an earthly friend we take great joy in carrying out his, or her, wishes. When effort and sacrifice are required our pleasure is increased. Such exertions are not burdensome. How much greater should be our joy in doing the will of the Saviour!

We ought to talk much more than we do of the love of God. Let us speak of the dimensions of this divine magnet that draws us from sin to salvation, from the sordid, hopeless elements of a woeful, weary world that is doomed, to the eternal joys of heaven. Looked at from the standpoint of eternity, we cannot view God's requirements as grievous. His commandments are practical and they are "holy . . . and just, and good" (Rom. 7:12).

Viewed from the vantage point of the ages, the law of God is composed of gentle, salutary pleadings instead of stern commands. The golden rule epitomizes His attitude toward us. "Love worketh no ill to his neighbor: therefore love is the fulfilling of the law" (Rom. 13:10). The indwelling Christ shines out of the heart in love, purity, honesty, truthfulness, and goodness. How then can anyone say that this divine law is against us?

Perchance you consciously harbor a deepening desire to love God with all your heart. A re-reading of the letters of the apostle Paul will intensify that aspiration. In his solicitous heart burned such a dedication to the Master that he could declare, "I determined not to know anything among you, save Jesus Christ, and him crucified" (1 Cor. 2:2). With such a motivation Paul and his co-laborers "turned the world upside down." When the same love constrains us, we, too, will go forth and turn our world God-side up.

JUST ONE GOD

Thou shalt have no other gods before me. Ex. 20:3.

Even a cursory review of the various religions of the world, their origins and history, will reveal that Christianity stands in the sharpest contrast with almost every other belief or faith ever known among men. Two paramount differences distinguish belief in the Jehovah-God of Israel from all other faiths. Our Jehovah is a supreme, exclusive God, and credence and faith in Him is monotheistic and all-embracing. As the Creator of the universe He alone can say with authority, "The Lord is God, . . . there is none else" (1 Kings 8:60).

More than this, Jehovah is a personal God and has chosen to reveal Himself in a personal way. This He did specifically when, in time of great need, His voice spoke His law at Sinai. Thus the Decalogue, there proclaimed with divine authority and twice inscribed on tablets of stone, is not only a transcript of God's character and His love, but also reveals His eternal standard of conduct for men. Christianity, thus specified on the Mount of the Law and as illuminated by the Saviour in His Sermon on the Mount, offers the solution to the basic problems of modern society. Unaltered by time, this "golden yardstick of human behavior" has provided dignity to man's endeavor whenever it has been exalted.

"Thou shalt have no other gods before me." This first commandment, spoken out of the fiery wonder of Sinai on "Decalogue Day," struck at the roots of evil in every generation since Adam disobeyed the Creator in the Garden. The iniquity that was born that tragic day is the sin of disbelief in God, in the worship of the creature rather than the Creator, in the denial of man's divine heritage, and in the self-service of the "me" generation of today.

The psalmist declared that "a good understanding have all they that do his commandments" (Ps. 111:10). To have this confident understanding is to find spiritual sustenance and peace. It means being in tune with heaven. An Arab legend describes a scarred and jagged rock along a desert path that presents a forbidding appearance except when approached from one direction. There an open door appears in the barren stone through which the famished traveler can pass into cool shelter from the heat and find an abundance of delicacies. Likewise the footsore pilgrim on this life's toilsome way may approach God and find his every need satisfied.

DON'T BOW DOWN TO THEM

Thou shalt not make unto thee any graven image . . . thou shalt not bow down thyself to them, nor serve them: for I the Lord thy God am a jealous God, visiting the iniquity of the fathers upon the children unto the third and fourth generation of them that hate me; and shewing mercy unto thousands of them that love me and keep my commandments. Ex. 20:4-6.

The commandments given to Moses on Sinai dispelled the obscurity Satan had generated to conceal God's real character. Of these ten precepts, the second is perhaps the most beautiful in its broad range—from stern authority to tender appeal, from solemn warning to loving promise. Here is the reminder that all men owe allegiance only to Him whose hands hold both justice and mercy.

Man is endowed with the spirit of worship as an innate characteristic. Like the heathen of old, modern man goes astray when he misplaces his adoration. The command cannot be misunderstood, whether the devotee be a Buddhist bowing in his gilded temple, the native Alaskan venerating his totem pole, the Yogi contemplating his own navel, or the bejewelled socialite smiling into her full-length mirror. In all such instances the distorted veneration is placed upon things of earth. Satan cares not at all that men worship, so long as they do not worship the true God.

Being weak in spiritual vision men provide visual aids: marble statues, gilded saints, masterful paintings, and miracle shrines in an attempt to focus worship. Before these they bow, forgetting the injunction, "Thou shalt not bow down thyself to them."

Professor W. S. Reid, of McGill University, says that the principal false god of today is our high "standard of living." He continues, "We forget that material possessions are the gift of God. . . . Man's chief end in life is to glorify God and enjoy Him forever, not to have a house with a swimming pool."

How can this generation be aroused to the solemn obligation and promised blessings of the second commandment? Perhaps by observing the first commandment, not in lip service, but through a daily communion with God through His Spirit. Church attendance, soulful music, and pulpit eloquence are not enough. These are all well and good, but cannot take the place of personal communion. Said David, "The sacrifices of God are a broken spirit: a broken and a contrite heart, O God, thou wilt not despise" (Ps. 51:17).

REVERENCE FOR HIS NAME

Thou shalt not take the name of the Lord thy God in vain; for the Lord will not hold him guiltless that taketh his name in vain. Ex. 20:7.

It is surprising to note the various ways this third commandment of the Decalogue is translated into English. In one version it is the misuse of God's name that He will not "leave unpunished." In another version taking His name in a "worthless manner" is condemned. In all cases, however, no doubt is left that God's name is to be honored and that those who dishonor it will not be held guiltless in the judgment.

The late novelist Eugene O'Neill spoke of this age as a "generation with a scant view of history but an abundance of irreverence." One need not travel far to recognize that disrespect at all levels of society has become a hallmark of our civilization. The close observer will notice, too, that in places where lawbreaking has grown so rank as to threaten the very existence of organized society there blasphemy and profanity thrive unchecked, unrebuked, and almost unnoticed. As with man so with God. When life loses its sanctity anything goes with men, and the Creator is either denied or ignored. A loss of faith entails a loss of knowledge that anything is sacred. Hosea's description applies to our times: "There is no . . . knowledge of God in the land. By swearing, and lying, and killing, and stealing, and committing adultery, they break out, and blood toucheth blood" (Hosea 4:1, 2).

With the loss of the least awareness of God, irreverence for His name follows, along with contempt for the attributes of His character. The names of Deity are heard with vile epithets to no purpose except to display a swaggering braggadocio.

The use of profanity exposes an imprecision of thought and a poverty of speech that are easily recognized by the cultured mind. Infinitely more important is its disclosure of spiritual poverty. God's holy name is taken in vain to bolster emphasis by those who do not know nor respect Christ as the living Saviour.

Fortunately, obedience to the third commandment carries its own rich reward. Nothing more effectively elevates the mind, purifies the speech, activates thought, and strengthens the vital forces than does this reverence for the Deity. All who wait in confidence for our Lord's return, every one who "hath this hope in him purifieth himself, even as he is pure" (1 John 3:3).

A DAY TO REMEMBER

Remember the sabbath day, to keep it holy. Ex. 20:8.

In my personal library are nearly a score of treasured volumes dealing with the Sabbath—historically, doctrinally, polemically, and persuasively. I have read them all, some several times. These books I value because, as a boy growing up in a Seventh-day Adventist home, I early realized that observing Saturday as our Sabbath set us apart religiously from most of our neighbors. Because we worked on their Sunday and they worked on our Sabbath I felt this denominational difference, this peculiarity, very keenly. Although I felt obliged to keep the seventh-day Sabbath with my family, I often felt isolated from the "outside" boys of my acquaintance. And sometimes I even felt ashamed to be so completely out of step with the religious practices of the community. I often thought, too, how comfortable and cooperative it would be, if in some mysterious way, we could change and honestly worship on Sunday like the majority.

With such reflections going through my young head I spoke at length with my parents, my teachers, and my friends about the matter. And I read histories, encyclopedias, and a host of various denominational publications on the subject. In time I gradually came to certain incontrovertible conclusions that the passing of the years and much study have served only to confirm. I list some of them here.

The first word of this commandment, "Remember," sets it apart from the others and gives it distinction. The Sabbath is a memorial of Creation. It is not Jewish for it was made 2,300 years before there was a Jew. The Sabbath was made in the Garden of Eden. God blessed and hallowed the Sabbath day and no other. Set in the bosom of God's unchangeable law it is binding upon all men during all time. Jesus kept the Sabbath and said it was made for man. It is the sign of the true God by which He is known from all false gods. God has promised to bless all who keep the Sabbath. All the holy prophets kept it. The seventh day is the Lord's day for Jesus is the Lord of the Sabbath. Nowhere in the New Testament is there a word about the seventh-day Sabbath being abolished or changed. Jesus condemned the Pharisees as hypocrites because they pretended to love God and yet made void one of the commandments by their tradition.

"Remember the sabbath day to keep it holy," for it will most assuredly be kept in heaven.

THE RESPECT DUE OUR PARENTS

Honour thy father and thy mother: that thy days may be long upon the land which the Lord thy God giveth thee. Ex. 20:12.

Without question the first four precepts announced from Sinai clarified the ideal relationship between God and man. This fifth commandment, with the five that follow, sets forth the duties that individual members in an ordered society owe one another. The Saviour expressed these six obligations thus: "Whatsoever ye would that men should do to you, do ye even so to them" (Matt. 7:12).

Be it noted that this is the first commandment with promise. A reward for its obedience is long life. Conversely, among the curses enunciated by Moses appears this: "Cursed is the man who dishonors his father or his mother." (Deut. 27:16, N.I.V.). Writing to the Colossians Paul told the children, "Obey your parents in all things: for this is well pleasing unto the Lord" (Col. 3:20).

Why should we honor our parents? In addition to the assurance of long life if we show them honor, we remember that they gave us birth, cared for us in infancy, nourished us and watched over us in illness, clothed us for years, educated us and guided us when our uncertain feet did not know the way. They hovered over us with unspeakable love and with the most intense interest opened our minds to truth, and still find in our happiness and prosperity their greatest joy.

How are we to honor them? Not by mere verbal expressions of respect but by true reverence, by constant affection, by unfailing obedience, and by every effort to enhance their welfare and delight. If we are so fortunate as to have them into their old age it is our privilege to care for them. Nor should we ever cause them pain by wrongdoing.

Mark Twain is reported as saying that when he was 16 he considered his father "a stodgy old mossback" but on seeing him again four years later, he was surprised how much the old man had learned. Like the prodigal son, too many youth of today look upon their home as a boring, unexciting place, and seek adventure in "a far country," perhaps a theater or a cheap night club. Sure, they love Pa and Ma but consider them of a generation gone and out of touch with today's world. Angela Morgan wrote that in every life is a little "imprisoned splendor." The Christian parent will find and release that splendor in their children. And these same children will eventually discover that there is a bit of imprisoned splendor in Mom and Dad, too.

THE SHEDDING OF BLOOD

Thou shalt not kill. Ex. 20:13.

Ever since that saddest of all days, when sin first desecrated Eden, the hideous visage of death has looked into the faces of all the sons of men. At that tragic moment life on earth was reduced to a somber tunnel with no escape save through the little gray door at the end. The courteous consideration of the most sympathetic mortician fails to dispel the gloom that envelops the open grave. However tactful and comforting, the language of consolation cannot diminish the dread of death nor assuage the grief of those who mourn. The beauty of the flowers mocks the pallor of death and the soft strains of the organ only intensify the stillness of the tomb.

This then is the dreadful penalty for sin that, as the Scriptures declare, passed upon all of Adam's heirs to the end of time. (See Rom. 5:12.) Yet, well-knowing death's conclusive finality, evil men, from Cain to today's killers, have not hesitated to shed blood like savage fiends. Because the murderer takes away what neither he nor anyone else can give back, the sixth commandment sternly and uncompromisingly enjoins, "Thou shalt not kill."

Emphasizing the broader scope of this commandment, the Saviour said, "Ye have heard that it was said . . . of old . . . "Thou shalt not kill . . . but I say unto you, that whosoever is angry with his brother without a cause shall be in danger of the judgment" (Matt. 5:21). He went even further in saying "Love your enemies, do good to them which hate you, bless them that curse you, and pray for them which despitefully use you" (Luke 6:27, 28). Thus He bids us bind those angry passions that lead to envy, jealousy, hatred, and murder.

The spirit of hatred and revenge originated with Satan and led him to put to death the Son of God. "All acts of injustice that tend to shorten life . . . or the indulgence of any passion that leads to injurious acts toward others, or causes us even to wish them harm . . . a selfish neglect of caring for the needy or suffering; all self-indulgence . . . that tends to injure health—all these are . . . violations of the sixth commandment."—*Patriarchs and Prophets*, p. 308. Furthermore, "those who corrupt the innocent and seduce the virtuous 'kill' in a . . . worse sense than the cutthroat and the bandit, in that they do more than to kill the body."—*SDA Bible Commentary*, vol. 1, p. 606. It behooves every believer to consider the broader implications of this commandment.

MORAL PURITY
Thou shalt not commit adultery. Ex. 20:14.

Oscar Jay tells of a Bible teacher who suggested to her class that the children make cards for Mother's Day. She said they might wish to illustrate their work with a Bible text. When she collected the cards she found that one of them had on the outside, "To My Mommy—Happy Mother's Day!" Inside, in block letters, it read, "Thou shalt not commit adultery." The implications are plain and sadly symptomatic of the prevailing immorality of our age.

History records that licentiousness put an end to Babylon, "the beauty of the Chaldees' excellency," when, in a night of obscene revelry, its final doom was decreed on Belshazzar's palace wall. Depravity tarnished the glory that was Greece and eclipsed the splendor that was Rome. Today the leer of lechery and the lure of licentiousness effectively undermine the leadership of scores of popular political, theatrical, and society "stars" whose shameful lives are exposed in disgusting detail in the daily press and weekly pulp magazines. Those with a concern for national morality point to the newsstands where obscene novels crowd out decent publications, to the adulation of immoral performing celebrities featured on television, and to unchecked adultery, rampant at motels everywhere. Pleas for a return to chastity are scorned as Victorian hypocrisy and any who dare raise a voice for purity are lampooned as absurd "squares."

Sexual promiscuity, winked at in sophisticated circles, has become a way of life for millions. Marital infidelity is considered as a badge of emancipation by "liberated activists" who insist that they represent "the wave of the future." Homosexuals, mistakenly called "gay," are gaining acceptance as "normal," and American divorce rates now lead the world.

Marriage was established at Creation to set a standard of social integrity. The family bond was instituted as the agent of love, making the home the basic unit of a God-fearing society. Through the marital union God's moral margins were to be maintained.

The seventh commandment roundly condemns smutty stories, foul jokes, filthy literature, lewd suggestions, and immorality in all its forms. It offers a princely reward for compliance with its lofty concepts. Therefore, "seeing . . . all these things . . . what manner of persons ought ye to be in all holy conversation and godliness?" (2 Peter 3:11).

THE PARAMETERS OF THEFT
Thou shalt not steal. Ex. 20:15.

Writing to the Ephesians, the apostle Paul gave dimensions to the eighth commandment with this exhortation: "Let him that stole steal no more: but rather let him labour, working with his hands the thing which is good, that he may have to give to him that needeth" (Eph. 4:28). Obviously, in his day as in ours there were professed Christians who were robbers, preferring to steal rather than work. Human selfishness prompts a man to look out for and live for himself as an individual and not as an integral part of the community. Yet, to promote one's true welfare is to promote the good of the society of which he is a part. He who wrongs others, wrongs himself and injures the body politic. By stealing, a person expects to enrich himself whereas, in the long run, he impoverishes all—including himself.

This commandment enforces the right to possess property. For society to prosper this right must be safeguarded. Otherwise anarchy prevails with no protection or safeguard for anybody. Yet stealing, in its multiple guises, has become big business in America as elsewhere. Lucrative thievery in high places, fraud, and extortion outmaneuver legal efforts to apprehend their perpetrators. By the enormity of their crimes governmental swindlers, income tax evaders, and corrupt labor union officials compete for headlines with notorious bank robbers and safecrackers. Looking at today's world of avarice it is not hard to agree with the apostle Paul that "the love of money is the root of all evil" (1 Tim. 6:10).

We knew of a prosperous farmer whose wheat invariably took the blue ribbon at the state fair. Because he refused to sell seed wheat to his neighbors they continued to raise inferior crops. In time, inter-pollination deteriorated this selfish farmer's wheat. Realizing the cause, he not only provided his neighbors with his best seed for planting, but also shared his better methods of farming with them too. If everyone appreciated this demonstrable truth, stealing, cheating, hoarding from others, and other forms of thievery would give way to generous sharing for the betterment of all.

"As we deal with our fellow men in petty dishonesty, or in more and more daring fraud, so will we deal with God. Men who persist in a course of dishonesty will carry out their principles until they cheat their own souls, and lose heaven and eternal life."—*Christian Service,* p. 142.

WITNESSING TO TRUTH

Thou shalt not bear false witness. Ex. 20:16.

The wise man, who was familiar with the ways of God and men, recorded that "a false witness shall not be unpunished, and he that speaketh lies shall not escape" (Prov. 19:5). Solomon knew that, although men may hide their evil deeds from human eyes, they cannot deceive God. "All things are naked and opened unto the eyes of him with whom we have to do" (Heb. 4:13). Ultimately every lie will be disclosed, all the dark things shall be made plain. What a revelation that will be!

One contemporary analyst has called ours the age of the monumental lie. You need but attend the hearings in an important lawsuit to realize that consummate perjurers take regular refuge behind the Fifth Amendment and present composed and smiling faces as masks for conspiracy, fraud, and deception. Is it any wonder that judges, after years on the bench, entertain a very low opinion of the integrity of their fellow men?

The motives of perjurers, whether in international relations or over the backyard fence, are designed to benefit the prevaricator by profit, face-saving, revenge, or for ingratiation with a view toward advancement. In the marketplace it is misrepresentation; in politics, impossible promises; in religion, hypocrisy. Like a Halloween pageant in reverse, every deceiver wears a comely mask.

Perfidy wears a thousand faces. Perjury, libel, slander, and the bribing of witnesses are against the law, but fewer than one in ten who are guilty of such offenses are ever convicted. These may escape civil punishment but not heaven's frown for "These six things doth the Lord hate: yea, seven are an abomination unto him, a proud look, a lying tongue, hands that shed innocent blood, an heart that deviseth wicked imaginations, feet that be swift in running to mischief, a false witness that speaketh lies, and he that seweth discord among brethren" (Prov. 6:16-19).

As with all ten commandments, there are privileges on the positive side of this one. The tongue can be used to glorify God and bless mankind. It can witness to the truth, instruct the ignorant, comfort the afflicted, and inspire the disheartened. It can benefit with reproof if given in love. If one has the mind of Christ the law of kindness will be in his tongue. Shall we not, therefore, pray each day, "Set a watch, O Lord, before my mouth; keep the door of my lips" (Ps. 141:3).

INORDINATE DESIRE

Thou shalt not covet thy neighbour's house, thou shalt not covet thy neighbour's wife, nor his manservant, nor his maidservant, nor his ox, nor his ass, nor anything that is thy neighbour's. Ex. 20:17.

"When Christ, who is our life, shall appear, then shall ye also appear with him in glory. Mortify therefore your members . . . fornication, uncleanness, inordinate affection . . . and covetousness, which is idolatry" (Col. 3:4-6).

There are two closely related Scriptural commands: "Thou shalt not covet thy neighbour's wife" and "Thou shalt love . . . thy neighbour as thyself." Here are the negative and the positive aspects of the life of a righteous man. "Thou shalt not" may do for children, but "Thou shalt" is a step higher. We must not only abstain from injuring a neighbor, but must embrace him in the arms of love.

Love is wholly compatible with desire, but it is inconsistent with inordinate desire. Love thinks no evil, does not behave itself unseemly, and seeks not her own. The covetous seek their own with great zeal, and also, by fair means or foul, seek to get their hands on what is not their own. Yet, in a sense, divine love makes the perfections I admire in my neighbor, mine. They can be rightly mine to the extent that I admire them unselfishly.

When we violate this commandment we question the wisdom of God in giving riches and beauty to some while withholding them from others. Covetousness impels the rich to oppress the poor, and the poor to combine for the destruction of the rich. The life of the covetous man is stripped of pleasure because the cup of envy he constantly drinks is very bitter. It robs a covetous person of that sweet and generous spirit without which even a very rich man is poor indeed.

That this dictum is of vast importance is seen by its position in the code. It is the last. Yet it deals with sin's beginning. Dark passions and shameful desires spring from within the heart. Temptation begins there. James says, "Let no man say when he is tempted, I am tempted of God: for God cannot be tempted with evil, neither tempteth he any man" (James 1:13).

Happily this injunction is not all negative. Fortunately, there are many lovely, desirable things we may eagerly covet with honor. There are the manifold gifts of the Spirit as enumerated in 1 Corinthians 12. Let us covet these "best gifts" and, possessing them, rejoice in the blessings of His peace.

THE SIMPLICITY OF THE LAW

The law of the Lord is perfect, converting the soul: the testimony of the Lord is sure, making wise the simple. Ps. 19:7.

In the *Congressional Record* appear page on page of long, drawn-out, cumbrous, obtuse statutes and laws, which often are couched in language so obscure and ambiguous that legal specialists and high-powered lawyers dispute endlessly regarding the true intent and meaning. Attempts to amend and clarify these laws more often than not succeed only in making them still more incomprehensible. No one familiar with the facts will dispute this.

By contrast how wonderful in simplicity, comprehensiveness, and clarity is the law of Jehovah! The Decalogue embraces every phase of human interrelationship and is the standard by which all who have ever lived in the earth will be either justified or condemned in the last great judgment. Therefore we have the admonition, "So speak ye, and so do, as they that shall be judged by the law of liberty" (James 2:12). Solomon said that God will "bring every work into judgment, with every secret thing, whether it be good, or whether it be evil" (Eccl. 12:14).

In the purposes and dealings of God and in the outworking of His will there are mysteries our finite minds cannot comprehend. But there is no mystery about His law. The simplest mind can understand these principles that regulate life and, when diligently obeyed, form characters after the heavenly model. "By obedience to this law the intellect is strengthened, and the conscience is enlightened and made sensitive." * It is the depravity of sin that causes men to look upon this moral law as an enemy blocking the way to freedom and joy. Actually it imparts the grand secret of successful living here and of immortal good hereafter.

If there ever was a time when the sincere believer needed an infallible doctrine that is above all doubts in its declarations that time is now. "The testimony, i.e., the revealed will, of the Lord is sure." We cannot believe in the infallibility of the church, nor of philosophers, for they often contradict one another. The best thinkers of one age are laughed at by those that follow. Nor can we believe in the infallibility of our own opinions arrived at outside of revelation. There remains no infallible guide save that declared on Sinai as recorded for all in Holy Writ. God give us the grace to believe and follow it.

---

* *The Youth's Instructor,* Sept. 22, 1903.

GOD'S LOOKING GLASS

But whoso looketh into the perfect law of liberty, and continueth therein, he being not a forgetful hearer, but a doer of the work, this man shall be blessed in his deed. James 1:25.

This emphatic scripture can be summed up in the warranty that there is blessing in obedience. We are not to be hearers only but also *lookers*. We are to review God's perfect law of liberty and continue our looking and our walking in His way. A blessing is assured when we do this. Instead of complaining that obedience is beyond attainment or criticizing the law as unattainable, as some do, the faithful believer will remember the words of the Lord, "This is the way, walk ye in it" (Isa. 30:21).

Anyone experienced in college administration knows that to accomplish its aims, any well-run institution of higher learning must operate in accordance with reasonable regulations. That students be expected to attend classes regularly and on time hardly needs explaining. To prevent pandemonium, dormitory life must be governed by rules so that study, rest, and worship can proceed in an orderly manner. There is ample reason to require quiet during certain hours so sleep can be restful and restorative. All of this seems to be reasonable enough. Yet human nature resists regimentation and protocol. The impulse to "do as I please" on the part of independent, inexperienced spirits stirs up rebellious passions.

A like spirit of rebellion toward God's requirements inclines opposers to withstand His perfect law of liberty. Because the transgressor finds his absolute freedom abridged he refuses to recognize that obedience to law is the only true freedom. But when, by the grace of God, any dissident member of the human race accepts the Saviour's sacrifice and looks into the law that was previously so repugnant to him, he finds that it accords with his best interests and that it is conducive to his highest happiness.

The law of God is "the great moral looking-glass into which the sinner is to look to discover the defects of his character. If all would study the law of God . . . as diligently and critically as many do their outward appearance by means of the looking-glass, with a purpose to correct and reform every defect of character, what transformations would most assuredly take place." * "God help us to take care of the inward adorning as carefully as we arrange the outward apparel."—*Ibid.*

---

* Ellen G. White, *Review and Herald,* Oct. 11, 1887.

WITH ALL THINE HEART

This day the Lord thy God hath commanded thee to do these statutes and judgments: thou shalt therefore keep and do them with all thine heart, and with all thy soul. Deut. 26:16.

During the American Civil War, after a surprising defeat of a large Northern army, President Abraham Lincoln learned that the Union general had been so confused and intimidated by his opponent, General Robert E. Lee, that he had held nearly a third of the men under his command out of the battle. Bitterly disappointed, President Lincoln wired his shamefaced commander, "Next time put in all your men."

In the personal warfare waged against wickedness, many a battle is lost because the timorous, halfhearted Christian fails to "put in" all his men. Again and again throughout the counsels of the Spirit of Prophecy appear appeals for deeper consecration, greater earnestness, and aroused enthusiasm. Not one soul need fail in this vital struggle. Nor will he when he determines to do God's will with all his heart.

According to our text, the Lord appealed again and again to Israel to give wholehearted obedience to His commandments. Had they been willing to obey Him, they would have been richly rewarded by both material and spiritual blessings. He said they would be blessed when they came in, and when they went out. Also, they would be blessed above all people if they kept His statutes with all their heart (see Deut. 28).

When Jesus walked among men, He called a certain man to follow Him. The man replied that he wished first to bury his father, who was not yet dead. Jesus answered, "Let the dead bury their dead: but go thou and preach the kingdom of God. And another also said, Lord, I will follow thee; but let me first go bid them farewell, which are at home at my house. And Jesus said unto him, No man, having put his hand to the plough, and looking back, is fit for the kingdom of God" (Luke 9:60-62).

The requests of these men seem reasonable enough to us, but to Him who reads the hearts of men, they indicated divided interests. God can accept no halfhearted obedience. We must "put in all our men."

By the sea can be found tiny purple shells clinging tenaciously to the rocks. No rushing tide can dislodge them. The secret is that there is nothing between them and the rock. This beautifully represents the believer who clings to the Saviour, allowing nothing to come between. There is security and joy in obeying Him with all our heart and with all our soul.

NO SUBSTITUTE FOR OBEDIENCE

Samuel said, Hath the Lord as great delight in burnt offerings and sacrifices, as in obeying the voice of the Lord? Behold, to obey is better than sacrifice, and to hearken than the fat of rams. 1 Sam. 15:22.

On the Israelites' hazardous journey from Egypt to the Promised Land the main body sometimes moved ahead while the feeble and weary fell behind. Thereupon the fierce and cruel Amalekites came out to smite them. Moses sent Joshua with soldiers to punish these marauders and a pitched battle ensued. After the Amalekites were driven off the Lord directed Moses to "write . . . a memorial . . . and rehearse it . . . for I will utterly put out the remembrance of Amalek from under heaven" (Ex. 17:14). In mercy this sentence was long delayed but repent they would not. Finally, when the cup of their iniquity was full, the Lord sent a message to King Saul saying, "Go and smite Amalek and utterly destroy all that they have" (1 Sam. 15:3). No command could possibly have been more specific.

Saul went energetically to his punitive task but he did not fully obey his commission. He spared Agag, king of the Amalekites, and drove off the best of the cattle and sheep. The next day, in high glee, Saul said to the prophet Samuel, "I have performed the commandment of the Lord." Samuel then asked, "What meaneth then this bleating of the sheep in mine ears, and the lowing of the oxen which I hear?" Attempting to justify himself, Saul said, "The people took of the spoil . . . to sacrifice unto the Lord thy God" (1 Sam. 15:21). No doubt Saul reasoned that, if the sheep and cattle were to be killed, they might better be offered as sacrifices. But God had said, "Destroy."

Sacrifices, gifts, and praises of all kinds are pleasing to God but none of these can atone for disobedience. True, Saul partially obeyed. But partial obedience is disobedience. The lesson stands for all time. God knows that nothing but implicit compliance with His commandments will safeguard our salvation.

There is nothing unreasonable or arbitrary in the Lord's doings. When a human magistrate gives an order, he cannot be satisfied if the one to whom he gives the command complies with it just so far as it agrees with him or suits his fancy. If a soldier is ordered to execute a specific movement, he is judged derelict of duty if he does anything but his best to fulfil his command to the letter. How much more obligatory it is upon God's children to do His will completely!

"ONE THING THOU LACKEST"

Whosoever shall keep the whole law, and yet offend in one point, he is guilty of all. James 2:10.

To some, particularly our youth, this verse seems like a hard saying. Yet, when we analyze it and comprehend its full meaning in the light of God's love, it shines forth as a most logical and reasonable utterance.

One day a lawyer came to Jesus with this question, "Master, which is the great commandment in the law?" Jesus answered, "Thou shalt love the Lord thy God with all thy heart . . ." and "Thou shalt love thy neighbour as thyself" (Matt. 22:36, 39). Thus the Saviour pointed out that love is the basis of all genuine obedience.

The Decalogue is not a collection of separate precepts. The commandments are, in fact, all the manifestations of love in action. They constitute a harmonious expression of the divine will. To choose to follow only that part of the law that is convenient to obey and ignore the rest is to do our own will and not God's. This substitutes our own will in place of God's will for us. This produces sin. We can see then that when one deliberately chooses not to accept any one of the ten precepts of the law, he does not accept God's great principles of love.

R. Lenski has written that "the law is not a set of ten pins, one of which can be knocked down while the others are left standing. A glass that is struck at only one point is nevertheless shattered. The law is a unit, its unity is love; to violate it at one point is to violate love as such, the whole of it." As a chain is snapped when one link fails, as one sour note spoils the whole harmony, as a wound to one member injures the whole body, or as leprosy in one part makes the whole man leprous, so one commandment, when disregarded neutralizes the effects of God's love for the transgressor.

The rich young ruler was troubled about his soul. After telling the Saviour truthfully that he had always kept the commandments, he asked, "What lack I yet?" He was a lovable young man and Jesus yearned to make him one of His disciples. But when told that he must divest himself of his wealth and give to the poor, he "went away grieved: for he had great possessions" (Mark 10:22). The Saviour could not give him eternal life because of one "lack"—his unwillingness to give up his riches.

Jesus looks lovingly upon us today. Do we "lack one thing?" Let us rejoice that God has provided us with His law of love, and if we are willing, His Son Jesus to be our substitute and surety for eternal life.

THE MOTIVE FOR OBEDIENCE

This is the love of God, that we keep his commandments: and his commandments are not grievous. 1 John 5:3.

In Phillips' translation this verse reads, "Loving God means obeying his commands, and these commands are not grievous." The New English Bible says "to love God is to keep his commands, and they are not burdensome." Without question, accepting Christ's righteousness and obeying His will go together. Nor can loving God and keeping His commandments ever be separated.

When I was a boy there were plenty of chores to do at our place. By the time I was 12, I had two brothers and two sisters, all eager to help with whatever small tasks they could do. I enjoyed working outside with my father, but washing dishes, making up beds, and sweeping floors didn't appeal to me. I was more interested in play. As "mother's little helper" I deserved no laurels. Still, I dearly loved my mother. One morning, when she wasn't feeling well and looked very tired, an unusual impulse struck me. I pitched in with a will. She assigned me task after task. As soon as one was finished, I ran to her to ask, "Now what can I do?" Because of my love for her these perfunctory jobs, for the first time in my life, took on significance and gave me immense satisfaction.

The noted evangelist Charles T. Everson used to say, "We are not saved *by* our works but we can be sure we cannot be saved *without* works." Although faith is assuredly the means of our salvation, it manifests itself in works. "Faith, if it hath not works, is dead . . ." (James 2:5). Faith makes believers such partakers of Christ's grace that His will becomes a delight to perform.

Any belief or motive that does not lead to obedience is presumption and wholly unacceptable to God. Acidity can be tested with paper. Our love can be tested by the litmus paper test of obedience. In Ingall's *Christian Harmony* is this stanza from the hymn, "I Love Thee:"

> "I love Thee, I love Thee,
> I love Thee, my Lord;
> I love Thee, my Saviour,
> I love Thee, my God.
> I love Thee, I love Thee,
> And that Thou dost know;
> But how much I love Thee
> My actions will show."

PRIVILEGES OF THE OBEDIENT

Ye are my friends, if ye do whatsoever I command you. John 15:14.

We can shout "Praise the Lord" and call Jesus our friend a thousand times; we may even sing loudly of His friendship, but if we overlook the "whatsoever" He commands us to do, for our own betterment, we cannot really be His friend.

What a privilege it is to have close friends! How empty and pointless life would be without them! When the evening sky is emblazoned with crimson by the setting sun and all the birds cease to sing, we know that day is done. It is then we ponder and, forgetting the cares of the day, realize that love and friendship are our greatest blessings.

In truth, friendship is about the closest mutual relationship possible between two individuals. The basis of friendship is a similarity of views, sympathy, and a fellow feeling of understanding and esteem. Originally the word *friend* meant *lover*. A friend loves for the sake of the other as well as for his own sake. A friend loves consistently and constantly regardless of any return. A greeting card, sent me by one such friend, has these lines:

"For come days happy, or come days sad
We count no hours save the ones made glad
By the wondrous good times we have ever had
——With a friend or two."

But friendship with the Saviour is higher and nobler than any earthly attachment can ever be. It is fruitful too. After calling His disciples "friends," Jesus reminded them that He had called them, and He told them why. "I have chosen you," He said, "that ye should go and bring forth fruit" (John 15:16). This divine friendship may be ours, too, that we may be active in bringing forth fruit for His kingdom.

There is joy and a rare satisfaction in obedient, fruitful service. "Sir," said the Duke of Wellington to an officer of engineers, who urged the impossibility of carrying out the orders he had received, "I did not ask your opinion. I gave you my orders, and I expect them to be obeyed." Such will be the loving obedience of every friend of Christ.

"I am the Lord your God, which have separated you from other people. . . . Ye shall be holy unto me" (Lev. 20:24). "This people I have formed for myself; they shall shew forth my praise" (Isa. 43:21).

NOTHING TO BE ADDED NOR SUBTRACTED

Ye shall not add unto the word which I command you, neither shall ye diminish aught from it, that ye may keep the commandments of the Lord your God which I command you. Deut. 4:2.

This text makes it plain that the Lord is not only "a jealous God" (Ex. 20:5), but also a particular God. He is what He says He is and He does what He says He will do. He does not want man to meddle with His Word. Because His law is a transcript of His character it is perfect and therefore not subject to improvement. To try to alter it in any way is to reflect on His character. And because it sets forth our obligations to Him and to our fellow men, any attempt to add or subtract from it is evidence of a desire to alter those obligations.

Altering or tampering illegally with human law is a common practice. The unilateral changing of any statute or even of a contractual obligation is a violation of law. Such an act also violates the Law of Nations. A classic historical example of such tampering happened in 1870 when the Prussian Chancellor Otto von Bismarck, deliberately altered a dispatch sent him from Ems by Emperor William II. Seeking a provocation to goad France into war, Bismarck recast the telegram just enough to make it sound like an insult to the French. As Bismarck hoped would happen, the French immediately declared war. This "slight alteration" provoked the Franco-Prussian War in which the French were soundly beaten. Bismarck's minor word changes ignited that gory holocaust.

To tamper with human law is invariably risky but to attempt to change divine law is inevitably fatal. The latter is so vital in God's sight that the Scriptures provide three warnings against it, once in the early part of His Word, once in the middle of it, and the third time in the last book of the Revelation. The first warning is in today's text. The second is Ecclesiastes 3:14, "Whatsoever God doeth, it shall be for ever; nothing can be put to it, nor any thing taken from it." The third warning reads in the Moffatt translation:

"I adjure all who hear the words of the prophecy of this book:
  If anyone *adds to them,*
God will add *to him the plagues described in this book,*
  And if anyone *removes* any words written in this book,
God will remove his share in *the tree of Life* and in the
  holy City described in this book" (Rev. 22:18, 19).

A CROWN OF RIGHTEOUSNESS

Henceforth there is laid up for me a crown of righteousness, which the Lord, the righteous judge, shall give me at that day: and not to me only, but unto all them also that love his appearing. 2 Tim. 4:8.

Recently my wife and I visited an affluent financier and his wife in their stately manor house in a fashionable, exclusive suburb of a great city. This imposing mansion lacked nothing of elegance or splendor, and the furnishings were sumptuously magnificent. As these obviously well-heeled people proudly walked us from one stately room to another we were visibly impressed. They were living like lords. Even so, because they had once been dutiful churchgoers, I sensed a strange dissonance, an absence of harmony between their former modest mode of living and this princely display of opulence. Finally we came to a showroom of glittering luster. There sat a pair of professionally carved, life-sized teakwood human statues each wearing a lavishly emblazoned golden crown encrusted with diamonds and rubies. I had not seen such glitter except in the British Museum. Turning to our host, I asked, "Why such extravagance?" As a shadow crossed his handsome face he said soberly, "It's because my wife and I know these are the only golden crowns we'll ever have." In all likelihood he spoke the truth.

Most people these days don't know much about crowns and couldn't care less. Yet, because the Bible often mentions them, we should understand their significance. Historically a crown is an ornamental headpiece worn as a symbol of authority. The blue band, or diadem, is the sign of kingship. In Israel of old the high priest wore a golden crown, and the famous Greek "crown of victory" consisted of a wreath of laurel or olive leaves presented to the winner as an emblem of victory in an athletic or military contest.

No doubt Paul knew that those who championed the athletes of his day could encourage them by their cheers yet could not help them win. But God, who offers the "crown of righteousness," supplies the strength to every one who strives.

When the aged apostle wrote these confident words of assurance to Timothy he himself was nearing the finish line in life's long race. Imprisoned and facing imminent execution, he had nothing on earth to look forward to. But the beckoning hand of God was all he needed to eclipse every earthly desire. May we, with him, receive the "crown of righteousness" that "fadeth not away."

SUCCESS AS A REWARD OF OBEDIENCE

This book of the law shall not depart out of thy mouth; but thou shalt meditate therein day and night, that thou mayest observe to do according to all that is written therein: for then thou shalt make thy way prosperous, and then thou shalt have good success. Joshua 1:8.

Our text treats of prosperity and success. Investigations have shown what most people intuitively know, that opinions vastly differ as to what constitutes success. Ask Sophocles and he replies, "Success is the reward of toil." Ask Andrew Carnegie and you get this answer, "Success in any line is to make yourself a master in that line." Dale Carnegie's answer is "The successful man will profit by his mistakes." Lord Dewar said, "The road to success is filled with women pushing their husbands along the road." Roger Bacon's opinion was that "success is the result of constant effort."

The different viewpoints from which success is considered also enormously influence the judgments of it. The carefree man who lived in a barrel offered a different definition of success from that of the overburdened king on his throne. A youth of 20 will evaluate success quite at variance with the views of a doctor or a lawyer on the threshold of retirement. Also, for the individual, the concept of success changes and too often palls as the years pass.

With insight born of experience Henry Ward Beecher said that "success is full of promise till men get it, and then it is as a last year's nest from which the bird has flown." With even deeper insight he wrote that "everybody finds out, sooner or later, that all success worth having is founded on Christian rules of conduct."

How eager was the Lord for Israel to succeed and how good He was to them! He chose them to be "a special people unto himself" (Deut. 7:6). He gave them a perfect law, which, when obeyed, assured them of prosperity and "good success." This included spiritual as well as temporal blessings. Through their prosperity God was to be honored, and through them all nations of the earth were to be blessed.

We, too, by diligently following the Lord's commandments, have the promise of prosperity and "good success" as truly as did Israel. "Blessed is every one that feareth the Lord, that walketh in his ways" (Ps. 128:1).

OBEDIENCE UNTO LIFE ETERNAL

Behold, one came and said unto him, Good Master, what good thing shall I do, that I may have eternal life? And he said unto him . . . if thou wilt enter into life, keep the commandments. Matt. 19:16, 17.

On the face of it this categorical reply from the lips of the Saviour would seem to mean that heaven is the reward meted out to the faithful for their obedience to the Decalogue. But it is not quite that simple. Hence the endless discussion in religious circles today centering on the proper relation of law and grace, the correct balance of obedience and love. A number of popular modern Christian advocates insist that we need love and practically nothing else. These would de-emphasize the ten commandments almost out of existence or, at least, reduce them to insignificance. Rejecting out of hand the stern Calvinistic doctrine that heaven is a fore-ordained reward for obedience alone, these enthusiastic espousers of "the new theology" go to the opposite extreme as they advocate their "advanced" views of Christian freedom. This liberating emphasis on a largely emotional response, rather than on a call to obedience, is eagerly espoused by youth who regard it as countenancing a permissive life of "love" wherein each can conscientiously "do his own thing" and still bask in the indulgent, approving smile of the Lord Jesus.

How then shall we relate to the words of Christ who said, "If thou wilt enter into life, keep the commandments?" Taken in context, it is clear that Jesus did not mean by this that anyone can *earn* eternal life. A home in heaven is God's crowning gift and, even by the strongest faith, we can but faintly appreciate the meaning of this great and wonderful prize—an endless life in which all is perfection. It means that we shall live as long as Christ shall live.

Lesson assignments to students are grievous when they are beyond their mental ability. Taxes are devastating when they are imposed arbitrarily beyond the capacity of people to pay. But the indwelling love of God solves this problem in the spiritual realm by enabling the believer to fulfill the righteousness of the law. (Rom. 8:3, 4.) Without His love the commandments are beyond our power to obey but this is where love comes in. Embued with divine love the believer is enabled to keep the law with ease and confidence. When the heart is filled with Christ's presence through the Holy Spirit, obedience follows. If we feel that the lofty standards of God are burdensome, the inner life probably needs attention, restoration, and rededication through the power of the Holy Spirit.

THE LAW OF THE WISE

The law of the wise is a fountain of life, to depart from the snares of death. Prov. 13:14.

In the bright morning of life many young people feel such strength and vigor, such energy and vitality that, briefly at least, they believe that they will live on and on and never die. Sooner or later, however, everyone born into this world of sin must face up to the stark reality that, no matter how we feel, this temporal life is a furtive, fleeting thing that inexorably slips through our fingers, and that no elixir or tonic known to man can ever recall it. This joyless moment of truth comes to some with a start when in the mirror the first silver hair appears among the darker strands. It may come on the playing field or during a hike when we first notice that our legs do not respond with the alacrity they had only yesterday. Perhaps on some ill-starred day we do not bound out of bed with our usual enthusiasm to challenge the tasks of the day. Whether this unexpected first sign of physical decline leaps upon us suddenly or by slow degrees is of no significance. In most cases the realization is a shock and, counting life dear, it is inevitable to do all we possibly can to delay declivity and postpone our decadence of powers.

From time immemorial men have sought in vain for the legendary Fountain of Youth, a never-failing spring reputed to have power to restore youth. In the sixteenth century it was thought to be somewhere on the tiny island of Bimini in the Bahamas. There the intrepid Spanish explorer Ponce de León looked for this ''marvelous fountain whose waters would rejuvenate all who bathed in or drank them.'' Failing, as have all others who ever sought it, Ponce de León lost his life in the attempt.

Our text declares that the ''law of the wise is a fountain of life.'' No one can safely despise this law for by obedience to certain physical laws of health our lives can be improved and extended. The laws of this life may not be universal, but we violate them to our hurt. The ''law of the wise includes God's moral law which *is* universal. There is no escape from it.

The wise live by rule according to law. A morally wise person will keep his powers of mind and soul in hand. This is the fountain that, both here and hereafter, delivers the obedient ''from the snares of death.''

THE DECEITFULNESS OF SIN

But exhort one another daily, while it is called To day; lest any of you be hardened through the deceitfulness of sin. Heb. 3:13.

The chameleon is a harmless little reptile that some people find interesting because it can almost instantly change its color from gray to green, red, or blue. A young woman once captured a small, salamander-like creature she thought was a chameleon. She enjoyed playing with it and, so as to display it for her friends, she put a tiny collar on it and pinned it by a little chain so it could crawl about on her shoulder. But, instead of being a chameleon as she thought, it was a poisonous kind of lizard that, despite its diminutive size, bit her one day, causing her death. What this girl did innocently millions are doing every day. They are toying with a viper called sin. Sin does not always appear sinful because, in one respect, it is like the chameleon, it can change its colors to fit any environment and appear to be what it is not.

"Nothing is more treacherous than the deceitfulness of sin. It is the god of this world that deludes, and blinds, and leads to destruction. . . . He [Satan] disguises these temptations with a semblance of good; he mingles some little improvement with the folly and amusements, and deceived souls . . . [engage] in them. . . . Satan's hellish arts are masked. Beguiled souls take one step, then are prepared for the next. It is much more pleasant to follow the inclination of their own hearts than to . . . resist the first insinuation of the wily foe. . . . Satan watches to see his bait taken . . . and to see souls walking in the very path he has prepared! . . . He unites his sophistry and deceptive snares with their experience . . . and thus wonderfully advances his cause."—*Testimonies,* vol. 2, pp. 142, 143.

Sin allures because it appears wonderfully desirable and appealing. When Eve looked at what God had warned her not to eat, she viewed it as "good for food," "pleasant to the eyes" and "desired to make one wise" (Gen. 3:6). She was totally deceived in each respect. Yet she stepped over the line that separates right from wrong, and by that fatal step flung open the floodgates of evil.

Today, as in the Garden, the most deceptive characteristic of sin is its almost irresistible fascination. But when Christ dwells within, the mask of evil fades, and we see sin as it is. We must ever be wary lest we lose our souls through the deceitfulness of sin.

THE WAY OF THE TRANSGRESSOR

Good understanding giveth favor; but the way of the transgressor is hard. Prov. 13:15.

The good understanding that brings favor corresponds with what, in an ethical sense, we call elevated culture. It shows how to take the right side and, in all circumstances, to exercise a kindly, heart-winning influence. This sound understanding is the kind Daniel had. It gave him favor in the Babylonian court. Such a good understanding removes a partition wall and brings people into easier relationships. Intelligence and sound judgment, by fitting a man to be a wise and prudent counsellor, win him favor and preferment.

Over the entrance arch at a state penitentiary appears the inscription, "The way of the transgressor is hard." I have wondered what this truism has meant to convicts entering. Some, no doubt, in turmoil of mind and distress of soul, heartily agree. Some may be so humiliated that they hardly see it at all. Others appear to be so set and so hardened as to seem already determined to prove it false. Yet, in spite of much evidence to the contrary, these words are still true. Paul wrote the Galatians that "whatsoever a man soweth, that shall he also reap" (chap. 6:7).

The word here translated "hard" denotes that which remains the same during the course of time. The fundamental idea is of remaining like itself, continuing uncultivated and incapable of cultivation. This is the way of the transgressors and the manner in which they interact with others—stiff, repulsive, and hard as stone. Such a way is hard for themselves, for the members of their families, and for society. The faithless Voltaire said, "I find myslf in a most deplorable condition, environed with the deepest darkness on every side. . . . In man is more wretchedness than in all other animals put together. Man loves life, yet knows he must die. I wish I had never been born."

True, the way of transgressors is hard. But not too hard. The very harshness of the path is intended to induce them to leave it. Because the end is worse than the journey, it is God's mercy to make it hard. The pain tells the sinner that he has taken the wrong road. The buffeting that wounds him is only the voice of God saying, "Turn back. Do thyself no harm." When a hazardous mountain pass looms ahead where every step is misery and the freezing cold threatens death, is it not suicide to continue? As in days of old, the Lord still calls, "Turn ye from your evil ways; for why will ye die, O house of Israel?" (Eze. 33:11).

GOD'S GIFT OF LIFE ETERNAL

For the wages of sin is death; but the gift of God is eternal life through Jesus Christ our Lord. Rom. 6:23.

Great as are the contrasts between light and darkness and between good and evil, none is greater—or more important—than between the two opposites, *life* and *death,* as set forth in this sublime passage. Sin repays its devotees with eternal death, which is what they have earned. In colossal contrast stands life eternal, the "unspeakable gift," for which Paul fervently thanked God (2 Cor. 9:15). This is the crowning gift that awaits all who are prepared to receive it.

This irreversible antithesis of destiny is inherent in the Biblical descriptions of the ultimate fate of the impenitent. They are compared to fat, which melts away in the fire (Ps. 37:20). They are likened to the chaff of a summer threshing floor (Dan. 2:35). They will be burned up root and branch (Mal. 4:1-3). They will disappear in unquenchable fire, not in the sense that it will burn throughout eternity, but that no power on earth can extinguish the flame until it has burned out completely (Matt. 3:11, 12). This destruction will be everlasting death (2 Thess. 1:9). And finally, they shall be as though they had never been (Obadiah 16).

In the sharpest possible contrast to the eternal extinction of the wicked stands the glorious gift offered in love to the faithful believers of earth. In the promised home of the saved every condition contributes to perfect happiness and everlasting joy. The curse of sin is obliterated. Satan has been forever destroyed (Rev. 20:10). Crime and vice are no more (Isa. 60:18). There will be no locks on the doors, no time vaults in the banks, no floods nor devastating fires, and no haunting memories. No tears nor sorrows, no growing old and infirm, no death and no funerals will mar the peace and tranquillity of that goodly land.

Have you ever tried to imagine the exhilaration the faithful reapers in the Lord's vineyard will experience as they greet again those for whom they have labored and prayed? Can you foresee the wordless emotion that will flood the hearts of long-separated loved ones cruelly torn from them by the pitiless hand of death?

This is the way God's purposes will be realized, and His great love for man be made manifest. The penalty for sin is death but, beholding man's helpless condition, He made a sure way of escape. He does not reward us according to our iniquities but according to His great love, for He is "very pitiful and of tender mercy" toward all who in sincerity call upon Him for salvation (James 5:11).

EVILDOERS CANNOT INHERIT HEAVEN

The righteous shall never be removed, but the wicked shall not inherit the earth. Prov. 10:30.

Traditionally, and to a mandatory degree, the estate of an English nobleman belongs to his family as they live on it, maintain it, and share its production. But the eldest son is the heir of the house which is his as a perpetual possession. It is, therefore, his in a sense that it is not the property of his brothers and sisters. Similarly, the psalmist says that "the earth is the Lord's and the fulness thereof" (Ps. 24:1). It is thus the property also of His children, of those who have been accepted as His sons and heirs (Rom. 8:17). To some extent all men enjoy the blessings of the earth, but it really belongs only to those Paul addresses thus, "All things are yours . . . the world . . . things present or things to come" (1 Cor. 3:21, 22). Again and again this assurance is repeated in the Scriptures. David said, "What man is he that feareth the Lord? . . . His seed shall inherit the earth" (Ps. 25:12, 13).

Clearly, the earth made new is to be the inheritance and the eternal abode of the righteous. Yet there will be that about it to enable the redeemed of this earth to recognize it. And if in this wonderful place there is to dwell righteousness it will be because it is the home of righteous beings.

It is the gracious will of the Father that not one should be shut out of this blessed abode under preparation for the righteous to occupy throughout eternity. He sent His Son into the world to live and die that even the vilest sinner might be saved. But the wicked shall not inherit the earth—unless they cease to be wicked. To emphasize this the apostle Paul wrote the Ephesians, "For this ye know, that no . . . unclean person . . . hath any inheritance in the kingdom of Christ" (chap. 5:5).

A profound love of home is a natural emotion in man and no people ever delighted more in home than did the Israelites. But even the adopted Israelite need not fear eternal expatriation. From that "home of the soul" the repentant sinner will never be excluded.

How different it is with the wicked who have their hearts set on an eternal existence where they may live as selfishly and as sensually as they have in this present life! Heaven would be no joy for them. "It is no arbitrary decree on the part of God that excludes the wicked from heaven: they are shut out by their own unfitness for its companionship."—*Steps to Christ*, p. 18.

WRONGING ONE'S OWN SOUL

But he that sinneth against me wrongeth his own soul: all they that hate me love death. Prov. 8:36.

From the time the devil deceived Eve and entrapped her in disobedience, he has made sin appear harmless and attractive. Had she foreseen the tragedy let loose upon mankind by that one transgression she would not have been so easily beguiled by the devil's falsehoods. From that day to this it has been this enemy's calculated plan to shield the eyes of his deluded victims from the end results of their own disobedience.

Our own fallible judgment is incompetent to evaluate the results of even one transgression. As our first parents learned to their incalculable sorrow, the sure fruit of sin is more monstrous sin. Like the huge wooden horse full of soldiers the Greeks used to enter and destroy Troy, so is sin when taken into the heart.

Had Cain perceived to what lengths of anger his jealousy would lead him he would have humbled himself before God and never would have killed his brother. Had Samson stopped to think of the degradation into which Delilah's forbidden charms would plunge him he would not have had to spend his last days as a blind slave grinding corn for his enemies. Had the prodigal son visualized himself, friendless, hungry, and in rags, feeding shucks to swine he would hardly have allowed the beckoning pleasures of sin to entice him away from his father's house. And certainly self-serving Judas would not have betrayed his Lord had he but looked ahead to his pitiful, suicidal death.

God is the fountainhead of life and when anyone turns away from Him and chooses the service of sin he separates himself from his only source of spiritual strength and cuts himself off from life. As Jesus said, he becomes "alienated from the life of God" (Eph. 4:18). In other words, all who reject God's mercy unwittingly embrace death. How sad that unrepentant sinners find this out too late!

God gives the rejecters of His mercy "existence for a time that they may develop their character and reveal their principles. This accomplished, they receive the results of their own choice. By a life of rebellion, Satan and all who unite with him place themselves so out of harmony with God that His very presence is to them a consuming fire. The glory of Him who is love will destroy them."—*The Desire of Ages,* p. 764.

FRIENDSHIP WITH JESUS

Know ye not that the friendship of the world is enmity with God? Whosoever therefore will be a friend of the world is the enemy of God. James 4:4.

Of the many names and attributes that characterize Jesus none carries quite the depth of meaning as does the word *friend*. He emphasized its special significance when, as He neared the close of His earthly ministry, for the first and last time He called His disciples "friends" (John 15:15).That left no doubt of His special feeling of endearment toward them. It may have given them a deepening insight into the intended slur of the Pharisees when they called Him a "friend of publicans and sinners!" (Luke 7:34). In any case they knew then that henceforth He was in truth the "friend that sticketh closer than a brother" (Prov. 18:24).

Many high, fulsome tributes have been paid to human friendships. Charles Gow wrote that "true happiness consists, not in the multitude of friends, but in their worth and choice." Another writer has it that "the strong, helpful grasp of the hand by a true friend is worth more than silver and gold." Robert Louis Stevenson said that a "friend is a present you give to yourself."

But the joys and benefits of sincere human friendship, however vast and inspiring, cannot compare with the friendship Jesus offers. His precious promises prove that His love is all-sufficient for every human experience, and that His gifts are bountiful beyond all human calculation. Before He left His disciples He promised them three things: absolute fearlessness, unutterable happiness, and that they would get into trouble. As their Friend He shared all three.

"The most striking characteristic and the most moving quality in the life of Jesus," says Joseph Sizoo, "was His capacity for friendship." The Lord's abiding good will ran across every racial, social, economic, and political frontier. He held all mankind in the embrace of His love. This included the rich and the poor, the old and the young, the moron and the savant. It is true that Christ had intimate friends. There were those who lived in the inner circle of His comradeship. His love could be manifest to some more than to others. But beyond these intimate friendships the Lord lived with a sense of good will toward all mankind.

Although many professed Christians know that the world is at enmity with God, they are disloyal to Christ. We cannot be friends both with Christ and the world. Today's text emphasizes that this is unthinkable.

WHICH MASTER?

No man can serve two masters: for either he will hate the one, and love the other; or else he will hold to the one, and despise the other. Matt. 6:24.

The Bible leaves no doubt that acceptable service to God requires complete devotion. No halfway dedication will do. Moses told Israel "that the Lord he is God; there is none else" (Deut. 4:35). The Almighty Himself asserted His exclusive, peerless primacy when He said at Sinai, "I the Lord thy God am a jealous God" (Ex. 20:5). In His masterful simplification of the Decalogue, Jesus emphasized this majestic certainty in the words, "Thou shalt love the Lord thy God with all thy heart" (Luke 10:27). As one author has put it, "God must be Lord of all or He is not Lord at all."

In heaven, when Lucifer sinned and was cast out with his angels into the earth he immediately claimed dominion over this same world in which Adam and Eve had been created and over which they were given dominion. Having failed in his bid for dominion in heaven, Satan made it his chief business to gain it here by securing the allegiance of our first parents. When they sinned by yielding to Satan's deception a conflict began that continues until now.

Through disobedience Adam yielded the dominion God had given him, whereupon Satan usurped man's overlordship and became the "prince of this world" (John 12:31). When, on the mount of temptation, Satan said, "All this is delivered unto me," Jesus did not dispute him (Luke 4:6). But the issue did not end there. Dominion still remained undecided. Three and one-half years later Jesus went to Golgotha and died there to reclaim it. He paid for it with His own blood.

The great controversy still rages. The battleground for uncontested dominion is the heart of man. Satan would dethrone God and assume complete control. The Saviour pleads, "Give me thine heart" (Prov. 23:26).

By His sacrifice Jesus made possible the restoration of the lost dominion. The decision as to who must be served—the Saviour or Satan—will be made individually in every human heart.

" 'Give me thine heart,' says the Saviour of men,
    Calling in mercy again and again;
  'Turn now from sin, and from evil depart,
    Have I not died for thee? Give me thine heart.' "

FELLOWSHIP WITH THE WORLD

Have no fellowship with the unfruitful works of darkness, but rather reprove them. Eph. 5:11.

In the *New English Bible* this text and the ones with it offer a little different interpretation thus: "Try to find out what would please the Lord; take no part in the barren deeds of darkness, but show them up for what they are. The things they do in secret it would be shameful to mention." The uncompromising exhortation expressed in these verses sounds clear and plain. Yet there are other scriptural instructions that deal with the Christian's proper associations in a somewhat different light. Jesus, who is assuredly our example, associated so much with those of questionable morals that He said of Himself that He "came, enjoying life, and people say, 'Look, a drunkard and a glutton—the bosom-friend of the tax-collector and the sinner'" (Matt. 11:19, Philips). To what end did He risk His influence with the better classes? "Jesus was eating with publicans and sinners in order to bring the light of heaven to those who sat in darkness."—*The Desire of Ages,* p. 276.

Conscientious Christians often find it perplexing to know for sure where to draw the line between avoiding, on one hand, fellowship with those who do shameful deeds of darkness and, on the other, engaging in authorized, uplifting witnessing before sinners. This question troubled me as a teen-ager. In college I had a friend called Averill who, although a gifted scholar, was not a Christian. One time in spring he asked me to take a long Sabbath walk with him. He proposed an all-day hike to the mountains and wanted me to ask permission of the dean of men for us to go. I did this, also asking for his advice. The dean said, "Ordinarily I'd say No but I believe you can go and keep the Sabbath. Besides you may be able to influence Averill." We hiked to the mountains, and I kept the Sabbath. For once, at least, so did Averill. The remembrance of that hike has remained a helpful guide to me ever since.

On sensitive issues such as this no one can be conscience for another. Each believer must needs examine the matter prayerfully and then decide for himself the proper procedure. This much is clear: we are to have no fellowship with "the unfruitful works of darkness" but we must not hold ourselves aloof from the world. Our influence, like that of Jesus, may be instrumental in leading unbelievers out of darkness into the light of the gospel.

UNSPOTTED FROM THE WORLD

Pure religion and undefiled before God and the Father is this, To visit the fatherless and widows in their affliction, and to keep himself unspotted from the world. James 1:27.

With the passing of the years little incidents of childhood sometimes seem to grow more vivid. One small occurrence of fleeting importance has remained long lodged in my mind, the result, no doubt, of its connection with today's text. It was my sister Ruth's seventh birthday, and mother had surprised her with a frilly white dress. The next Sabbath she wore it proudly but, as she walked home after church a passing vehicle splashed inky-black mudspots all up and down one side. Certain that her new gown was ruined, little Ruth ran home in tears. Mother's careful washing later removed the ugly stains completely, but I shall never forget how punishing was Ruth's distress that day nor how deep was my sympathy for her. Our Sabbath school memory verse that morning was today's text. This phrase, "keep . . . unspotted from the world," has had emphasis from this episode ever since that day.

The Lord has not left us in doubt as to what constitutes pure and genuine religion. It assuredly involves doing humble, loving service such as showing kindness to neighbors, orphans, and widows. Unfeigned religion, when free from pretense and hypocrisy, will also keep the heart pure and free from the corrupting influences of the world. A mere outward profession is valueless in the sight of God.

At the close of a great revival in New York City the far-famed evangelist D. L. Moody called his new converts together to impart some "advice to young Christians." In part he said, "Let your friends be those who are in the church. Select for your companions experienced Christians. Keep company with those who know a little more than you do. . . . You get the best of the bargain; but from my own experience I know it is the best way to make advances in religious life. And fall in love with the Book, and the world will lose its hold on you."

After his first public concert, the eminent composer Giuseppe Verdi was loudly applauded. But no evidence of satisfaction crossed his countenance until he saw an appreciative smile on the face of his teacher. The approval of the world ought not move us. Instead our greatest satisfaction and joy should come from pleasing the Saviour while guarding against those things that forfeit His smile. In this way we can keep ourselves "unspotted from the world."

HATRED WITHOUT CAUSE

"If the world hates you, it hated me first. . . . He who hates me, hates my Father. . . . However, . . . 'They hated me without reason.'" John 15:18-25, N.E.B.

In Phillips' translation these words of Jesus are expressed thus: "The man who hates me, hates my Father as well. . . . They hated me without cause."

In the beginning of the world love reigned. Looking at His creation God "saw everything that he had made, and, behold, it was very good" (Gen. 1:31). But when sin entered hatred opposed love and evil grew predominant. Referring to this colossal tragedy, Jesus used the word "world" to represent the evil and sinners in it. "Marvel not, my brethren," said He, "if the world hate you" (1 John 3:13). "You know that it hated me before it hated you."

We may sometimes wonder why the world manifested such hatred toward Christ. It was truly "without cause." Yet wicked men did hate Him. It was because His life, His words, and everything He ever did testified that they and all their works were evil and would end at last in the lake of fire. Jesus came to reconcile the world to God. But the blameless life He lived and the gospel He proclaimed were so opposite to the desires and practices of the world that, in towering hate, it rose up to oppose and destroy Him.

Today the world hates Christ's followers for the very reasons it hated Him. Worldlings want to believe Satan's claim that no man can live uprightly. That claim is given the lie by every Christian who brings forth the fruits of righteousness. This is maddening. So, with no cause at all, the wicked man or woman mortally hates Christians as Christ was hated in His day.

When brotherly kindness is repaid with hatred, when the misfortunes of the righteous are met with derision, when piety is made the object of scorn, then the Christian "enters into Christ's suffering" and that of the Father, for Jesus said that those who hate Him hate the Father also.

Christ was *in* the world but, by His example, he showed us how not to be *of* the world. He was no recluse shut away in holy meditation. He made contacts with all classes of men, making a powerful appeal to them to live a holy life as He did. With this peerless example to guide us we need not fear whatever hatred the world manifests, and like Him we must remember not to hate in return.

AFTER LAUGHTER, TEARS

Woe unto you that laugh now! for ye shall mourn and weep. Luke 6:25.

In all God's vast creation man alone was endowed with a sense of humor. He is the only creature that laughs. Humor surfaces in a hundred ways, and laughter takes a thousand forms. There is the innocent laughter of the little child, the lilting laughter of the happy young girl, the deep-throated laughter of manhood. There is a laugh for surprise, another for disappointment, a different one for pure joy and even a sighing laugh for sorrow. There is laughter for every known mood of man. Mark Twain said, "The human race has only one really effective weapon and that is laughter."

In our text, Jesus was not referring to the wholesome laughter of the Christian but to the coarse, raucous guffaw of the wicked of which the wise man said, "It is mad" (Eccl. 2:2). Solomon also sensed that "the heart of fools is in the house of mirth" (Eccl. 7:4). He also observed sadly that "even in laughter the heart is sorrowful; and the end of that mirth is heaviness" (Prov. 14:13).

Looking at the enthralled multitude, many of whom He had just healed of their diseases, the Saviour recognized the narrowness of their minds and the shallowness of their gratitude. He foresaw their sufferings, the carnage and annihilation ahead, which they did not anticipate, despite all His warnings. Saddest of all He knew that nearly all within the range of His voice would turn aside from His free offer of salvation and be consumed at last in the lake of fire.

The Saviour's call still reechoes above the barren hills over Jordan, beyond troubled Galilee into anxious Europe and teeming Asia and up and down the aging New World. Jesus invites all who will hear Him to spurn the allurements of the deceitful enemy of souls and to reply to his temptations:

> "Nay, world! I turn away,
> Though thou seemest fair and good:
> That friendly outstretched hand of thine
> Is stained with Jesus' blood.
> If in thy least device
> I stoop to take a part,
> All unaware, thine influence steals
> God's presence from my heart."—Margaret Mauro

BLAMING SOMEBODY ELSE

And the man said, The woman whom thou gavest to be with me, she gave me of the tree, and I did eat. Gen. 3:12.

We cannot go back farther in the history of the world than to Eden where transgression originated, and along with it the sin of blaming others. When God asked Adam about his disobedience, he blamed Eve, thus indirectly placing the blame on the Creator. Eve, in turn, blamed the serpent, saying he had beguiled her. Here at the very beginning we find man dodging responsibility for his misdeeds. He has been doing it ever since. Few indeed are willing to stand up manfully and accept responsibility for their acts when things go wrong and their plans fail.

Many instances of blaming others are recorded in Holy Writ. None is more instructive than that of Aaron who was left in charge when Moses went to receive the Decalogue on Mount Sinai. Since their leader did not return when they thought he should, the people demanded a replacement. "Make us gods," they cried to Aaron, "as for this Moses . . . we wot not what is become of him" (Ex. 32:1). Lacking sanctified backbone and wanting to please the people, Aaron made them a golden calf, which they danced around, having quite forgotten the God who had brought them out of Egypt. But when Moses returned those pagan-minded Israelites scurried to their tents leaving Aaron to confront his wrathful brother alone. Aaron pleaded, "Let not the anger of my lord wax hot: thou knowest the people . . . I said unto them, Whosoever hath any gold, let them break it off . . . : then I cast it into the fire, and there came out this calf" (verses 22-24). What a stupid explanation! He would have Moses believe that the golden calf came walking right out of the fire.

In attempting to justify himself Aaron tried to conceal facts, which is what all do who blame others. Yet people still try to live in this make-believe world. In politics the governor blames the legislature and the legislators blame the voters. When the conference gets into trouble the president blames the pastors and the pastors blame the members. In the school the students blame the teachers, the teachers blame the principal and the principal blames the board. In the home the children blame one another and the parents blame each other. It is a familiar merry-go-round.

Yet, both God and man, even husbands and wives, are quick to forgive the one who admits, "I was wrong." To blame others is human, to forgive is divine.

CARNAL PLEASURE IS VANITY

I said in mine heart, Go to now, I will prove thee with mirth, therefore enjoy pleasure: and, behold, this also is vanity. Eccl. 2:1.

This verse summarizes the chapter it introduces. It is a personal monologue or soliloquy of Solomon with himself. Its significance lies in the fact that this wise and wealthy king had ample opportunity to taste every pleasure his age could offer. He did not, like the esthete, judge life from some obscure retreat and despise its glories he could not share. Instead he tried them all. He tried unrestrained indulgence of the lower appetite in drink. He explained it thus, "I sought in my heart to give myself unto wine" (Eccl. 2:3). In its intoxication he could forget the miseries and painful aspects of life and see it as if illuminated with some bright glare. But with the sober reawakening to reality he experienced a towering repugnance toward sottish inebriation. In strong drink he found no pleasure. He concluded that "wine is a ridiculer, intoxicating liquor is boisterous, and everyone going astray by it is not wise" (Prov. 20:1, N.W.T.).

Solomon also experimented with unrestrained indulgence of animal instincts. The unleashing of wild passions left him the nauseating spectacle of a great soul debased through unbridled gratification. He demonstrated that in the throbbing excitement of pleasure for its own sake rationality gives way to mad infatuation, that to forsake duty and allow the carnal senses to run riot is to dethrone reason. Surely, for a man with a mind like his to allow the sirens of desire to debase that intellect until reality became an illusion is sheer madness.

Coming to himself, Solomon saw that when reason deserts her throne the image of God is marred and man falls below his proper dignity. The scepter falls from his hand and his sovereign powers vanish.

Solomon finally concludes that worldly pleasure promises much but benefits little. He who tries in the polluted pools of sin to drown out the sad facts of life becomes disenchanted. He first suspects and then knows himself befooled. Although sinful pleasures promise to entertain the whole life through, they early clog the senses and wear out life's resources. The power to enjoy the world passes away. Pleasure casts away her worshipers when they have toyed with her for a season. Then all these transient joys turn into disgust and loathing. "Behold, this also is vanity."

WISE WORDS TO YOUTH

Rejoice, O young man, in thy youth; and let thy heart cheer thee in the days of thy youth, and walk in the ways of thine heart, and in the sight of thine eyes: but know thou, that for all these things God will bring thee into judgment. Eccl. 11:9.

One of the saddest and most tragic realities of this life is the undeniable fact that many crucial decisions are made at the least advisable time. Youth make vital choices in the springtime of their lives when wisdom is yet in the bud and there is little or no experience on which to draw. The unbounded confidence and impetuosity of youth add to the danger of making unfortunate decisions.

Many are the youth who, without sufficient consideration and on impulse, choose a profession with little regard for their natural talents and capacities. An ill-advised choice often results in a lifetime of boredom and acute unhappiness. Like "a square peg in a round hole," they simply do not fit in, and the fruitage of their unwise choice is discouragement and dissatisfaction.

Similarly, in the early, throbbing thrill of young love, adolescent couples see in each other the hopeful realization of all their fondest dreams and, without considering any other factor, rush into matrimony only to discover that they are utterly unsuited for each other in the most important ways. As someone has said wisely, "Many a young man falls in love with a dimple or a curl and then foolishly marries the entire girl."

Possibly the aging Solomon remembered some unhappy experiences and observations. There may have been a rueful smile on his lips as he recalled how often headstrong youth insist stubbornly on learning by their own experience. So he solemnly warned of the coming judgment. In that day how will our pleasure appear in God's sight when every character is weighed for eternity?

"Sometime your last song will be sung;
I wonder what song it will be:
The song that was heard at the dance last night,
Or the holy "Abide With Me"?

"And when your last word has been said,
In breathing of time or of trust,"
Will it tell of a hope in that heavenly land,
Or of treasures lost in the dust?"

—Robert Hare

PLEASURES KNOWN AND UNKNOWN

There is nothing better for a man, than that he should eat and drink, and that he should make his soul enjoy good in his labour. Eccl. 2:24.

Once while I was visiting with one of my sisters we were suddenly interrupted by her 10-year-old son who burst into the house with a perturbed expression on his face. He ran to her and asked, "Mamma, why is it that the bad boys have all the fun?" She explained that because the older boys down the street used foul language and played rough and dangerous games in the street she did not want him with them. This explanation seemed to satisfy him, at least in part. She then gave him a new book she had just bought for him. He took it and went to his room. After he closed the door his mother said to me, "I've been asking that same question all my life: 'Why is it that worldly people seem to enjoy life a lot more than Christians do?'" We talked about that and agreed that worldlings only *seem* to get the most pleasure out of life.

What my nephew at 10 did not know is that he was asking a question that has puzzled the hearts of men for ages. Job asked it in his day, and David admitted that his steps "well nigh slipped . . ." when he saw the prosperity of the wicked. But the psalmist's doubts vanished when he went into the sanctuary of God where he clearly foresaw the coming annihilation of the wicked (see Ps. 73:3, 17).

One of the more prevalent deceptions of the devil is his constant portrayal of the Christian life as a joyless way. Actually Christianity thoroughly encourages the exercise of every healthful practice that enhances the value of life. It does not in any way incapacitate the believer for the fullest enjoyment of true happiness. "It does not mantle the life in sackcloth; it is not expressed in sighs and groans. . . . Those who in everything make God first . . . and best are the happiest people in the world."—*Fundamentals of Education,* pp. 83, 84.

Were there no life eternal beckoning on the believers of earth, were there no paradise ahead where pleasures are so great that "eye hath not seen nor ear heard" of them, it would still be far better to live uprightly among men. Enduring happiness is found only in doing and being good. Instead of seeking what fleeting pleasures the world provides, the Christian will remember that the amusements of earth are never satisfying nor healing to the sinsick soul. In Christ is fullness of joy forevermore.

LUSTS OF THE SPIRIT
The spirit that dwelleth in us lusteth. James 4:5.

The Bible warns repeatedly against the dangers of the lusts of the flesh. It calls these carnal temptations deceitful, unclean, hurtful, and foolish—and so they are. Drunkenness, dissipation, and the numbing of the senses from riotous living are devastating and foolish to the participant, and are saddening and pathetic to the observer. But the more pernicious evils of the world stem not from the indulgence of the fleshly appetites but from the more insidious and deceptive lusts of man's spirit.

The vaunted military conqueror Alexander the Great was proud of his personal chastity. Contrary to the custom of his time, he refused to violate the wives and daughters of his captives. Yet Alexander's over-weening ambition to conquer the world constituted a more monstrous wickedness than yielding to the lusts of the flesh could ever be. The murder, rapine, and arson that devastated the regions that Alexander's armies subjugated left a harrowing record of destruction that appalls all who read of these atrocities.

Adolf Hitler boasted of his admirable qualities. He was a sober, continent vegetarian living a Spartan personal life. But no more vicious, evil man ever lived. Like Alexander, his myriad atrocities were the mortal sins of the spirit.

Whether it be in commerce, politics, or religion, it is the man with a lust for power, with an overgrown desire for honor or glory, with a maniacal need to manipulate and overcome all who stand in the way, whose curse is the lust of the spirit. Such are the men who do the greatest harm. In comparison the weak people, those who easily succumb to the lusts of the flesh, cause relatively small trouble.

Physical sin shows how far man has fallen from what he was in Eden. But spiritual sin repudiates and perverts all Ten Commandments. This malignant perversion repeatedly has brought men and nations to the brink of catastrophe. Any number of libertines and wastrels cannot do the damage perpetrated by misguided, self-serving sadists or bigots.

Jesus was accused by respectable citizens of consorting with publicans and harlots. Could it be that He was pointing out that such people are more savable than those who publicly called Him "Master" while secretly violating the basic tenets of His kingdom? Think it over.

DOING YOUR OWN THING

As Moses lifted up the serpent in the wilderness, even so must the Son of man be lifted up. John 3:14.
And I, if I be lifted up . . . will draw all men unto me. John 12:32.

In sharp contrast with the aimlessness and uncertainty of the youth of the world, who insist doggedly on "doing their own thing," Christian young people have an aim, a standard to repair to, and a Leader who never fails them. These have a purpose in life that centers on things other than themselves. They have a trust in God's eternal purpose that shifts their gaze from themselves to others. More than the worldling, the Christian knows reality. Faith in the Scriptures provides stability and brings life into perspective and balance. Christ lived for us and our aim is to live for others.

Of late there has been a concerted drive on the part of youth to "do our thing." Statistics show that more and more are doing it. Why are so many smoking "pot," injecting narcotics, and going in for uninhibited living? Why do they seek their "kicks" in pill popping and imbibing mind-crippling "angel dust"?

The answer to these grave questions lies in the fact that modern youth have continued to lose faith in the Bible until young infidels and pagans far outnumber those who believe, or even know, that Christ died for their sins. Two anti-Christian ideas lie at the base of their self-destructive philosophy. One is the theory of evolution, which sweeps away belief in the God of the Bible. For decades the notion that the earth and all life on it evolved from the simple to the complex has been taught as truth in the classroom. The other pernicious, soul-destroying theory is believing Satan's lie that death does not follow disobedience. Under this two-pronged attack, youth come into captivity to error and, as night follows day, the true aims of all purposeful living are lost. And the essential concepts of duty, destiny, responsibility, and judgment cease to exist.

For the followers of Him who was "lifted up," this life has meaning and so has the future. This makes the difference between thoughtlessly "doing one's thing" and clinging to the immutable plans of the Almighty.

Christians do not lack for things to do: a smile to smile, a lesson to learn, a song to sing, a load to lift—and an eternity to anticipate. Is your thing the thing God would have you do?

THE PREEMINENT QUESTION

What shall it profit a man, if he shall gain the whole world, and lose his own soul? Or what shall a man give in exchange for his soul? Mark 8:36, 37.

Anyone familiar with college students knows that some who are mentally superior like to baffle their less gifted colleagues with hard questions. An apt scholar in mathematics who was not a Christian often stumped his classmates in this way. One day, however, the tables were turned when one of his Christian friends said to him, "John, I have an important problem that I'd like you to solve." He then handed him a folded paper and left the room. John expected a tough problem in mathematics. Instead he unfolded the paper and read, "What shall it profit a man, if he shall gain the whole world, and lose his own soul?" John recognized the ploy as an appeal. He thought about the question and gave his heart to God.

This solemn question was first asked by the Saviour of His disciples after telling them that "whosoever will save his life shall lose it; but whosoever shall lose his life for my sake and the gospel's, the same shall save it" (Mark 8:35). And it remains the supreme question which, sooner or later, in one way or another, everyone must answer.

What a mistake it is to undervalue our souls! Esau sold his for a mess of pottage. The prodigal son sold his for pleasure. Samson sold his for the sultry charms of Delilah. And before all that, Adam and Eve sold their souls for what they mistakenly believed would make them wise. How sad that millions of people today are selling their souls for property, power, or fame and bartering away eternal life for ephemeral baubles that crumble at the touch!

In these lines Jessie Belle Rittenhouse epitomizes the fatal mistake of minimizing eternal values:

> "I bargained with life for a penny,
>> And life would pay no more,
>> However I begged at evening
>> When I counted my scanty store;
>
> "I worked for a menial's hire,
>> Only to learn, dismayed,
>> That any wage I had asked of Life,
>> Life would have paid."

SHOW US THE FATHER

Philip saith unto him, Lord, shew us the Father. . . . Jesus saith unto him, . . . he that hath seen me hath seen the Father. John 14:8, 9.

From ancient coins and statues we know something of the faces and figures of renowned men who lived in Christ's time and before. But of so obscure and unworldly a personage as was the humble Man of Nazareth no known likeness in wood, paint, or stone survives. Even so, many all-but-inspired artists and sculptors have so uniformly portrayed His noble visage that it is instantly recognized the world around. Have you ever wondered how accurate a likeness of Jesus is His generally accepted picture? No one living today can know the answer. But all will know it—and before long. None will fail to recognize Him when He comes again as King of kings and Lord of lords, for "every eye shall see him."

One of the kindest and most wonderful things God ever did for men was to send His Son into the world so that through Him and in Him we might see and understand the Father. With the Saviour's first coming among men in the form of man we have been provided insights into the infinite mind and the loving heart of the eternal Father. Of the significance of all this an unknown author has written, "Until Jesus came, we knew that God could build a universe, but we never dreamed He would be willing to labor with carpenter's tools. We knew He was surrounded by angels, but never thought He would condescend to eat with publicans and sinners. We believed He held the world in space by His power, but we never suspected that He would consider a sparrow's fall important. Jesus associated with us here that through His actions, teachings, and death we might come to a better understanding of the One who inhabits the entire universe. The Saviour Himself exclaimed, 'He that hath seen me hath seen the Father.' "

Before he was cast out of heaven Lucifer stirred up rebellion against God by proclaiming a falsehood. He charged the Almighty with despotism, malevolence, and cruelty. A third of the angels believed him. On earth he continued to promote this despicable lie, and more than a third of the sons of men have believed it. Then, so that men might look into the face of the Father through Him, the Son came. For thirty-three years the wonder-working Man of Galilee showed that the Almighty is not vindictive or punitive, but that He is tender, compassionate, and forgiving. If you want to see a true picture of the Father, take a long look at the life of His Son, who said, "He that hath seen me hath seen the Father."

THE HEALING TOUCH

And there came a leper to him, beseeching him, and kneeling down to him, and saying unto him, If thou wilt, thou canst make me clean. And Jesus, moved with compassion, put forth his hand, and touched him, and saith unto him, I will; be thou clean. Mark 1:40, 41.

Leprosy is a chronic infectious disease affecting the skin, the nerves, and finally the deeper tissues of the body. This deadly ailment is still prevalent in certain parts of the world, but its disastrous effects have been greatly mitigated by the use of a synthetic drug, Avlosulfon, truly a wonder treatment for this offensive malady. In Bible times the term *leprosy* was used in a more general sense than today and probably included psoriasis and other similar but less serious diseases.

One day a leprous outcast from society came to Jesus and asked for cleansing. He believed that Christ had the power to heal him but seemed not to have been sure whether the Saviour was willing to do so. Knowing that he was loathsome and repulsive in appearance, he probably wondered whether the merciful Master would be concerned about him. Although a leper was excluded from direct contact, Jesus gently reached out His hand and deliberately touched the infected body of this man who felt totally rejected. New hope was born, for that one touch proved that the Master did care. "Immediately the leprosy departed . . . and he was cleansed" (Mark 1:42). The despair rolled from the healed one's soul, and gratitude shone in his countenance. In fact, he was so very grateful that despite Jesus' caution to "say nothing to any man," he rushed out and began to "blaze abroad the matter" (verse 45).

From of old, leprosy has been a symbol of sin. There are many today as lonely and distraught as was the leper Jesus healed. But since the Saviour is not now on earth, He has asked His followers to be channels through which His love can flow. As a teen-ager I was convicted that I should be baptized and join the church. Then a beloved teacher put his hand on my shoulder and urged me to do so. I could tell from the way he looked at me that he was in earnest. That was all I needed to give me the courage to take that vital step.

There is nothing this old world needs more than a sincere display of Christian compassion. If believers would show deeper personal concern, multitudes in despair would respond and be won to the Saviour.

DECISIONS! DECISIONS!

And if it seem evil unto you to serve the Lord, choose you this day whom ye will serve; whether the gods which your fathers served . . . , or the gods of the Amorites . . . : but as for me and my house, we will serve the Lord. Joshua 24:15.

Life would be simpler, and superficially a lot easier, if we didn't have to make decisions all the time. From as early as we can remember to as far as we can see into the future, a succession of choices constantly confronts us. From the childhood choice of a toy to the selection of friends, to a curriculum, a lifework, and a life partner—there is no end to picking and choosing.

Indecisive, uncertain fence straddlers are to be pitied even as we deride them. In John Bunyan's *Pilgrim's Progress* we read of Mr. Facing-Both-Ways, who never wanted to commit himself.

Accepting decision-making as an inescapable duty is an important characteristic of adulthood. Unfortunately, many who hesitate fail to perceive that to make no decision is in itself a decision and that to fail to choose the right is to choose the wrong by default.

Joshua was a colorful, forthright leader. He is remembered for his generalship in conquering the Amalekites, for standing staunchly with Caleb and encouraging the Israelites to "go in and possess this land," for his obedience to God and for his audacity before men in subduing Jericho. But the supreme strength of Joshua was in none of these. As an aged man, he stood as firm as ever and made his position clear to all Israel. He reviewed their spiritual decline in spite of God's providences in their behalf and reiterated the covenants and promises of the Lord. Then, in a strong voice and with a flinty face, he declared, "Choose ye this day whom ye will serve . . . : but as for me and my house, we will serve the Lord."

As Lee and his army marched up the road toward Gettysburg, a local girl grabbed a poker and started down the road to meet the approaching forces. After the memorable battle, a neighbor asked this girl what she had planned to do to the Southern army with that poker. She replied, "Nothing, except to show them which side I was on."

In making today's decisions let us be as decisive as was Joshua when he said, "As for me and my house, we will serve the Lord."

ENDURING HARDNESS

Therefore endure hardness, as a good soldier of Jesus Christ. 2 Tim. 2:3.

Timothy probably needed toughening for the difficult life of proclaiming the gospel. So Paul told him that faithful Christian service is like being in the army and that he must accept hardships "as a good soldier of Jesus Christ." It is a fitting comparison that is still applicable today.

True soldiers are devoted to duty, and they obey orders with stamina, courage, and unswerving loyalty. This demands a willingness to endure hardship.

D. D. Rees told of an army lad who was sent during World War II to North Africa, then to Sicily, and finally to Italy. On going ashore his amphibious tank was blown up by a hidden mine and every member of the crew was killed except this young soldier, who was frightfully wounded. With both legs broken and other severe injuries he dragged himself into a shell hole, where he lay praying until the enemy was driven back and he was rescued. Placed on a small boat to be taken to the hospital ship, he was thrown violently into the sea by a direct hit followed by an explosion from which he alone survived. Clinging to his stretcher, he was picked up by a patrol and eventually taken to a San Diego hospital for a long recuperation. There he remarked to a friend that the Lord surely had use for him, considering these two miraculous deliverances.

The apostle Paul knew about hardships too. Of his experiences he wrote that he had been "in prisons more plentifully, in blows to an excess, in near-deaths often. By Jews I five times received forty strokes less one; three times I was beaten with rods, once I was stoned, three times I experienced shipwreck, a night and a day I have spent in the deep: in journeys often, in dangers from rivers, in dangers from highwaymen, in dangers from [my own] race, in dangers from the nations, in dangers in the city, in dangers in the wilderness, in dangers at sea, in dangers among false brothers, in labor and toil, in sleepless nights often, in hunger and thirst, in abstinence from food many times, in cold and nakedness" (2 Cor. 11:23-27, N.W.T.).

After all these astounding tribulations Paul could call them "light afflictions" (chap. 4:17). He knew how to endure "hardness, as a good soldier of Jesus Christ." Do we?

PERFECTION FROM HARDSHIP

Take, my brethren, the prophets, . . . for an example of suffering affliction, and of patience. Behold, we count them happy which endure. James 5:10, 11.

Only the young and the inexperienced can look upon life as a perpetual joy ride. They have yet to learn that living brings to most of us trials, hardships, heartaches, and many sorrows. To anticipate and be prepared for the difficult vicissitudes that lie ahead, the Christian will be wise to develop courage and endurance. Strength to persevere can be ours by taking the prophets as "an example of suffering, affliction, and of patience." We also have the Saviour's promise that "he that endureth to the end shall be saved" (Matt. 10:22).

A useful epigram says that "the quitter never wins and the winner never quits." Endurance not only proves the inner presence of nobility but aids mightily in developing it. Any man who has never known want, difficulty, severe toil, or affliction is not likely to be of much worth, nor is he fitted for a useful place in society. The worthwhile man is the one who, along with his share of proper pleasures, has suffered hard toil, privation, and disappointment.

The story is told of a farmer who needed a new wagon tongue and sent his son to find a suitable timber. The boy returned bringing a smooth, straight pole. When his father asked where he had found it, the lad said it had grown in a clump surrounded by other trees. There it had been protected from the winters' blasts and the summers' storms and largely deprived of sunshine. On that account the father rejected the pole as being too soft and tender. Then he said to his son, "Go down into the pasture and get that tree that stands all alone. It has been toughened by strong winds, bent and bowed by the storms, and has stood them all. I think it is well suited for the stress a wagon tongue needs. Bring it." The rampaging gales it had withstood prepared that tree for its task, and it served well.

Think of the angry threatenings made against God's prophets because they spoke in the name of the Lord. Consider the indignities they endured at the hands of His chosen people.

Do not let anyone tell you that the Christian life is easy. Yet accepting the refining influence of trials develops Christian polish through the grinding effects of adversity. "Behold, we count them happy which endure."

SOME ENDURED

What shall I more say? for the time would fail me to tell of Gedeon, and of Barak, and of Samson, and of Jephthae; of David also, and Samuel, and of the prophets: who through faith subdued kingdoms, wrought righteousness, obtained promises, stopped the mouths of lions, quenched the violence of fire, escaped the edge of the sword, out of weakness were made strong, waxed valiant in fight, turned to flight the armies of the aliens. Heb. 11:32-34.

This is one of the most sublime and moving passages ever to flow from the mind and pen of the apostle Paul. Each of these heroic exemplars constitutes a shining demonstration of faith in action with this transcendent thought in them all: by perseverance strength came from weakness. If you study the cases one by one, you will find weakness in each and will marvel how strong these people became through the indwelling power of Christ. In every instance out of weakness and tribulation came triumphant victory at last. This was possible because when they fell, God did not desert them, but graciously brought them back to Himself, even though they had to walk the path of trial, hardship, and suffering. The dogged perseverance of these worthies of old is recorded "for our learning, that we through patience . . . might have hope" (Rom. 15:4).

Courage and persistence were often manifested during World War II. Lt. R. J. Albano, of the Ninety-fifth Division, U.S. Army, explained that the way to win is to "keep moving, keep firing; but especially, keep moving . . . and if you keep on firing they either duck or sweat it out, break and run, or give up." That's the way his division operated. After the war many prisoners said that when their commanders learned that they were facing the Ninety-fifth Division, "they would take off for the rear with their hands up. They didn't like that marching fire."

The importance of facing the foe and keeping on the move is given in less sanguinary terms in Joseph Conrad's *Typhoon*. When danger was greatest the captain would call out to the mate: "Keep her facing it. They may say what they like, but the heaviest seas run with the wind. Facing it—always facing it—that's the way to get through. You are a young sailor. That's enough for any man. Keep a cool head and face it."

"The cause of thy Master with vigor defend;
Be watchful, be zealous, and fight to the end;
Wherever He leads thee, go, valiantly go,
And stand like the brave, with thy face to the foe."

—Fanny J. Crosby

COURAGE IS HONORABLE

Wait on the Lord: be of good courage, and he shall strengthen thine heart. Ps. 27:14.

These words are found at the close of one of the most exalted tributes found in all the Bible. Clearly courage is a virtue to be coveted. Yet it is one of the simplest, most straightforward of the Christian graces. It is both necessary and possible for every true and noble life.

Courage is a quality of the heart more than of the mind. The word is derived from the Latin *cor,* which means heart. To have courage means that we have our hearts in our work. David says it becomes ours when we wait patiently on the Lord for it.

We admire courage by instinct. We need no teacher to tell us it is a fine thing to be brave. Lack of courage is regarded as a grave defect of character. If we feel in our hearts a lack of it, if we cannot summon enough of it to face the dangers and fight the battles of life, we feel not only sorry but secretly ashamed. The absence of courage is a fault hardly anyone is willing to admit. We invent favorable names for it and try to keep it secret even from ourselves. We call this cowardice prudence or respectability or conservatism or economy or worldly wisdom or the instinct of self-preservation. Nothing is harder to confess than cowardice. No virtue do we more gladly possess and prove than courage.

Men have always loved and praised courage. It lends a glory and a splendor to the life in which it dwells, lifts it up and ennobles it and crowns it with light. The world delights in heroism, even in its rudest forms and lowest manifestations. Among the animals we create an aristocracy on the basis of courage. We recognize in the supposed fearlessness of the lion, the tiger, and the eagle a right to claim superiority to the timorous, spiritless, and furtive members of creation.

In men bravery is always fine. We salute it even in our enemies. A daring foe is respected, and although we fight against him, we still honor his courage. The foe who slinks and conceals and makes ambuscades seeking to entrap his opponent in dangers he himself would not dare to face is dishonorable and contemptible. But he who stands up boldly against his opponent and deals fair blows or presents honest arguments is a man to respect across the chasm of strife.

Let us with God's help determine to honor fearlessness and promote within us the peerless virture of courage.

LEADING OUT WITH COURAGE

Only be thou strong and very courageous, . . . that thou mayest prosper. Joshua 1:7.

Moses was dead. Now the burden carried so long by that intrepid man devolved upon Joshua. At once the new leader faced his first and greatest assignment. He was to get the vast host of Israelites across Jordan and into the Promised Land. At that season the stream was formidable, and there were no bridges or barges. But at his right hand Joshua had God, and he did not quail. Had not the Captain of the Lord's host commanded him? Also in his mind remained the miracle of the passage of the Red Sea. In comparison, what was Jordan? Israel would cross the river on dry land with the priests leading the way. Joshua knew that faith and courage would win where the world's finest engineers would have failed.

Humanly considered, the crossing of the Jordan with the hosts of Israel seemed impossible. But Joshua remembered that the Lord had told him to be courageous and that He would be with him. That constituted his orders, and that was enough for Joshua. Summoning the officers of the people, he told them forthrightly, "Within three days ye shall pass over this Jordan, to go in to possess the land, which the Lord your God giveth you" (Joshua 1:11). His enthusiasm and dauntless courage took his anxious hearers by surprise. But his certain faith strengthened theirs, and soon the word was passed around among the people that a thrilling event was just before them. They came together and assured Joshua of their cooperation. Already his own courage was reflected in his followers. We can imagine how he felt when they said, "All that thou commandest us we will do, and whithersoever thou sendest us, we will go. According as we hearkened unto Moses in all things, so will we hearken unto thee" (verses 16, 17). It must have been a marvelous sight. The record reads that "all the Israelites passed over on dry ground, until all the people were passed clean over Jordan" (chap. 3:17).

This life too has many swollen streams, many swift rivers to cross before, under God's leading, we come to the Promised Land. The Israelites following Joshua had to cross the Jordan but once. In the spiritual life, however, there are many rivers. You may even come to a crossing of your Jordan today. If so, remember to be "strong and very courageous." In this way lies success and prosperity. God is at your right hand. If you step courageously into the murky, frightening current, faith will open up a way for you.

IN CONTRAST TO COURAGE

Be ye strong therefore, and let not your hands be weak: for your work shall be rewarded. And when Asa heard these words . . . he took courage, and put away the abominable idols out of all the land. 2 Chron. 15:7, 8.

When admonished by the prophet Azariah to take courage, King Asa did so and put away the "abominable idols" that had for years desecrated Judah. The people responded and "entered into a covenant to seek the Lord God of their fathers with all their heart and with all their soul" (2 Chron. 15:12). Asa's courageous reforms were judicious and extensive. The Lord richly blessed Asa and amply rewarded Israel for this badly needed reformation.

If the leaders of Israel had always faced idolatry with similar fortitude they would not have so often fled before their enemies, as they did when they saw that King Saul and his sons were dead. The spirit of fear opposes courage and is apt to take charge in times of crisis or confusion.

There are sharp differences too between courage and some other things that are sometimes mistaken for it. What a vast contrast there is between courage and recklessness! The drunk who runs, in the delusion of intoxication, into a burning house is not brave. He is only befuddled. But the clear-headed individual who with every nerve alert makes his way carefully into a sea of flame to rescue a little child proves his courage.

Courage consists not of the absence of fear, but of the mastery of it. Never was there a better soldier than the French marshal Montluc, who said that he often had gone into battle shaking with fear and had recovered courage only after saying a prayer. This shows that the keener we are to the perils of life, the nobler is the exercise of courage. To drift along in this world of sin as if there were nothing in it to fear, and to slide downward easily, as some do, to the gate of death as if there were nothing beyond to fear under all the arch of heaven is but to say with the fool, "There is no God." But to face the temptations and the dangers of this life without yielding to fear; to pass without trembling the portals of death with a faith that is stronger than fear; to live in the presence of a just God in the confidence of a love that casts out fear—this is courage.

GOLIATH OF GATH

And all the men of Israel, when they saw the man, fled from him, and were sore afraid. . . . And David said to Saul, Let no man's heart fail because of him; thy servant will go and fight with this Philistine. 1 Sam. 17:24-32.

It was a climactic day in the protracted conflict between the armies of Israel and of the Philistines. For forty days they stood arrayed against each other. Day by day the confidence of God's people eroded. The daily challenge and wild boasts of the giant warrior, Goliath, unnerved the Israelitish soldiers. They cringed with fear, and their timid hearts, including that of King Saul, turned to water.

Then came David, the shepherd boy from the hills of Bethlehem. His heart too was stirred when he saw the fearsome Philistine champion and heard his profane boasts. David felt the shame of his people, but instead of cowering before this challenge, he was fired with zeal to avenge their shame. He also knew that the honor of the living God was at stake. His thoughts were on the national disgrace and how he might save the honor of Israel and of Israel's God. His life had been one of faith that fits a man for any emergency, a faith in the Unseen that had saved him in prior dangers. Goliath's confidence was in his own extraordinary physical size and strength and in the false gods he worshiped.

Wearing only his simple shepherd's garb, David carried the one long-range weapon he knew. It was well adapted for the task at hand. As he ran to meet his towering challenger, he was probably thinking of the dead lion and bear. Suddenly one smooth, small stone let go, and the loud, angry boasts ceased in mid sentence. Goliath was stunned, for such a thing had never entered his head before. As the armorbearer fled, David ran to the prostrate giant, whose great sword he took from its sheath; using both hands, he severed the head of his fallen foe. The contest was ended.

Sacred Writ records this episode so that we also might cultivate godly courage. Secular literature offers other examples: the lad Casabianca keeping the solitary deck of the burning vessel rather than disobey his father; Leonidas at Thermopylae; Horatius at the bridge; the brave six hundred at Balaklava; Florence Nightingale risking death fever in Crimean hospitals; Martin Luther at the Diet of Worms.

The Christian way demands Christian courage. Do we have it?

COURAGE IN THE LORD

Though an host should encamp against me, my heart shall not fear: though war should rise against me, in this will I be confident. Ps. 27:3.

Like Israel passing through the territory of the Amalekites, today's believers are strangers here passing through the enemy's land. The foes of the Christian lurk in the shadows and behind hidden obstructions ready to pounce upon the unwary travelers on the way to the heavenly Canaan. These emissaries of Satan hate God and all who bear His name. But our enemies are God's enemies too, and although they are shrewd and skillful, we can vanquish them with the help of the divine arm. "As the sun disperses the clouds. . . , so will the Sun of Righteousness remove the obstacles to our progress. We may cheer our souls by looking at the things unseen which will cheer and animate us in our journey."—*Our High Calling,* p. 22.

In many respects the moral trials of the Christian life are more frequent and more dangerous and require greater fortitude than occasional physical perils. There are some people to whom reproach, ridicule, and condemnation mean little. They simply do not care. But to others the sharp, unkind word is like a blow, and the sneer like a sword thrust, and the breath of contempt like the heat of flames. When such endure these things and face up to them and will not be driven by them from the path of duty, they are truly courageous.

Elijah on Mount Carmel, was full of boldness. There the Lord stood by him and blessed him. But when the prophet began to trust in his own strength and then received word from Jezebel that she was about to kill him, he became afraid. He had shown no fear of Ahab and all his minions. He had stood as bravely before the king as he had on Mount Carmel. What came over him we don't know, unless it was that he took his eyes off the Lord. This is the problem of a good many of God's people today. We lack moral courage. When the apostles were brought before the council, their boldness was perceived, and the members of the council were impressed. The Lord could and did use them then because they were fearless and bold.

The true believers have always been in the minority in this world and always will be. But if faithful, we are in the majority with God. Majorities do not count with Him by whom men were weighed as well as numbered. Thus we have reason to say with David, "My heart shall not fear."

COURAGE OF THE COMMONPLACE

After he had patiently endured, he obtained the promise. Heb. 6:15.

Writing to strengthen the faith and courage of the Hebrew believers, Paul cited Abraham, "The father of the faithful," as one who "patiently endured" and so "obtained the promise" of salvation. Reared among idolatrous kinsmen, he was never an idolator. Continually withstanding temptation and tried more severely than Adam, even to the point of sacrificing his own son, Abraham endured patiently. "All heaven beheld with wonder and admiration Abraham's unfaltering obedience."—*Patriarchs and Prophets*, p. 155.

Abraham's life could hardly be called commonplace. It embraced trial, disappointment, and delay. Yet many of his 175 years must have been routine, ordinary, and even dull. I like to think that the rare heights of faith he reached sustained him during his many commonplace years.

Occasionally those of us who live so-called commonplace lives experience a sudden glimpse of inspiration that makes life meaningful and precious. This gleam may come from a sunrise, a drifting cloud, the pure infinity of blue sky, a baby's smile, a tree, a poem, a flower, or maybe a long-dormant thought awakened by a bird's song or the casual remark of a friend. It is like a rift in the fog. Suddenly goodness and beauty obliterate the sorrows of life and the ugliness of sin. At such times our courage is replenished.

Robert Louis Stevenson wrote that "the world has no use for cowards. We must all be ready to toil, to suffer, to die. And yours is not the less noble because no drum beats before you when you go out to your daily battlefields, and no crowds shout your coming when you return from your victory or defeat."

No duty is so small that it needs no courage. There is a courage for the battlefield, for the thronged city and the lonely desert, for the sickroom and the marketplace, for the study and the kitchen, for the pulpit and the pew. There is a man's courage, a woman's courage, and a child's courage, for courage is strength of heart and there is a place for the strong in heart everywhere.

"The Christian who is such in his private life, . . . in sincerity of purpose. . . , in meekness under provocation, . . . in fidelity in that which is least, . . . such a one may in the sight of God be more precious than even the world-renowned missionary or martyr."—*Christ's Object Lessons*, p. 403.

COURAGE DESPITE LOSS

Though he slay me, yet will I trust in him. Job 13:15.

Even in times of seemingly total loss, faith and a clear conscience are courageous (see 1 John 3:2). "The righteous are bold as a lion" (Prov. 28:1). Virtue promotes boldness, and, like love, courage casts out fear. Despite his colossal calamities, Job's case before God was similar to Esther's before King Ahasuerus: "I will go, and if I perish, I perish" (Esther 4:16). Likewise Paul, on the grounds that he was ready not only to be bound but also to die for the name of the Lord Jesus, forbade his friends to weep for him as he was about to go up to Jerusalem to face persecution (see Acts 20:22-24). Such is true courage.

The time of loss is the testing time for courage. When Thomas Carlyle had completed the first volume of his monumental history of the French Revolution, he handed the manuscript to a friend, the economist John Stuart Mill, for criticism. Some days later Mill came to him in fear and trembling to confess that his careless maid, thinking that the manuscript was merely scrap paper, had used it to start a fire. The author, although inwardly distraught, concealed his feelings so as not to hurt his friend. But when Mill had gone, Carlyle gave way to despair. He was in desperate financial straits and had not even kept his precious history notes. In his diary he wrote, "It is as though the great invisible Schoolmaster had torn up my book when I showed it to Him, and said, 'No, boy, thou must write better.' " After agonizing for a time, Carlyle recovered his courage and came to realize that in his loss there was gain. He laboriously rewrote the volume, and went on to complete his great history, doubtless doing a much better job of it the second time.

An aged farmer laid a trembling hand on the knee of his grandson and said, "I have found this a good world. It has contained more of happiness than despair. With my good wife I have faced lean years but I have always had faith in the future. I have been through panics when money almost entirely disappeared. I have seen the potatoes rot in the ground and the oats sprout in the shock. Many of our weaker neighbors fell by the wayside, not having the courage to go on. But the ones with the iron wills stuck to the land and prospered. It has not been an easy life, but it has been a good one. If I could live my life over I would bend my back to my burdens, treat every man fairly, earn good neighbors by being one, and go forward unafraid." It takes the night to bring out the stars.

COURAGE LEADS SKYWARD

How then can I do this great wickedness, and sin against God? Gen. 39:9.

Joseph's loyalty and tact had won the confidence of the chief captain, who looked upon him more as a son than a slave. Now he faced an unexpected temptation. By yielding to sudden, seductive enticement he could foresee pleasures, favors, and rewards. To resist courageously meant demotion, disgrace, and possibly death. Joseph's religious experience and integrity were evident in his prompt response, "How then can I . . . sin against God?" Because Potiphar knew Joseph better than his wife did, he did not believe her accusations, and Joseph, a man of unshakable courage and character, went on to fulfill God's mighty purposes.

Sooner or later courage invariably leads skyward. Scores of graduating classes have selected the Latin motto *per aspera ad astra,* "Through hardship to the stars." No other virtue, save goodness, leads ever upward.

Neither courage nor danger are new in the human equation. Has life on earth ever been other than fleeting and fragile? Has not everything held dear and precious always teetered on the razor's edge of danger? Being intensely personal, most of this life's acts of courage remain obscure and go unheralded. But they form the spiritual backbone of every person, the sheet anchor of the soul.

Unshakable courage is an essential quality of leadership. "Courage is rightly esteemed the first of human qualities," Winston Churchill said, "because it is the quality that guarantees all others." Gen. W. T. Sherman said, "I would define true courage to be a perfect sensibility of the measure of danger, and a mental willingness to endure it."

All who have gained a measure of courage through the experiences of the years know that this precious virtue is born of genuine faith and that it cannot be acquired in a moment. Nor can the inexperienced in faith or in years be expected to own the courage of veterans.

In his sermon *Going Up to Jerusalem,* Phillips Brooks said this: "Do not pray for easy lives. Pray to be stronger men! Do not pray for tasks equal to your powers. Pray for powers equal to your tasks. Then the doing of your work shall be no miracle, but you shall be a miracle. Every day you shall wonder at yourself, at the richness of life which has come to you by the grace of God."

TRIUMPHS OF COURAGE

I can do all things through Christ which strengtheneth me. Phil. 4:13.

This was no proud boast. When Paul wrote it, he was a prisoner in Rome. He knew what it was to be friendless, falsely accused, and hated. He endured cold, hunger, and privation. Yet he was able to say, "I have learned, in whatsoever state I am, therewith to be content." He was content because he knew that his tribulation helped to further the gospel. He witnessed so effectively during his imprisonment that several servants in the imperial palace accepted Christ. This was a triumph of courage.

In 1919 Gov. Calvin Coolidge, of Massachusetts, trusted in God and read his Bible, as was his custom. A crisis developed when, in violation of their oath, Boston policemen joined a trade union and then went out on strike. More than a thousand officers left their jobs. Without law enforcement, the city was quickly taken over by rioters and gangsters. There was no one to stop them. Lives were lost. The governor brought in militia to restore order and sent a telegram to the union chief saying, "There is no right to strike against the public safety by anybody, anywhere, anytime." The union leaders called on the governor and pointedly reminded him that he would be up for reelection soon and that unless he relented, he would never hold another elective office in Massachusetts. He quietly replied, "It is not necessary for me to hold another office." Shortly thereafter Coolidge was reelected by an unprecedented majority. Four years later he was President of the United States. He who follows the dictates of his own conscience need never fear the consequences.

It is recorded of the Saviour, "He shall not fail nor be discouraged" (Isa. 42:4). Think of what He accomplished in just thirty-three years—the redemption of the world. The same spiritual resources that were His are available to His followers, for He said, "Greater works than these shall he do; because I go unto my Father" (John 14:12). The work of the believers really is greater because it reaches out to all the world, whereas Christ's personal ministry was confined to Palestine.

There remains much to be done to finish the work. Perhaps God is calling you, as a herald of the gospel, to do a greater service. Have you the courage to heed His call?

SANCTIFIED GUMPTION

We are made partakers of Christ, if we hold the beginning of our confidence stedfast unto the end. Heb. 3:14.

As a youth growing up in a Christian home I had the incomparable advantage of the sound advice, whenever I asked for it (and sometimes when I didn't), of a loving, consecrated mother. Often when I was facing problems and when choices had to be made, she would help me decide. Sometimes, as I wavered in doubt, she would ask, "Where is your sanctified gumption?" It was a good question then, and it is a good question now. When I see young people—and some no longer young—about to make even small choices that are nevertheless important because they involve issues of morality, I am tempted to ask, "Where is your sanctified gumption?"

Over and over in the Word of God we are encouraged to remain steadfast. Jesus said, "He that shall endure unto the end, the same shall be saved" (Matt. 24:13). He promised a crown of life to all who are "faithful unto death" (Rev. 2:10). He admonishes, "Behold, I come quickly: hold that fast which thou hast, that no man take thy crown" (chap. 3:11). How pathetically sad it is that many who start out strongly in the Christian pathway eventually grow weary in well doing and drop out! No reward is promised to those who begin courageously and endure for a while and then fall by the way. But every incentive is offered to anyone who will remain steadfast as long as he lives.

An ancient French legend contains an important truth: we need sanctified gumption enough to say No. As the story goes, a peddler called to the birds, "A worm for a feather!" A lark heard and said to himself, "The loss of one feather will not hinder my flying." So he traded a feather for a worm. When he could fly as well as before, he came back. Day after day he kept on trading because the worms were so good. Finally he found himself featherless, unable to fly, and doomed to a dangerous existence on the ground.

The wise man said, "My son, if sinners entice thee, consent thou not" (Prov. 1:10). Consent involves the will. If Satan can secure the consent of the will, he can assuredly overcome us. But if our will is surrendered to God, He will strengthen us to say No to Satan. With His help and with sanctified gumption we can keep our confidence steadfast to the end.

JESUS AND ALEXANDER—I

He that is not with me is against me. Luke 11:23.

Many authors have pointed out the few similarities and the many striking differences between Jesus Christ and Alexander the Great. There is a lesson in this for all Christians.

First, consider Alexander, who was called "the Great" because there was much greatness in him. He was the restless, flaming youth of all time. Fearless, ruthless, and heroic to the verge of insanity, he was a slave to his passion to conquer. Blood was the fuel of his life, and death was his daily companion. At 12 he subdued the wild stallion Bucephalus, which no one else could handle, and at 20 he set out to conquer the world.

Gold and silver lost their luster when they threatened Alexander's ambition. After he had conquered Persia, his loot-laden soldiers were so bogged down they could scarcely walk. So their commander had their booty burned. Once more the men became warriors. In India, Alexander paraded with a hundred white elephants, each with gilded tusks, and followed by enormous bulls with jeweled horns. Next in the procession marched hordes of black elephants, red camels, and multicolored horses. Then came Alexander on an ivory throne drawn by forty jet-black stallions. His chariot was escorted by four hundred tame male lions. Flowers festooned the trees overhead, and the streets were strewn with blossoms.

In flamboyant words Alexander proclaimed that he was now ready to conquer the stars. "I am my own law," he said. "I am the embodiment of wind and light, born from the breath of fire."

Not long after this matchless triumph the mind of the young commander began to waver and weaken. After two nights of dissipation he died in Babylon at age 33.

The other world Conqueror, who was born at Bethlehem and died just outside old Jerusalem, also lived thirty-three years. Alexander's body was embalmed and entombed in a golden casket. But the casket has long since disappeared and the bones within have crumbled with the years. Their whereabouts are unknown today. Although the body of Christ lay two nights in a borrowed tomb, it never knew corruption. For a brief three years the Son of God laid siege to the forces of evil and conquered them forever for all those who trust His name. His sword was the power of His perfect Word. His victory was the sacrifice of a perfect heart.

JESUS AND ALEXANDER—II

Because I live, ye shall live also. John 14:19.

A thoughtful poet has written the following meaningful lines fittingly contrasting Jesus and Alexander.

"Jesus and Alexander died at thirty-three;
One lived and died for self; one died for you and me.
The Greek died on a throne; the Jew died on a cross;
One's life a triumph seemed; the other but a loss.
One led vast armies forth; the other walked alone;
One shed a whole world's blood; the other gave His own.
One won the world in life and lost it all in death;
The other lost His life to win the whole world's faith.

"Jesus and Alexander died at thirty-three;
One died in Babylon; and one on Calvary.
One gained all for self; and one Himself He gave;
One conquered every throne; the other every grave.
The one made himself God; the God made Himself less;
The one lived but to blast; the other but to bless.
When died the Greek, forever fell his throne of swords;
But Jesus died to live forever Lord of Lords.

"Jesus and Alexander died at thirty-three;
The Greek made all men slaves; the Jew made all men free.
One built a throne on blood; the other built on love;
The one was born of earth; the other from above.
One won all this earth, to lose all earth and heaven;
The other gave up all, that all to Him be given.
The Greek forever died; the Jew forever lives;
He loses all who gets and wins all things who gives."

—Charles Ross Weede

The casual student reads of the exploits of Alexander and marvels at what he accomplished. The searching Christian reads of the perfect life of Jesus Christ and wonders at its matchless beauty. He allows Christ's love to cover him, and becomes acceptable to God. In the end, there is actually very little in Alexander that compares with the Saviour.

WE SHALL SEE HIS FACE

As for me, I will behold thy face in righteousness. Ps. 17:15.

In *The New English Bible* this confident verse carries a slightly different meaning: "I shall see thy face, and be blest with a vision of thee when I awake." What a blessed day is coming when all the saved of earth will, with the psalmist, be blessed with a vision of the Saviour. Here we see all things as "through a glass, darkly," with less than perfect sight. Less perfectly still do we perceive the things of the Spirit. But at the moment when "this mortal must put on immortality" the mists and fog that cloud our sight and insights here will all be cleared away. And best of all is that promise, according to the revelator, to the redeemed that "they shall see his face" (Rev. 22:4).

Queen Elizabeth I said that "a good face is the best letter of recommendation." When President Lincoln refused to appoint to a Government position a man recommended by a Congressman, the latter asked why. Lincoln said, "I don't like his face." The Congressman said, "Surely you would not reject a man on that account." The President explained, "Every man over 40 is responsible for his own face."

The Bible speaks often about the face. When Nehemiah came to see King Artaxerxes, he was asked why his countenance was sad, seeing he was not sick. His face had betrayed his inner sorrow (see Neh. 2:2). When brought before the council, Stephen witnessed courageously, and the members, "looking stedfastly on him, saw his face as it had been the face of an angel" (Acts 6:15).

An artist's daughter lost her sight in infancy. Her blindness was considered incurable, and for years after her mother died her father was her constant companion. Then a new surgical technique promised to restore her vision. While she lay recuperating in her hospital bed with eyes bandaged, her brightest thought was, Now I shall see my father. At last she saw the face she had so longed to see. As he embraced her, she exclaimed, "I've had a good-looking father all these years and I didn't even know it!"

Although we see dimly now, we shall see "the king in his beauty" (Isa. 33:17). No wonder Charles H. Gabriel wrote exultantly,

"When, by the gift of His infinite grace,
I am accorded in heaven a place,
Just to be there and to look on His face
Will through the ages be glory for me."

BEAUTY FOR ASHES

The Spirit of the Lord . . . hath sent me . . . to give unto them beauty for ashes. Isa. 61:1-3.

To exchange with the Lord our ashes for His beauty would seem to be a marvelously good bargain. The proposition is even more attractive when we compare beauty with ashes. Yet this, and more, is the offer that is made to every Christian.

Every normal person loves beauty. Heaven intended us to enjoy the things that are lovely, else the Creator would not have adorned nature so lavishly. Keats declared that a "thing of beauty is a joy forever." But we must not forget that the capacity to appreciate the glories of nature is a God-given talent that everyone should enjoy and cultivate. Fortunately this ability can be educated and developed. One can derive the keenest delight from the colorful scenery that surrounds us: the trees and their foliage, the bird songs and wildflowers, the vault of blue sky, fleecy clouds, tumbling waves, the sparkle of the sea, the glint on the river, the moving shadows on the hills, the moon and stars at night. The gifted architect Frank Lloyd Wright said, "The longer I live, the more beautiful life becomes. The earth's beauty grows on men. If you foolishly ignore beauty, you'll soon find yourself without it. Your life will be impoverished. But if you wisely invest in beauty, it will remain with you all the days of your life."

An elevated sense of the beautiful is Godlike. "He who created for man a beautiful world . . . with every variety of trees for fruit and beauty, and who decorated the earth with most lovely flowers of every description and hue, has given tangible proofs that He is pleased with the beautiful."—*Testimonies,* vol. 2, p. 258.

The Saviour regarded His surroundings when presenting truths to the multitude. The surrounding scenery appealed to the eyes of His hearers and stirred admiration in the hearts of the lovers of the beautiful. Jesus pointed to the wisdom of God in His creative works and bound up His "sacred lessons by directing their minds through nature up to nature's God. Thus the landscape, . . . the flowers of the valley, . . . and the beautiful heavens were associated in their minds with sacred truths which would make them hallowed in memory as they should look upon them after Christ's ascension to heaven."—*Ibid.,* p. 580.

Who would not gladly exchange the ashes of our poor human endeavors for all this beauty that the Lord offers along with the beauty of His holiness?

OUTWARD VERSUS INWARD BEAUTY

The Lord said unto Samuel, Look not on his countenance, or on the height of his stature; . . . for man looketh on the outward appearance, but the Lord looketh on the heart. 1 Sam. 16:7.

These words were spoken by the Lord to His servant Samuel, who, like many others, rushed to judgment. There is a tendency in even the best of men to be carried away by appearance. Jesse's eldest son, Eliab, was handsome and his stature imposing. He looked every inch a king. But the Almighty, who knows what lies in the hidden recesses of every heart, had a more youthful and humbler candidate in mind for the throne. One by one, seven of Jesse's sons passed before Samuel only to have God tell the prophet, "The Lord hath not chosen these." At Samuel's request the puzzled Jesse then sent for his youngest son, who was keeping the sheep. When David came in, the Lord told Samuel, "Arise, anoint him: for this is he." Jesse had failed to mention David because he considered him just a shepherd boy. But God had His eye on this lad who was faithfully looking after the sheep.

David's seven older brothers were all rejected because of their spiritual unpreparedness. The lives of men are an open book before God. Grace, charm, and decorum may be all that could be wished for, yet because of hidden inner defects, such are passed by in favor of others less outwardly qualified.

The Taylor family had two sons. The older boy chose to enter politics; he was elected to Parliament and achieved a certain limited fame. The other son dedicated his life to Christ and became a missionary. He founded the far-famed China Inland Mission, and when J. Hudson Taylor died he was known and revered on every continent. "But," wrote his biographer, "when I went to *Who's Who* to see what the other had done, I found there, 'The brother of J. Hudson Taylor.' " Even here eternal values are sometimes recognized as above earthly accomplishments.

However wide of the mark man's opinion of men may be, God's estimate is the final arbiter of everyone's destiny. The God of time will place each one where he ought to be, often making the first last and the last first. Many of merit, who go unappreciated here, may not reach their destined throne until all shall "know even as" they "are known." Appearances were strongly against it, but the despised and crucified Nazarene is the One who sits at the right hand of God to judge the world. He will see to it that no justified, however obscure, prince of earth shall miss his throne.

THE PRODIGAL'S BROTHER

Where envying . . . is, there is confusion and every evil work. James 3:16.

In many respects the prodigal son's brother was an admirable young man. He stayed home. He worked, obeyed his father, and, no doubt, saved his money. Yet he had one mean-spirited trait of character. He was envious. When his wayward brother came home, he was very unhappy and refused to join his parents and their guests in the welcoming banquet. In effect he was saying, "Why all this costly to-do about my brother? He is a profligate and has wasted his own and our father's wealth in riotous living. He doesn't deserve a feast. Look at me. I have lived honorably and worked hard, but nobody has ever thought of killing the fatted calf for me."

He was envious, all right, but on top of that, the green-eyed dragon Jealousy had taken up abode in his heart. He had not learned that envy and jealousy are twins, conceived in iniquity and nurtured by selfishness.

John Bunyan wrote, "Envy is the very father and mother of a great many hideous and prodigious weaknesses. It both begets them and nourishes them up till they come to their cursed maturity in the bosom of him that entertains them."

The author of the Proverbs said: "A sound heart is the life of the flesh: but envy the rottenness of the bones" (Prov. 14:30). He also said, "Jealousy is cruel as the grave" (S. of Sol. 8:6). And in another verse he asks, "Who is able to stand before envy?" (Prov. 27:4).

Theogenes of Thasos won a notable victory in the Olympic games. To honor him, the citizens of his city had a statue erected to commemorate his triumph. This so incited the envy of his rival that the enraged man went every night and tried to pull down the statue. Finally he succeeded, but was crushed to death beneath the falling monument.

Prof. Richard E. Burton made this cogent observation: "Every other sin hath some pleasure annexed to it, or will admit of some excuse, but envy wants both.—We should strive against it, for if indulged in, it will be to us a foretaste of hell upon earth." Envy is self-consuming. In the end it dwarfs and crushes and ruins the soul of him who harbors it.

We wonder whether the prodigal's brother repented of his corroding jealousy. Concerning this, Christ was silent. The parable was still enacting, and it rested with His hearers to determine the outcome. It is still enacting today.

BROKEN DREAMS

But what things were gain to me, those I counted loss for Christ. Phil. 3:7.

Looking back on his life of peril and persecution from his dungeon in the Mamertine prison—from which he was soon to go to a martyr's death—the apostle Paul might well have been disillusioned. As a young man he had advantages of education, wealth, and position for which others, could they have gained them, would have given much. Yet Paul had forsaken all this to advance the gospel and "for the excellency of the knowledge of Christ Jesus," his Lord. What looked like miserable human failure to the world was heavenly success to the great apostle. On balance, he was "rich toward God."

Unnumbered other godly men and women have gone into the shadows with their broken dreams, counted by the world as failures, or at best, as insignificant nonentities. However, some whose early hopes were broken are still remembered despite their unfulfilled dreams.

One day a dejected man rode out alone through the gates of the beautiful Alhambra in Granada. His hair had turned gray and the light of hope had gone out of his eyes. But he still believed in his dream of a round world and a western route to the Spice Islands. For more than six years he had pleaded in vain for help from the sovereigns, Ferdinand and Isabella. Now his wife was dead. His friends had abandoned him, and he was forced to beg for bread. Although the queen was almost persuaded, she had refused to help him.

But as Columbus rode away, he heard a voice calling to him. A friend had just convinced Isabella that should this dreamer's idea prove to be correct, it would be a marvelous thing for Spain. Suddenly she said, "It shall be done. I will pledge my jewels for the money." Columbus came back.

After more than two months of sailing westward, the man at watch on the flagship *Pinta* at two o'clock in the morning shouted, "Land! land! land!" Columbus had not found the Indies, nor had he proved the world to be round. Instead he had discovered an immense new world.

When the plans our hearts are set on are thwarted, we experience keen disappointment, but in the end the alternate course often proves the better one. Julius Rosenwald wanted to remain a clothier, but when this plan failed he tried something else. He built the huge Sears, Roebuck organization. It was infinitely better so.

FAMILIARITY BREEDS CONTEMPT

Jesus said unto them, A prophet is not without honor, but in his own country, . . . and in his own house. Mark 6:4.

It is unlikely that the axiom "Familiarity breeds contempt" was known in Christ's day, but it seems that His statement in today's text was a familiar proverb to His hearers. If Jesus' brothers did not recognize His divinity, His neighbors and townsmen could not be expected to believe.

Jesus was well known in the rustic little village of Nazareth, where He had grown up, worked in His father's carpenter shop, and participated to a limited degree in the social activities of this pastoral town in the uplands of Galilee. From His boyhood there was a typical Jewish familiarity with the other dwellers in the adjacent or attached stone-and-plaster houses on the narrow streets. It was a close-knit society. What one knew, others were not long in finding out.

A warm hearth, the tumbling and scampering of childhood, boyhood duties, conversation at table, a dependable and provident father, a tender mother: these may well be the memories Jesus had of His childhood. He ever cherished the recollections of those early years. Later He said of the children, "Of such is the kingdom of heaven." Yet, in strange ways, the marks of an alien were upon Him almost from the beginning.

There are similarities with the obscure Italian dreamer Christopher Columbus, who after diligent study decided that the East could be reached by sailing west. His compatriots said that suicide awaited anyone stupid enough to sail "over the edge of the sea," and made jokes about his "crazy" notions. Furthermore, it nettled them that such an obscure theorizer should dare to presume that he knew more than all the esteemed scholars of the time. The Italian reject then left his homeland and eventually claimed a new world for the Spanish crown, which underwrote his expeditions.

Like Columbus' countrymen, Jesus' neighbors were offended by His life and doctrine. They underrated His divine wisdom by recounting that He was a hometown woodworker. Disdainfully they asked, "Is not this the carpenter, the son of Mary?" (Mark 6:3).

How easy it is to overlook the people we know best while lavishing attention on casual acquaintances! The members of our families and the friends we meet every day are the most important people in the world. By neglecting them, we may also be overlooking the very ones with the highest potential for encouraging us on the pathway to heaven.

THE COURAGE OF GRATITUDE
She hath done what she could. Mark 14:8.

No forgiven sinner could ever love Jesus more than did Mary of Magdala. She had her reasons. He had pardoned her sins, freed her from devil possession, and raised her brother Lazarus from the tomb. No wonder her heart overflowed with appreciation and love. In fearful apprehension she then heard Him speak of His approaching crucifixion and death. In her sorrow and gratitude she determined to manifest her affection by securing an expensive fragrant oil with which to anoint His dead body much as people today lay flowers on the casket as a tribute to those they have loved and lost. So, at great personal sacrifice, she bought an alabaster box containing "ointment of spikenard, very costly."

Promptly a great clamor arose among the people in enthusiastic demonstrations to crown Christ as king. Mary's grief dissolved in joy. She wondered how she might show Him royal honor. Then she heard of a banquet for Jesus to be given by Simon of Bethany, a Pharisee the Saviour had healed of leprosy. Simon too had reason to show his gratitude.

As Mary pondered these matters, her eye fell on the beautiful alabaster box. She wouldn't need it now to anoint His dead body. Could it not serve far better to anoint Him as a king? Quickly she clasped it to her breast and made her way to the banquet room, where the dinner was already in progress. There she stepped to the couch where Jesus reclined and broke the seal. As she spread the costly perfume on her Lord, its fragrance filled the room. In the presence of the surprised guests she could not utter a word, but she spoke with her eyes as her tears of gratitude fell on the Saviour's feet. Then she wiped them with her hair. The drops of nard and her tears were so many thank offerings for the great salvation with which He had blessed her.

A murmur of disapproval swept the room. It was Judas who audibly objected. He piously asked, "Why was not this ointment sold . . . and given to the poor?" Mary heard these words of criticism, but the Saviour's glance at Judas convinced that thief that his hypocrisy was evident and his contemptible character disclosed. Then to the hushed room of critical guests He spoke words that echoed in Mary's ears as she went out: "She hath done what she could."

THE FRAGRANCE LINGERS

Verily I say unto you, Wheresoever this gospel shall be preached throughout the whole world, this also that she hath done shall be spoken of for a memorial of her. Mark 14:9.

The fragrant oil Mary had expected to spread upon Jesus' dead body she poured upon His living form. His approval was evident when He told His roomful of guests, "She hath done what she could." But Mary's tears fell not alone for her own sorrow and her own joy. The tears that bathed the feet of Jesus were also shed for Him. She anointed His head as the high priests had anointed the kings of Judea. She anointed His feet as the lords and their guests anointed themselves on festal days. Yet symbolically Mary had also prepared Him for death and burial. At His burial its fragrance could only pervade the tomb, but now it gladdened His heart with the assurance of her love and gratitude.

Nicodemus and Joseph of Aramathea loved Jesus too and believed in His divinity. But their timidity before men stood in the way of their witness while He lived. Nor did they manifest gratitude until, with bitter tears, they brought expensive spices to spread on His cold, unconscious form. But Mary had the courage to pour out her thankfulness while He could sense what He had meant to her. "And as He went down into the darkness of His great trial, He carried with Him the memory of that deed, an earnest of the love that would be His from His redeemed ones forever."—*The Desire of Ages,* p. 560.

As Mary anointed Jesus, that old hypocrite Simon thought, If Jesus were a prophet, He would have known who and what kind of woman she is. He had for Mary the scorn of those who have a lot to do with women of the street or else know nothing about them at all. Like many others Simon belonged to that vast cemetery of white sepulchers that contain corruption. There are those today who avoid physical contact with the impure, not realizing that their own souls are polluted vessels.

Jesus spoke with certainty of the future spread of the gospel into all the world. That far the memory of Mary's gift would spread and hearts would be touched by her fortuitous deed. As long as time lasts, the story of her broken alabaster box will tell of God's abundant love for a fallen race.

ISAAC AND ISHMAEL

"You will have a son. . . . He will be a wild donkey of a man; his hand will be against everyone and everyone's hand against him, and he will live in hostility against all his brothers." Gen. 16:11, 12, N.I.V.

Abraham was 75 and his wife ten years younger when the Lord called him out of Haran and promised to make him the father of a very great nation. When another decade passed during which the promised heir did not appear, they grew weary with waiting and their faith wavered. So they took matters into their own hands. Eager for Abraham to have a son, Sarah arranged for him to become a father by her Egyptian servant Hagar. The little boy born of this faithless union was named Ishmael. Because his father loved him, God told Abraham, "I will make him a great nation." This promise was abundantly fulfilled, for Ishmael became the father of the Arabic peoples of today.

Later on, in God's own time, the child of promise was born to Sarah. His name was Isaac and he became the mighty ancestor of the Jews. But what is all-important is that in him flowed the covenant promise of the Lord to bless all the world.

Ishmael and Isaac were half brothers. The angel of the Lord predicted that Ishmael's hand would be against everyone and that everyone's hand would be against him, also that Ishmael would "live in hostility against all his brothers."

For more than half the world's history Arabs and Jews have hated each other, insulted each other, harassed each other, and warred on each other. Peace between them has been tenuous and fleeting. Given world conditions today, it seems highly unlikely that they will ever be friends. They came close to being united as God's covenant people, yet they tragically failed.

When they are not fighting, the descendants of these two half brothers glower at each other across barbed-wire barricades. Their restless, unstable, and suffering land is the focal point of man's uneasiness today. Sarah's impulsive act and Abraham's supine submission still bear their sting. Their lack of faith at a critical turning point in history unleashed untold misery upon mankind. The visiting of the "iniquity of the fathers upon the children unto the third and fourth generation of them that hate" God has extended beyond twenty times the extent of that prophecy. In this, as in all else, God's word stands sure.

A SENSE OF VALUES

The statutes of the Lord are right. . . . In keeping of them there is great reward. Ps. 19:8-11.

In a society of abundance, where on every hand are so many things that gratify the eye and delight the senses, the call of the gospel to a life of selfless Christian devotion is all but drowned out by the loud mirth and clamor of temporal pleasures. Many are so engrossed with the pleasant interests and activities around them that they come almost to believe they can have "all this and heaven too."

A Bible teacher told the parable of the rich man and Lazarus to the children in her class. She then asked one interested little girl which she would rather be: the rich man or Lazarus. The child replied, "I'd rather be the rich man in this world and Lazarus in the next."

The response of this little girl is typical of the attitude of the masses of our day. It is saddening to realize that many church members reason the same way. We meet them every day seeking to get all they possibly can in this world and somehow hoping to do the same in the next as well, which cannot be because it is contrary to God's plan.

The rich man in this parable represents those whose interests are centered in this world. They devote their thoughts almost exclusively to the joys, comforts, and delights of worldly things. These are the things they think about, talk about, even dream about. The next world hardly ever comes into their thinking. It is foreign to them, a thing apart. It was like this with the man in the parable. What he had, what he wore, what he ate, and how to enjoy himself—these are what he lived for. What a shortsighted vision as compared with that of those who are preparing to inherit the next world!

Even when attained, most of the things that tempt the natural heart are disappointing in the end. Wealth and opulence, luxury and display, entertainment and excitement, do not satisfy the inmost longings of the soul. Man was made for better things. A man advanced in years and rolling in money suffered an ailment that caused him to lose much weight. He expressed his disappointment with the fallacy of living only for "things," in these words: "I'm old and can't enjoy my riches; I'm thin and my clothes don't fit; I'm weak and my food doesn't agree with me." "A man's life consisteth not in the . . . things which he possesseth" (Luke 12:15).

ILLUSIONS OF PROGRESS

But speaking the truth in love, . . . grow up into him in all things, which is the head, even Christ. Eph. 4:15.

The other day at the Seattle airport I hurried down the ramp fearing I would miss my flight to San Francisco. The smiling stewardess, who was about to close the door, welcomed me in. I sighed in relief and took my seat. For the next hour the plane sat dead still on the ground. When I finally sensed movement I thought we were on our way. But, as I glanced out the window, I realized we were not moving at all. The plane alongside was backing out. This is a common illusion to those who travel.

One time a kindhearted Scottish minister taught an illiterate parishioner to read. His pastor found the man to be an apt student who quickly learned to read the Bible. After a few solo flights into the exhilarating air of letters, the fellow was left to his own preferences. Meeting the man's wife on the street, the pastor asked how her husband's Bible reading was progressing. She replied, ''The Bible, sir! Bless you, he was out of the Bible and into the newspapers weeks ago!''

Too many people here and everywhere mistake movement for progress and motion for advancement. Because there is activity and bustle they think this means headway. Far too many heads are buried in newspapers instead of in Holy Writ. Too many ears tune to the frivolities and indecencies of television rather than listening for the still, small voice of God. There are too many hearts clamoring for the fleeting satisfactions of the hour instead of inviting in the presence of the Holy Spirit.

How many there are who profess the Christian way of life yet have no relish for Bible study, no joy in communing with nature's marvels that speak of God's love, no interest in daily worship, no genuine recognition of God's claim upon them nor of His unfolding providences. It should occasion no surprise when church members, having only shallow roots in spiritual matters, are carried away by winds of spurious doctrine.

Nothing is sadder than to lose the eternal glow out of the heart. When the Christian loses that gleam, the ongoing years touch with gray his symbols of faith that once glowed with glory. When the preacher loses it, his sermons become arid rhetorical wastelands. When the traveler toward Zion loses it, his footsteps falter. When love loses it, the heart soars no more and time becomes a dread interlude between two eternities. But those who look up in faith can behold the light of holiness still shining on the eternal hills. All who press on will be welcomed there.

NEVER REALLY LOST

They have taken away my Lord, and I know not where they have laid him. John 20:13.

These are the words of Mary Magdalene as she stood weeping by the empty tomb. Her eyes were so dimmed with tears that she failed to recognize Him who had asked her, "Why weepest thou?" She was sorrowing because she had lost the body of Jesus, and she failed to realize that it was the risen Christ who was speaking to her. In her seeming loss she had gained everything—even life eternal.

Something else of far lesser importance seems to have been lost that same early morning. This was the cask of aromatic spices the two Marys and Salome brought to embalm the body of Jesus. But the spices were never used. They may have been stolen or simply lost. We do not know. The popular radio speaker Paul Harvey likes to tell with dramatic effect "the rest of the story." What became of these spices is one Biblical incident about which I should like to know the rest of the story. Among other things, I would also like to know what became of the two tables of stone upon which were first written the Decalogue at Sinai, and what happened to Joseph's coat of many colors and to Elijah's mantle that fell on Elisha. I would like to know what became of the four stones that were left in David's sling, and who finally got away with Goliath's mighty sword. And I wonder, too, where the stone is that the builders rejected.

These things are all lost, including the spices. Yet, they are not really lost, because, as far as the resurrection story is related, so far will also be told the loving intentions of those early-morning visitors to the tomb. This instance also shows how frustrated hopes sometimes lead to more glorious achievements. When the motive is pure, even the most grievous disappointment can turn out to be the most splendid surprise. True love's labor is never really lost.

Some feel that their life's purposes have been thwarted. This life abounds in incompletions. Moses never reached the Land of Promise. He could only look from Pisgah's height to the "sweet fields" over Jordan. But God had a better place for him in the land of everlasting day.

Sometimes our costly preparations to serve the Master seem utterly wasted. Yet earth's thwarted hopes often become glorious fulfillments. Then the myrrh of our efforts and the spices of our devotion will arise before God as incense on His altars.

BY HIS POWER

Not by might, nor by power, but by my spirit, saith the Lord of hosts. Zech. 4:6.

Christ is the head of His church. He always has been and always will be. Any true spiritual fulfillment will come by the power of His Spirit and in no other way. Vance Havner in his *Pepper 'n Salt* says, "We spend much of our time in church these days trying to work up what is not there. Song leaders try to create a joy the singers do not really feel. Church workers try to create an enthusiasm, . . . a zeal for God's house that does not exist."

A church service where doctrinal tensions and deadening influences prevail recalls the word of the Lord through Amos, "I despise your feast days, and I will not smell in your solemn assemblies" (Amos 5:21).

Faithfulness in the mere externals of religion cannot win divine favor. Worship can no more be evaluated by the order and beauty of its outward form than can the nutritional value of any fruit be determined by its size and color. Without the indwelling Spirit from heaven, pomp, dignity, and eloquence have no power to move hearts, and a religious ceremony, however colorful and enchanting, becomes "as sounding brass, or a tinkling cymbal" (1 Cor. 13:1). Under such conditions the participants become playactors pretending what they do not feel and what only the Holy Spirit can provide and maintain.

If souls are to be genuinely converted and if believers, both young and old, are to be saved for the kingdom of heaven it can only be accomplished by the power of the Holy Spirit. Where there is humility, dedication, and spiritual growth, the Holy Spirit is the motivating power. If true Christian love exists it is the fruitage of this divine Spirit. A worked-up, forced, carnal emotion and enthusiasm never produce spiritual results nor heart renewals.

"Instead of man's speculations, let the word of God be preached. Let Christians put away their dissensions, and give themselves to God for the saving of the lost."—*The Desire of Ages,* p. 827.

"Neither wicked men nor devils can hinder the work of God, or shut out His presence from His people, if they will, with subdued, contrite hearts, confess and put away their sins, and in faith claim His promises. Every temptation, every opposing influence, whether open or secret, may be successfully resisted, 'not by might, nor by power, but by my Spirit, saith the Lord of hosts.' "—*The Great Controversy,* p. 529.

A TIME FOR SILENCE

But Jesus still made no reply, and Pilate was amazed. Mark 15:5, N.I.V.

With good reason no doubt, my father once cautioned me to weigh well my words. He said, "It will be much better for people to wonder what you would have said than why you said it." The passing years have proved that this was—and still is—excellent counsel, though I have not always had the wisdom to follow it.

Of one distinguished general it was said that he could "hold his tongue in ten languages." A. G. Gouthey lauded the virtue of silence in these words: "There is no explanation quite so effective as silence. . . . If you are right your life will do its own explaining. If you are wrong you can't explain." The British historian Thomas Carlyle left these sage words: "This is such a serious world that we should never speak at all unless we have something to say."

We are all prone to speak out hastily in reply to unfair criticism. Even those who usually have control of the tongue find it difficult to keep quiet when unjustly accused. When under provocation, we are mightily tempted to defend ourselves against false and spiteful misrepresentations, insinuations, and denunciations. At such times we should remember the example of Jesus, who "when he was reviled, reviled not again; when he suffered, he threatened not" (1 Peter 2:23). When outrageously aggrieved and piteously provoked He kept His peace. Pilate, that unprincipled Roman puppet, asked Him, "Art thou the King of the Jews?" Jesus did not answer the question. How could He explain to this pagan cultist of Tiberius that His kingdom was a spiritual kingdom that would consume all human kingdoms? Reading the depths of the shallow mind and sullied soul of the procurator, the Saviour kept silent as He had before Annas and before Caiaphas. Vain Pilate could not fathom this silence. It caused him great amazement. The noble appearance and solemn dignity of Jesus, in the face of death, was a silent witness more expressive far than any words even He could have uttered.

When we are mistreated and deserted by our friends and scorned by the world, our reaction and response will show how Christlike we are. Paul told Timothy that "the servant of the Lord must not strive" (2 Tim. 2:24). David prayed, "Set a watch, O Lord, before my mouth; keep the door of my lips" (Ps. 141:3). Clearly, a godly life speaks loudest when the tongue is still.

THE FIRE WITHIN US

The discretion of a man deferreth his anger; and it is his glory to pass over a transgression. Prov. 19:11.

Someone has said that temper is one of the few things that improve the longer they are kept. Every Christian strives to control this fire within. Because a violent temper betrays a grave character weakness those who can control their own spirit are marked for preferment. Yet, many good-natured people lose their "cool" in a crisis. To be equipped for emergencies when they come is possible by learning to exercise self-control in the lesser crises of daily life.

Practical Christianity makes a man a gentleman, and "gentle men" know that temper outbursts are highly unbecoming to them. The passions we control, and not those that control us, distinguish us as "doers of the word, and not hearers only" (James 1:22). When Gideon and his little band returned from defeating the Midianites the conceited Ephraimites asked why they had not been includ   Their pride was hurt "and they did chide with him sharply" (Judges   Gideon was tempted to lose his temper. He hadn't taken these men because they had not been ready to go when he needed them. But when the battle had been won they appeared greatly miffed. With serene self-control Gideon replied, "What have I done now in comparison of you? Is not the gleaning of the grapes of Ephraim better than the vintage of Abiezer?" (verse 2).

Gideon's soft answer to the Ephraimites was a beautiful exercise of self-control under provocation. The victorious commander granted his critics the place of honor by underrating himself in comparison with them. Knowing their sensitivity, without argument he acknowledged their superiority. "Then their anger was abated toward him, when he had said that" (verse 3). His control of his own spirit and courteous humility were as victorious as his sword, and his pacification of his brethren was a greater accomplishment than the destruction of their enemies.

In his allegory *Pilgrim's Progress,* John Bunyon says of Talkative that he was "a saint abroad, and a devil at home." Many others, who own a public image of self-discipline, are anything but exemplary at home. James pointed out that an untamed tongue can bless God and in the same breath curse men, "who have been made in God's likeness" (James 3:9, N.I.V.). There are some who can voice pious faith one moment and then tell a vulgar story the next. What finer Christian virtue is there than consecrated, consistent self-control?

A SOFT ANSWER

**A soft answer turneth away wrath: but grievous words stir up anger.
Prov. 15:1**

An elderly couple purchased a home and moved into it. As they were
arranging their furniture they had their first visitor. He was the man living
next door and he had fire in his eyes. He had come to talk to them about a
tree on the driveway of the newly-acquired home. He wanted that tree out
of there. The recent arrivals regarded the angry neighbor in silence for a
few moments. Then the husband said, "Sir, this tree is on our property
but I can see it irritates you. My wife and I would like to keep it but you
are our neighbor and your friendship is worth more than the tree. After we
have gotten settled and have rested a little, you and I will take axes and
shovels and remove it."

Those conciliatory words softly spoken took all the wind out of the
sails of the irate neighbor. He gulped and said, "I don't want to be nasty
about it. The tree may not be so bad really. Anyway, let's wait and see."
This once-angry man turned out to be a splendid neighbor and the tree was
never mentioned again.

In ancient times the most feared and effective engine of warfare was
the Roman battering ram. This huge, clumsy machine could usually
effect a breach in a massive, solid wall of stone. But defenders found that
when the breach was nearly made the powerful mechanism could often be
baffled by bags of straw and thick beds of down let down to receive the
stubborn blows. By this stratagem the besieged could endure until the
huge engine was withdrawn and the thwarted besiegers obliged to depart.

The apostle Paul could have easily exasperated his heathen hearers at
Athens by a direct disavowal of their gods. Instead he tactfully indicated
that they had overlooked one important god, the true God, whom they
were ignorantly worshiping (Acts 17:23). In this way, and without
offense, Paul was able to introduce the true God, whom he loved and
served. A little later he plucked at the conscience of Agrippa by kindly
mentioning that magistrate's intelligence and candor (chap. 26:26-29).

The Christian often finds need to turn away wrath for there is much
wrath in the world to turn away. That effective shield is the soft answer.
On the other hand, when harsh and grievous words have stirred up anger,
no later association can ever completely obliterate their baleful influence.
Let us employ the soft answer.

THE POWER OF WORDS—I

By thy words thou shalt be justified, and by thy words thou shalt be condemned. Matt. 12:37.

Few pay more than fleeting thought to the power and the potentiality of the tongue. "Talk is cheap," we say, or "He's just a talker." Such expressions are common and underscore our failure to realize the discretion we exercise when we speak. An oblique caution against such a lighthearted attitude is a succinct epigram: "Be careful of your tongue; it's in a wet place and liable to slip."

Neither does the Bible regard loose words as a light thing. With inspired insight Solomon said, "He who keeps his mouth and his tongue keeps himself out of trouble" (Prov. 21:23, R.S.V.). Paul told the Ephesians to "let no evil talk come out of your mouths, but only such as is good for edifying, as fits the occasion, that it may impart grace to those who hear" (Eph. 4:29, R.S.V.).

Care in speech is essential for the Christian, but a greater reason for choosing our words wisely is given by James, who said, "The human tongue is physically small, but what tremendous effects it can boast of! A whole forest can be set ablaze by a tiny spark of fire, and the tongue is a fire, a whole world of evil. . . . It can poison the whole body, it can set the whole of life ablaze, fed with the fires of hell" (James 3:5, 6, Phillips).

When a man is in serious earnest about his faith he bridles his tongue. During World War II a famous American general was said to be a colorful personality who was, at one and the same time, deeply religious and violently profane. How could this be? If one is deeply Christian in belief he cannot be profane. If he is profane his religion is feeble and defective. Our speech and our profession are closely linked, and the man who is careless about what he says shames and disgraces the faith he professes.

If we are Christ's, people will recognize us by our speech. They will mark what we say as well as what we don't say. Our conversation will either be of the earth, earthly or of heavenly things, heavenly. Which is it?

> "Dear Lord, I would be silent
> When slander's hurled my way,
> Forgiving with forbearance now
> Like Christ did in His day."

THE POWER OF WORDS—II

Let the words of my mouth, and the meditation of my heart, be acceptable in thy sight, O Lord." Ps. 19:14.

The Christian must respect the power of the tongue. With it we can praise God and witness for Him. With it we can bring comfort in sorrow and lift the spirit of those in despair. The tongue is essential in effective preaching and teaching. Eloquent, forceful words can uphold justice, inspire deeds of valor, and move hearts to repentance.

The words of the tongue sometimes live longer than the works of the hands. What we do is often forgotten whereas what we say frequently lives on forever in the recesses of memory. Abraham Lincoln was seldom wrong, but in his famous Gettysburg address he made one statement that time has invalidated. He said, "The world will little note, nor long remember, what we say here, but it can never forget what they did here." Because he was too modest he was only half correct. The world will never forget that the battle at Gettysburg was the turning point of the Civil War but neither will it ever forget the noble words Lincoln spoke there. The smoke of that battle and the stench of that field are gone but the telling words spoken by the President of a smitten land in the sorrows of war live on. That address, now regarded as a masterpiece of English literature, is engraved in the hearts of the American people forever.

Words have unlimited power. England has never known a darker hour than during World War II when Europe was overrun, France defeated, British armies about to be driven into the sea, her native soil devastated, and her great cities laid in ruins. Britain stood with her back to the wall. But the indomitable Winston Churchill still had one effective weapon— his tongue. With resolute voice he said, "We shall not flag or fail. . . . We shall go on to defend our island, . . . we shall fight on the beaches, we shall fight on the landing grounds, we shall fight in the fields and in the streets, we shall fight in the hills; we shall never surrender." His beleaguered people heard him with streaming eyes, and they took heart. The world knows the result of Churchill's peerless words.

With His tongue the Saviour emphasized divine truth, exposed sin, and extolled God's love. So remarkable was His power of speech that when the Pharisees berated the Temple police for not arresting Him, the officers replied, "No man ever spoke like this man!" (John 7:46, R.S.V.).

WORDS TRUE AND CLEAN

Let thy word, I pray thee, . . . speak that which is good. I Kings 22:13.

King Ahab's false prophets were encouraging him to go on what proved to be a fatal errand. His henchman, who held a low opinion of prophets generally, was sent to fetch Michaiah, a true prophet of the Lord. Ahab's lackey advised Michaiah to speak soothingly to the king. But Michaiah was not about to do this. He was resolved to speak the truth as revealed to him, though he well knew he risked death for it. His warnings were rejected and Ahab lost his life.

What is good is not always what men wish to hear and good does not always sound good. In contrast with the advice of the false prophets, Michaiah's bold declaration revealed that he stood far above any fear of his fellows. To speak truthfully before all men, whether they be clothed in silks or in rags, is the hallmark of the brave. Far better is unpalatable truth than welcome untruth.

A person's speech reveals his character. Words are tools of the mind and careless, slouchy speech betrays a poverty of thought. A lovelorn adolescent, badly hampered for lack of suitable words, proposed to his girlfriend thus: "I get a kick out of you and you get a kick out of me. Can't we get a kick out of stickin' together?" He lacked even the verbal resources to suggest that they ought to be sidekicks for the rest of their lives!

So as to think and speak clearly the ordered mind will try to have at command well-defined, forceful, and elegant words. Like other tools they must be kept clean and sharp. To be content with slang, to employ superlatives for what is commonplace, to soil what is pure, noble, and divine with vulgarity and profanity is to enfeeble and cripple the soul. It is as foolish and dangerous as for a dentist to use his forceps to pull a nail or a surgeon to use his scalpel to whittle. You would not trust a man who was so abusive and careless with his tools.

Above the question of economy of words and the proper adjustment of expressions to ideas stands the fact that the abuse of holy names blunts the sense of the sacred. It also deprives one of the verbal means to express it. To parody a sublime hymn is to destroy its sacred influence and to associate divine names with the commonplace leaves the practitioner impoverished in mind and spirit. May God grant us to recognize the gulf between the sacred and the profane and to be guided thereby.

THE DEADLY VENOM

Deliver me, O Lord, from the evil man: preserve me from the violent man. . . . They have sharpened their tongues like a serpent; adders' poison is under their lips. Ps. 140:1-3.

Elder G. H. Minchin once told of a vicious fight that took place in South Africa between a cobra and a black mamba. The cobra seized the mamba in a death grip and soon the black serpent relaxed and died. Thereupon the cobra proceeded to swallow it. But the mamba's venom began to take effect and the cobra, with the mamba half swallowed, heaved a convulsive shudder and died too.

In today's text is David's prayer to be delivered from perverse men whose lips he compares to adders' poison. Hateful, evil enemies of the psalmist had invented and published lies against him in order to ruin his reputation. Like all kinds of sin, jealousy and hatred, even though unprovoked, grow with self-propagating power and increase with lightning speed. Their natural outlet is the tongue.

People with unregenerate hearts cannot for long govern their violent tempers. Neither can they control their tongues, the handiest and most convenient "valve" for releasing the poisonous product of their selfishness. So, when a Christian reaches the place where he can control his tongue he has become indeed Christlike and, in the words of James, "is a perfect man" (James 3:2).

As has been noted, the tongue can move men and nations. Like all God's gifts, its potentialities run in two directions. It can produce both good and evil. Unfortunately, according to James, it tends toward evil. He calls it a "world of iniquity." The corrupt man uses his corrupt tongue to dispense his corruption. Anyone, who deals much with people, knows how venomous words can destroy friendships, break up homes, and divide churches. They can inflame mobs, incite riots, and instigate wars. Nobody outside of Germany paid much attention to the fanatical paperhanger who arose to influence in the postwar 1920s. But, with the dangerous gift of eloquence, Hitler seized the imagination of a defeated people, promised them a new and better day, and then set the world on fire.

The corruption of the tongue can be complete. James says that it can set on fire the entire cycle, or wheel, of nature (verse 6). The implication is that the entirety of our being is poisoned by the tongue's depravity. Only with the indwelling of the divine Spirit can we ever expect to control the tongue.

TAMING THE TONGUE

No human being can tame the tongue. James 3:8, R.S.V.

If no human being can tame the tongue are we then helpless? By no means! After Jesus had told His disciples that it would be hard to enter the kingdom of God, they asked, " 'Then who can be saved?' " Jesus replied, " 'With men it is impossible, but not with God; for all things are possible with God' " (Mark 10:27, R.S.V.). That is the secret. James doesn't say the tongue cannot be tamed; only that no *man* can tame it. Man cannot do it because his heart is sinful and "out of the abundance of the heart his mouth speaks" (Luke 6:45, R.S.V.). So we see that control of the tongue can never happen until control of the heart is achieved, and only Christ can do that.

James said that the wisdom from above is "first pure, then peaceable, gentle, open to reason, full of mercy and good fruits, without uncertainty or insincerity" (James 3:17, R.S.V.). Such wisdom is obtainable only through Christ. Therefore the key to tongue control is heart control, making "every thought captive to obey Christ" (2 Cor. 10:5, R.S.V.).

Accepting Christ as Lord and Saviour does not mean that tongue control will be easy. The sorest trials often follow conversion. Until we invite Christ into the heart the forces of evil are not concerned, but when He comes in they marshal their armies to attack. Yet, although the struggle may be greater, the resources of heaven are at our command and while we in our own strength cannot tame the tongue, Jesus can.

The Saviour told His disciples that it isn't what goes into us that defiles us "but those things which proceed out of the mouth come forth from the heart; and they defile the man" (Matt. 15:18). It is astonishing to stop and consider what comes out of the mouth. It has been estimated that the average person speaks enough in a week to fill a five-hundred page book. In a lifetime, that adds up to three thousand volumes. It is sobering to remember that by these words we shall either be condemned or justified (see 1 Cor. 3:15).

> "O that my tongue might so possess
> The accents of His tenderness
> That every word I breathe should bless!
> O that it might be said of me,
> Indeed thy speech betrayeth thee
> As friend of Christ of Galilee."
>
> —Robinson

CONTENDING WITH SLANDER

Slander drives a wise man crazy and breaks a strong man's spirit. Eccl. 7:7, N.E.B.

Solomon was probably thinking of the calumnies heaped upon his father, David, when he wrote the words of today's text. In the Psalms there is certainly ample evidence that David's enemies persecuted him unmercifully with their tongues. Complaining bitterly of this slander, he wrote, "I have borne reproach. . . . They that sit in the gate speak against me; and I was the song of the drunkards. . . . Reproach hath broken my heart" (Ps. 69:7-20). In Psalm 41 he detailed how his enemies came before him with flattery, their real object being to gather materials for slandering him and that they then went out to publish their base and dastardly misrepresentations. He lamented the betrayal and ingratitude of those he had befriended in these words, "Yea, mine own familiar friend, in whom I trusted, which did eat of my bread, hath lifted up his heel against me" (Ps. 41:9).

To an honorable man nothing is more bitter, unless it be ingratitude, than malicious slander. The psalmist was smarting severely under unjust defamations that seemed to assail him from every direction and in every form. But David is not the only one to be crushed by derision. The good still suffer from assaults by slanders. Misrepresentations assume many forms of which the most perilous are the most subtle.

Frederick the Great, while riding one day in Berlin, noticed a crowd gathered before a vile caricature of himself hanging high on a wall. The onlookers feared a violent outburst from their monarch. Frederick looked at the slanderous exhibit then said quietly to his attendant, "Place it lower so all can see it." Then, as his subjects gained a new admiration for their ruler, he calmly rode away.

It is the lot of most leaders to suffer wounds from malicious tongues. I have learned that it helps very little to reply in kind or to refute lies. If you are made the target of slander remember that Jesus endured colossal "contradiction . . . against himself" (Heb. 12:3). Yet He triumphed magnificently.

THOUGHTLESS WORDS

I tell you this: there is not a thoughtless word that comes from men's lips but they will have to account for it on the day of judgment. Matt. 12:36, N.E.B.

In other versions of Matthew this expression "thoughtless word" as used here is rendered "careless," "useless," "pernicious," "trifling," "unprofitable," and "idle." The fact that words can be unnecessary, damaging, and trifling is obvious. The great significance of the verse is further evident when the setting in which Jesus spoke these words is considered. It was His reply to the Pharisees who had just charged Him falsely with casting out demons by the prince of demons, the devil. They knew it was an insulting falsehood when they angrily flung it into His face. Instead of directly denying their slurring accusation Jesus' reply neatly turned it aside by implying that the charge was "an unprofitable saying" for which they would be held strictly accountable in the judgment.

The Pharisees were sobered—and visibly chilled—by the Saviour's fiat that all their perfidious and unprofitable utterances would be up for review in the judgment. And so should we. "The words we utter today will go on echoing. . . . The deeds done today are transferred to the books of heaven, just as the features are transferred by the artist onto the polished plate. They will determine our destiny for eternity, for bliss or eternal loss."—*Testimonies to Ministers,* pp. 429, 430.

Since World War II the opinion of astronomers has radically changed about the size of the universe, which is now thought to be at least ten times more vast than it was believed to be fifty years ago. Sensitive, sophisticated devices, capable of gauging remote nebular impulses and almost imperceptible outer-space emanations, have been rescued from the domain of science-fiction and brought into the realm of possibility. Apparatus is anticipated that can recoup every word ever spoken so that history can be heard all over again. Could it be that all past words, like light emitted centuries ago, are still traveling somewhere in space where science may yet catch up to them for replay that all may hear?

Skeptics doubt that heaven is big enough to hold all the words ever spoken. But heaven is a more commodious place than finite minds can conceive and "the words we utter today will go on echoing when time shall be no more."—*Ibid.,* p. 429. The *how* of it remains as yet unrevealed but the truth of it could not be more clearly stated.

PEACE

These things I have spoken unto you, that in me ye might have peace. In the world ye shall have tribulation: but be of good cheer; I have overcome the world. John 16:33.

On this date, November 11, in 1918, after almost four years of unprecedented bloodletting, peace came to the world. Although I was only in the seventh grade I was old enough to maintain a lively interest and concern about the progress of that world war. I was also old enough to work at a sawmill at a railroad siding near our home in Montana. As we had no radio or television to keep us up to date, the first news of the Armistice arrived when a lone railroad locomotive came up the line with its whistle wide open. We shut off the machines and hurried to the trackside to receive the newspapers the engineer tossed to us. He called out above the din of hissing steam, shouting with exultant voice, "The war is over!" Then he touched the throttle and roared up the track to bring the same good news to the next station. It is impossible to adequately depict the sense of relief and satisfaction that spread over the nation and the world. At long last the guns were still.

That same evening, a German farmer living nearby, who had lost one son in the conflict and had two others in the trenches in France, came to our place to see my father. He could scarcely contain his joy. Tears welled up in his blue eyes and his voice trembled. He embraced my father in a burst of emotion as he said several times, "O peace! She is vonderful!" The whole world felt the same way.

For years after that conflict, November 11 was commemorated by Americans as Armistice Day in honor of the dead of that war. But as multiplied more laid down their lives in World War II, Korea, and Vietnam the name of the remembrance day was changed to Veterans' Day, thus to honor the fallen of all America's wars.

As we celebrate Veterans' Day this year it is little joy to realize that hatred, strife, and bloodshed prevail in many places throughout the world. The love of peace is swallowed up in the prevailing hatreds that threaten civilization itself. How strange that, while men talk of peace, conflicts rage, savagely consuming lives and property and banishing happiness for everyone! Of course, there can be no peace so long as iniquity abounds. Jesus said there could be peace only in Him. Whatever our troubles, let us embrace His peace.

THE HIGH ROAD

I will cause thee to ride upon the high places of the earth, and feed thee with the heritage of Jacob thy father: for the mouth of the Lord hath spoken it. Isa. 58:14.

Because this bountiful promise is God's reward for keeping the Sabbath holy most commentators emphasize the preceding verse and underrate the grandeur of this one. It is a sublime thought that the Lord will cause His people to ride "high" as they partake of the princely abundance of Jacob.

Elbert Russell tells of his visit to the Giant's Causeway in Northern Ireland. It had been raining and the members of Russell's party were fearful of getting wet feet on the uneven path. Their Irish guide noticed their concern and confided a secret saying, "If ye'll step on the hoigh places, ye'll kaip yer feet dry." This solicitous guide spoke more wisely than he knew, for a person can go safely through the perils of the world, keep his spirit safe and maintain his self-respect if he is careful to walk on the high places.

Mankind has come to regard certain virtues—faith, honesty, kindness, love—as high motives, worthy and noble. The general judgment—whether of youth, middle age, or advanced years—knows intuitively and honors these high motives in contrast to the low motives of mean and selfish men.

Attending sales conferences has impressed me that, while in many respects similarities pertain to them all, there are nevertheless, sharp inherent differences among tradesmen depending upon the character of their merchandise. For example, the clean, wholesome atmosphere that usually characterizes a boat and automobile show is similar to that where book companies display their publications. A far different tone is at once recognized on entering an exhibition staged by the tobacco or alcoholic beverage companies. Those that contribute to the betterment of mankind occupy "the high places"; those that are deleterious tend downward toward what is low.

Enoch and Noah walked with God. To walk with God is to keep the life consonant with His will. To walk with God means to follow the path toward the peaks, for the Lord walks upon high places. There we can go securely without giddiness, well guarded from falling, for His people are assured safety "upon the high places of the earth."

WE LIVE TODAY

Do not be anxious about tomorrow; tomorrow will look after itself.
Each day has troubles enough of its own. Matt. 6:34, N.E.B.

Fortunately, we have to live only today. That is all God expects. This is all the time allotted to us. Many people are so occupied with yesterday and tomorrow they don't have time for today. For them today's plans are thwarted, because their eyes are focused on yesterday or tomorrow. One old epigram has it that "well spent days bring happy nights and glad tomorrows." If we live today as we should there will be no yesterdays to regret or repair and we won't have to worry about tomorrow.

Confident religion bids us to forget the past. Too often brooding over what is gone breeds discouragement. Because we did not altogether utilize yesterday when it was today we tend to be unhappy with it. Paul knew he had no need to worry over the past. So he said, "Forgetting those things which are behind, . . . I press" forward (Phil. 3:13).

Someone is sure to ask, "Shouldn't we plan for the future?" The answer is, "Yes, indeed!" The best way to do that is to do our best today. If we squander time and put off for tomorrow today's duties then today will be a disaster, tomorrow still worse, and discouragement will follow us all our days.

The Secret*

"I met God in the morning
When my day was at its best,
And His presence came like sunrise,
Like a glory in my breast.

All day long the Presence lingered,
All day long He stayed with me,
And we sailed with perfect calmness
O'er a very troubled sea.

* * * * *

So I think I know the secret,
Learned from many a troubled way:
You must seek Him in the morning
If you want Him through the day!"

—Ralph Spalding Cushman

---

* From *Spiritual Hilltops*, by Ralph S. Cushman, copyright © 1932 by Abingdon Press. Used by permission.

RESISTING THE DEVIL

Stand up to the devil and he will turn and run. James 4:7, N.E.B.

This is a most encouraging text for the tempted, harassed pilgrim on the rough road toward the eternal city.

James states positively that by resolutely resisting the tempter he can be forced to turn and retreat. Let us never forget this.

To continue to be a successful prize fighter the contender must be capable of delivering hard blows. But it is just as important for him to be able to absorb hard blows and still stand up. Likewise in the spiritual contest the successful adversary against evil must not only take the aggressive approach but he must also be prepared to stand up boldly to resist temptation. The consecrated will, with courage, stamina and divine help, can make the devil turn and run every time.

In the French town of Aigues Mortes, stands the ancient Tower of Constance, which for centuries served as a cold and dreary prison. For eighty-two years, until 1768, Huguenot Protestant reformers were incarcerated in this wretched place. Along with many other staunch Christians, 15-year-old Marie Durand was put into this tower. She remained there for the next thirty-eight years. When her fellow captives were offered their freedom if they would recant their faith, Marie inspired them to continue to resist. Near a trap door on a rude stone she worked for years carving the letters *R E C I S T E R*, resist. There this word remains today, a mute yet living witness to the courage and faithfulness of a steadfast girl who could say No and persist in it.

Marie Durand lived on in prison, and eventually God softened the heart of the ruling prince, who released her and her companions from their living death. His brief order to them was, "You are free." When criticized for releasing them from the foul jail, this considerate prince said, "I have ordered it closed in the hope that it will never be opened again for such a cause."

Temptation is the common lot of mankind. When Joseph said No the hand upholding the world upheld him. Daniel's greatest hour was not in the palace of Belshazzar, but years earlier when he "purposed in his heart" not to defile himself. Moses' finest hour was not when he talked with God on Sinai but when, in his youth, he "refused to be called the son of Pharaoh's daughter" and chose instead to suffer affliction with the people of God.

All who choose to serve God must resist the devil. They must be able to say No.

A COLONY OF HEAVEN

Our commonwealth is in heaven, and from it we await a Savior, the Lord Jesus Christ. Phil. 3:20, R.S.V.

In the King James Version this text states that the believer's citizenship is in heaven. Moffatt's translation reads, "A colony of heaven." Philippi, where this letter was sent, was a colony of Rome. The people of the city were proud that they were Roman citizens, that Philippi was ruled as a Roman city and that they were governed under Roman law.

Writing to the Philippian believers Paul reminded them that they were not only Roman citizens but also a colony of heaven existing in a non-Christian world. The thought that Christians live in the midst of an unbelieving world, somewhat like a colony under a different set of laws and observing a different standard of conduct, is an idea fraught with tremendous meaning.

As a modern example of a small, distant, yet loyal, colony one may consider Belize, formerly called British Honduras, and now independent. Although the streets are bordered with palms instead of oaks and the flowers bear tropical rather than English blooms, the atmosphere is definitely British. The colonists brought with them English ideas, customs, and habits. They lived under British law and held the privileges of British citizens, including the right to attend English schools. The spirit and tempo of the capital city is still British to the core, for this has been a British colony, where English is the spoken language.

Paul looked upon Christian believers on earth as a colony of heaven. However pagan the civilization in which they dwell, Christians ought to live among men as citizens of heaven. The rule of every man for himself, greed for gain, cutthroat competition and shameful immorality characterize earthly life. But the citizen of heaven is obedient to a different governing law as outlined in the Decalogue and in the Sermon on the Mount.

Attachment to and citizenship in a country leads one to be loyal to it. Even in a far-off colony he will live so as to honor his country's name. The kind of life the Christian plans to live in heaven serves as a guide to living here. The English of Belize did not ignore the nationals about them. Instead they endeavored to bring them the benefits of the British Commonwealth. A true colony of heaven must not withdraw from the world but regard itself as an outpost of a better kingdom and seek to draw all men into it.

THE DOCTRINE OF THE DEVIL

Ye are of your father the devil, and the lusts of your father ye will do. He was a murderer from the beginning, and abode not in the truth, because there is no truth in him. When he speaketh a lie, he speaketh of his own: for he is a liar, and the father of it. John 8:44.

A stanza committed to memory in childhood says

> "The devil is voted not to be,
> And, of course, the devil is gone:
> But many people would like to know
> Who carries his business on."

Belief in a personal devil doesn't sit well with modern philosophers. But their views, however deeply held, are daily disproved by the prevailing evidence that his nefarious business is thriving. Those who like to believe Satan doesn't exist outside of lively imaginations are engaging in deceptive, wishful thinking. Of course, this is nothing new, for Jesus vehemently told the Pharisees that, from the very beginning, Satan was the incarnation of all evil.

Soft-pedaling in dealing with the harsh truth is not new either. One time, during a heated discussion, a church leader seemed surprised when someone inadvertently used the word *liar*. He reacted with, "Oh, don't use that word! It's too harsh." I said, "Jesus used it when it fit the case. Why shouldn't we?" He gave me a long look and said no more.

In all Holy Writ there is no sharper depiction of unrestrained hostility than is portrayed by the gentle apostle John in today's text. It was unparalleled, eyeball to eyeball, confrontation and defiance. The Pharisees were enraged because Jesus had just told them that their claim to be Abraham's children was false and that their plotting to murder Him proved it. In seething resentment they shot back: "Now we know you are mad [crazy]." Jesus retorted by telling them who they were. He told them they were sons of the devil. Taking up stones to kill Him, they could not find Him in their blind rage. He passed out "through the midst of them" and went His way.

It is the doctrine of the devil to prevaricate and kill and then pretend nonexistence. Martin Luther knew better when he hurled the ink bottle at him. The Wesleys knew better when he opposed them on two continents. Billy Sunday knew better when he wrestled with him in the night as did Jacob of old. The devil still "works to do us ill." Jesus came into the world to destroy the devil and all his works.

HE TOOK A TOWEL

Jesus rose from supper, . . . and girded himself with a towel. Then he . . . began to wash the disciples' feet. John 13:4, 5, R.S.V.

On this last evening with His disciples Jesus had much to tell them. Had they been prepared to hear Him they would have saved themselves much anguish and disappointment later. But as He looked into their faces He could see that His words pointing to His imminent death had made little impression, because of the pervading atmosphere of contention and jealousy. A dispute had arisen earlier over who was the greatest. This rivalry showed up again at the table over the seating arrangement. Apparently Judas had come in and had taken Peter's place at Jesus' left. Then, when Jesus rebuked them, Peter took Judas' place at the other end. Obviously, each disciple, even at that most solemn hour, was eager to hold on to whatever position of prominence he could get.

The servants had placed the victuals on the table and then had gone to their own homes to observe the Passover. There was no one to do the servants' work. None of the disciples would forgo his claim to greatness enough to wash the others' feet. Sensing the situation, the Saviour showed them how to do a humble service divinely. He washed those twenty-four dusty, calloused feet in order to engrave on those envious, unwilling hearts, still swollen with vanity, the truth His lips had so long in vain pronounced: " 'Whoever would be great among you must be your servant' " (Matt. 20:26, R.S.V.).

After performing the menial task of a servant, Jesus said, "If I, then, your Lord and Master, have washed your feet; ye also ought to wash one another's feet. For I have given you an example" (John 13:14, 15). In this way Jesus reversed the world's idea of greatness. He both taught and practiced the humility of self-forgetting service and love.

Although He knew Judas was about to betray Him to death, Jesus washed the traitor's feet. He had said, "Love your enemies." Now He practiced it.

The other eleven had some claim to Jesus's cleansing. For many weeks their feet had trod the dust of Judea with Him. Afterward, year after year, those feet were to tread longer, rougher roads, taking them as pilgrims and strangers proclaiming the gospel of the crucified One.

Jesus entered the world through a very lowly door. Yet He made the streets to shine with holy service. Can we learn to perform ordinary duties as steps of spiritual ascent leading up to heaven?

A NEW SONG

He put a new song in my mouth, a hymn of praise to our God. Ps. 40:3, N.I.V.

David was no ordinary musician. He could play the harp beautifully, and he had a soothing singing voice. He was also a gifted composer. The Psalms testify to the power and thoughtfulness of his lyrics. One day something came into his life that gave him a desire to sing a new song. He had come closer to God and this experience put a new song into his heart. In this instance it was a song of deliverance. From despair and gloom the Lord had saved him. So he sang, "He brought me up also out of an horrible pit [of sin], out of the miry clay" (Ps. 40:2).

Because most of us are not as musically gifted as was David we sing songs composed by others. By pushing a button or twisting a knob we can flood our houses and cars with music of every conceivable type. Much of it is good, but of late there has been so much jarring disharmony and bumping, jumping rock-and-roll that a good many listeners switch it off faster than they switched it on. At such times a person wishes ardently to hear a new song.

While David's song was new to him, it was not new to mankind. It was not new in the sense that it had never been sung before. But it was new to him because it sang of a new experience. Hearses have been passing our doors ever since sin entered Eden. Yet to those who followed one to the cemetery yesterday it was as new and painful as if it had been the first one on earth. Mothers have been singing the same sweet, ungrammatical gibberish to their babies ever since Eve rocked her firstborn, yet it is ever a new song. It comes from experience.

No new song could thrill anyone more than those composed by Pastor William C. Jensen.

"Sometimes when strife seems more than I can bear;
No one to understand, no one to care;
Comes then a voice from out the long ago,
'This was for thee, My child, My shame, My pain, My woe.'

"Sometimes when on my pathway shadows fall,
I hear the Saviour gently, softly call,
'One day I walked through shadows deep for thee.
Can'st thou not walk this shadowy way for Me?' "

—William C. Jensen

PEARLS BEFORE SWINE

Give not that which is holy unto the dogs, neither cast ye your pearls before swine, lest they trample them under their feet, and turn again and rend you. Matt. 7:6.

This text is a unique saying of our Lord. Part of it has become proverbial. Actually it is an inverted quatrain, with the real meaning becoming clearer when the first and fourth lines are put together thus:

"Give not that which is holy unto the dogs
Lest they turn again and rend you.
Neither cast ye your pearls before swine
Lest they trample them under their feet."

Jesus spoke knowingly of dogs and pearls. For the Jews the dog was ceremonially unclean, an animal that was considered contemptible. Even today in much of the Orient dogs are the half-wild, mangy scavengers of the streets and are avoided as dangerous spreaders of disease, and also because they have been known to attack, and sometimes kill, children. In contrast to dogs, pearls, even small ones, have intrinsic value.

The Saviour was warning against wasting spiritual treasure upon those lacking spiritual perception, upon those who are intentionally and completely in the wrong and have no desire to depart from sin. There is a subtle contrast here too, for while dogs lack the capacity to appreciate spiritual realities and swine cannot comprehend the value of pearls, if men lack these capacities it springs from neglect and not from inherent disability. Christ's sharp warning is needed today because of the social influences and peer pressures that cause people to overlook or to depreciate spiritual values that are of supreme importance.

The Saviour's warning assails today's misnamed realism, the view that considers "real" only the sensuous and sensual, what can be weighed, measured or observed. This view is as blind to spiritual values as are dogs to the concept of holiness or swine to the importance of pearls. Those thus orientated think of Thanksgiving in terms of a five-course dinner, Christmas as the prospect of receiving gifts, Memorial Day as an automobile race, and July 4 as an outing with fireworks. Confining themselves to what is earthly, they regard time spent in spiritual matters as simply wasted. The Saviour's words were His way of reinforcing the divine principle that "the things which are seen are temporal; but the things which are not seen are eternal" (2 Cor. 4:18).

THE LIGHT THAT SHINES

Let your light so shine before men, that they may see your good works, and glorify your Father which is in heaven. Matt. 5:16.

During his later years Charles Ruskin sat one evening by a window overlooking a distant hill where a lamplighter was lighting one street lamp after another. The darkness hid the man himself, but his progress could be traced by each new gleam. Turning to a visitor, the author said, "That illustrates what I mean by a genuine Christian. You may not know him, . . . but his way has been marked by the lights he leaves burning."

Light has ever been a symbol of the divine Presence. John called Jesus "the light of men" shining forth in the darkness of this world (John 1:4). Every Christian who is true to his profession becomes a reflector of that light. It is not necessary for the light to be seen, for it shines, not to shed light on itself, but so that others may see in the darkness because of the light. Our light is to shine, not to attract attention to ourselves, but that those our light illuminates may be attracted to Christ, "the true Light, which lighteth every man that cometh into the world" (verse 9).

In his *Works Count Too,* Charles Pickell insists that there never was a time when positive witnessing was more needed than in our day. On the eve of the first world war, Britain's Sir Edward Grey remarked that "the lamps are going out all over Europe." As the lights of Christianity are extinguished all over the world today the hearts of millions grow dark. The result is frustration, anxiety, and despair. Some speak of our age as the twilight of civilization. In many fields we can point to admirable achievements by man, but we do so against the background of spiritual, moral, and social decay. Achievement? Yes, but achievement enveloped in darkness and threatened with the terrible possibility of total annihilation. Of no other period of history could it more accurately be said than of ours that darkness covers the earth and "gross darkness the people" (Isa. 60:2).

A Christian builder I knew moved, with his wife and two daughters, next door to a family of nine, none of whom was interested in religion. But the light of the exemplary family so illuminated these neighbors that, within four years, every one was baptized into Christ. From then on these two families faithfully attended church together every Sabbath. Even when we do not speak about it the Lord wants us to be His light and shine for Him.

LIGHT AT EVENING

At evening time it shall be light. Zech. 14:7.

Without electricity to turn night into day, the setting sun over ancient Israel brought darkness down like a shroud. Except when the fitful light of the moon relieved the blackout, darkness reigned. While the words of our text were directed to Israel of old, they could have no better application than to those who live today "upon whom the ends of the world are come" (1 Cor. 10:11).

The prophecies all point to the last days of earth, the evening of God's great day of salvation, as days of doom, disaster, and darkness. Daniel said there would be "a time of trouble, such as never was since there was a nation even to that same time" (Dan. 12:1). Paul spoke of the sunset hours of world history as "perilous times." Of moral conditions he wrote, "Evil men and seducers shall wax worse and worse, deceiving, and being deceived" (2 Tim. 3:13). Speaking of the churches he says, "Having a form of godliness, but denying the power thereof" (verse 5). Isaiah pictures the earth just before the end of time as one of deepest darkness. "Behold, the darkness shall cover the earth, and gross darkness the people" (Isa. 60:2). Just before the dawn of His eternal day, Jesus described "men's hearts failing them for fear, and for looking after those things which are coming on the earth" (Luke 21:26).

There was probably never a time when everything on earth seemed as unreliable and uncertain as now. Pronouncements by world leaders are highly unsettling to all who cherish tranquillity. Yet, despite the uncertainties that creep in the darkness, God's people can trust His promise that there shall be light. This is the light of salvation. Many hearts now in darkness will be set aglow with the light of God's truth coming to them from His Word in the sunset hours of time.

In vision John saw the earth at eventide set ablaze with the glory of God. Every Christian may be a light-bearer. By a blameless life of nobility, by speaking "a word in season," by sympathetically aiding the needy and afflicted, by distributing gospel literature, the followers of Jesus may have lights burning in many a dark heart. Can you say, with Isaiah, "Here am I; send me"?

AFTER MANY DAYS

Cast thy bread upon the waters: for thou shalt find it after many days. Eccl. 11:1.

In the *New English Bible* this familiar text reads "Send your grain across the seas and in time you will get a return."

Imagine that while living in the South Seas you should scatter a few bunches of breadfruit on the waves. They disappear, and the winds eventually waft them ashore on a distant isle. There, under a brilliant sun, they take root and grow to a stand of trees. After long years, when the trees are grown and their clusters are ripe, you are shipwrecked and stranded on that same shore. Until rescued, your life is preserved by eating of the breadfruit you cast on the waters long before.

Such are the providences of God's husbandry. Do the generous deed in faith and commend it to His care. Though the winds of circumstance may waft it away, the effect is not lost. Those same winds of circumstance that bear it away will in time bring it to the place prepared by Him. Whether the seed comes to an earthly or heavenly shore, after many days the result will come to light. Then the reaper will rejoice that he was once the sower.

Mrs. Lucile Meyer tells of an early experience when the Adventist leaders in the Philippine Islands felt the time had come to replace their modest medical dispensary with a modern sanitarium-hospital. But Dr. H. A. Hall, the medical director, was frustrated because of repeated delays in securing permission to build. The local authorities refused to approve the plan. Months went by with no consent in sight. Then one day, as the downhearted doctor sat at his desk wondering what to do, a dapper, flashily dressed Filipino businessman breezed into Dr. Hall's office. Waving a big cigar, this self-confident caller said, "I hear you want a hospital and can't get a permit to build it. I'll see you get it right away." The long-delayed permit was issued the next day.

Later when asked why he came forth with his badly-needed help, this man said that years before, while attending college in Colorado, he had been befriended by an Adventist student. This friend was a delight to know, a man who lived his religion yet was careful not to impose his opinions on others. He said he had decided then that if ever the opportunity arose to help Adventists he would act. This was that chance. The Filipino's friend was the late well-known and highly respected Dr. A. W. Truman.

A BOOK OF REMEMBRANCE

They that feared the Lord spake often one to another: and the Lord hearkened, and heard it, and a book of remembrance was written before him for them that feared the Lord, and that thought upon his name. Mal. 3:16.

As a boy was about to leave the hospital, where an operation had been performed to restore the use of his arm, he looked gratefully into the face of his surgeon and said, "My mother is never going to hear the last about you." Most people like to receive remembrances on their birthday and at Christmas time, but this little lad was so appreciative of his benefactor that he wanted to remember him all the time. We hope he did.

Malachi says that they who feared the Lord and thought about Him "spake often one to another." What did they speak about? They talked about God's love, His protecting care, and their hope in the coming Redeemer. And because God, who was listening to their conversation, was pleased, He had "a book of remembrance" written before Him.

The wicked talk a lot. When we hear them speaking things against God it is the Christian's duty to speak out for Him. Conversation about spiritual matters is all the more needful because of the world's chill that surrounds us. When a fire burns low in the grate, we bring together the embers that glow so that they may be coaxed into a flame. So, when so much of life around us is cold and dead spiritually, Christians ought to rekindle one another's faith with encouraging words.

Many of my friends take pleasure in maintaining personal remembrances called diaries. Such records often prove of key importance in criminal cases and in the probate of wills. When I began to put together the life story of Pastor V. T. Armstrong, late outstanding minister and missionary, I had the assistance of his daily doings written by his own hand. These diaries reveal where he was and what he was doing every day for more than forty years. They record in simple yet most moving words the many providences of God in his life.

The Lord keeps a record too.

> "The chronicles of heaven keep
> Our words in transcript fair;
> In heaven's sacred book of life
> Which names are written there?"

THE LORD'S JEWELS

And they shall be mine, saith the Lord of hosts, in that day when I make up my jewels. Mal.3:17.

In Yo Go Gulch on the eastern fringe of the Belt Mountains of Montana lies a strange deposit of dun-colored clay, the only such alluvium known in the United States. Embedded and hidden in this terra cotta are deep-blue sapphires of the rarest hue. When washed and screened these precious little gems shine like cobalt diamonds, as though each were lit by an inner light of its own. To hold and admire a handful of these exquisite stones is an experience. It explains why they are assiduously sought and are so expensive.

The Lord is coming soon from heaven to gather His "jewels" so that, with undimmed luster, they may shine eternally for the glory of His kingdom. This expression "my jewels" is an assertion of high personal esteem. Although God condemns much in this world, He attaches great worth to His jewels, which He distinguishes from all that sparkles with material glitter, the things that carnal man idealize, covet, and worship.

At the present time God's jewels are scattered here and there among earthly things and not collected except in God's view. But by Him they are seen as one precious company. Differing in degrees of purity, often considered as dross by contemporary society, He to whom they belong looks upon them in a different light. His radiant beam falls on each one and they shine. There will come an assembling as the grand act of redemption takes place. None will be lost, not one missing, despite the obscurity of mortal life, not even one in the remotest corner of the earth or the islands of the sea.

Think of the stupendous knowledge, the vigilance, the affectionate care and the mighty power that will bring His jewels together after preserving them separately in an infinite variety of circumstances and for so many ages. Then, when the jewels are all collected, He will pronounce, "They are mine." What a triumph to hear the words! What tears of joy as congratulations are extended! What a situation of place, felicity, and glory! Then He will assign each jewel its "setting" in the abode of the blest.

Looking at this prospect, what soul would choose to be absent when the Lord of hosts makes up His jewels? Who can bear the thought of being rejected with the baser things of creation and hear with inexpressible sorrow His voice saying, "This is *not mine,* take it away"?

A THANKSGIVING PRAYER

Offer unto God thanksgiving; and pay thy vows unto the most High. Ps. 50:14.

From stacked-up cities that once were strong and proud,
And from far hills half hid by fleeting cloud,
From fallow farms by dusty crooked roads
Where oaken wagons bent 'neath heavy loads,
Where curling leaves on yellow stubble lie,
Where geese wing far in azure-tinted sky,
From woodland smoke that floats on pungent air,
Great God of life, accept our humble prayer!

Lord, guard our feet from sting of wayside thorn,
Grant that our pride be undefiled by scorn,
And that our eyes shall not be blind to shame,
That our chill souls shall kindle to Thy flame.
Be deaf to boasts of what our hands have made
For naught shall be the palaces we rear
If lurks within our hearts a gnawing fear
—and we're afraid.

Pray grant today the warmth of heart we felt
In simple faith that blessed us as we knelt
In faith that fell like dew at early morn
When first we reaped the ears of rustling corn,
The childlike sense of latent inner power,
Wit wise enough to glory in a flower,
The peace that eases every numbing pain
—and joy of rain.

Up from thronged cities, such as cities are,
From o'er far hills where springs one twinkling star,
From youthful laughter like a hidden stream,
From aging hearts that faltering still can dream.

* * * * *

Our thoughts, our souls, our thankful hearts we raise Giver of every good,
our gratitude and praise.

LAST WORDS

Yea, though I walk through the valley of the shadow of death, I will fear no evil; for thou art with me. Ps. 23:4.

Listen to most any conversation and you will soon discover that many people like to have the last word. It is said that women usually get it. Lawyers scheme to take it. A good many long distance telephone calls would cost much less if the parties at the ends of the line were not trying to get in the last word. Television round tables often are cut off while someone is trying to get in his final "clincher." A popular newspaper series is called "Famous Last Words." But the last word will not be spoken until the end comes when time shall be no more. Meantime I have been noting the last words of various persons of importance.

In their final conscious moments military men usually revert to their field experiences. Dying on the island of Saint Helena, Napoleon gasped, "France! . . . Army! Head of the army!" Knowing that his hours were numbered, General Douglas MacArthur said shakily, "I've looked that old scoundrel death in the face many times. This time I think he has me on the ropes."

There is a vast contrast between the dying words of nonbelievers and the last utterances of those whose faith endured as they walked through "the valley of the shadow of death." The atheist Thomas Hobbes said, "I shall be glad then to find a hole to creep out of the world at." Voltaire, the French infidel, said, "In the name of God, let me die in peace!" The non-Christian rationalist Sir Francis Newport wailed, "Oh, that I could lie for a thousand years upon the fire . . . , to purchase the favor of God and be united to Him again."

By contrast the last words of Sir David Brewster were "I will see Jesus, see Him as He is. Oh, how bright it is!" Facing death, the evangelist D. L. Moody declared, "Earth recedes; heaven opens . . . Don't call me back." As we near our closing days the child of God knows that the Father will walk that shadowy way with us and give us dying grace so that, with the psalmist, we can say "I will fear no evil."

THE FUNERAL OF A CHRISTIAN
Precious in the sight of the Lord is the death of his saints. Ps. 116:15.

At the end of the Civil War, Robert E. Lee was offered a position by a New York firm at a salary of $10,000 a year. He was also invited to become president of the near-bankrupt Washington College at Lexington, Virginia, at $1,500 a year. He took the work at Lexington. For five years he toiled incessantly—and successfully—to restore Washington College. He also lived a most exemplary and spotless Christian life.

Now it was October 12, 1870. In the fields and woods of the impoverished Southland men were busy with ax and hoe. Across the campus of Washington College students were passing to their classes. In a room overlooking the college its careworn president lay dying. From his lips came the words "Strike the tent." He breathed a long sigh and was gone.

A recent flood had swept away every casket in town, but two boys found one waterlogged on the bank of the swollen river. It was cleaned and prepared for the frail body. Two days later a long procession of teachers, students, and townspeople formed before the chapel. Most noticeable were the rustic veterans who had followed Lee. They had come there from cove and mountain to pay final tribute to their valiant leader. In threadbare clothes, battered hats, and worn-out shoes they rallied for the last time around the man who had held their trust in the hollow of his hand.

As they assembled a reverent silence prevailed, but when the procession moved out one veteran began to sing a hymn they all knew. Others joined in and from the throats of Lee's old soldiers rolled the confident words of hope:

> "How firm a foundation, ye saints of the Lord,
> Is laid for your faith in His excellent Word!

> * * * * *

> "The soul that on Jesus doth lean for repose,
> I will not, I will not desert to his foes;
> That soul, though all hell should endeavor to shake,
> I'll never, no, never, no, never forsake!"

That was all.

THE COMFORT OF HIS COMING

The Lord himself shall descend from heaven . . . : and the dead in Christ shall rise first: then we which are alive and remain shall be caught up together with them in the clouds, to meet the Lord in the air: and so shall we ever be with the Lord. Wherefore comfort one another with these words. 1 Thess. 4:16-18.

A few years ago, while waiting on Fiji for the refueling of our trans-Pacific plane, I was told of a strange custom of the islanders known as calling the dead. The person most bereaved climbs to the top of a cliff or a tall tree. There he calls, again and again, the name of the recently deceased one and then shouts pathetically, "Come back! Come back!" The heart-rending wail is full of despair, with only mocking echoes to emphasize the depth of the bereavement.

All who have lately lost a dear companion, a close friend, or a much-loved child can sympathize with this Fijian, who, with tears on his cheeks, pleads hopelessly for the return of the one he loved so much.

Few indeed are they that do not deeply grieve when the merciless hand of death snatches from us the ones who are more precious to us than our own lives. Yet, despite tear-filled eyes and breaking hearts, we do not suffer and mourn "as others which have no hope." For we have the inflexible promise that all who die in the Lord will "be raised incorruptible" (1 Cor. 15:52). This marvelous assurance by the apostle Paul has been the infallible mainstay of the faith of true believers since it was written twenty centuries ago. And it will buoy up all who trust in God until Jesus comes again. And on that glorious day of resurrection all our dearly beloved of earth who sleep in Jesus will be reunited. Looking for that day is the blessed hope. What a reunion! What a clearing of tear-dimmed eyes as the saints go marching in!

> "The days that waft us onward
> Across life's ocean broad
> Bring us ever nearer to
> The kingdom of our God.

> * * * * *

> "Then haste, O haste, ye moments,
> And bear us swift along
> Until the Saviour greets us
> Mid bursts of angel song."
> —Edward J. Urquhart

SPECTATOR OR PARTICIPANT

And as they led him away, they laid hold upon one Simon, a Cyrenian, coming out of the country, and on him they laid the cross, that he might bear it after Jesus. Luke 23:26.

Curious to see the spectacle of a crucifixion, a crowd followed as Jesus was taken toward Golgotha. Many who had hoped in Him now despised Him. But a few, moved mostly by pity, still felt a little love for Him who had loved the poor. They did not realize that He was about to offer up His life for the sins of all the world.

As the procession came to the gate of Pilate's court the cross was placed on Jesus' bleeding shoulders. In His weakened state He crumpled under the weight of the massive cross. His strength was utterly exhausted, and there He lay near death. The retinue paused and the circle of spectators jeered, "He is only pretending." But the centurion, anxious to be done with his distasteful task, saw that his chief captive would never be able to drag the heavy load to Calvary. Then the centurion's eye fell upon a Cyrenian from the country who was looking with astonishment and pity on the prostrate form panting beneath the two beams. One glance told the centurion that this kindly looking man was strongly built, so he called to him, "Take the cross and come after us." The Cyrenian obeyed. In an instant, Simon changed from a spectator to a participant. With the cross on his sturdy shoulders, he saw the scene from a different point of view. Being a part of the act made a big difference in Simon.

Little else is known of the merciful-hearted man who lent his strong shoulders to lift Jesus' load, except that his two sons were Christians.

It makes a world of difference today whether a person looks from the sidelines or participates in the performance. A situation looks vastly different to those who merely look on than it does to those who carry the load. Unregenerate human nature sees flaws more quickly than virtues. The caliber of a man can often be determined by the way he looks at others. The little fellow measures everybody by himself, for he is his own yardstick.

Likewise, the view of the church is different from the outside than from the inside. No one should judge it until he has sensed its strength and beauty from the inside. What is of the most importance outsiders never see. Are you a spectator or a participant?

WHY HE CAME

To this end was I born, and for this cause came I into the world, that I should bear witness unto the truth. John 18:37.

It is often declared—and rightly so—that Jesus came into the world to save sinners. No assertion could more clearly epitomize His mission to earth. Yet, in His own words, there were at least two other purposes that activated His life among men. He came to bear witness to the truth and He came to please His Father. He said, "I do always those things that please him (John 8:29).

The majestic statement in our text for today was the Saviour's reply to Pilate's inquiry. If, in all things, we are to emulate Christ then we too must bear witness to truth and endeavor to live always to please our heavenly Father. Wordsworth's immortal lines suggest that at our genesis we stood, as it were, before God to receive our commission even before we were clothed with this body of humiliation. Whether or not the poet was right in his surmise that "not in utter nakedness or forgetfulness do we come from God, who is our home," we need not argue. It is enough for us that God, who "doeth all things well," sent us forth to fulfill a purpose, to realize an ideal and to bear witness to the truth. Should we not therefore ask ourselves, as if in His actual presence, whether we are fulfilling the divine purpose that the apostle Paul calls our "high calling" (Phil. 3:14)?

As he takes up a lump of clay the potter means to make of it either a vase to adorn a palace or some simpler household vessel. The revolving wheel and his hand will serve his purpose. "Cannot I do with you as this potter?" asks the Lord (Jer. 18:6). David acknowledged also the Lord's high purpose in his life in these words: "Your eyes saw my unformed body. All the days ordained for me were written in your book before one of them come to be" (Ps. 139:16, N.I.V.).

If, as we consider our modest endowments, we humbly ask, "Why hast thou made me thus?" God's reply is sometimes voiceless as it steals insensibly into our consciousness and we perceive that we are fulfilling His purpose.

The Christian should live, work, and even suffer if need be, so as to please our heavenly Father. Then we shall be like Jesus, who said of His earthly mission, "I do always those things that please him."

GOD'S GIFT OF SNOW

He showers down snow, white as wool, and sprinkles hoar-frost thick as ashes; crystals of ice he scatters like bread-crumbs; he sends the cold, and the water stands frozen. Ps. 147:16, 17, N.E.B.

Every year, about this time or earlier, a blanket of mantling snow comes sifting down over much of the Northern Hemisphere. There are those who dread the coming of winter because of the shivering cold it introduces and the danger of winter traveling to life and limb. But the first snowfall is exciting to children. They love the exhiliration of winter sports that puts zest into the blood, paints youthful cheeks with scarlet, and adds sparkle to clear, young eyes.

John W. Watson exulted thus: "Beautiful snow! it can do nothing wrong." And John Ruskin's appreciation of nature's coverlet of white was expressed in these words: "I doubt that any object can be found more perfectly beautiful than a fresh, deep snowdrift, seen under warm light. Its curves are inconceivable perfection, . . . its lights and shadows, sharp, pale, and of heavenly color, the reflected light intense . . . mingled with the sweet occurrences of transmitted light."

It is an inspiration to stand atop a lofty mountain range and see the heights below capped with perpetual snow. Tall peaks are especially beautiful on a clear morning when the snowy crests reflect the rising sun. They are lovely when draped with fleecy clouds. Somehow though, they seem most awe-inspiring at sunset, when a soft rosy glow tips them with incandescent fire.

When we pause to reflect, we realize that everything in which we delight and which we reckon as "ours" is really a gift from God, who "is a generous giver who neither refuses nor reproaches anyone" (James 1:5, N.E.B.). When we appreciate this great truth we will consistently and humbly bow our heads before every meal to thank the heavenly Giver.

> "Tis God who causes rain to fall
> And sends the winter's snow,
> Who puts power in the soil
> That makes the corn to grow.

> "He takes time to paint the roses.
> He marks the sparrow's fall.
> He bedecks the clouds at sunset
> And watches over all."
>
> —Leonard C. Lee

OUR UNFALTERING TRUST

Woe to them that . . . trust in chariots, because they are many; and in horsemen, because they are very strong; but they look not unto the Holy One of Israel. Isa. 31:1.

Newspapers and colorful picture magazines are continually featuring fanciful new religio-pseudo-scientific notions and strange far-fetched conceptions of deity in which to trust. Millions place their confidence in one or more of these outlandish, supposedly rational, modern ideas. The amazing range of these ideologies embraces astrology, witchcraft, voodooism, black magic, exorcism, sorcery, numerology, neophrenology, divination, and many more. New ones spirng forth every day.

This entire galaxy of occult beliefs and manifestations betrays a rising erosion of faith in the traditional virtues and values and in the God who is the Creator of all. Nationally the original, sturdy confidence in the benefits of honest work, in saving for a rainy day, in the belief that right makes might, in the invulnerability of our safety due to continental isolation—all once thought invincible—are in process of erosion.

In Israel's time national leaders depended on military might composed of horses, chariots, and armed men. Except that tanks replaced chariots and rockets succeeded swords, that concept prevailed from the time of Alexander the Great to that of Adolph Hitler. But today all is changed. Hitler's boast that he was strong enough to rule the world sounds hollow now. With human inventive ingenuity turning toward mass annihilation our pride in vaunted progress is withering and the peoples of the world are asking in paralyzing fear, "What now?"

But, instead of looking to "the Holy One of Israel" they look to a conglomeration of strange, occult deities spawned by the god of this world. Christian believers still look up to God as did the founding fathers of America. From Washington on they voiced with ringing words their trust in divine Providence. Dwight D. Eisenhower expressed it in these words: "You can't explain free government in any other terms than religious. The founding fathers . . . wrote their faith into our founding documents, stamped their trust in God on the faces of their coins . . . and put it boldly at the base of our institutions. . . . Our forefathers proved that only a people strong in godliness is strong enough to overcome tyranny and make themselves and others free. . . . Prayer today is a necessity."

SUSTAINING RIGHTEOUSNESS

Righteousness exalteth a nation: but sin is a reproach to any people. Prov. 14:34.

Astute scholars who have studied and written the lives of kings and rulers and have produced volumes of history detailing the story of the nations, disagree on many matters. But they remarkably concur on one point, namely, that high moral standards of a citizenry constitute a formidable bulwark of strength in both peace and war. Indeed, some standard of right and wrong is essential to national existence. No nation lacking some such standard has ever been known. Rome and Greece had systems of laws based on reason and a common sense of what is right. Without that they would never have become nations. And the principle of righteousness exalted and taught in the Schools of the Prophets laid a solid foundation for the marvelous prosperity that attended God's people during the reigns of David and Solomon.

The philosophy of history is a well-worn subject among historians who have discussed, dissected and reviewed it from many viewpoints. But the true philosophy of history is that "righteousness exalteth a nation." To recognize this and that the "throne is established by righteousness," to acknowledge the outworking of God's power to remove and set up kings, "this is to understand the true philosophy of history" *(Prophets and Kings,* p. 502).

"In the word of God only is this clearly set forth. Here it is shown that the strength of nations, as of individuals, is not found in the opportunities or facilities that appear to make them invincible; it is not found in their boasted greatness. It is measured by the fidelity with which they fulfill God's purpose."—*Ibid.*

The prosperity and influence of a nation is in proportion to its righteousness. France once turned away from this divine principle. She might have been a magnificent example among the nations, but selfishness, vanity, and venality held sway. The national prosperity vanished and the country eventually reaped in blood the harvest that had been sown.

During these same years beyond the Atlantic a new nation was emerging with freedom on its banner and righteousness as its resolute foundation. Within a century the United States progressed from a few scattered settlements on the fringe of a continent to a mighty nation stretching "from sea to shining sea." Righteousness does exalt a nation.

A CASTLE IN SPAIN

And the peace of God . . . shall keep your hearts and minds through Christ Jesus. Phil. 4:7.

Like many others, I once dreamed of owning a castle in Spain. But I had no very clear mental picture of such a castle. Then came good fortune, a chance to visit not only one but several very ancient castles in very ancient Spain. Was I impressed!

In many of these old castles is an inner keep or stronghold that is protected not only by the outer walls and bastions but by a strong portcullis of heavy iron bars at each of the gates. Armed sentries stood at every approach to challenge all who came to enter or to leave. This was a reminder that, in a similar way, the heart is continually approached by good and evil, by the frivolities and vanities of the world, impelled by the insidious promptings of the flesh and the devil.

It is said that one time a heartless enemy hired a ruffian to murder the lord of a certain castle. The paid assassin tried various ways to get inside, but the alert guards always turned him back. Observing that a cartload of hay was about to be driven in for the lord's mount, this knave took his dagger and hid himself under the hay. By this ruse he entered the castle undetected and stabbed to death the unsuspecting noble.

The heart too can be entered stealthily. At any hotel guests throng in and out, and some may intend to steal or do arson. When an enemy sets fire in the heart the entire being is swept with passion and in an hour the fabric of years can be consumed to ashes. We must therefore be alert to guard the heart, for "out of it are the issues of life" (Prov. 4:23).

Men of great wealth trust in their riches, which they pile around them like a fortress within which they fancy they have security and defense, with every want satisfied. But ill health stalks the castle as often as it does the cabin, and the peace and happiness of the affluent usually fall short of that enjoyed by the lowly—and often prove more ephemeral.

Sursum corda is a Latin motto meaning "Lift up your hearts." When we lift up our hearts unto the Lord He becomes the warden protector of our lives and gives us a "peace . . . which passeth all understanding." With His protecting arms around us we are safer than in a moated castle in Spain.

WAITING ON THE LORD

Therefore will the Lord wait, that he may be gracious unto you, . . . that he may have mercy upon you: for the Lord is a God of judgment: blessed are all they that wait for him. Isa. 30:18.

This verse speaks of two kinds of waiting: God's and ours. God's waiting is real and earnest, not a passive loitering like a man waiting for a bus, but with expectation and desire. What is He waiting for? Surely not for the humble and repentant. No, He waits patiently for the careless, the erring, and the scoffers to hear His voice saying, "Come unto Me."

As a diamond sparkles more brightly in its setting and the rose appears lovelier with its green leaves so this text gains force in the light of its setting. In the preceding verses the Lord witheringly exposes human wickedness then suddenly changes the tone with the sweet invitation, "Come now, let us reason together." The voice of mercy is the more appealing because of the thunderings immediately preceding it. As lightning is more brilliant during darkness, so God's mercy shines more gloriously against the background of human guilt. The marvel is that He is waiting still.

The Lord has done a lot of waiting for men. The angel at Jabbok waited until Jacob, exhausted by his struggling, could wrestle no more. Then the angel whispered in Jacob's ear his mystic name and blessed him there. The Saviour waited until the Syrophenician woman fell helpless at His feet, then He granted the boon she craved for her child. He waited over Jordan, ignoring entreaties to hasten and save Lazarus (and at no small cost to His heart), so that He might work a greater miracle than had been asked. He waited until the apostle Paul's energy was utterly exhausted, then imparted His power as He whispered, "My grace is sufficient for thee."

Too often we misinterpret God's delays. They are not denials, not neglectful nor unkind. He is waiting for just the right moment to flood our lives with such plenteous blessings that eternity will be too short to utter all our praise.

God waits patiently to bestow His grace on us. We should wait patiently to receive it. "Blessed are all they that wait for him."

THY WILL BE DONE

Then Job arose, and rent his mantle, and shaved his head, and fell down upon the ground, and worshipped. Job 1:20.

In the *King James Version* quoted here there are nineteen words in this verse, five of which are verbs in the active voice. Job arose, rent, shaved, fell, and worshiped. Each verb records an act of the will on Job's part. He kept his self-control in the midst of the worst crisis imaginable.

It is an oriental custom for persons to react to tragic news by sitting alone for long periods with heads bowed and eyes closed. The silence is broken at intervals by sighs, groans, and muted lamentations. Then the suffering mourner falls silent again. No doubt Job was following this practice. Although he was shaken to the depths by his grief he roused himself from this wonted calmness. In spite of his calamities Job was not prostrated by them. He arose.

Job rent his mantle. Wealthy Arabs still do this as a token of sorrow and humiliation. Thus Job showed that he was neither insensible to grief nor too proud to show it. There is as little virtue in not showing grief as there is in being overwhelmed by it. Someone once said that not to feel is to be either more or less than a man. Jesus wept. Grace teaches us not to be without sorrow, but to learn from it penitence, submission, faith, and hope.

Job had his head shaved, which is another token of mourning. Some such external sign of grief was expected, and the Christian religion does not forbid it.

Job fell down upon the ground. Falling prostrate signified grief, humiliation, or adoration. In this instance it seems probable that all three were involved. They are not incompatible. Trouble can be a blessing when it leads to self-abasement before God. Satan expected to see Job standing on his feet and cursing God as the author of all his afflictions. But Job's mind was on nobler things.

Then Job worshiped. There could be no finer example of complete resignation to the will of God. He did not know why the floodgates of disaster had broken upon him. He did not realize that he was on exhibition before the universe as a man who trusted God implicitly. He was in the dark but depended on God where he could not see and believed when he could not understand. Instead of cursing God he praised Him.

When trouble comes let us learn from Job's experience to say with him, "The Lord gave, and the Lord hath taken away; blessed be the name of the Lord" (Job 1:21).

GREAT IS HIS FAITHFULNESS

May God himself, the God of peace, make you holy in every part, and keep you sound in spirit, soul, and body, without fault. . . . He who calls you is to be trusted; he will do it. 1 Thess. 5:23, 24, N.E.B.

In the *King James Version* verse 24 reads "Faithful is he that calleth you, who also will do it." The antecedent of the word *it* is Paul's statement in the preceding verse: He will "make you holy, . . . and keep you sound in spirit, soul, and body, without fault, . . ." If we couple with this Jeremiah's earnest assertion that great is God's faithfulness (Lam. 3:23), we have a ringing declaration of heaven's determination to save His own. It is assurance that the unwavering Almighty will do the necessary sanctifying and keeping. The Lord is resolute to use His power to see to it that every true believer *here* will be sanctified and saved for *over there*. There is no doubt about it. The Lord is going to save His people and Satan and all his legions of death cannot prevent it.

Sometimes, even within the circle of the saved, some confident "achievers" develop such strength in themselves that they lose faith in God. Others grow so weary bearing their heavy loads that their faith falters too. Many unintentionally permit the advances of modern civilization that surround us to diminish devotion. We push a button to start the furnace in the morning. Touch a little switch and the house is flooded with light. Automatic toasters and poachers prepare our breakfasts. Mechanical carriers whisk us to school or office where blinking-bright new "systems" regulate the day. The God of heaven is thus, through neglect, excluded from our lives. Only in emergencies is He thought of or remembered.

The archdeceiver commandeers the wizardry of today's computerized civilization to turn men from God and from dependence on Him who created and sustains the universe and from the Saviour who loves us and gave Himself for us. Though unseen and largely out of mind, the Almighty still stands just beyond the shadows keeping watch above His own.

A mighty God "is able to deliver" (Dan. 3:17). He shields "them that are tempted" (Heb. 2:18) and is able "to save them to the uttermost" (chap. 7:25). He is able to do "abundantly above all that we ask or think" (Eph. 3:20). Shall we not trust Him to see us through to victory!

THE FORGIVENESS OF GOD

In whom we have redemption through his blood, the forgiveness of sins, according to the riches of his grace. Eph. 1:7.

God can forgive sin only by the tragedy of the cross. There is no other way. If there had been, the Father would not have permitted His Son to die on Golgotha. Forgiveness, which is so easy to accept, cost agony untold. As we accept God's forgiveness, a gift of the Holy Spirit, we should consider at what a price it was made ours. The magnitude of the forgiveness of sins awakens the deepest sense of gratitude in the human heart. The apostle Paul never forgot this and, as he pondered it, he was held as in a vice, constrained by the love of God.

There is no such thing as an unforgiven Christian. Nor is there one unforgiving Christian. Jesus said that God can forgive only the sins of those who forgive their brethren. "If ye forgive not men their trespasses, neither will your Father forgive your trespasses" (Matt. 6:15).

Peter's association with Christ made him see that a man must practice forgiveness if he is to be a follower of Him. But it was not clear to Peter how many times a person should be forgiven in one day. Like the Pharisees, he thought there ought to be a limit. He asked, "Lord, how oft shall my brother sin against me, and I forgive him? till seven times?" (chap. 18:21). While Peter was seventy times wrong about God's plan of forgiveness he was seven times ahead of most people today. Many, otherwise good, kind people, find it very hard to forgive just once those that have injured them. Jesus taught that the forgiveness we extend to others should be without limit. We should rejoice over this because "With what measure ye mete, it shall be measured to you again" (chap. 7:2).

Frederick of Prussia carried on an extended correspondence with the French philosopher Voltaire. Each considered the other his friend. But when some minor disagreement developed they became alienated and their friendship turned to antipathy. This terminated their correspondence. Some time later Frederick fell ill. Fearing he might not survive, he called his orderly and said, "If I die you will notify Voltaire that he is forgiven. If I recover send him no message." A conditional forgiveness is no forgiveness at all, for the Lord says, "He shall have judgment without mercy, that hath shewed no mercy" (James 2:13).

God has forgiven us so much, we should do in a small way what He does so abundantly.

THE ACT OF FORGIVENESS

Forgive, I pray thee now, the trespass of thy brethren, and their sin. Gen. 50:17.

These words of the dying Jacob were to his absent son, Joseph, whom he did not expect to see again. Jacob, the last bond between Joseph and his brothers, was attempting to reconcile them. As he was dying, his sons, who had so grievously wronged Joseph, feared that the old wound would rupture and that their brother would take vengeance on them. They suspected that the recent kindnesses shown them were for their father's sake only and feared that, with his restraining influence removed, they would suffer the punishment they so richly deserved.

So the brothers brought forth the appeal of their dying father. They asked that his words be held sacred. At the same time they confessed their guilt with humility. In effect they were saying, "As we have one father so we have one God. Forgive us for His sake." By uniting the tie of religion with that of nature they were making the best approach they knew.

Joseph had already forgiven his brothers. He reminded them that God brings good from evil and was turning calamity to deliverance. Now they realized that their exalted brother was not a hypocrite, that there was no revenge in his heart and that his gifts had been sincere. He proved his forgiveness by his actions. "And Joseph wept when they spake unto him" (Gen. 50:17). All their fearful suspicions were banished by the quiet testimony of his tears.

In *Proving the Promises,* the life story of Elder V. T. Armstrong, is a record of the hatred he had for his cruel stepfather, who, with little or no reason, often horsewhipped the boy mercilessly. Victor was impressed that he ought to join the church but the verse, "If ye forgive not . . ." stood in his way. He later told how one morning he settled the matter: "I stopped under a tree and asked God to take all the hatred out of my heart and to give me love for my enemy instead. . . . He took away the hatred, and from that moment I had only love for my stepfather. . . . Never again did this hatred return. From then on I prayed for his salvation."

Every Christian faces the vexing problem of forgiveness. There are so many things to be forgiven, many too grievous to bear until they are held up to God. "As we forgive . . ." is a shattering dictum to the proud. It is humiliating to recall our feeble attempts at forgiving others. Bleak, unconvincing confessions are worthless. Then let us, on our knees, lay hold of the promised power to "do all things." This includes forgiving.

WHEN OUR SHIP COMES IN

My people shall be satisfied with my goodness, saith the Lord. Jer. 31:14.

This prediction of the ingathering of the Jewish nation is capable of wider application. "My people shall be satisfied with my goodness," says Jehovah. Experience teaches that the soul, even in the midst of riches, honor, and luxury, is still unsatisfied. God alone can satisfy it because our souls were designed originally for a life of infinite good in paradise. But even there sin erupted in dissatisfaction and mankind has been largely unhappy and dissatisfied ever since. Most people do not know how very deep and widespread that dissatisfaction is.

In the days of sailing ships the safe arrival in port of a white-winged merchantman was a long-anticipated, joyful event. If the homecoming was overdue the anxious owners were jubilant. Many a fortune was made from the sale of merchandise brought in the hold of such a vessel. For days they had talked of the day "when our ship comes in."

The ships that come in for us are those we launch ourselves. We may dream of the day when vessels loaded with cargoes of fame, fortune, position, and power sail in. But we wait in vain unless we have launched them. It may be pleasant to dream, but dreaming is only a delusion. Dream ships will never come in.

The person who lives beyond his means cannot expect the ship of fortune to dock at his port. But he who takes care to always live within his means launches a ship that will come sailing home with a precious cargo. In this life little comes by chance, and the vessels and the shipments that come to us are usually the ones we ourselves have launched.

There are those who launch ships they anticipate will return with a valuable cargo. Then, by unworthy conduct and dissipation, they bore holes in the hulls and thus sink their own ships and scuttle their hopes by forgetting God and His ideals for them.

There are spiritual ships we must all launch if we expect to receive a returning cargo of power and influence to enable us to do our part in proclaiming the message of salvation. All those who commit their ways to the Lord early in life can rest assured that the ships they launch in faith will, if not in this life, then in the port of eternity, come sailing home to them. We shall be satisfied then.

MORE THAN CONQUERORS

Who shall separate us from the love of Christ? Shall trouble or hardship or persecution or famine or nakedness or danger or sword? . . . No, in all these things we are more than conquerors through him who loved us. Rom. 8:35-37, N.I.V.

In 1927 students of the carpentry class at the Japan Mission Training College were invited to take on the construction of the projected Tokyo Adventist Sanitarium. It was a big order and their director, Dr. Andrew Nelson, wasn't sure they should attempt it. But the mission president, Elder V. T. Armstrong, had confidence they could do the job. So they went to work with a will. One day, after they had been at work for a couple of weeks, Elder Armstrong came out to see how they were getting along. During their lunch break several of the boys were singing a song with words that roughly translated went "Maybe we can do it. Maybe we can't do it." When Armstrong heard it he got others to reply with the same tune "Yes, we can! Yes, we can! Yes, we can!" Everyone had a good laugh, then they all joined in and sang Armstrong's version heartily and loudly. The encouraging spirit thus engendered animated these workers and they finished the task in record time.

A life that is hid with Christ in God will stand up against surprises and attacks. In a world beset with alarms, ill tidings, sickness and change, the heart that is fixed and stable is also serene and quiet because it knows that "they that be with us are more than they that be with them" (2 Kings 6:16).

After the battle of the Nile, Lord Nelson sent word of the triumph of the British fleet over the French navy. In exultant language he said that *victory* was not a big enough word to describe it. Likewise Paul, writing of the remarkable spiritual battles he had won through the power of the Redeemer, declared, "We are more than conquerors through him who loved us."

What could be more comforting than knowing that nothing can separate us from God's love? Whether we ride high on the crest of good fortune or bend beneath a burden of calamity and despair He is there all the time. But His presence does not always ward off disaster. This is true because man and the devil try to run this world their way. But no one can be separated from God's love. You and the Almighty have the last word. It is a shout of victory.

INASMUCH

And the King . . . shall say unto them, Verily I say unto you, Inasmuch as ye have done it unto one of the least of these my brethren, ye have done it unto me. Matt. 25:40.

This well-known verse preaches in one sentence the substance of the gospel of Jesus. Here is the key to a life like His. The Scriptural equivalent of service to Christ is unselfish service to our fellow men.

The King might have said, "You have kept the Sabbath; you have paid a faithful tithe; you have prayed many prayers; you have given liberally to the church building fund and you have attended church faithfully." A genuine Christian will be an active church member and will eagerly and faithfully perform these duties and many more. But it is a significant and telling fact that the King does not mention any of these obligations. He mentions only the duties that Christian love induces.

"Duty, stern duty, has a twin sister, which is kindness. If duty and kindness are blended, decided advantage will be gained; but if duty is separated from kindness, if tender love is not mingled with duty, there will be a failure, and much harm will be the result. Men and women will not be driven, but many can be won by kindness and love." *Testimonies,* vol. 3, p. 108.

Edwin Markham wrote a poem about Conrad, an old cobbler, who dreamed one night that the Master was to be his guest. Early the next morning Conrad decorated his little shop with bright blooms thinking to himself, When the Master comes I will wash His spike-pierced feet and kiss His wounded hands.

But the Master did not come. A beggar came. So the cobbler gave him shoes. An old woman came bending under a heavy load. Conrad took the burden from her back and shared with her his simple meal. Finally, as the day was fading into darkness, there came a little child, her eyes wet with tears. In his pity he tenderly led her home to her mother. But the divine Guest never came.

> "Then soft in the silence a Voice he heard:
> 'Lift up your heart, for I kept my word.
> Three times I came to your friendly door;
> Three times my shadow was on your floor.
> I was the beggar with bruised feet;
> I was the woman you gave to eat;
> I was the child on the homeless street!' "

THE INCOMPREHENSIBLE ONE
Whence hath this man this wisdom? Matt. 13:54.

The Nazarene congregation was dumfounded. Jesus' hearers did not know what to think. It was baffling. The sermon they had just heard was a world apart from what they were accustomed to hearing from the scribes. This sermon soared to the heights and plumbed the depths. It throbbed with power and stabbed at their hearts. "Whence," they asked, "hath this man this wisdom?"

They began by wondering at the sermon and ended by wondering about the young Preacher. What astonished them was that He was no stranger. They knew His family and were cognizant of the fact that for years He had worked right there in Nazareth as a carpenter. Now He had taken to preaching, and this was His first sermon to the home congregation. It left them stupefied with amazement.

Ordinarily we can account for a unique person either through his parentage, environment, or both. Biographers usually write in this vein: "He inherited his mental powers from his father. He derived his gentle nature from his mother." When this fails to provide the key we examine the influences of the early years. But the Nazarenes were astonished because they knew that Jesus' parents, sisters, and brothers were simple Galilean peasants like themselves. As for His education, this was an even greater conundrum. He had not studied in the rabbinical schools nor sat at the feet of the learned Gamaliel. The people did not know what to make of it.

The impression Jesus made at Nazareth was repeated everywhere He went. At age 12 He had amazed the great doctors of the law. After coming to Him the palsied man strode away with his bed on his back. When the Pharisees tried to trap Him with words His answers so surprised them that they left him and went their way. Even the Roman officials were profoundly perturbed. And at last, as He stood before Pilate as a lonely, friendless prisoner, His demeanor caused that callous functionary to marvel greatly (see Matt. 27:14).

The world's great can all be explained. But Jesus can be understood only by accepting His verdict on Himself: that He was what He said He was, the Son of God. Were the apostle Paul to come into the room we would all stand in his honor. But if the Incomprehensible One were to come in, we should fall down and worship Him. Like Thomas of old we would say, "My Lord and my God"!

OUR DAILY CHOICES

A good man out of the good treasure of his heart bringeth forth that which is good; and an evil man out of the evil treasure of his heart bringeth forth that which is evil: for of the abundance of the heart his mouth speaketh. Luke 6:45.

Man's physical diet is under scientific scrutiny today as never before. Specialists in nutrition are coming out with new theories every day and new best sellers every week. This concentrated attention on the merits or demerits of various foods has made people more careful than in the past about what they put into their mouths. But Jesus said, " 'Listen, and understand thoroughly! . . . It is what comes *out* of a man's mouth that makes him unclean' " (Matt. 15:10, 11, Phillips). This verse is usually construed—and rightly so—as a condemnation of improper, vulgar, and profane language. But there is a deeper significance to it. A person's character is what he has become by the successive choices he has made, day by day, through the years. The words of his mouth and his daily life mirror these inner qualities.

When life is reduced to a simple, day-to-day formula it can be said to be a matter of choosing. We need to realize that the choices we make mold our characters. They make us what we are. A Christian's life, therefore, is the product of the ability to choose wisely and solve life's daily problems with right decisions. This cumulation of right choices, small and great, forges a successful life.

Savonarola once asked, "Would you rise in the world? You must work while others amuse themselves. Are you desirous of a reputation for courage? You must risk your life. Would you be strong morally and physically? You must resist temptation. All this is paying in advance. Observe the other side of the picture: the bad things are paid for afterward."

Anyone who has greatly achieved will agree with Savonarola: "You must work while others amuse themselves." He was right too in saying that we pay for the good in advance while bad choices are paid for later. This latter may be termed the devil's credit plan, his installment system: always postponing payday, indefinitely if possible. Sometimes, in this life, payday never comes. But in spiritual matters none can avoid payment for bad choices—often with compound interest.

Let us never underestimate the importance of the choices we make today.

ORGANIZATION ISN'T ENOUGH

"It is the Spirit which gives life. The flesh will not help you." John 6:63, Phillips.

Recently I was included in a small group of local citizens who were invited by our regional electric company to visit and inspect the nuclear energy facility at Diablo Canyon near San Luis Obispo. It was a memorable experience because that gigantic plant and the prodigious energy potential overwhelm the mind. On the return trip I sat on the bus with one of the other guests, one who knew of my church affiliation. After discussing the impressive operation we had just visited this man suddenly changed the subject. He said, "You know, I admire that tremendous establishment but I admire just as much your magnificent church organization." This unsought, unexpected tribute so surprised me that I could only reply, "I am glad you think so. I only wish your commendation were better deserved."

Thinking later about this conversation I began to wonder. I realize we have more church members than ever before. But numbers do not necessarily mean divine approval. Other things than churches grow.

We have never had more denominational institutions than today. But however impressive they may be, the number and grandeur of buildings do not signify growth in grace.

We never had more money as a church than now. A portion of this money is donated to advance the gospel and does much good. But money alone can never solve our problems nor save one soul for the kingdom.

We never had more or better church buildings than at the present time. While some individual congregations need better places for worship, our church bodies as a whole are better housed than ever in the past.

We have never had finer educational institutions than now, nor a better-trained ministry. Most of the key positions in the church are held by specially trained workers.

But more members with better churches, more money, and a better-trained ministry will never meet our needs. Towering above all else is our need of God's Holy Spirit. Some years ago Charles Spurgeon wrote, "Unless the Spirit of God come upon us, baptizing our manpower, our organized efforts, our pulpit, and our pew, we might as well close our church door and write upon it, 'God, have mercy upon us!'" "Not by might, nor by power, but by my spirit, saith the Lord of hosts" (Zech. 4:6).

ACTIONS TELL

Whoever claims to live in him must walk as Jesus did. 1 John 2:6, N.I.V.

An old Spanish proverb warns that "If you live like wolves you will learn to howl." Benjamin Franklin commented that "none teaches better than the ant, and she says nothing." Albert Schweitzer, who was short on words but long on deeds, went even further when he said that "example is not the main thing in life—it is the only thing." In the same vein is Longfellow's quatrain from his famous "Psalm of Life."

> "Lives of great men all remind us
> We can make our lives sublime,
> And, departing, leave behind us
> Footprints on the sands of time."

Of more than one prominent person it has been said that his life speaks louder than his words. Nor is this always said with a derogatory implication. I have known many indifferent preachers but none, I think, less naturally suited for the pulpit than my uncle, Elder C. H. Rittenhouse. He had little formal education, and, until in his 30s, lived the outdoor life of a North Dakota cowboy. Then he accepted Christ and was converted—thoroughly. He promptly sold his cattle holdings and headed for Walla Walla College, where for a year he studied for the ministry, especially Bible. Then he and one of the art teachers were married and they entered earnestly into the gospel ministry. Although he was an outstanding Bible student, his public messages were halting and far from eloquent. But his Christian witness and love for sinners have seldom been excelled. After he had labored in Idaho for eight years I attended the Idaho camp meeting near Boise. At one service the conference president asked members to stand according to whichever minister had baptized them. When he called the name of his poorest preacher more than half of those present rose to their feet. From that revealing moment I looked upon my fumbling uncle with enhanced respect. All who attended that service took away impressive proof that actions tell.

The eminent missionary Adoniram Judson was distressed when he read a newspaper article comparing him to the early disciples. He said, "I do not want to be like Paul, nor Apollos, nor Cephas. . . . I want to be just like Christ. . . . I want to follow Him only. . . .O, to be more like Christ!" The secret of a successful Christian life is faithfully following the Saviour and walking as He walked.

ACTIONS STILL TELL

I . . . beseech you that ye walk worthy of the vocation wherewith ye are called. Eph. 4:1.

We are admonished by Paul to walk worthily in our vocation. A vocation is a life's profession. What is important is not the particular profession we have but the way we walk in it. Christ requires that those who take His name honor it by their deportment.

Happily the lives lived by many youth today prove that they walk worthily. A recent news brief from Michigan illustrates this. The report states that a sizable bequest had just been received by Andrews University from the estate of a South Bend businessman. That is the end of the story. Here is how it began.

While I was serving at Andrews University my family shopped in South Bend, Indiana, much of it at a general store where other members from Andrews also traded. One afternoon the proprietor of the store, who recognized me from my speaking at the Rotary Club, invited me into his office. He said, "I want you to send me one of your needy students, perhaps a worthy young lady who is in financial straits. I'll help her."

The next day, at my request, the dean of women recommended a girl for this benefit. I took her to meet this merchant, who said to her, "If you'll go to such-and-such a store and get yourself a new wardrobe, I'll foot the bill." She replied, "That's very kind and generous of you, but if you'll just pay for some material I'll make the dresses myself. It will cost much less." He agreed.

A few weeks later I took this young lady back to see the kindly-disposed gentleman. She showed him three beautiful dresses she had made. The cost was well under a hundred dollars. The satisfaction that showed in his face was a joy to behold.

Shortly thereafter a lawyer telephoned, asking me to come by his office "on important business." When I went this same South Bend merchant was there. He said, "My attorney here has prepared a large trust to Andrews University. It's the best way I know to dispose of my estate when I am gone. The life style and the appreciation of that girl I helped is all the testimony I need about your school." His generous gift was recently received. That is the rest of the story.

When Christians of all ages "walk worthy of the vocation" for which they are called many observers looking on—and their wealth—are "added unto" us.

GOD'S WAY OF PROVIDENCE

We know that in everything God works for good with those who love him. Rom. 8:28, R.S.V.

In his meditative *Bridge of San Luis Rey,* Thornton Wilder deals directly with the theme of God's providences among men. This absorbing historical novel is based on an actual event, the collapse of a suspension bridge that spanned a fearsome chasm near Lima, Peru, in the early seventeenth century. In this accident five persons lost their lives. The explanation advanced is that the five who died that day were blessed in dying when they did, that their end was designed by Providence.

Because man is mortal and finite we cannot always recognize God's providences as time unrolls the tapestries of our lives. He does not always permit us to know the end from the beginning. Yet His "providence, though unseen, is ever at work in the affairs of men."—*Testimonies,* vol. 3, p. 547. And, from time to time, we can discern His manifestations in our own daily experiences.

There are those who face their daily lives as they face the phenomena of the universe, finding no meaning or superior guidance in either. Life is full of mysteries both within and without but there is a vast difference between viewing it as forever incomprehensible and accepting it as something yet uncomprehended.

It is interesting, at first even astounding, to see young fellows flying toy airplanes that take off, circle about, and land again all by radio control. But the guidance is not in the graceful little plane, but in the hand of the lad who holds the control mechanism. The direction is not in the mechanism of the machine at all. It resides in the intention of the intelligence piloting it.

According to God's eternal purpose, all things contribute to the good of those who love Him. Even the troubles, sufferings and sorrows of this life, instead of hindering our salvation, help it forward. At each step the Christian is courageously doing his part to carry out the divine plan.

> "All chance and change His love shall overrule.
>> What though today
> Thou canst not trace at all the hidden reason
> For His strange dealings through the trial season?
>> Trust and obey;
> In afterlife and light all shall be plain and clear."
>> —Author Unknown

HIS BLESSED QUIETNESS
Be still, and know that I am God. Ps. 46:10.

One hot summer my work took me for a few weeks to a thickly-populated Eastern city. The only rooming house where I could find accomodations I could afford was at a crossroads where two busy thoroughfares met. The stark, three-story frame structures housed a score of workers, all single like myself. I soon discovered that about half of them could play, were learning to play, or thought they could play some sort of musical instrument. From dawn to midnight seven days a week, horns were tooting, violins screeching, and drums beating. At rare intervals when this raucous disharmony died down the roar of traffic outside took up the refrain. The consequence was that quiet thinking was untenable and restful sleep impossible. Although my rent had been paid for the month, I fled that house—and the city too—at the end of two weeks. I was very glad to go, and I haven't been back there since.

Barbarians make hideous music and devil worshipers love ear-splitting syncopation. In recessed retreats Haitian voodoo drums pound through the long nights to appease native spirits, and along the China coast fishermen beat gongs with hammers to drive off evil spirits. Some leave their wheelbarrows ungreased to create screeching sounds deemed offensive to lurking ghosts. In the days of Ahab the priests of Baal made hill and dale echo with their drunken cries, which were heard for miles.

In sharp contrast to the babel that evildoers create we have the assurance that our "God is not the author of confusion, but of peace" (1 Cor. 14:33). To the Christian believer, above the discord of pagan noises and beyond the clamor and jostlings of men, God is found in the quiet sanctuary of the heart. There His still, small voice can be heard.

God's faithful servants of all ages, those mighty in spiritual power, all knew by daily experience the reality of Isaiah's affirmation that "in quietness and in confidence shall be your strength" (Isa. 30:15). Bishop Ken arose at three to pray, John Wesley at four. Martin Luther spent never less than three hours daily on his knees.

> "Drop Thy still dews of quietness,
> Till all our strivings cease;
> Take from our souls the strain and stress,
> And let our ordered lives confess
> The beauty of Thy peace."
> —J. G. Whittier

THE GRACE OF QUIETNESS

And he said to them, "Come away by yourselves to a lonely place, and rest a while." Mark 6:31, R.S.V.

Unfortunately many dedicated workers for the Lord, who are surely zealous in good works, never experience the blessings and the grace of solitude. They overlook the example of Jesus in today's text. He not only told them to isolate themselves ''apart'' but He led them ''into a desert place . . . privately'' (Mark 6:32). It is understandable that at times during His arduous ministry the Saviour felt the need and the necessity to get away from it all.

It has been my distressing experience to see a number of devoted laborers in the Lord's vineyard becoming so involved in doing good works, so determined to expend their every ounce of energy in advancing the ''cause'' that they far overdid their strength and went to an early grave at a time when it seemed that their potential for leadership and service was at full tide. On one occasion I remember an inspiring sermon delivered at camp meeting by the conference president. But as he spoke I noticed that his unstinted, long-sustained efforts had wearied him to the point of near collapse. Afterward as I looked at him close range I could see that his eyes were bloodshot from lack of sleep, that his shoulders drooped from weariness, and that an involuntary twitch had developed at the corner of his mouth. Trying to be tactful, I said, ''Elder, you need to relax. Can't you take off a week or so and go to the mountains and just rest?'' He roused himself and replied, ''I couldn't do that. I am starting an evangelistic effort the day after camp meeting closes.'' The pleading of his wife and others went unheeded. Within a year this faithful, upright man was laid to his earthly rest, a victim of his own self-imposed overdoing. Scores of similar instances could be cited.

There is a boon in quietness that can only be appreciated by those who live with turmoil and incessant activity. Tranquillity is a gift from God. Sometimes it comes in the early morning, when streets are empty and no raucous sounds disturb. At such a time a deep all-enveloping quietness enfolds the soul with peace and sweet stillness.

In darker hours one place offers refuge for regaining perspective. It is the quiet retreat with God. You can get away from it all ''near to the heart of God.''

STANDING READY

God called unto him. . . . And he said, Here am I. Ex. 3:4.

Tending his flocks one day near Horeb, Moses saw an astounding sight. A bush was in flames, with leaves, trunk, and branches all burning, yet it was not consumed. He came closer to better see the mysterious spectacle. Suddenly there came a voice from the fire calling, "Moses! Moses!" The Lord was calling the shepherd to do a great and wonderful work. Recognizing who had called him, Moses responded in a manner demonstrating that, after forty years of preparation, he was ready and willing to accept the challenging assignment. He said, "Here am I."

A somewhat similar experience is recorded of the child Samuel, whom the Lord called by night. Thinking that the voice calling him was that of the aged prophet Eli, Samuel ran to him and said, "Here am I." Eli said he hadn't called and told him to go on back to bed. The same thing happened again. "Now Samuel did not yet know the Lord" (1 Sam. 3:7). When the voice called the third time "Eli perceived that the Lord had called the child," and he instructed him how to answer should he be called again. "And the Lord came . . . and called." Then Samuel answered "Speak; for thy servant heareth" (verse 10). Then the Lord revealed that such a terrible thing was about to happen to Eli and his sons that on knowing it "both the ears of every one that heareth it shall tingle" (verse 11). Samuel was only 12 years old, but he was chosen of God to do marvelous things as a mighty prophet "and the Lord was with him."

When God calls, many today are like men in a fog who do not answer. Readiness means a living relationship with God. Some are so busy telling Him—and others—where they want to serve that they do not hear His call. Others wait for some great opportunity or position, sure that when such a call comes they will quickly reply, "Here am I." Yet they seem deaf when a call comes to any obscure post. Dedicated readiness to God's service means a willingness to respond to duty, lowly or great. A ready person never needs much time to get ready. The burning bush stands a symbol of God's presence confronting the ready soul. It is ablaze with the presence of God.

AVAILING PRAYER

The effectual fervent prayer of a righteous man availeth much. James 5:16.

This is a stirring, straightforward declaration that the right prayer by the right man "availeth much." There is power in prayer and only in eternity will we know how much and how many of life's blessings and benefits here result from earnest prayer.

"Prayer is the opening of the heart to God as to a friend. Not that it is necessary in order to make known to God what we are, but in order to enable us to receive Him. Prayer does not bring God down to us, but brings us up to Him."—*Steps to Christ,* p. 93.

There are many conditions, however, to true prayer. It must be earnest. At times, when we know we are in line with God's purposes, we may dare to be importunate. Prayer must be offered in God's name. Praying in His name will screen out selfishness in the petitioner. Prayer must be based upon a definite promise of God, which we can present in confidence like a check at a bank. The things we pray for must be of a nature to advance righteousness in the world.

In his sermon on prayer a veteran minister I knew emphasized three provisions of prevailing prayer. He said we let loose of the hand of God too soon, that a whim or a selfish motive does not warrant our calling God about it, and that when we pray we should petition in confidence, believing that we shall receive.

George Müller, who remains today a shining example of a godly man whose prayers were answered, said, "There are five conditions which I always endeavor to fulfill. In observing these I have the assurance of an answer to my prayer: 1. I have not the least doubt, because I am assured that it is the Lord's will to save men and to bring them all to a knowledge of the truth (1 Tim. 2:1). 2. I have never pleaded in my own name, but in the blessed name of the Lord Jesus and on His merits alone (John 14:14). 3. I always believe firmly in the willingness of God to hear my prayers (Mark 11:24). 4. I am not conscious of having yielded to any sin, for 'if I regard iniquity in my heart, the Lord will not hear me' (Ps. 66:18). 5. I have persevered in believing prayer for fifty-two years for some, and shall continue until the answer comes (Luke 18:7)."

ANSWERED PRAYER

And he spake a parable unto them to this end, that men ought always to pray, and not to faint. Luke 18:1.

Prayer is not a formal or fixed speech to God, though many a humanly acceptable prayer will be found among the "wood, hay, stubble" because it is little more than a stilted or grandiloquent invocation to be heard of men (see 1 Cor. 3:13). A prayer is a cry. A newborn baby cries as first evidence of life. If it does not cry, the doctor shakes or spanks it to make it cry. If it continues silent it will soon be dead. Peter says we are "newborn babes." "Because ye are sons," says Paul, "God hath sent forth the Spirit of his Son into your hearts, crying, Abba, Father" (Gal. 4:6). *Abba* means "papa." This is the cry of the childlike heart that knows little except that it is alive and needs the tender care of the heavenly Father.

Jesus received answers to His prayers. He taught us that, through prayer, we can receive answers too. But to prevail, prayers must be in Christ's name, must glorify God, and be uttered by sincere lips.

Elder E. E. Cleveland tells of visiting the Adventist hospital in Seoul, Korea. The nurse who showed him around asked him to pray for a boy emaciated so far by cancer that he was beyond the aid of physicians. As they entered the lad's dimly lighted room his orphaned sister sat silently crying. The minister and the nurse knelt beside the bed. They appealed earnestly to God for His mercy and healing power. They then slipped out quietly. Months later, after Elder Cleveland reached home, he received a letter from this boy. He wrote that his body was healed and that he was in school preparing to become a minister. That was twenty years ago. Today that young man is healthy and happy in the work of God.

We need to pray about difficult daily problems. Recently, as we were renovating Elmshaven, the last home of Ellen G. White, a perplexity arose. The committee voted to reinstall twenty-six window shutters. Except for a piece of one, the originals had disappeared. Opha Mayes and I searched in vain. Such shutters are not made today. Custom built they would have cost $3,000, which was prohibitive. So we prayed about it. Then, at a venerable lumberyard the manager said, "We may have something." The boy he sent to look came back with a shutter of the exact measurement. Sent again, he returned to report, "There are twenty-five more." They were installed by Mr. Mayes at a cost of $600. A small thing? Oh, no! God answers prayers.

CHRISTMAS: GIVING OR GETTING?

And when they were come into the house, they . . . fell down, and worshipped him: and when they had opened their treasures, they presented unto him gifts: gold, and frankincense, and myrrh. Matt. 2:11.

Christmas Day will soon be here, and just as soon, gone. Its mirth and music, bounties and blessings, charities and carols, generosity and good cheer, will pass as quickly as they came. As you look back upon it all what will you remember? Will it be what you got or what you gave? What treasure will you have laid beside the cradle of the infant Redeemer?

The first visit paid Him was made memorable by precious gifts. Meditating on His prophesied glory and the splendor of His future reign, the wise men came to adore a king. Instead they found an infant poorly swaddled and lying in a manger. But they knew that the newborn Baby was the Prince of heaven. So they knelt by His cradle and gave gifts of gold, frankincense, and myrrh.

At this late point of time, far removed from the birth of the baby Jesus, we marvel at the magnitude of the life then beginning. We bow before the grandeur of His saving grace and rejoice at the multitude of souls transformed by His saving power. So we turn once more to the cradle scene and celebrate the advent of that transcendent life. And, in the tradition of the Magi, we bring gold, frankincense, and myrrh.

What meaning do these gifts hold for us? We bring gold, the precious metal of value in every land. Gold signifies the high worth that must mark our gifts to Christ. Baser gifts would be less than the gold the Magi brought.

We bring the frankincense of self-denial willingly accepted for His sake. This gift He prizes, for it follows His example and His sufferance with us for whom He was "marred more than the sons of men" (Isa. 52:14).

There is also the precious ointment myrrh, symbolizing the prayers and praises of His earthly children that are prompted by a sincere and uncorrupted faith. A box of precious ointment was once broken for Him on earth, a sacrifice for a sweet-smelling savor. In gratitude we too bring and break it for Him.

At Christmas, as with every other day in the year, it is not what we get, but what we give, that makes us rich.

THE GREATEST GIFT EVER GIVEN

For unto us a child is born, unto us a son is given: . . . and his name shall be called Wonderful, Counsellor, The mighty God, The everlasting Father, The Prince of Peace. Isa. 9:6.

We realize that it was not on December 25 that God's gift of His Son was made to men. But it is inspiring to know that such a gift was given. Prophets and seers had been looking for Him for millenniums, yet on that hallowed day when He came, there were few to lift up their voices and say "Thank You, God, for Your unspeakable Gift." In the weeks that followed Jesus' birth, only a small troop of shepherds who came from their nearby pastures, a few wise men from a far country, an old man and woman in the Temple—only these came to thank God for the greatest Gift ever given. Countless gifts of great worth are given on this day every year all over Christendom, but no gift, before or since, could ever match that one. Johnson Oatman asked the question and then answered eloquently: "Was ever gift like the Saviour given? No, not one! no, not one!"

Luke quotes the angel to the virgin Mary, "That holy thing which shall be born of thee shall be called the Son of God" (Luke 1:35). Jesus was born *into* the world, not *of* nor *from* it. He did not arise out of history; He came into history from eternity. He was not a man becoming a god but God becoming a man. Thus, by human calculation alone, He cannot be accounted for at all.

As Jesus came from outside to enter the world, so must He come into our hearts from the outside. This is the new birth whereby Christ is formed within us, and His Spirit then works from us for others. In these words a poet has nicely pointed the way:

"For somehow not only for Christmas
But all the long year through
The joy that you give to others
Is the joy that comes back to you;
And the more that you spend in blessing
The poor and lonely and sad,
The more of your heart's possessing
Returns to make you glad."
—Selected

As yuletide bells ring out again and we are sobered by the sweet strains of "Silent Night," may our thoughts and our footsteps turn to the Redeemer. And may there be no slackening of pace until we come to Him.

DEFEATING DESPONDENCY
Bless the Lord, O my soul, and forget not all his benefits. Ps. 103:2.

Now that Christmas has come and gone you may be feeling a little low in spirits. It is easy to get the blues after the partying, the excitement, the gift-giving, and the gift-receiving are over and you sit looking, in the light of day, at the various presents you got and the crumpled wrappings lying about in disorder. You can regain your optimism and buoyancy by following the example of the psalmist who asked himself, "Why are you downcast, O my soul? . . . Put your hope in God" (Ps. 43:5, N.I.V.). You will find that getting the blues saps your confidence in Him who has promised to supply all your needs, but by making hope in God your motto you will soon recover your good cheer.

Believers who become despondent tend to overlook the favorable aspects of their situations. But when they begin to count their blessings, rather than nursing their dissatisfactions, life takes on a brighter hue. Delighting in the Lord and His benefits is a marvelous tonic to take for the disillusion and discomfort of despondency.

Think of the exhausted prophet Elijah who sank down under the juniper tree because Jezebel had threatened his life. Then God sent an angel to minister to him and assure him that he still had a great work to do. Remember Paul, facing the perils of shipwreck, whereupon the Lord told him to be of good cheer, that He would not allow His servant to perish. In like manner, Joshua, lying face down in despair, was imparted new confidence when the Lord appeared and said to him, "Get thee up."

Another good way to help banish the blues is to break out in song—whether you feel like it or not. Lift your voice in a gladsome hymn such as this one from the pen of Fanny Crosby (if you can't sing, you can ponder the words):

> "Never be sad or desponding,
> Only have faith to believe;
> Grace, for the duties before thee,
> Ask of thy God and receive.
>   * * * * *
> Never give up to thy sorrows,
> Jesus will bid them depart;
> Sing when your trials are greatest,
> Trust in the Lord and take heart."

LOVE'S ARGUMENT

He [the lord] loves Israel for ever. 1 Kings 10:9, N.E.B.

Some attributes of God are so universally and luminously evident that they need no proof. His power and wisdom are accepted, for they are "past finding out." Paul declared that the love of Christ may dwell within us with "all the fulness of God" (Eph. 3:19). Today's text emphasizes its endless extent, showing how long that love will endure. He loves "for ever."

Some facts seem to argue against God's love. There is ceaseless struggle for existence. Man fights with man, beast with beast, bird with bird, and fish with fish. Among them there is endless strife. Aldous Huxley once wrote to Charles Kingsley that in nature he could find no proof of the fatherhood of God, that he couldn't reconcile what God's supposed children were doing to one another with what his, Huxley's, children wouldn't dream of doing to each other.

It is true that today all over the world victims of war and starvation are crying for deliverance. And in our bewilderment we weep too when the chair of the one desperately needed is empty and the grave is full. "Can it be," we ask, "that love is still on the throne?"

The unanswerable proof is in the Bible. It does not say that God's love is in the lovely summer day (though it is), because before sunset an earthquake somewhere may take the lives of many innocent people. The Bible doesn't tell the mother to look for love in the face of her child (though she can find it there), because she or the child or both may soon be sleeping in death. But the Bible does tell us where to find the proof we seek. It is at the cross. "But God commendeth his love toward us, in that, while we were yet sinners, Christ died for us" (Rom. 5:8).

Once we fully understand what was accomplished on the cross and have grasped the scope of its spiritual meaning we can nevermore doubt the love of God. Whatever trials and sorrows may yet await us the fact of Calvary remains.

Our text is in the timeless present tense, and spiritual Israel embraces every Christian. Human thought may range far and knowledge widen. Science may unlock mysteries our fathers never dreamed of. But standing unshakable forever is the cross of Christ, the undeniable evidence that God is love.

GOD'S INSCRUTABLE WAYS

Seek ye the Lord. . . . For my thoughts are not your thoughts, neither are your ways my ways, saith the Lord. For as the heavens are higher than the earth, so are my ways higher than your ways, and my thoughts than your thoughts. Isa. 55:6-9.

When I was a university student I took a couple of courses in philosophy. For collateral reading I was assigned tomes by Alfred North Whitehead, A. S. Eddington, Albert Einstein, and other renowned dialecticians and savants. I confess that I found some of their fine-spun reasoning a little too much. I felt I had ventured into intellectual waters too deep for me. But my failure to altogether comprehend their rationalizations doesn't necessarily invalidate them. My lack of understanding proves only my incompetence in an unfamiliar field of thought, nothing more.

Likewise, "the word of God, like the character of its divine Author, presents mysteries that can never be fully comprehended by finite beings. The entrance of sin into the world, the incarnation of Christ, regeneration, the resurrection, and many other subjects presented in the Bible, are mysteries too deep for the human mind to explain, or even fully to comprehend. . . . The difficulties of Scripture have been urged by skeptics as an argument against the Bible; but so far from this, they constitute a strong evidence of its divine inspiration. If it contained no account of God but that which we could easily comprehend; if His greatness and majesty could be grasped by finite minds, then the Bible would not bear the unmistakable credentials of divine authority."—*Steps to Christ,* pp. 106, 107.

The very limited nature of human understanding may be illustrated by an ant moving over the uneven surface of the pillars of the Parthenon. What can the ant know of the magnificently sculptured friezes of Phidias when it sees only the scarred face of the ancient stone on which it crawls? To the ant the beautiful carvings and ornamental designs are only mountains and valleys hindering his progress. In a similar way, the trusting believer in the midst of God's colossal universe sees only the diminutive space around him.

For the nonce we perceive but a glimmer of the purposes of the Eternal, whose movings, even His grace, may be viewed as mountains of difficulties. Yet God provides the assurance that if we will but trust Him and follow His leadings all will work out for our eternal good.

SUSTAINING OUR HOPE

We will not hide . . . his strength, and his wonderful works. . . . [We] should make them known . . . and declare them to their children: that they might set their hope in God. Ps. 78:4-7.

Christian courage is a rock-ribbed foundation on which the noblest life structures have been built. And when at last the gates of pearl swing open to welcome the saved of earth not one will enter there who has not maintained a massive courage, which is the essential attribute enabling the redeemed, having done all, to stand. No coward will enter in. But courage alone cannot suffice. With it the overcomer must have the hope that motivates courage. Even when the future looks darkest, hope animates the faltering soul and beckons the pilgrim on. Oliver Goldsmith wrote that

> "Hope, like the gleaming taper's light,
>   Adorns and cheers our way;
> And still, as darker grows the night,
>   Emits a brighter ray."

In the Scriptures hope is frequently praised. It is linked with faith, patience, and endurance. In Psalm 31:24 David shows that hope bulwarks courage. "Be of good courage, and he shall strengthen your heart, all ye that hope in the Lord."

The essential bond between hope and courage is illustrated in an incident that came about in the 1920s in Japan. The new Adventist sanitarium there was nearing completion, the first such hospital to be built in that island kingdom. Elder V. T. Armstrong, mission president, was worried because funds were running low. His hopes revived when Elder W. A. Spicer, General Conference president, made a surprise visit. With pride Elder Armstrong showed his important guest the new institution, tactfully mentioning that a grant of $7,500 would complete the project. Elder Spicer looked grave and remained noncommital. The next day at the wharf, as Armstrong waved goodbye, President Spicer called back, "Keep up your courage, Brother Armstrong!" He stood there until long after the big liner had vanished from view and wondered why Elder Spicer had urged courage when an appropriation was so badly needed to bolster that courage. Six weeks later a check for $7,700 arrived from Washington. The link between courage and hope was reestablished.

Paul says that hope is the anchor of the soul (see Heb. 6:19). We should learn, and then teach our children, to hope in God.

GLEAMS OF THE GOLDEN MORNING

Christ, having been offered once to bear the sins of many, will appear the second time . . . to save those who are eagerly waiting for him. Heb. 9:28, R.S.V.

In His final discourse before His crucifixion the Saviour promised to come back again. He said, "Then shall they see the Son of man coming in the clouds of heaven with power and great glory" (Matt. 24:30). Jesus' first coming set the world's pyramid of values on its apex; His second coming will abolish every false value and annihilate every evil work. It was a marvelous day when the announcement was made to the shepherds by angels, "Unto you is born this day . . . a Saviour, which is Christ the Lord" (Luke 2:11). It will be an even more glorious day when He comes again with power and great glory. At the time He first came the world desperately needed a Saviour.

Two thousand years ago the transcendent need was for a Saviour who could accept man's guilt and submit to man's punishment, One who could transform abject sinners into His own likeness and point them to a path to paradise. Only One could do this, the Son of God. So He "took upon him the form of a servant, and . . . humbled himself, and became obedient unto . . . the death of the cross" (Phil. 2:7, 8). For thirty-three years Deity, veiled with humanity, walked sinlessly with men. In one hand He held the throne of heaven. With the other He grasped perishing mankind. Then, after showing men how to live, He showed them how to die. Eternity alone can disclose the wonders of God's love as demonstrated by this "unspeakable gift" of the first advent.

In His first coming Jesus shed a gleam of heavenly light on this sin-shadowed world. Then He said, "I go to my Father." On Olivet He told His followers they must "bear witness" and He blessed them. Then He was lifted up and a cloud hid Him from their sight. As they gazed upward in astonished awe two men in white appeared and said, "This same Jesus . . . shall so come in like manner" (Acts 1:11).

Christ then became man's Intercessor. Heaven is not since as cut off as before. He dwells in the heart of every believer. The promise He made His disciples to come again is the blessed hope.

When Christ comes again He will appear to take His ransomed sinners home. He comes to raise the saints that sleep and to reunite those who have long been parted. He says, "Be ye also ready" (Matt. 24:44).

THINGS TO LEAVE BEHIND

Lay aside every weight, and the sin which doth so easily beset us, and let us run with patience the race that is set before us, looking unto Jesus. Heb. 12:1, 2.

As this last day of the old year dawns it is wiser to look to the future than to the past. If we really intend to make the new year better than the old one there are some things that had best be left behind: bagatelle and impedementa that only encumber us and hinder our progress toward the heavenly Canaan.

First, let us leave behind past sins. There may have been more than you can remember, but if you have confessed and forsaken them they are put away forever. It is useless to brood over what is past. God has buried it out of our sight and His. Why should we remember what He forgets?

You should also leave behind accomplished ambitions and goals that have been reached. They were once ahead, but now, by God's grace, estimable things once dreamed of have been largely or completely accomplished and you have reached the coveted tableland you once despaired of attaining. Now is a good time to look up and forward. At age 80 Edwin Markham wrote:

"I am done with the years that were: I am quits:
I am done with the dead and old.
They are mines worked out: I delved in their pits:
I have saved their grain of gold.

"Now I turn to the future for wine and bread:
I have bidden the past adieu.
I laugh and lift hands to the years ahead:
'Come on! I am ready for you!'"

We must leave what is behind and not turn back. Challenges lie ahead. To turn back is to expose oneself to attack and encourage the backward drift. The apostle bids us "run . . . the race that is set before us." We are to look to Jesus, for He is our forerunner. His crest is like that of Henry Navarre, always in the thick of the conflict. Following Him helps us become oblivious to the past. He holds out to us "the crown of glory that fadeth not away" (2 Peter 5:4).

SCRIPTURE INDEX